SOCIOLOGICAL READINGS IN THE CONFLICT PERSPECTIVE

SOCIOLOGICAL READINGS IN THE CONFLICT PERSPECTIVE

Edited by
WILLIAM J. CHAMBLISS
University of California, Santa Barbara

ADDISON-WESLEY PUBLISHING COMPANY
Reading, Massachusetts
Menlo Park, California • London • Don Mills, Ontario

 Printed in the United States of America. Published simultaneously in Canada. Library of Congress Catalog Card No. 72-579.

FOR JACKIE

Is there such a place as heaven? No, Jonathan, there is no such place. Heaven is not a time or place. Heaven is being perfect.

PREFACE

There is a plethora of readers introducing the student to sociology, but in my view these readers suffer from two major shortcomings: they fail to present a coherent theoretical system, and they do not begin to represent the richness of the research methods employed by sociologists. These two shortcomings I have tried to rectify in this book.

Theoretical perspectives do not exist in isolation. Every issue in any discipline is always a response to some opposing view. To fail to communicate this to beginning students is to rob them of that basic insight from which all inquiry flows—that scientific inquiry is a series of confrontations and refutations. Unfortunately, social science has been slower to recognize this than other sciences. As a result, students have often been confused by the appearance of harmony in the face of undeniable conflict.

Yet it is not enough to simply communicate to students that there are competing and conflicting views. We must, as social scientists, assess the relative merits of the opposing views. This collection of readings attempts to do this and in the process comes to the conclusion that what has come to be called "the conflict perspective" is at the moment the best general perspective we have for explaining social phenomena. To say that it is the best perspective we have means that the implications of the conflict theory are more compatible with the known facts about society and human behavior than are the implications of other general theoretical frameworks—especially the perspective variously known as equilibrium, functional, or structural-functional theory.

Fitting the facts is the ultimate test of a theory's utility. How well we can assess this ultimate test depends on the logical structure of the theory and the research tools we have available for gathering the facts. Both aspects of the sociological enterprise are dealt with in the articles included in this volume. We have purposely included researches which use participant observation, historical data, survey research, and a host of other research tools as a basis for gathering the information the investigator seeks.

It is thus the intention of this book to provide students of sociology with an introduction that contains the central issues of the discipline and a sense of the process by which the discipline changes, grows, and develops. In this way the excitement, the promise, and the achievements of sociology are conveyed without distortion.

August 1972 W.J.C.
Santa Barbara, California

CONTENTS

INTRODUCTION

Today people everywhere are groping almost desperately for a perspective from which to understand the world's current circumstances. Sociology, as the most general of the social sciences, is quite naturally at the forefront of this quest. No single social theory can begin to come to grips with the many perplexing and complex problems calling for insight and analysis. It is increasingly apparent, however, that the theoretical framework known as the conflict perspective provides a point of view from which the contemporary world can most fruitfully be studied, analyzed, and understood.

No doubt one of the advantages of the conflict perspective over other extant models is its interdisciplinary character. As reflected in the readings in this book, historians, economists, philosophers, geographers, as well as sociologists, are continually engaged in testing, modifying, and applying the conflict perspective. This interdisciplinary cast is absolutely essential for understanding the complex and dynamic issues of today. Attempts at a general understanding of society and human behavior from the vantage point of a single discipline are doomed to failure at the outset.

Having said this, however, it is necessary to interject a quick disclaimer lest one be led to think that the conflict perspective represents nothing but an eclectic, unorganized, but varied approach to the study of man and society. Quite the contrary is the case. At the center of the conflict perspective is a core of ideas which direct us to look at certain features of society and man's environment in order to understand it. The conflict perspective also provides us with a set of concepts which can be used for explaining the events we choose to investigate.

MODELS OF SOCIOLOGICAL INQUIRY

Sociology, in common with all other scientific enterprises, conducts its work within the confines of general theoretical models. As Barber has said:

> Each sociologist carries in his head one or more "models" of society and man which greatly influence what he looks for, what he sees, and what he does with his observations by way of fitting them along with other facts, into a larger scheme of explanation. In this respect the sociologist is no different from any other scientist. Every scientist holds some general conception of the realm in which he is working, some mental picture of "how it is put together and how it works."[1]

A model, then, is a very general set of ideas and concepts—a point of view—that the scientist uses to select his problems, organize his thoughts, and pursue his inquiries. A model is not a theory—it is more general and unlike a theory, it cannot be proved wrong. A theory, by contrast, answers a specific question and, if it is to be scientifically useful, must be capable of being proved wrong. A model is more or less productive of useful theories; it may be misleading or fruitful, or it may be more or less complete. We choose one theory or another because it has stood the test of empirical research. Data support the theories that stand the test of time and refute the theories that do not. Models, however, are chosen because they direct us to the issues that seem most important; because they lead us to the data that prove most fruitful; because they are productive of useful theories.

Throughout sociology's history two general theoretical perspectives have been ubiquitous: functionalism and conflict. Each perspective accepts the challenge of all sociological inquiry—to study and make sense of social phenomena. But within this very broad field of inquiry there are an almost infinite number of variables that might be selected for study, unending questions to be asked, and a host of possible concepts and ideas that might be sensibly selected as explanatory tools. The advantages to be had from using the conflict model of society rather than the functional are that it raises questions which are more crucial to the relevant issues of the day, that it directs our attention to those variables which are most important in determining the important events in men's lives, and that it provides a more powerful explanatory model.

The German sociologist Ralf Dahrendorf has observed that the question in sociology for the past fifty years has been "what holds societies together," *not* "what drives them on."[2] The prominence of the question "what holds society together" is perhaps seen most clearly in the voluminous works of Emile Durkheim, whose entire life as a scholar was devoted to searching for those elements in social life that provide the glue to the fabric of society. He investigated various types of division of labor and their relationship to law, the way the morality of the community affects professional life, and the characteristic ways that the norms and values of society affect the rates of deviant behavior (particularly suicide). In the end his most seminal work was an attempt to trace the roots of behavioral norms in the primitive religions from which modern society inherited its religious forms and consequently its conceptions of right and wrong, of good and bad.

From Durkheim and sundry other sociologists, we inherited the functionalist perspective, which focuses on what produces stability and continuity in society rather than what produces change and alteration. The functionalist model emphasizes those aspects of society that are harmonious, whereas the conflict perspective which is more concerned with change and alteration than with stability and continuity, focuses on the disruptive aspects of society—conflicts inherent in any human group, but especially those in modern industrialized societies, where the society is divided according to such critical characteristics as power, wealth, prestige, way of life, and perception of the world.

Dahrendorf has suggested that the essential elements of the structural functional model can be summarized as follows:

1. Every society is a relatively persisting configuration of elements.
2. Every society is a well-integrated configuration of elements.
3. Every element in a society contributes to its functioning.
4. Every society rests on the consensus of its members.

The conflict model, on the other hand, takes as its point of departure disagreement with every one of these assumptions in postulating that:

1. Every society is subjected at every moment to changes; social change is ubiquitous.
2. Every society experiences at every moment social conflicts; social conflict is ubiquitous.
3. Every element in a society contributes to its change.
4. Every society rests on constraints of some of its members by others.[3]

More generally, we can discern a whole series of disagreements between the functional and conflict models, which can be summarized as follows:

1. Functionalists view society as a social system with various needs of its own which must be met if the needs and desires of its members are to be met. Conflict theories tend to view society more as the setting within which various struggles take place.

2. The governing bodies of every society—the state—are viewed by functionalists as value-neutral agencies within which various struggles take place. The conflict perspective sees the state as a most important agent participating in the struggle on the part of one side or another. Conflict theories emphasize coercion (usually in the form of law or war-making institutions) as the chief factor undergirding and maintaining social institutions such as private property, slavery, and other institutions which give rise to unequal rights and privileges. Functionalists have argued that coercion plays only a minor role and that inequality arises as a necessary consequence of the fact that there is a general consensus within society on its most important values.

3. Social inequality, in the conflict view, arises because of the operation of coercive institutions, which lay great emphasis on force, fraud, and inheritance as the chief avenues for obtaining rights and privileges. Functionalists have stressed such things as hard work, innate talent, and selection by others as the route by which economic advantages are obtained by some and not by others.

4. The conflict perspective sees social inequality as being a chief source of social conflict. Functionalists generally minimize the existence of social conflict and see whatever conflict there is as stemming from man's nature, not from the structured inequality of society.

5. Conflict theories regard the state and law as instruments of oppression employed by the ruling classes for their own benefit. Functionalists see them as organs of the total society, acting basically to promote the common good.

6. Functionalists tend to regard the concept of social class as a heuristic device calling attention to aggregations of people with certain common characteristics. Conflict theorists are inclined to view classes as social groups with distinctive interests which inevitably bring them into conflict with other groups with opposed interests.

7. Both functional and conflict theorists seem to understand the consequences which particular social events have for the society. The functionalist analysis generally stops when the consequences have been described.

The conflict analysis goes on to ask who benefits from the established social relations that produce those events.
8. Whether they are studying war, social class, or deviant behavior, the functionalists typically ask what functions it serves; the conflict approach adds: for whom is it functional?[4]

The importance of these various disagreements is best seen in the study of particular social phenomena. The concepts used, the questions asked, and the empirical data gathered are all conditioned by the model from which we begin our inquiry. Nowhere is this more clearly illustrated than in the study of social inequality.

THE STUDY OF SOCIAL INEQUALITY

According to the conflict model, social class and social inequality (that is, inequality in wealth, power, prestige, and privilege) are among the most important features to be studied if we are to understand society. The existence of social classes leads to certain recurring conflicts, certain persistent tendencies to use force, and the emergence of laws and rules to control threats to the established unequal relations and the like. Although not accepting the dictum of Karl Marx that all of human history is but a reflection of class struggle, the conflict perspective nevertheless gives social class a place of great importance in the analysis of human society.

The functionalist perspective, by contrast, either ignores social class entirely (as does Emile Durkheim)[5] or approaches it as one of the static characteristics of society that are "necessary and inevitable." For the functionalists, what makes social class necessary and inevitable comes down to two arguments, frequently joined but sometimes separated. The first argument is that inherent differences in ability make different individuals (and collectively different classes) mutually dependent on one another. The classic illustration of this notion of mutual dependence is Aristotle's analysis of the relationship between master and slave. Aristotle saw the master as providing the necessary intellect and guidance which the slave was incapable of providing for himself. The slave, for his part, contributed the physical strength which was necessary for the master's well-being. Thus the master and the slave (or the wealthy and the poor), like the shark and the pilot fish, live in a symbiotic relationship of mutual benefit and harmony.

The second argument contained within the functionalist perspective is that social inequality is necessary in order to motivate people to occupy more demanding positions. Davis and Moore have articulated this position most explicitly in laying down "some principles of stratification" to "explain in functional terms, the universal necessity which calls forth stratification in any social system."[6] The explanation offered by Davis and Moore is as follows:

> A society must somehow distribute its members in social positions and induce them to perform the duties of these positions. [Society] must thus concern itself with motivation at two different levels: to instill in the proper individuals the desire to fill certain positions, and, once in these positions, the desire to perform the duties attached to them.[7]

Members are motivated to work hard in positions filled by society's unconsciously devised system of social inequality! "Social inequality is thus an unconsciously evolved device by which societies insure that the most important positions are conscientiously filled by the most qualified persons."[8] It follows from this that "those positions convey the best reward and hence have the highest rank, which (a) have the greatest importance for the society and (b) require the greatest training or talent."[9]

These propositions, which represent a theory of social inequality, derive quite logically from the assumption that whatever consequences we can impute to a social phenomenon must be the cause of its presence in society.[10] Thus since there *is* inequality, we need only "discover" (or imagine) what good this does for society to have laid bare its reason for being. Yet this logic leads to erroneous conclusions.[11]

The first issue is how to determine what constitute the most important positions. As Davis and Moore recognize, this is a difficult task, but even more, it requires an acceptance of the prevailing values of the particular society. For example, during colonial times the most highly placed Africans were those who worked hand-in-glove with the foreign colonial powers. By the logic of the functional argument, they must have been the functionally most important members of the African society. Yet the opposite case could easily be made; by cooperating with the colonials these persons were, in fact, forcing the exploitation, impoverishment, and sometimes the enslavement of the bulk of their African brothers.

To be sure, these African elites were very important to the *colonial governments* and to the people in Europe and America who benefited economically from the exploitative relationship. But one could argue that the most important positions in African society at this time were held by a handful of revolutionaries who were trying to overthrow the colonial governments. The revolutionaries' actions were crucial to the larger historical process which was to culminate in the demise of most colonial empires (or more accurately, a shift in the form of colonization). But these revolutionaries would have to be seen as the least important members of society from the functionalists' point of view, because they were imprisoned, executed, and kept at the bottom of the economic and social hierarchy. The point, of course, is that what is functionally important depends on what you *see* as important to the society. If the maintenance of the status quo is "most important," then the argument has some consistency; but one can argue just as logically that what is most important is to change the society.

Granting that the functionalist argument has greater consistency if contribution to the maintenance of the society as a smoothly functioning, unchanging, predictable system is the criterion by which the importance of jobs is evaluated, many problems are left unsolved. In England during 1970 the sewerage workers went out on strike. Overnight the major sources of drinking water for millions of people became polluted, fish died by the hundreds of thousands, and diseases began spreading rapidly as sewage backed up and infested populations, thus making the "functional importance" of the sewerage workers readily apparent to everyone. Yet these workers were striking to achieve a raise in their minimum pay from thirty to forty dollars a week. This occurred in a society where an actress, whose principal contribution to the social order is displaying her large breasts on film, was robbed of one million dollars worth of jewels the same week that the sewerage workers struck. By contrast, large corporations' top executives, who earn three and four thousand dollars a week, could go on strike and the consequences would certainly be no more serious. Indeed, when the London School of Economics was closed for six weeks due to student political activities, no fish died, no diseases spread, and no one's water was polluted. Some even argued that the pollution of the youths' minds was stopped for this period. Yet professors are paid quite high salaries and enjoy great prestige and even, occasionally, considerable power.

When the garbage collectors in New York City went on strike, the heart, as well as the health, of the city was severely threatened. Large cities everywhere come to a virtual standstill, and inhabitation is impossible when streetcar conductors, taxi drivers, streetcleaners, or rubbish collectors refuse to do their jobs. Yet these jobs, which require their own sorts of talent, inconvenience, and training (if nothing else, considerable training in alienation is required to be able to retain one's self-esteem while working at such poorly rewarded jobs) are given the lowest rewards of any in society. And other positions which are highly rewarded and presumably demand greater talent and sacrifice can go unfilled for long periods of time—perhaps even forever—and there is little effect on society. When Columbia University was shut down by student demonstrations, there was hardly a ripple of inconvenience or loss of a heartbeat in the city of New York. When "Broadway Joe" Namath, who is paid more for throwing an egg-shaped piece of leather filled with air for one hour than the average garbage collector makes in an entire year, fails to throw for a day, there is no threat whatsoever to America's well-being. Athletics and entertainment are among the highest paid occupations in America; yet they must rank as among the most expendable as well. These same occupations have a limitless supply of talent which could easily be tapped whenever desired; and the "training period" surely requires more play than work. Such income inequality can be seen as deriving from the differential importance of the jobs, the scarcity of talent, or the necessity for arduous training which requires "deferring gratification" only by tautology. That is, the only way a case can be made for the greater functional importance of entertainers and athletes is by arguing that their undeniable position at the top of the social and income hierarchy is the evidence for their importance. But to make such an argument is, of course, to explain nothing, since it becomes true by definition.

The functional argument can also be dismissed by looking at it cross-culturally. Occupations that are highly rewarded and highly regarded in one society do not necessarily share the same position in other societies. Physicians and medical doctors are among the most highly paid workers in America; one assumes, therefore, that they are also among the functionally most important. In Britain, however, they are paid far less, even taking into account the lower standard of living there. Surely it does not make sense that the medical doctor is less important to British society than to American.

The reason for these differentials in socio-economic status among different positions within a country or the same positions in different countries is far more likely to be found in the variances in political power, organization into interest groups, and the power of the different social classes generally than in the functional importance of the positions. The differences are, in fact, explained much more rapidly and sensibly from the perspective of the conflict model, which emphasizes interests, social class differences in power, and class conflict. The political influence of the American Medical Association and the relative weakness of proletarian political organizations in the United States as contrasted with the relative strength of the proletariat in England (only in comparison with the United States) goes much farther to explain the different incomes of doctors in the two countries than does any argument about the relative importance of the roles.

It can also be argued that a system of inequality leads to strangulation, rather than discovery, of talent. For where some positions are afforded high esteem while others are not, the pressure to ensure that one's offspring inherit the high position is intense. Persons occupying positions at the top will thus take whatever measures they can to keep other, possibly more talented, people from replacing their heirs. Given that those at the top do in fact possess the wherewithal to at least influence and at times completely control the selection of their replacements, a structural tendency to eliminate a true search for talent necessarily arises.

A wealth of untapped and unuseable talent exists in every society, for there is always more talent than the society can possibly use. Even if certain talents are more important than others to society, the fact remains that the people who are provided an opportunity to use their talents are selected in ways that must be understood if we are to unravel the mysteries of the society. We can hardly claim to understand them simply by arguing that people with talent are enticed by higher rewards to develop their talents. People with talent are also enticed to waste it or to channel it into being thieves, revolutionaries, or workers performing routine, mechanized tasks in factories.

Finally, we turn to a basic assumption of the functional theory of social inequalty, i.e., that inequality is necessary to motivate people to perform "functionally important" jobs. In one sense we have already answered this by pointing out that many functionally crucial jobs (e.g., sewerage workers, rubbish collectors) are rewarded very poorly but are nonetheless filled.

Richard Schwartz provides further confirmation in his study of two kibbutzim in Israel.[12] Schwartz found several positions in these two communities that were essential if the communities were to continue as they were. In one community (Orah) the essential positions were those of routine workers; in the second community (Tamim) the functionally important roles were those of the decision-makers. Schwartz notes that "each position, whether or not the 'most important' in the society, is important so that failure adequately to fill it results in dissatisfaction for the members and a threat to the survival of the settlement."[13] Contrary to what would be expected from the functional theory of inequality, these communities do *not* find it necessary to create economic inequality in order to motivate people to fill these jobs. This is clear in both communities; here we shall look only at Orah.

In Orah such things as rotating the routine tasks to be done, providing outside work that requires nonroutine actions, and continually attempting through mechanization to reduce the amount of routine work necessary to the community's survival make routine jobs sufficiently attractive to motivate people to occupy them. None of those features of work organization includes an unequal distribution of rewards. Inequality, then, is not a necessary ingredient of society; its cause must be sought elsewhere.

A corollary of this functionalist argument is that since the more prestigious, more rewarding positions require more training, society must build into the socialization process a willingness in some of its members to "defer gratification" before they become economically and socially independent. People will be motivated to make this sacrifice only if the carrot at the end of the stick is juicier than is the one to be had immediately. In other words, people can be induced to go to college or to seek specialized technological training only if the positions open to them when they complete their training bring greater wealth, power, prestige, and privilege. Going to university, then, is deferring gratification, and this is why university graduates make more money and have more prestigious positions than people who do not go to university.

It is difficult to see how anyone who has even walked through a university campus in America, Europe, Asia, or Africa could take such a view seriously. Can it be reasonably argued that college students would really prefer (and choose) to be working on a farm or in a factory with their lower-class age-peers if the job prospects after college were more promising than for those who are working in the fields and factories?

First of all, university and college education is primarily for the children of persons of considerable economic standing. The youths who attend college and university do so quite comfortably. In point of fact in most countries the people who attend the universities have a higher standard of living during their attendance than do their age-peers who join the labor force. Even lower-class youth who occasionally slip into the university or college system are afforded a higher standard of living through loans, grants, and scholarships than are their working-class peers. It is nonsense to say that students living in comfortable apartments or dormitories, with access to automobiles and a life of considerable leisure are "deferring gratification." There would doubtless be no shortage of eager applicants to university or college even if the jobs that one qualified for afterwards were no more rewarding than those available without higher education.

It is even arguable that the bulk of the university-trained students have not learned any skills that are particularly useful for the society as it is constituted. Most graduates of universities must be completely trained for their jobs after they leave college or university (excepting, of course, that minority of students who specialize in engineering or natural science). The training the functionalists see as so necessary is for the most part superfluous.

The final argument of the functionalists is that the jobs that receive the greatest rewards are the most demanding of personal sacrifice and this is why they must be rewarded more highly. While this may be true for some jobs, it certainly is not true for others. The laborer who is partially deaf by age forty from having worked next to noisy machinery has made every bit as much of a personal sacrifice as has the business executive who must pamper his ulcer. The beggar who stands in the rain, snow, and sleet for long hours is every bit as hard pressed as is the professor who faces students. The laborer who runs a jack hammer all day is making as great a sacrifice (if not greater) as is the judge who sentences him to jail for being drunk.

Following the tradition of Tocqueville and Durkheim, the functionalists tend to see modern democratic societies as becoming increasingly egalitarian. The functionalist view is frequently linked to the emergence of a large middle class which, in combination with strong labor movements in industrial societies, has greatly reduced economic differences among social classes. Lipset and Rogoff expressed this view as follows:

The assembly line and mass production, with the higher wages and more equal distribution of wealth that they make possible, are thus probably more responsible for the development of the American "classless" society than trends in social mobility.[14]

Significantly, these remarks are derived not from empirical data, but rather from the model with which Lipset and Rogoff viewed society, a model which incorporated a belief that what *ought* to be taking place in America was *in fact* taking place. It remained for a historian, Gabriel Kolko, whose model of society was not quite so tinted by rose-colored glasses, to study the distribution of incomes as they are in fact and not simply in the imagination.

While the income share of the richest tenth has remained large and virtually constant over the past half century, the two lowest income-tenths have experienced a sharp decline. In 1910, the combined income shares of the two poorest income-tenths were about one-quarter that of the richest tenth; by 1959, their share had dropped to one-seventh. During this same period, the percentage of the next lowest tenth also decreased, while the fourth and fifth from the lowest tenths (the sixth- and seventh-ranking) neither gained nor lost ground appreciably. Together these five groups, which constitute the poorer half of the U.S. population, received 27 per cent of the national personal income in 1910, but only 23 per cent in 1959. Thus, for the only segments of the population in which a gain could indicate progress toward economic democracy, there has been no increase in the percentage share of the national income.[15]

A recent Census Bureau report further supports Kolko's conclusions. This report shows that there were 900,000 American families whose income exceeded $50,000 in 1968 and that these 900,000 people accounted for eleven per cent of the total national income. The analysis, conducted by the chief of the U.S. Census Bureau's population division, disclosed that in 1968 five per cent of the families controlled twenty-two per cent of the total national income.[16]

The myth of increasing equality is based in part on the assumption that graduated income taxes, inheritance taxes, and estate taxes effectively control the concentration of wealth. In fact the income tax structure is riddled with loopholes that can be used by the wealthy to *legally* avoid paying taxes. Writing in 1969, Phillip Stern noted:

There are, in this land, some 381 rich or super-rich Americans who can look back upon April 15, 1968 with satisfaction, if not smugness—and who are probably facing this Tuesday's midnight tax deadlines with near or total

Table 1. Percentage of national personal income, before taxes, received by each income-tenth

	Highest tenth	2nd	3rd	4th	5th	6th	7th	8th	9th	Lowest tenth
1910	33.9	12.3	10.2	8.8	8.0	7.0	6.0	5.5	4.9	3.4
1918	34.5	12.9	9.6	8.7	7.7	7.2	6.9	5.7	4.4	2.4
1921	38.2	12.8	10.5	8.9	7.4	6.5	5.9	4.6	3.2	2.0
1929	39.0	12.3	9.8	9.0	7.9	6.5	5.5	4.6	3.6	1.8
1934	33.6	13.1	11.0	9.4	8.2	7.3	6.2	5.3	3.8	2.1
1937	34.4	14.1	11.7	10.1	8.5	7.2	6.0	4.4	2.6	1.0
1941	34.0	16.0	12.0	10.0	9.0	7.0	5.0	4.0	2.0	1.0
1945	29.0	16.0	13.0	11.0	9.0	7.0	6.0	5.0	3.0	1.0
1946	32.0	15.0	12.0	10.0	9.0	7.0	6.0	5.0	3.0	1.0
1947	33.5	14.8	11.7	9.9	8.5	7.1	5.8	4.4	3.1	1.2
1948	30.9	14.7	11.9	10.1	8.8	7.5	6.3	5.0	3.3	1.4
1949	29.8	15.5	12.5	10.6	9.1	7.7	6.2	4.7	3.1	0.8
1950	28.7	15.4	12.7	10.8	9.3	7.8	6.3	4.9	3.2	0.9
1951	30.9	15.0	12.3	10.6	8.9	7.6	6.3	4.7	2.9	0.8
1952	29.5	15.3	12.4	10.6	9.1	7.7	6.4	4.9	3.1	1.0
1953	31.4	14.8	11.9	10.3	8.9	7.6	6.2	4.7	3.0	1.2
1954	29.3	15.3	12.4	10.7	9.1	7.7	6.4	4.8	3.1	1.2
1955	29.7	15.7	12.7	10.8	9.1	7.7	6.1	4.5	2.7	1.0
1956	30.6	15.3	12.3	10.5	9.0	7.6	6.1	4.5	2.8	1.3
1957	29.4	15.5	12.7	10.8	9.2	7.7	6.1	4.5	2.9	1.3
1958	27.1	16.3	13.2	11.0	9.4	7.8	6.2	4.6	3.1	1.3
1959	28.9	15.8	12.7	10.7	9.2	7.8	6.3	4.6	2.9	1.1

Source: From Gabriel Kolko, *Wealth and Power in America,* New York: Praeger, 1962, p. 14. Reprinted by permission.
"Income tenths" are for "recipients" for 1910-37 and "spending units" for 1941-59.

Notes: Data for 1910-37 are from National Industrial Conference Board, *Studies in Enterprise and Social Progress* (New York: National Industrial Conference Board, 1939), p. 125. Data for 1941-59 were calculated by the Survey Research Center. Figures for 1941-46 are available in rounded form only. Previously unpublished data for 1947-58 are reproduced by permission of the Board of Governors of the Federal Reserve System, and data for 1959 by permission of the Survey Research Center.

equanimity. The reason: even though each had an income in excess of $100,000, not one of the 381 paid a penny of Federal income tax last April. Indeed, 21 of them had incomes of more than $1 million in 1967 but contrived to pass the 1968 deadline wholly unscathed. And they are likely to have equal success this year.

> In 1966, four lucky Americans, each of whom drew an income in excess of $5 million, clearly escaped taxation. Even that achievement is dwarfed by the gentleman who a few years ago enjoyed an income of more than $20 million and shared not a penny of it with Internal Revenue.[17]

These "rich and super-rich" legal tax evaders are joined by thousands of others who to a greater or lesser extent pay taxes far below the "official" rates announced by the government.

Equally important are the large numbers of the wealthy who devise various illegal means of avoiding the payment of taxes. At a conference on "crimes of corporations," the U.S. Attorney for the Southern District of New York, Robert M. Morgenthau, pointed to the use of secret, unnumbered Swiss bank accounts for crimes such as income tax evasion and the manipulation of stock values.

> We have discovered during the course of our investigation that persons who illegally use these secret accounts are all too frequently highly respectable corporate executives, businessmen, brokers, accountants, and lawyers—men who would be the first to complain about a robbery or a mugging in their neighborhood.[18]

Comparable resistance to any substantial redistribution of wealth is also apparent in other industrialized democracies. John Strachey examined the distribution of wealth in Great Britain and found that from 1911–1939 only 10 per cent of the total population received 50 per cent of the total income while the remaining 90 per cent of the population shared the other 50 per cent. From 1939 to 1951 there was a slight redistribution of income in favor of the wage earners, but this trend was probably reversed after 1951.[19] Strachey concludes that "all this is evidence that capitalism has in fact an innate tendency to extreme and ever-growing inequality."[20] These conclusions, based on incomes reported to the tax offices no doubt underestimate the real inequality—the ability of the wealthy to hide real income, to take advantage of untaxable capital investments, to benefit from insurance programs, etc. Any estimate of their share of wealth is therefore likely to underestimate the inequality. Richard Titmuss' more recent analysis of income distribution in Great Britain takes such things into account, and he concludes that "there is more than a hint from a number of studies that income inequality has been increasing since 1949 while the ownership of wealth . . . has probably become still more unequal, and, in terms of family ownership, possibly strikingly more unequal, in recent years."[21] Similar trends and tendencies seem to be true in other democratic countries as well.[22]

The view that social inequality is functional is more akin to an apologia for the status quo than it is to a sociologically useful model. It suggests that validity of Ossowski's observation:

> Wherever there is a tendency to efface the distinctness of social inequalities —whether this is motivated by a desire to deaden the sensitiveness of the oppressed classes or to appease the conscience of the privileged and reconcile the existing state of affairs with the theology which they profess—we find in the image of the social structure an inclination to give priority to mutual dependence in the inter-class relationship.[23]

With the same sort of logic, functional models are developed for "understanding" war, deviance, law, and virtually any other social phenomena as functional. To argue that these social events serve some "purpose" can be cogent only if we ask the further question, which derives from the conflict model; whose purposes do these social phenomena serve? The conflict model also suggests a hypothesis in answer to that query; they serve the purpose of the ruling classes, whose sons do not fight the wars but whose way of life is protected as a result of these wars;[24] whose children do not experience the sting of law enforcement or suffer for their deviance;[25] and whose children do not have to be taught to "defer gratification" in order for them to inherit their parents' position in society.[26]

THE RELATIONSHIP BETWEEN NONINDUSTRIALIZED AND INDUSTRIALIZED SOCIETIES

It is commonplace to refer to nonindustrialized societies as forming "the third world." The fact that the nonindustrialized societies are so perceived is in and of itself indicative of the kinds of errors that derive from a failure to bring to bear the conflict perspective in analyzing events. The concept of a "third world" suggests implicitly (and inevitably leads to explicit theories) that: (a) the nonindustrialized nations form a sociological unit that has developed independently of the industrialized nations, and (b) such independence is true today. It also suggests that the nonindustrialized nations share certain unique characteristics (which the industrialized world has "outgrown" or "gone beyond") that allow them to remain autonomous. As Pierre Jallee writes:

> To accept too easily the term (third world), to introduce it into ordinary language, means to introduce insidiously the idea that the group of countries about which we have spoken constitutes a particular entity, a world in itself, in regard to which the theories and reasoning applied to the group of capitalist (industrialized) countries should be revised, adapted, and more or less adulterated.[27]

Merely to accept the terminology of "the third world" (the least industrialized countries of Latin America, Africa, and Asia) is to open ourselves to the reasoning that the "first world" became industrialized of its own accord. Yet no one can fail to recognize the fact that the industrialized world's superior war-making technology at a particular point in history allowed it to exploit and convert to its own uses the resources of three-fourths of the world.[28]

Similarly, nonindustrialized nations are frequently called "dual societies." According to this view, the key feature of a nonindustrialized society is its division into: (a) a small, industrialized, westernized, "modern" population centered in the cities, and (b) a large, rural, agrarian nonindustrialized, traditional society. To characterize nonindustrialized societies in this way is not so much an error as it is a blindness to the fact that the undeveloped areas of nonindustrialized societies furnish the resources which enable the elites of these countries to live in the style of their peers in industrialized societies. This situation allows the industrialized societies to maintain their exploitative relationship with the nonindustrialized. As Frank notes:

> Those people in the underdeveloped countries who were not or are not at any one time incorporated into the capitalist system's market as visibly direct sellers of labor or buyers of products are not for all that unintegrated into, isolated from, or marginal to the capitalist system. Theirs is another rate which is a no less necessary result of the essential internal contradiction of the capitalist system . . . they have witnessed the capitalist system produce its sometimes sudden, sometimes slow, but always inevitable world, national and regional shifts in supply and demand for their former output of spices, sugar, cocoa, coffee, tea, rubber, gold, silver, copper, tin and other raw materials, and of industrial goods as well, which for months, years, decades, or even centuries transform whole populations of once independent producers or dependent workers into the "floating" or "marginal"

bare or nonsubsistence populations of the capitalist system's ubiquitous underdeveloped rural and urban slums and ghettos.[29]

These are egregious errors; they preclude any realistic understanding of the relationship between industrialized and nonindustrialized societies. To make such errors leads us to develop theories of development which border on the ludicrous. Two theories of development deriving from a perspective of nonindustrialized society as "the third world" are illustrative.

Achievement Motivation and National Development

Viewing nonindustrialized societies as "the third world" leads us to look within those societies for the causes of nonindustrialization. It may lead us, as does one prominent theory, to ask what it is about the individual psyche of populations that differentiates industrialized and nonindustrialized societies. From such a perspective comes David McClelland's theory of achievement motivation. "In its most general terms, the hypothesis states that a society with a generally high level of achievement will produce more energetic entrepreneurs who in turn, produce more rapid economic development.[30] McClelland's theory of economic development is based on the assumption that "it is values, motives or psychological forces that determine ultimately the rate of economic and social development."[31]

With a swift swipe of the pen McClelland has provided a theory of development which implicitly denies the importance of four hundred (or more) years of history. The enslavement of Africans is not connected with their failure to industrialize; the economic dependency of Latin America created, fostered, and maintained by the United States is not relevant to economic development; the unquestioned ability of the industrialized societies to manipulate governments and fight wars against nonindustrialized nations that balk at exploitation has nothing to do with development. All that one need know is that nonindustrialized nations lack the proper amount of "achievement motivation." Had they had a sufficient amount, presumably, the slave ships of England, France, and America would never have been able to ply the waters of Africa. Yet strangely, it was the high achievement motivation of some African tribes (from McClelland's perspective) that made them slave traders while others were slaves.

Such a perspective also implies what is not true—that underdeveloped nations have always been that way. In fact, of course, many currently nonindustrialized societies were at one time highly developed and in many cases dominated a good part of the world as a result of their superior technology, much as the west does today. Their underdevelopment was created by western expansionism and imperialism, *not* by a lack of "achievement motivation":

> To extract the fruits of their labor through pillage, slavery, forced labor, free labor, raw materials, or through monopoly trade—no less today than in the times of Cortez and Pizarro in Mexico and Peru, Clive in India, Rhodes in Africa, the "Open Door" in China—the metropolis (the urban centers of industrialized societies) destroyed and/or totally transformed the earlier viable social and economic systems of these societies, incorporated them into the metropolitan-dominated worldwide capitalist system, and converted them into sources for its own metropolitan capital accumulation and development . . . [The people in these societies] have, as in India, seen imperialism destroy the organization, handicrafts, industry and trade as well as the livelihood they derived from these . . . The resulting fate for these conquered, transformed, or newly established societies was and remains their decapitalization, structurally generated unproductiveness, ever increasing poverty for the masses—in a word, their underdevelopment.
>
> Underdevelopment, far from being due to any supposed "isolation" of the majority of the world's people from modern capitalist expansion, or even to any continued feudal relations and wars, is the result of the integral incorporation of these people into the fully integrated but contradictory capitalist system which has long since embraced them all.[32]

Pattern Variables and Underdevelopment

Following the theoretical perspective of Talcott Parsons, Bert Hoselitz has argued that nonindustrialized societies, unlike industrialized societies, exhibit the characteristics of particularism, ascription, and functional diffuseness. Industrial societies, by contrast, exhibit the opposite of these variables—universalism, achievement orientation, and functional specificity.

A complete analysis of these variables and their theoretical utility is beyond the scope of this introduction and can be found elsewhere.[33] We shall take only the first presumed difference between industrialized and nonindustrialized societies, namely, the particularistic-universalistic dimension.

Stripped of its comprehensive aspects, the theory suggests that in nonindustrialized societies, the criteria of achievement are particularistic. In other words, people become leaders, are employed or fired, are wealthy or poor, not because they deserve it—not because they have earned it—but because they are chosen for personal reasons by those already in power. The argument is that "success" in nonindustrialized societies depends on "connections," whereas success in industrialized societies depends on merit—on ability. The argument is also made that "first world" societies industrialized because they always emphasized merit (a universalistic principle) rather than, say, kinship ties (a particularistic principle). The falsity of this notion is apparent by looking at either the presumed "meritocracy" in industrialized societies or the presumed particularistic criteria in nonindustrialized societies.

One of the "miracles" of economic development in the last seventy-five years has been Japan. Yet this has been accomplished, as most observers agree, because particularistic criteria were used. Factories are organized around the principle of hiring entire families rather than individuals. One is employed, in other words, because of his kinship ties, not because of his own abilities or aspirations.[34]

Particularistic criteria also abound in Europe and the United States among the working classes as well as the elites.[35] The children of the wealthy inherit wealth and power in industrialized societies irrespective of their ability. The best education in industrialized societies goes to the children of the well-to-do, not to the most intelligent or most deserving. Power and wealth perpetuate themselves in *all* societies. All societies are, in this sense, particularistic. To argue that industrialized societies are less particularistic than nonindustrialized societies is to perpetuate myths.

Particularism works blatantly at the highest levels of decision-making in industrialized societies.

> Roosevelt's and Kennedy's brain trusts co-opted all sorts of American social scientists. Harvard historian Arthur Schlesinger, Jr.'s aid to the development of underdeveloped countries has so far consisted in writing the now famous White Paper on Cuba which was intended to justify the coming invasion of that country at the Bay of Pigs. He later admitted lying about the invasion in the "national interest." Stanford economist Eugene Staley wrote *The Future of Underdeveloped Countries* and then planted it in the renowned Staley-[General Maxwell] Taylor Plan to put 15 million Vietnamese in the concentration camps they euphemistically christened "strategic hamlets." Since the failure of that effort at development planning, M.I.T. economic historian Walt Whitman Rostow has escalated the effort by writing *The Stages of Economic Growth: A Non-Communist Manifesto.* He wrote of these stages at the CIA-financed Center for International

> Studies on the Charles River and has been operationalizing them on the Potomac as President Kennedy's Director of Policy and Planning in the State Department and President Johnson's chief adviser on Vietnam. It is on behalf of Vietnamese economic growth that Rostow has become the principal architect of escalation, from napalming the South to bombing the North, and beyond. Then, doubtless due to universalist particularism and achieved ascription, Eugene Rostow moves from professing international law at Yale University to practicing it at his brother's side in Washington. Meanwhile, after performing his role as Dean of Humanities at Harvard University, McGeorge Bundy becomes W. W. Rostow's superior in Washington and goes on television to explain to the misguided and incredulous why this economic development theory and policy is humanitarian (after which he goes on to direct the Ford Foundation and its influence on education and research). In the light of the manifest and institutionalized role-summation and diffuseness of these deans of humane scholarship and professors of applied social science, the clandestine direction of Project Camelot by the Department of Defense and the financing of the United States National Student Association by the CIA pale into the shadows.[36]

I am not arguing that adopting the conflict perspective makes one immune to theoretical errors. But it does protect one from the kinds of errors consistently made by Western social scientists who look at nonindustrialized societies with the wrong model in mind. It forces one to look at societies as forming part of a whole system. To speak of underdevelopment without taking into account the relationship between the underdeveloped and the developed is to invite the kinds of narrow-visioned errors contained in the theories of Hoselitz and McClelland.

A second feature of the conflict perspective which helps it to avoid some of the errors frequently made by social scientists is its emphasis on history. The conflict perspective insists that the history of any contemporary society must be taken into account in trying to understand that society. Certainly this is obvious when we are dealing with the question of industrialization.

A third feature of some importance in the context of this discussion is the emphasis on looking at both one's own society and others in the same light. To see "particularism" in other societies and universalism in our own is to look at our own with blinders. Indeed, it denies the validity of centuries of sociological research, which has consistently shown how wealth protects poorly qualified persons from failure and how poverty commits highly talented people to wasting their talents. If we are blinded by a model of society that makes such observations inconsistent with the perspective, it is possible to grossly misrepresent our own way of life.

BUREAUCRATIZATION

Max Weber is rightly renowned for seeing the extremely important role bureaucracies and bureaucratization would play in industrial society.[37] He, more than any other sociologist, devoted time and attention to the characteristics and effects of bureaucracy on society. He provided us with a conceptual framework for thinking about bureaucracies which has dominated most thinking on the subject since his initial observations were made. For Weber the chief indentifying characteristic of bureaucracy is that it has clearly specified areas of jurisdiction which are (usually) ordered by explicit rules—either laws created by the state or regulations stipulated by administrative units. Concomitant with this is the fact that the rules are enforced and lived up to by persons who occupy positions within the bureaucracy. These persons gain their authority by virtue of occupying roles in the organization. They do not have authority because they have inherited it (which would be traditional rather than rational authority); they do not have authority because they are chosen as leaders or because people can be swayed to follow them (which would be charismatic authority). Their authority must rest, according to Weber, on the fact that they occupy a role with specified duties and obligations in a bureaucratic structure. Their authority, then, is neither traditional nor charismatic; it is legitimate. Thus, legitimate authority becomes the defining characteristic of the positions that constitute the bureaucracy.

Nisbet has summed up other characteristics of bureaucracy that were of importance to Weber:

> From the basic principle of fixed and official jurisdiction flow such vital practices and criteria as the regularization of channels of communication, authority, and appeal; the functional priority of the office to the person occupying it; the emphasis upon written and recorded orders in place of random, merely personal commands or wishes; the sharp separation of official from personal identity in the management of affairs and the superintending of finances; the identification of, and provision for the training of "expertness" in a given office or function; the rigorous priority of official to merely personal business in the governing of an enterprise; and finally, the conversion of as many activities and functions as possible to clear and

> specifiable rules; rules that, by their nature, have both perspective and authoritarian significance.[38]

Weber's analysis goes farther than simply this description of bureaucracy. The process of bureaucratization

> becomes for Weber a powerful manifestation of the historical principle of rationalization. The growth of bureaucracy in government, business, religion, and education is an aspect of the rationalization of culture that has also transformed . . . the nature of art, drama, music and philosophy.[39]

Weber's followers have often translated "rationalization" as meaning "good" in contrast to "irrational processes," which were bad. Surely no one would want to argue that irrational authority is better than rational authority. But Weber in fact did just that.

> It is horrible to think that the world could one day be filled with nothing but those little cogs, little men clinging to little jobs and striving towards the bigger ones—a state of affairs which is to be seen once more . . . playing an ever-increasing part in the spirit of our present administrative system.[40]

Judging from the excruciating experiences modern man undergoes at the hands of the "rational" bureaucracies, it is easy to see that Weber's fear prognosis of the terrors of "rational" ordering of activities through bureaucracies was quite justified.

But our concern here is not with the consequences of bureaucratization. Our concern is to point up the difference between conflict and functionalist approaches, and this becomes clearest when we try to explain *why* bureaucratization has taken place. Weber was more concerned with describing the process of bureaucratization than with explaining why it had taken place. To the extent that Weber offered an explanation of why bureaucratization occurred, he emphasized two different reasons. First and foremost was the fact that a tendency to rationalization was simply part of the inevitable process of history. Second, Weber imputed the cause of bureaucratization to the fact that in the modern world, organizations tended to be large; largeness, he argued, led to bureaucratization.

Neither of these arguments is very compelling. Bureaucratization as a fact is not really explained adequately simply by saying that it is part of a historical process. To suggest the historical process as an explanation is really only to describe what is happening in different words. The problem for sociologists is to explain what it is in the structure of society that is bringing about this change in society.

To see the cause of bureaucracy in the mere size of social groups is perhaps more akin to an explanation, but it is no more viable. As Gouldner has pointed out,

> Weber's emphasis on size as the crucial determinant of bureaucratic development is unsatisfactory for several reasons. First, there are historic examples of human efforts carried out on an enormous scale which were not bureaucratic in any serious sense of the term. The building of the Egyptian pyramids is an obvious example. Second, Weber never considers the possibility that it is not "large size" as such that disposes to bureaucracy; large size may be important only because it generates other social forces which, in their turn, generate bureaucratic patterns.[41]

The implications of Weber's analysis were not fully appreciated until the more recent efforts of functionalists to explain bureaucratization. Talcott Parsons exemplifies this position among contemporary sociologists:

> Technological advance almost always leads to increasingly elaborate division of labor and the concomitant requirement of increasingly elaborate organization. The fundamental reason for this is, of course, that with elaborate differentiation of functions the need for minute coordination of the different functions develops at the same time.[42]

Parsons' argument (unlike many of his others) is quite clear in this passage. Technological advance necessitates bureaucratization. Bureaucratization (like pollution) with all its faults, then, is a price we must pay for advancing technology.

Such an explanation leaves out more than it includes. The typical functional analysis (as the arguments of Weber and Parsons illustrate) ends precisely where the most compelling and challenging questions lie. For real insight into the process of bureaucratization, it is necessary to ask why the decision to bureaucratize is made by those responsible for the shape of the organization. It must also be asked what meaning bureaucratization will have for the people at all levels of the organization. In short, a consideration of the dynamic process of bureaucratization must be a part of any responsible sociological analysis; it is simply not enough to point to the correlates of the process (technological advance and bureaucratic organization) and to suppose that you have thereby explained the process.

Furthermore, the alleged cause of bureaucratization does not hold up in the face of empirical data. As Weber himself recognized, bureaucratization occurs in organizations where technological "advance" is completely lacking—religious and charitable organizations, for example—and in contemporary western societies whose agencies administer social services or agencies that enforce the law.

How might the process of bureaucratization be approached from the conflict perspective? More insight into the bureaucratic process would be gained by asking whose interests are served by this phenomenon. Who, in the last analysis, benefits from the bureaucratization of industry and organizations? And how are the decisions to bureaucratize made? Who pays what price for bureaucratization, once established, and who is responsible for perpetuating bureaucratic organization in the face of opposition? By asking such questions, much can be learned about the bureaucratic process that remains hidden if we accept too readily the superficial explanation that bureaucracies emerge with increased size; or that bureaucracies are necessary ingredients in advancing technology; or that bureaucracies simply reflect inevitable historical processes.

The fact is that bureaucracies do *not* represent "rational" organization in one sense of the word; they are not always the most sensible way of reaching the goals for which the organizations ostensibly exist. For example, there is good reason to doubt that bureaucratization is in fact the most efficient or, in Parsons' terminology, a functionally necessary way to organize the production of material goods. Bureaucratization interferes rather basically with the process of education, as is becoming increasingly clear to everyone involved with modern-day universities. And recent analyses of the legal system have demonstrated how the bureaucratic demands of the law-enforcement agencies tend to usurp the goals of the law in democratic societies.[43] Indeed, it is not too much of an exaggeration to say that in law enforcement, bureaucratization has been the principal cause of a breakdown in the legitimacy of law in the eyes of many members of society. In short, bureaucratization has served to *lessen* the legitimacy of the social institutions, not to enhance it, as Weber would have us believe it should.

In the face of such high costs and inevitable contradictions of bureaucratic organization, we must explain the continuation and expansion of bureaucracy. The place to look for an explanation of this apparent paradox is not in the lives of people who must cope with bureaucratic red tape, but rather in the needs of those in power to maintain their positions of power. And for this purpose bureaucracies are incredibly fit. Where traditional authority justified the exploitation of the masses during feudal times, bureaucratic organization serves that purpose in the modern world. In days gone by, it was the crown's right to punish people who did not accept the prevailing moral order; today, the interests of the state and of the elites are perpetuated by bureaucracies which claim to be (but in fact are not) impartial administrators of morality and justice.

Bureaucracies, in short, persist and are perpetuated because they serve the interests of those in power. They do this by:

1. Fuzzing the lines of power so that those who benefit most are not so visible to those who benefit least.
2. Making decisions appear rational and universal and fair when they are in fact whimsical, particularistic, and consistently biased.
3. Making the exploitation of those who get the least out of the available resources of society appear to be a consequence of "the organization" rather than of "managers," "capitalists," "elites," or "the haves."

HOLISM

Both the functional and conflict approaches claim to be "holistic." Yet their holisms, it turns out, are of quite different cuts. The discussion of the relationship between industrial and nonindustrial societies exemplifies one such difference. The functionalist approach is to look at each society as though it were a self-contained unit (thus leading to such explanatory theories about developmental rates as achievement motivation, amount of particularism, etc.). The conflict perspective, starting from the vantage point of the relationship between the nonindustrial and industrial societies, looks at *all* countries as comprising the unit of analysis for understanding why they are where they are. The conflict perspective leads one to see the all-important relationship between the underdeveloped nations as satellites of the developed (European and North American) nations, which is at the root of their relative positions as industrialized countries.

This basic difference in approach is also clear in evaluating one of the propositions of Marxian theory.[44] Marx asserted that one of the characteristics of capitalism is an increasing proletarianization and increasing misery for the masses of the people. In attempting to deny that this has occurred, functionalists point to the fact that within the United States (or Great Britain, West Germany, and France), this has not occurred. Yet if one looks at the entire world and not just at particular societies, then Marx's assertion is not so easily dismissed. For Latin America his prophecy has proved quite true: for Africa, India, and most of Asia there has been an increasing proletarianization and increasing misery for the vast majority of people. There is some evidence, in fact, that Marx's expectation has also been realized in Eastern Europe. In short, for most of mankind there has been increasing misery and increasing proletarianization. Most of mankind has been subjected by the capitalist economic system to precisely the kind of exploitation that Marx saw as inevitable, given the structure of capitalism. Only if our "holism" is strangely restricted to looking at *one* society and not at the relationships among all societies can we sustain the argument that Marx was in this instance wrong. There is indeed quite a difference in the holistic approach of the conflict perspective and the holistic approach of functionalism.

ON POWER

The interpretations and interest in power of the conflict and functional models parallel rather closely the earlier discussion of social class and social inequality. Two related points of difference, however, bear special mention. In general, the conflict model sees the upper classes of the society as a ruling class. The functional model emphasizes instead the diversity of interests of the ruling class. In other words, the conflict perspective emphasizes the cohesiveness and unity of interests of the upper classes, whereas the functional perspective emphasizes the divisions within the upper classes and (ironically) their conflicting interests.

The conflict perspective also gives primacy to the role of money and wealth in the determination of social power. The functionalists' view is more eclectic and emphasizes a variety of types and sources of power. This difference between functional and conflict models comes out clearly in a comparison of Marx's conflict approach and Weber's functionalist perspective:

> Max Weber, who was the first to present a comprehensive alternative to Marx's theory, did so by distinguishing, in the first place, between different modes of stratification which coexisted in modern societies: class stratification with which Marx had been primarily concerned, and stratification by

> social prestige or honor. He also treated as an independent phenomenon the distribution of political power in society, which Marx had viewed almost exclusively as the product of class stratification.[45]

The functionalists, following Weber, tend to analyze power, if at all, as a problem of how different types of power are diffused throughout the society. Conflict theorists, following Marx, tend to concentrate on those groups that control the "big decisions" in modern society. The title of C. Wright Mills' best-known book, *The Power Elite,* points to the essential difference between conflict and functional models in this regard.[46] Not only would someone working with a functional model avoid such a title, he would not, in all likelihood, be led to even research the question of whether there is a ruling elite. Instead, he would assume that power is diffuse and that the appropriate study of power should concentrate on who wields power in what particular situation over what particular group.

In part, this conception of power harkens back to our earlier discussion of different conceptions of the "whole." The conflict theorist is continually looking from very large social units (all societies or all of a particular society) and attempting to explain the behavior of the parts (the family, community, law, individual) as a reflection of the characteristics of the whole. The functionalists' holism, by contrast, is in fact more a particularism wherein the whole of society or of all societies is thought to be understood by examining the parts.

The answer to issues raised here concerning power are contained in the articles to follow. At this point, however, it may be well to quote the argument of Bottomore in support of the conflict approach to the study of power:

> If power is really so widely dispersed (as the functionalists would have it) how are we to account for the fact that the owners of property—the upper class in Marx's sense—still predominate so remarkably in government and administration, and in other *elite* positions; or that there has been so little redistribution of wealth and income, in spite of the strenuous and sustained effort of the labour movement to bring it about? Is it not reasonable to conclude ... that notwithstanding political democracy, and despite the limited conflicts of interest which occur between *elite* groups in different spheres, the upper class in capitalist societies is still a distinctive and largely self-perpetuating social group, and still occupies the vital positions of power? Its power may be less commanding, and it is certainly less arrogantly exercised, than in an earlier period, because it encounters an orga-

> nized opposition and the test of elections, and because other classes have gained a limited access to the *elites;* but the power which it has retained enables it to defend successfully its most important economic interests.[47]

THE QUALITY OF LIFE

In keeping with their general orientations, the conflict and functionalist perspectives take quite different stances with regard to the quality of life. In general, the conflict model leads one to investigate and emphasize the disruptive, inherently contradictory features of modern civilization. The inability and unwillingness of states to solve problems of ecology and psychological well-being are of paramount importance to those who view social life from the vantage point of conflict. The presumed tendency of man to solve his problems and his willingness to do so is the point of departure for the functionalist.

The general conclusion that man faces ecological disaster is a viewpoint increasingly voiced by politicians and scholars alike. It is, indeed, becoming so apparent that the environment is being spoiled irretrievably by man that even the functionalists can be expected to begin paying some attention to this problem in the near future; though predictably, they will not stress the fact that the interests of some segments of society conflict with those of others. Rather, their emphasis, when it comes, will doubtless be on the tendency of "man" (not the business elite or the political power holders) to exploit "cheap resources" and thereby to despoil his environment. The clear advantage of the conflict model is that it first leads one to ask questions about the misuse of the environment before it becomes a political and moral issue, and it focuses attention on those parts of the society that are responsible for the despoilation. To link the leaving of paper on the roadside with the dumping of pollutants into the water and air is to completely misunderstand the problem and to create impotence in the face of the necessity for change.

The problem of modern man's estrangement from his world is also an integral part of the conflict model. Karl Marx put the point succinctly in writing about the workers in capitalist societies:

> In what does the alienation of labor consist? First, that the work is external to the worker, that it is not a part of his nature, that consequently he does not fulfil himself in his work but denies himself, has a feeling of misery, not of well-being . . . the worker therefore feels himself at home only during his leisure, whereas at work he feels homeless.[48]

Elsewhere in his writings, Marx extends this notion of alienation (he refers to it elsewhere as "estrangement," a term which is in many ways preferable to "alienation," since the latter has been so butchered by social researchers) to apply to all of modern man. He sees not only the worker but also the capitalist and the bourgeoisie as suffering estrangement from life and his fellow man. In addition to accepting the broader application of its prevalence of estrangement, modern conflict theories also apply Marx's broader application to all men in industrialized society.

The functionalist perspective, although not uniformly arguing that modern man is content and finds meaning in the quality of his life, does tend to see the quality of life as generally high in modern industrialized society. The functionalists' emphasis is on the cohesive nature of norms and the meaning given to life by the belief systems which prevail.

It is doubtless safe to say that no empirical evidence exists for this argument. Social-science techniques have proved grossly inadequate to the task of assessing the quality of life. Questionnaire attempts to assess the general "happiness" of the people have been abysmal failures;[49] efforts to determine objectively the presence or absence of "alienation" among workers or other groups have been contradictory.[50]

Those who generally favor the conflict perspective point to such things as the amount of crime, the high suicide and alcoholism rates, and the disappointment of adults with youth and vice versa as indications of a general state of unhappiness and estrangement. Functionalists point to rising wages, presumed increases in social mobility, and an improvement in the standard of living for more and more people as indications that the quality of life has improved and that alienation has declined.

It is at this point pretty much a matter of taste which approach one chooses. Historian William A. Williams' excellent book *The Great Evasion,* stresses the quality of life in modern capitalist societies and argues persuasively for the validity of the conflict perspective.[51] We are nevertheless left with the distinct feeling that as yet the evidence is not complete on either side of this argument (if, indeed, it is on any of the arguments which divide the conflict and functionalist perspectives), and as a result whether one sees the quality of life in modern industrialized society as "strained" or "satisfactory" depends more on disposition than fact. The disposition of the conflict approach is more pessimistic; that of the functionalist more optimistic. It comes down, in this case, to more a matter of style than logic or fact.

At a time when students and hordes of adults are deeply concerned about the meaninglessness of life—when they are vocally and overtly expressing estrangement from modern society—it is perhaps unnecessary to defend the conflict position with any further evidence. Certainly the minority groups that have been most exploited by the modern system —the rural poor, the small farmers, the blacks, the Indians, the Puerto Ricans, and a host of others—share this intense dissatisfaction with the modern world. Their voices speak for the validity of the conflict perspective, but the voices of the "hard hats" and the complacent middle class contradict them. The tool of the debate is evidence of the utility of the conflict perspective, but the resolution of the debate is not forthcoming.

INTERESTS AND HUMAN ACTION

Marx put the point succinctly when he noted that "history is not like some individual person, which uses men to achieve its ends. History is nothing but the actions of men in pursuit of their ends."[52] The psychological implications of this point of view have not been traced very systematically; though some of the writings included in Part 6 touch on it. More often the emphasis among conflict theorists has been on the role of groups of men who are acting in their own interests. Consistent with the conflict model, the emphasis has been on groups which grow out of economic divisions of society into social classes.

The contrast with functionalist thinking is striking. Where conflict emphasizes the inherent conflict of interests among different groups in the society, functionalism emphasizes the mutuality of interest. Where conflict emphasizes the role of the state in expressing the interests of particular groups (especially the elites), functionalism tends to see the state as a value-neutral setting in which interest groups share a more or less equal footing and some form of balance or homeostasis is reached through the state.[53]

In the abstract either point of view may appear equally defensible. When one gets down to particulars, however, it is difficult to find substantiation for the functionalist perspective. In the section on problems of industrialized societies, we shall trace a number of particular issues of industrialized society, and it shall become clear from these analyses how the conflict model approaches the problem.

At this point it may be useful to discuss one illustrative case before leaving the issue. For some time now sociologists have been exploring and proclaiming the explanatory utility of the "theory of status inconsistency." The crux of this "theory" is that people who occupy conflicting statuses (such as having a good deal of education but a poor-paying job) are less content than the average with their lives and with the political order. They are, in this argument, thus more susceptible to extreme political viewpoints such as the John Birchers or the communists.

The view has a good deal to recommend it from the functionalists' point of view. It reinforces the idea that it is disharmony (a lack of status consistency) and not poverty, lack of power, or conflicts inherent in the society that leads men to take something other than the "rational" or "normal" course of nonradical political views.

The evidence in support of the theory of status inconsistency is conflicting, but one attempt to assess the theory's utility concludes that

> comparisons between the relative ability of social class membership and status inconsistency to predict political attitudes quite clearly demonstrate the superiority of social class as a predictor . . . Social class membership and minority group status appear to be far superior explanatory concepts. These concepts may be time-worn and smack of Marxism. But if they are in fact the kinds of sociological variables that determine the behavior of men then we should use them. Concepts like status consistency . . . unquestionably have a more sophisticated sound to them. But if we sacrifice substantive usefulness for sophisticated appearance then our contribution to knowledge will be meager indeed.[54]

This investigation and a number of others have suggested that the notion of social classes acting according to their own interests is a far more useful predictor of political predispositions than is the inconsistency of statuses. It is unlikely that those who wear the functionalists' bifocals will cease attempting to construct "alternatives to a Marxian interpretation," but nonetheless it seems clear that the alternatives offered fall short of supplying very satisfactory explanations.

The Relative Importance of Culture and Social Structure

Every sociological perspective finds it analytically useful to distinguish between culture and social structure. Culture refers to the prevailing ideas of right and wrong, the belief systems, and the rules for interacting with other people and institutions. Culture also includes the "baggage," or "tools," with which people adjust, drop out of, or attempt to change established relationships in the society. Language, technological know-how, religious dogma, and legal rules are among the most important elements of a society's culture.

Social structure refers to the rather more substantial, nonideological aspects of society, e.g., the fact that the economic system is organized around private property. The belief that this is good, and the laws that protect and establish this relationship are part of the culture. But the fact that individuals own private property and that this ownership determines their "web of life"—their day-to-day patterns of existence—is the social structure, just as the fact that the world of business and large corporations exists and dominates the decision-making processes in contemporary western societies is part of that social structure. The fact that the western world controls 60 per cent of the world's natural resources and uses it to support 10 per cent of the world's population is a fact that is built into the structure of contemporary life. It may or may not be supported by values that depict these relationships as right, but their existence is a fact of life and is part of the social structure.

The functionalist and conflict perspectives place different emphasis on the relative importance of culture and social structure. Both perspectives, to be sure, have a place for these aspects of society. But the functionalists tend to emphasize the primacy of culture, whereas the conflict perspective emphasizes the primacy of social structure. Marx's view of religion as "the opiate of the masses"—that is, his view that religion derives from the established exploitative relationship between those with property and those who live by labor—makes religion (part of the culture) dependent on the established economic relationships (the social structure). This contrasts rather dramatically with our earlier discussion of Durkheim's search for the "glue" of society, which led him to seek the foundation of society in the religious beliefs that had developed through the centuries. To be sure, Durkheim talked about and emphasized structural characteristics just as Marx and conflict theorists after him talked about and emphasized culture. Rather, the point of departure tends to be the relative importance placed on these different facets of society. As a rule the functionalists see culture as shaping social structure; the conflict model sees the reverse.

Which view is more useful can be judged only by the explanations and researches it produces. Time and a willingness to look open-mindedly at the merits of each position will be the final judge of the relative merits of each.

SOCIAL ENGINEERING

Functionalists either deny that social scientists should concern themselves with social engineering or insist that the recipe for change is to tinker with the prevailing culture or structure. Conflict theorists tend to see the need for change as involving wholesale alterations to the primary institutions of the society—economic relationships, for example. The conflict perspective is also rather more likely to place social engineering as a legitimate and necessary component of the social science enterprise.

Functionalists often accuse conflict sociologists of being "unscientific" because of their social engineering. Yet certainly in one respect they are much more scientific. Conflict theorists more often than functionalists admit explicitly to a set of values that govern their work. These values, then, become part of the package that can be refuted by empirical evidence. The functionalists more often than not deny that they are imposing any values on their study at all, a claim which has been shown time and again to be but a delusion. One example may suffice to make the point.

In his discussion of the study of underdevelopment, Rinehard Bendix argued that social scientists should submerge theory and approach the study of developing nations "objectively."[55] Yet when one pursues his argument, it becomes apparent that Bendix has smuggled in an inherent conservatism in the guise of "objectivity." For as we have argued before, what is looked at, what is selected for study, and the way these things are viewed all depend on the application of a perspective. The problem is to make that perspective explicit so that the conjectures contained in the perspective can be open to refutation if they do not square with the facts that emerge from our inquiries. Functionalists, who hide behind the thin facade of being "scientific" because they do not express any theory, have in fact the complete reverse of a scientific approach. Their ideas, which are never tested, are only smuggled in through the back door of description. But description is impossible without some general perspective. To be scientific, a perspective must be explicit and capable of being judged.

WHAT FOLLOWS: THE PLAN OF THE BOOK

Sociology is in some respects like a three-ring circus; not because what goes on inside is particularly entertaining, but because there are so many acts taking place at one time that one can scarcely see them all as a unified show. Until recently, however, American sociology did possess one unifying characteristic—a strong urge to avoid at all costs any interpretation of society which smacked of conflict theory.[56] The inability of conventional, inherently conservative, functional theory to account for, predict, or make sense of the myriad of violent and unanticipated events in America in the sixties, however, has provided new breath for the conflict perspective. What the historian William A. Williams has aptly called "the great evasion" of American intellectuals has, at long last, begun to break down.

The articles, research findings, and essays that follow describe the fundamental characteristics of modern societies. They represent some of the products of conflict-oriented social science inquiry. The first and most important reason for studying these articles is to gain an understanding of the contemporary world. It will also be important to be sensitive to the concepts used in the quest to gain this understanding—social class, power, interest groups, bureaucracy, cultural pluralism and, of course, social conflict—all of which are foundation blocks to an understanding of the contemporary world.

Finally, attention should be called to the variety of research techniques used. Analyses of the historical trends are complemented by survey researches of modern society, and participant observation studies provide data which supplement both. The articles illuminate the studies, techniques, interests, skills, and conclusions of research in all of the social sciences. Taken together, they represent the best available evidence for the potency of the conflict perspective.

NOTES

1. Bernard Barber, "Resistance by Scientists to Scientific Discovery," in Robert B. Seidman, "Law and Development in Africa." Unpublished manuscript. University of Wisconsin, 1971. Reprinted by permission. For the use of models in scientific inquiry, see also: Norwood Russell Hanson, *Patterns of Discovery,* Cambridge: Cambridge University Press, 1959; Karl Popper, *The Logic of Scientific Discovery,* New York: Basic Books, 1959; and Thomas S. Kuhn, *The Structure of Scientific Revolutions* (2d ed.), Chicago: University of Chicago Press, 1970.
2. Ralf Dahrendorf, "Toward a Theory of Social Conflict," *Journal of Peace and Conflict Resolution,* **XI,** 1958, pp. 170-183.
3. *Ibid.*

4. For these points, I am heavily indebted to observations originally made in Gerhard Lenski, *Power and Privilege: A Theory of Social Stratification,* New York: McGraw-Hill, 1966.
5. Robert A. Nisbet, *The Sociological Tradition,* New York: Basic Books, 1966.
6. Kingsley Davis and Wilbert Moore, "Some Principles of Stratification," *American Sociological Review,* **10,** April 1945, pp. 242-249; Kingsley Davis, "A Conceptual Analysis of Stratification," *American Sociological Review,* **7,** June 1942, pp. 309-321; Kingsley Davis, *Human Society,* New York: Macmillan, 1949.
7. Davis and Moore, *op. cit.,* p. 242. Reprinted by permission.
8. *Ibid,* p. 243.
9. *Ibid,* p. 244.
10. Walter Buckley has quite rightly pointed out that the Davis-Moore theory is a theory of inequality, *not* a theory of stratification. We shall therefore refer to it in this way rather than the more general term used by Davis and Moore. See Walter Buckley, "Social Stratification and the Functional Theory of Social Differentiation," *American Sociological Review,* **23,** August 1958, pp. 369-375.
11. For detailed criticisms of the Davis-Moore theory see: *ibid.;* Melvin Tumin, "Some Principles of Stratification: A Critical Analysis," *American Sociological Review,* **18,** August 1953, pp. 387-394; *idem.,* "Rewards and Task-Orientations," *American Sociological Review,* **20,** August 1955, pp. 419-423; Richard D. Schwartz, "Functional Alternatives to Inequality," *American Sociological Review,* **20,** August 1955, pp. 424-430; and Richard L. Simpson, "A Modification of the Functional Theory of Social Stratification," *Social Forces,* **35,** December 1956, pp. 132-137.
12. Schwartz, *op. cit.*
13. *Ibid.*
14. Seymour Martin Lipset and Natalie Rogoff, "Class and Opportunity in Europe and the United States." Reprinted from *Commentary,* p. 568, by permission; Copyright © 1954 by the American Jewish Committee.
15. Gabriel Kolko, *Wealth and Power in America,* New York: Praeger, 1962, p. 15. Reprinted by permission.
16. *International Herald Tribune,* March 16, 1971.
17. Phillip M. Stern, "How 381 Super-rich Americans Managed not to Pay a Cent in Taxes Last Year," *New York Times Magazine,* April 13, 1969, p. 30. © 1969 by The New York Times Company. Reprinted by permission.

18. *Los Angeles Times,* June 27, 1969.
19. John Strachey, *Contemporary Capitalism,* London: Gollanz, 1956, ch. 8.
20. *Ibid.,* p. 146.
21. Richard M. Titmuss, *Income Distribution and Social Change,* London: George Allen and Unwin, Toronto: University of Toronto Press, 1962, p. 198.
22. T. B. Bottomore, *Elites and Society,* New York: Basic Books, 1965, pp. 40-42.
23. Reprinted with permission of the Macmillan Company from *Class Structure in the Social Consciousness* by Stanislau Ossowski, p. 90. Copyright © The Free Press of Glencoe, a Division of The Macmillan Company, 1963.
24. Fred J. Cook, *The Warfare State,* New York: Macmillan, 1964; Tristram Coffin, *The Armed Society: Militarism in Modern America,* New York: Penguin, 1964.
25. William J. Chambliss, "Two Gangs," unpublished manuscript summarized in William J. Chambliss and Robert B. Seidman, *Law, Order and Power,* Reading, Massachusetts: Addison-Wesley, 1971.
26. Robert S. and Helen M. Lynd, *Middletown,* New York: Harcourt Brace & Co., 1929.
27. Pierre Jalle, "Third World: Which Third World?" *Revolution,* **1,** no. 7, 1968 (English edition).
28. This discussion owes much to Andre Gunder Frank, "Sociology of Development and Underdevelopment of Sociology," *Catalyst,* Summer 1967. This article is also reprinted in *idem., Latin America: Underdevelopment or Revolution,* New York: Monthly Review Press, 1969; see also *idem., Capitalism and Underdevelopment in Latin America,* New York: Monthly Review Press, 1967.
29. Andre Gunder Frank, *Latin America: Underdevelopment or Revolution, op. cit.,* pp. 225-226. Reprinted by permission.
30. David C. McClelland, *The Achieving Society,* New York: Van Nostrand Reinhold, 1961, p. 205.
31. David C. McClelland, "Motivational Patterns in Southeast Asia with Special Reference to the Chinese Case," *Journal of Social Issues,* **29,** no. 1 January 1963, p. 17.
32. Andre Gunder Frank, *Latin America: Underdevelopment or Revolution, op. cit.,* pp. 28-29. Reprinted by permission.
33. Andre Gunder Frank, "Sociology of Development and the Underdevelop-

ment of Sociology" in *Latin America: Underdevelopment or Revolution, op. cit.,* pp. 24-48.

34. James C. Abegglen, *The Japanese Factory,* Glencoe, Ill.: The Free Press, 1958.
35. David Granier, *The European Executive,* Garden City, N.J.: Doubleday, 1962; Ferdinand Zweig, *The British Worker,* Penguin Books, Ondon, 1962; Ferdinand Zweig, *The Worker in An Affluent Society,* London: Heineman, 1962; Raymond Williams, *Culture and Society,* London: Penguin, 1961.
36. Andre Gunder Frank, *Underdevelopment or Revolution, op. cit.,* p. 28. Reprinted by permission of Monthly Review Press. Copyright © 1969 by Andre Gunder Frank.
37. Max Webcr, "Bureaucracy," in Hans Gerth and C. Wright Mills, (ed.) *From Max Weber: Essays in Sociological Theory,* New York: Oxford University Press, 1946.
38. Robert Nisbet, *op. cit.,* p. 46. Reprinted by permission.
39. *Ibid.,* p. 146. Reprinted by permission.
40. *Ibid.,* pp. 292-293. Reprinted by permission.
41. Alvin W. Gouldner, "Metaphysical Pathos and the Theory of Bureaucracy," *American Political Science Review,* **49,** 1955, pp. 496-507. Reprinted by permission. The entire article is reprinted in this volume on pp. 337-352.
42. Talcott Parsons, *The Social System,* Glencoe, Ill.: The Free Press, 1951., p. 507.
43. For examples of how bureaucratic goals come to replace the ostensible and agreed-upon goals of law enforcement agencies, see William J. Chambliss and Robert B. Seidman, *Law, Order and Power, op. cit;* William J. Chambliss, *Crime and the Legal Process,* New York: McGraw-Hill, 1969, pp. 98-346; Jerome Skolnick, *Justice Without Trial,* New York: John Wiley, 1966; Abraham S. Blumberg, "The Practice of Law as Confidence Game," *Law and Society Review,* **1,** June 1967, pp. 15-39.
44. William Appleman Williams, *The Great Evasion,* Chicago: Quadrangle Books, 1964.
45. Robert Nisbet, *op. cit.,* p. 214. Reprinted by permission.
46. C. Wright Mills, *The Power Elite,* New York: Oxford University Press, 1956.
47. T. B. Bottomore, *Classes in Modern Society,* London: George Allen and Unwin, pp. 63-64. Reprinted by permission.

48. Karl Marx, *Economic and Political Manuscripts.* Translated and edited by T. B. Bottomore in *Karl Marx's Early Writings,* p. 127, New York: McGraw-Hill Book Company, 1964. Reprinted by permission.
49. *Reports on Happiness,* National Opinion Research Center, Chicago, 1962.
50. Ely Chinoy, *Automobile Workers and the American Dream,* Boston: Beacon Press, 1965; Richard Hamilton, *Affluence and the French Worker in the Fourth Republic,* Princeton: Princeton University Press, 1967.
51. William A. Williams, *op. cit.*
52. Karl Marx, "The Holy Family," in Lloyd Easton and Kurt Guddat, *Writings of Young Marx on Philosophy and Society,* New York: Doubleday-Anchor, 1967.
53. William J. Chambliss and Robert B. Seidman, *op. cit.*
54. K. Dennis Kelley and William J. Chambliss, "Status Consistency and Political Attitudes," *American Sociological Review,* **31,** no. 3, June 1966, p. 382. Reprinted by permission.
55. Rinehard Bendix, "Concept in Comparative Historical Analysis," in Stein Rokkan, *Comparative Research Across Cultures and Nations,* The Hague: Mouten, 1968. pp. 67-81.
56. See the excellent treatment of this in Robert W. Fredericks, *A Sociology of Sociology,* New York: The Free Press of Glencoe, 1970. See also Alvin W. Gouldner, *The Coming Crisis in Western Sociology,* New York: Basic Books, 1970.

Part 1
THE CONFLICT PERSPECTIVE

THE NATURE OF SOCIETY

Gerhard Lenski

There is a basic conflict between the views of conservatives and radicals and between their intellectual heirs, contemporary functionalists and conflict theorists.

In the conservative tradition human societies have been repeatedly compared to biological organisms. Like organisms, (1) they are systems made up of specialized and interdependent parts, (2) the whole normally outlives the various parts which are continuously being replaced, and (3) the whole has needs which must be met if it is to survive and thrive, and it is the function of the parts to satisfy these needs through their specialized activities. In short, societies, like organisms, are systems in which the survival and well-being of the whole is achieved through the mutual cooperation of the parts. Through such cooperation the good of the whole is obtained and, as a consequence, the good of all the parts.

It is no coincidence that one of the major statements of modern functionalist theory is entitled *The Social System.*[1] Functionalist theory is usually *systemic* theory, positing the systemic character of human societies at the outset and then seeking to explain the action of the parts in terms of the needs and requirements of the whole.

Conflict theory, in contrast, is usually *antisystemic* in character. It emphasizes the conflicts and struggles which constantly threaten to destroy the fabric of society. It is much less concerned with the total society and its needs than with the subunits within societies, the classes, parties, factions, and interest groups, which are forever contending for the advantage. Radical theorists tend to view human societies as settings within which the conflicts of life are acted out. They are important chiefly because their characteristics, e.g., their level of economic development,

---

affect the outcome of the struggles. The struggles and the struggling factions, not society, are the central object of concern.

Both of these views strike a responsive chord in an open-minded student of society. Both clearly contain an element of truth. Cooperation is certainly a pervasive feature of all human life and so, too, is conflict. Some patterns of human action make sense only when interpreted in the light of the needs of society as a whole, while others make sense only when interpreted in the light of individual needs and desires. To the degree that any theory denies the importance of either the social or the antisocial elements in human societies, it ignores an important aspect of life and becomes an unreliable interpreter of the human scene.

In order to integrate and synthesize the valid insights of both these traditions, it is necessary to reexamine with some care the concept of "systems," which is so important to conservative theorists. This is a concept which social theory cannot ignore; but neither can it be accepted uncritically as is usually done today.

Basically the concept refers to an organization of interdependent parts possessing a unitary character. Sociologists have borrowed it from other disciplines, such as astronomy, physics, and biology, in an endeavor to combat the extreme individualism and psychological reductionism of so much of popular thought, especially in the United States. As a weapon in this struggle it has been extremely effective; as a tool in social analysis its record is less impressive.

The greatest source of difficulty is that this concept is normally conceived of in *categorical* terms. Either something is a system or it is not. There is no middle ground. If an aggregation of people are interdependent to any appreciable degree, modern functionalists feel justified in analyzing their way of life in systemic terms. Building on this foundation they then proceed to develop their elaborate analyses, which strain to find social utility in every established pattern of action.

This usage ignores two important facts. First, *systems vary greatly in the degree of the interdependence and integration of their parts.* The constituent parts of human societies enjoy a measure of independence and autonomy which far exceeds that of the parts of most biological organisms or mechanical systems. To ignore this is to invite confusion. Second, *there is no such thing as a perfect human social system in which the actions of the parts are completely subordinated to the needs of the whole.* This is a theoretical construct which has no counterpart or even remote approximation in the real world.[2]

These facts have important implications for social theory. In the first place, if there is no such thing as a perfect social system, we should stop spinning theories which postulate their existence and direct our energies toward the building of theories which explicitly assume that all human organizations are *imperfect systems.* Second, social theorists (and researchers too) should stop trying to find *social* utility in all the varied behavior patterns of men; they should recognize that many established patterns of action are thoroughly antisocial and contribute nothing to the general good. Third, we should expect to find *both* cooperation and conflict as continuous and normal features of human life and should stop viewing conflict as a pathological or abnormal condition, as is often done in contemporary functionalist theory. Fourth, we should devote more attention to the causes and consequences of variations in the degree of group integration. Finally, we must learn to think of distributive systems as reflecting *simultaneously* system needs and unit needs, with each often subverting the other.

This last point deserves special attention since conservative theorists so often deny that there is any basic conflict between the interests of the group and the interests of the individual, asserting that what is good for society is good for the individual, and vice versa. The classic effort in modern times is Adam Smith's famous treatise, *The Wealth of Nations.* The father of modern economics developed a very impressive case for the thesis that, through the alchemy of the market, the single-minded pursuit of self-interest by each of the members of society redounds to the benefit of society as a whole. A century later the Social Darwinians developed a similar thesis. They maintained that as a result of the operation of the laws of natural selection, only the fittest survived, so that once again the pursuit of self-interest redounded to the benefit of society as a whole.

While it is surely true that the destinies of an individual and his society are linked, there is no simple 1-to-1 relationship between them. This can be illustrated in a number of ways. When a society prospers, some of its members may even experience financial disaster. Conversely, when the economy of a society declines, some of its members may benefit greatly, as shown by the stock market crash of 1929.

Logically, it is not possible for the interests of society to be compatible with the interests of all its members if the interests of these members are themselves incompatible to any appreciable degree. Yet, as we have seen, this is precisely the case. Under such conditions, the most that is possible is that the interests of society are consistent with the interests of *some* of its members. As we shall see later, there is good reason to believe that in many societies throughout history the interests of only a small minority of the members were significantly identified with the interests of the total society.

The conflict between societal interests and individual interests can be shown in yet another way. From the standpoint of society as a whole, it is desirable that the key positions be filled by the best qualified men. From the standpoint of the individual motivated by self-interest, it is usually desirable that he fill one of these positions himself. In most instances, the interests of the individual will be subversive of the interests of the society and vice versa.

NOTES

1. Talcott Parsons, *The Social System* (New York: The Free Press, 1951).

2. Hobbes saw this clearly as his comparison of man with the bees and ants indicates. Of the latter he wrote, "among these creatures the common good differs not from the private; and being by nature inclined to the private, they procure thereby the common benefit. But man, whose joy consists in comparing himself with other men, can relish nothing but what is eminent." Thomas Hobbes, *Leviathan* (New York: Liberal Arts, 1953), chap. 17.

DIALECTIC AND FUNCTIONALISM: TOWARD A THEORETICAL SYNTHESIS

Pierre L. van den Berghe

Functionalism and the Hegelian-Marxian dialect each stress one of two essential aspects of social reality, and are thus complementary to one another. My procedure will be to examine in turn the basic postulates of functionalism and the Hegelian-Marxian dialectic, show the limitations of each theory as a complete model of society, examine some of Dahrendorf's[1] reformulations, and, finally, by retaining and modifying elements of the two approaches, search for a unified theory.

FUNCTIONALISM

With the rapidly growing body of literature on functionalism,[2] that theoretical position has become both more sophisticated and more elusive of definition. Davis even goes so far as to argue that, irrespective of what they call themselves, all sociologists use much the same analytical framework.[3] Adherence to Davis' viewpoint can result in either optimism or dismay. I shall try to show, however, that functionalism is not a myth, but an important though fragmentary approach to social reality.

One must reject at the outset facile criticisms based on beating the dead horse of extreme Malinowskian functionalism. Such criticisms as that societies are never perfectly integrated, that not every element of a social system is functional or essential, and that functionalism cannot account for change have been satisfactorily answered and shown to be untrue or irrelevant by leading exponents of the "school," notably by Merton.[4]

Our concern, then, is with the more recent brand of functionalism in its most sophisticated and cautious form, and as represented by Parsons, Merton and Davis. Reduced to its common denominator, the

Reprinted by permission of author and publisher from the *American Sociological Review* **28**, No. 5, October 1963, pp. 695-705.

functionalist or "structure-function" approach seems to involve the following postulates or elements:

1. Societies must be looked at holistically as systems of interrelated parts.
2. Hence, causation is multiple and reciprocal.
3. Although integration is never perfect, social systems are fundamentally in a state of dynamic equilibrium, i.e., adjustive responses to outside changes tend to minimize the final amount of change within the system. The dominant tendency is thus towards stability and inertia, as maintained through built-in mechanisms of adjustment and social control.
4. As a corrollary of (3), dysfunctions, tensions and "deviance" do exist and can persist for a long time, but they tend to resolve themselves or to be "institutionalized" in the long run. In other words, while perfect equilibrium or integration is never reached, it is the limit towards which social systems tend.
5. Change generally occurs in a gradual, adjustive fashion, and not in a sudden, revolutionary way. Changes which appear to be drastic, in fact affect mostly the social superstructure while leaving the core elements of the social and cultural structure largely unchanged.
6. Change comes from basically three sources: adjustment of the system to exogenous (or extra-systemic) change; growth through structural and functional differentiation; and inventions or innovations by members or groups within society.
7. The most important and basic factor making for social integration is value consensus, i.e., underlying the whole social and cultural structure, there are broad aims or principles which most members of a given social system consider desirable and agree on. Not only is the value system (or ethos) the deepest and most important source of integration, but it is also the stablest element of socio-cultural systems.

The first two postulates are useful and provisionally acceptable, although we shall formulate reservations about the first one later. Any wholesale rejection of the holistic approach leads to sterile classification of cultural items torn out of context (as represented for example by diffusionism in anthropology). A rejection of the model of multiple and reciprocal causation entails all the pitfalls of the many different brands of one-sided determinism.

The other five elements of functionalism outlined above are further reducible to two basic postulates, those of consensus and of dynamic equilibrium or integration. Both of these assumptions can be traced back to Comte, and have permeated much of British and American sociology and anthropology via Durkheim, acquiring the sanctity of tradition. The two postulates lead to a self-created *impasse* by making certain problems insoluble and by presenting a partially valid but slanted concept of social reality.

In a nutshell my argument is that, while societies do indeed show a tendency towards stability, equilibrium, and consensus, they simultaneously generate within themselves the opposites of these. Let us begin with the assumption that value consensus constitutes the most basic focus of social integration. Consensus is certainly an important basis for integration, but it is also true that societies (except perhaps the least differentiated ones) fall far short of complete consensus, and often exhibit considerable dissension[5] about basic values. To generalize from the Trobrianders and the Arunta to complex, stratified and culturally pluralistic societies is clearly unsound. Numerous societies (e.g., colonial countries) integrate widely different cultures possessing quite different value systems. Even in culturally homogeneous societies, various social groups such as classes can hold antithetical political and economic values (as shown by class conflicts in nineteenth century Europe). Conversely, consensus such as is found in charismatic movements of a revivalistic or messianistic type can precipitate the disintegration of a society, as we shall see later.

What remains then of the consensus assumption? Clearly, to make value consensus a prerequisite to the existence of a social system (as Parsons does, for example) is untenable.[6] Granting that consensus is often an important (but not a necessary) basis of social integration, one has to accept that consensus can also have disintegrative consequences, that most complex societies show considerable dissension, and that there are alternative bases of integration to consensus (e.g., economic interdependence and political coercion). Consensus, then, is a major dimension of social reality, but so are dissension and conflict. Furthermore, there is no necessary direct relation between consensus and equilibrium or integration.

The postulate of consensus, however, is logically gratuitous to functionalist theory, i.e. one could logically retain a functionalist model of integration while rejecting the consensus assumption. We must therefore examine separately the postulate of dynamic equilibrium, the real logical cornerstone of the "structure-function" approach. Here a common confusion must be dispelled at once. The concepts of equilibrium or integration are distinctly different from those of stability and inertia. Relatively integrated societies can change faster than societies in a state of strain and conflict. The model of dynamic equilibrium has change built into it, albeit a minimization thereof. Adjustive change of the social system, in response either to exogenous change, or to endogenous change in one of its parts, is a condition to the maintenance of equilibrium. Conversely, increasing disequilibrium or malintegration can result from stability and inertia in certain elements of a society (e.g., the political systems) which fail to adjust to changes in other parts of the society. However, a simple inverse relation between equilibrium and stability is likewise untenable, as not all change is adjustive. We shall return to this point later.

The usefulness of the integration or equilibrium model (in its sophisticated and minimal form) suggests that it must be salvaged, at least in part. A minimum of integration must certainly be maintained for any social system to subsist. Furthermore, far from making the analysis of change impossible, functionalism has proven a powerful instrument in dealing with at least two major types of change: growth in complexity through differentiation, and adjustment to extra-systemic changes (e.g., problems of acculturation). At the same time, the equilibrium model cannot account for certain phenomena, and, hence, cannot be accepted as a complete and satisfactory representation of society.

More specifically, a dynamic equilibrium model cannot account for the irreducible facts that:

1. reaction to extra-systemic change is not always adjustive,
2. social systems can, for long periods, go through a vicious circle of ever deepening malintegration,
3. change can be revolutionary, i.e., both sudden and profound,
4. the social structure itself generates change through internal conflicts and contradictions.

The fourth shortcoming of functionalism results from looking at social structure as the static "backbone" of society, and considering structural analysis in social science as analogous to anatomy or morphology in biology. More than anybody else, Radcliffe-Brown is responsible for this one-sided outlook which has blinded functionalism to the conflicts and contradictions inherent in social structure.[7] In short, through its incomplete emancipation from organicism, functionalism has systematically overlooked one of the crucial sources of endogenous change. Insofar as functionalists have had to take cognizance of problems of conflict and dissension, they have done so in terms of "deviance," or "variance," i.e., an unaccountable aberration from, or modification of, the "dominant pattern" which somehow tends to resolve itself through "institutionalization." To account for endogenous change through conflict and contradiction, the dialectic must be introduced to complement functionalism. We shall return to that point later.

Related to, but analytically distinguishable from, the problem of endogenous change are the difficulties arising from the functionalist assumption that social systems adjust gradually to changes from outside, and uniformly tend towards equilibrium or integration. Basically, I believe that it is correct to speak of a long-range tendency towards integration. Functionalism is slanted in that it underrates conflict and disequilibrium, and assumes too much continuity, gradualness and uniformity in the process of change. Rather than scrapping the equilibrium model, however, we must try to modify it.

An expanded model of equilibrium has to allow for at least two alternative sequences of change. A social system can, and often does, gradually adjust to external changes, and hence, tend fairly uniformly towards integration. But a social system can also resist exogenous change and fail to adapt, either by remaining static or by introducing reactionary change. In this case, a cycle of cumulative dysfunction and increasing malintegration is initiated, which beyond a certain point, becomes irreversible, and makes drastic revolutionary change inevitable. This second alternative is compatible with a postulate of long-range tendency towards equilibrium. Indeed, revolution is fundamentally a process whereby accumulated imbalances between major elements of society (e.g., the political and the economic system) are eliminated, and a new state of relative integration achieved. This expanded equilibrium model meets the first three objections to the "classical" functionalist position: it allows the possibility of maladjustive change, of vicious circles of malintegration, and of abrupt "social mutations" through revolution.

At the same time, the revised model raises new problems which must be answered if it is to be heuristic. What forces "push" a society towards either the adjustive or the maladjustive alternative? In the latter case, what are the symptoms that the vicious circle is irreversible, short of revolution? What is the empirical range of variation on the dimension of integration (i.e., how closely can a system approximate perfect equilibrium), and, conversely, how much disequilibrium can it tolerate?

I can only suggest tentative answers. As regards the first question, we may hypothesize that the probability of entering a maladaptive cycle increases to the extent that the *status quo* is rewarding (or, conversely, that innovation is perceived as threatening) either to the society as a whole, or to its ruling group or groups (i.e., those who have the power to determine and enforce policy). While this statement appears tautological, I must stress that the notions of "reward" and "threat" are much broader and less mechanistic than the Marxian concept of "class interests," and include such diverse things as prestige, emotional or physical security, power, wealth and values. Likewise, I make no assumption that a single ruling class automatically acts in conformity with its "objective interests."

As symptoms of the inevitability of revolution (by which I do not necessarily imply physical violence), I would suggest lack of communication, unwillingness to compromise, disagreement about the "rules of the game," and reciprocal denial of legitimacy between the opposing groups. Finally, concerning societal tolerance for disequilibrium, the limits appear much wider than a functionalist position would lead one to expect. For many different reasons (such as efficient repression, strong ties of economic interdependence, or a complex crisscrossing of lines of conflict and cleavage), social systems can show great resilience to malintegration.

THE HEGELIAN-MARXIAN DIALECTIC

Let us now turn to the dialectic and see what it can offer social theory. Facile rejection of the dialectic method based either on vulgar Marxism, or, at a more sophisticated level, on the failure of Marxian orthodoxy to explain certain facts and predict certain developments has led many sociologists to throw out the baby with the bath. A detailed critical examination of dialectical materialism and Hegelian idealism is plainly out of place here: first, because there is no point in beating the dead horse of orthodoxy; second, because the task has been successfully accomplished by countless people.[8]

What can usefully be salvaged of the dialectic? Marx himself shows us the way here by rejecting Hegelian idealism and retaining the dialectic outlook. The irony is that Marx then fell into the dialectic trap by advancing his own brand of one-sided determinism as an antithesis to Hegel's idealism. Clearly, Marx's economic determinism (and hence much of the complex theoretical edifice built upon it) is as untenable as the idealism of Hegel which Marx ridiculed with ponderous sarcasm. There is no logical reason, however, why the dialectic method or outlook should be tied to any one-sided determinism, and why discarding the latter should entail a rejection of the former.

Hegel's great insight consisted in conceiving of change as inherent in the nature of ideas. Marx, in turn, showed the applicability of the thesis-antithesis-synthesis sequence to social structure. Two important limitations to the dialectic suggest themselves at this point. First, any claim that the dialectical process is the *only* source of change is untenable. The dialectical analysis of change complements and does not supplant the functionalist view of change through differentiation and adaption to external conditions. Any approximation to a satisfactory model of social dynamics requires at least these three distinct sources of change (not to mention individual invention or innovation which is at a different level of analysis because of its psychological dimension, and which is difficult to integrate into either the dialectic or the functionalist model).

The second limitation of the dialectic is its dualistic view of social reality. The difficulty seems to be that Hegel and Marx confused an empirical tendency for contradictions and conflicts to polarize into pairs of opposites, with a logical necessity to do so. In the realm of ideas, a thesis can give rise to several different antitheses and syntheses. Similarly, Marx ran into insuperable, self-created *impasses* by trying to cling to his binary class model, and, in fact, he often was forced to speak of "intermediate" classes (e.g., the petty bourgeoisie), or remnants from precapitalistic classes (e.g., the feudal nobility). As to the peasantry, it still remains the *Poltergeist* of Marxian class analysis.

What is left of the dialectic, one may legitimately ask, if one accepts all the above restrictions? Admittedly not very much, but the residual core is of great importance. As a reformulation of a "minimum" dialectic, the following elements appear both useful and valid:

1. Change is not only ubiquitous, but an important share of it is generated within the system; i.e., the social structure must be looked at, not only as the static framework of society, but also as the source of a crucial type of change.
2. Change of intra-systemic or endogenous origin often arises from contradiction and conflict between two or more opposing factors. These "factors" can be values, ideologies, roles, institutions or groups.

This minimum dialectic approach (if it can still be called that) seems applicable at three different levels of analysis. The first level, that of values or ideas, corresponds to Hegel's use of the dialectic, and includes the study of contradictions and conflicts between values, political or religious ideologies, and scientific or philosophical theories. In short, it is concerned with all conflicts involving abstract but explicitly formulated cultural concepts, viewed in isolation from concrete participants.

The other two levels of dialectic analysis are intertwined in Marx's writings, but it is essential to distinguish between them. One of them deals with institutionalized principles or forces arising out of the social structure, or, in different words, with the internal contradictions (generally latent, i.e., unrecognized and unintended) growing out of institutionalized processes of interaction. For example, the principle of authority is essential to the maintenance of structural stability and functional efficiency of practically all human groups; but, at the same time, authority generates conflicts and tensions which can threaten the disruption of groups. Finally, the third level of analysis concerns group conflicts. In any society, different groups (defined by sex, age, "race," culture, education, relation to the means of production, wealth, power, prestige, descent, etc.) have, by virtue of their differing roles and statuses, interests which often are conflicting.

Obviously, a binary model of group opposition based on the relation to the means of production (as advanced by Marx) or on the exercise of power (Mosca), or on any other single factor, is untenable. While some oppositions are inherently dualistic (e.g., those based on sex), and while conflict often favors polarization into two camps, there is no magic in the number two. Conflicts arising from differences between age groups, for example, often follow a three-fold division (young, adult, old). Furthermore, societies invariably have several lines of cleavages which may, but often do not overlap. Neither is it permissible to assume that groups in different positions *necessarily* have conflicting interests, or that they are always *conscious* of "objectively" antagonistic interests, or that, if groups have *some* conflicting interests, they cannot simultaneously share interests that override differences.

A CRITIQUE OF DAHRENDORF

Having sketched the main lines of theoretical house-cleaning in relation to functionalism and the dialectic, and indicated which elements of both should be retained, we can turn to Dahrendorf's work. While Dahrendorf's central concern is much the same as ours, and while he reaches a number of similar conclusions, his reformulations are slanted more in favor of the dialectic and against functionalism.[9] After criticizing functionalism and Marxian orthodoxy, Dahrendorf pleads for a development of conflict theory. He considers the two theoretical approaches valid and complementary (with many of the same limitations dealt with here), but leaves open the question whether the thesis and the antithesis can be integrated into a grand theoretical synthesis. Dahrendorf then assigns himself the task of developing one circumscribed aspect of conflict theory, namely class conflict as a special case of group conflict, which, in turn, is a special case of an all-encompassing conflict model.

Within present space limitations, I could not do justice to Dahrendorf's valuable contributions. Suffice it to say that he rejects Marx's definition of class as determined by the relation to the means of production, and Marx's notion that complex societies can be analyzed in terms of a basic dichotomy.[10] Dahrendorf then substitutes his own definition of class as determined by the unequal distribution of authority.[11] From that concept of class, he derives a binary model of class conflict, but unlike Marx, he does not apply it to total societies. Each "imperatively coordinated association" (Weber's *Herrschaftsverband*), which can be anything from a chess club or a nuclear family, to an industrial organization or a state, has its own dichotomous class structure; those who exercise authority, and those who are excluded from it. A total society thus has a multiplicity of "class-pairs" which may or may not overlap.[12] The distribution of authority within a given association is always dichotomous, different positions in relation to authority necessarily involve conflicting interests, and class conflict revolves around the struggle for authority.[13]

Dahrendorf then refines his analysis by introducing several variables (such as intensity and violence of conflict, and suddenness and radicalness of change) from which he derives a set of testable propositions.[14] Many of the latter withstand the test of my South African evidence and prove quite useful, while others call for refinement and modification. But a detailed examination of them would be out of place here. Instead, I want to question two of Dahrendorf's most basic notions, namely his concept of class and his postulate of the dichotomous nature of conflict.

The central importance that Dahrendorf assigns to authority in his analysis of class is open to question. He reverses the Marxian chain of causation and considers economic factors as derivative from the unequal distribution of authority.[15] To be sure, Dahrendorf's political determinism is more cautious than Marx's economic determinism, insofar as

Dahrendorf admits the existence of many other types of conflict group besides "classes." But he neither demonstrates why authority is prior to the relation to the means of production, nor convincingly shows how "classes" are different from other conflict groups, and, hence, why they should constitute a special analytical category. I would therefore suggest a more general theory of group conflict, where authority would not occupy a privileged position, but would rather be one of many desirable "goods" (along with material rewards, control of the means of production, power, prestige, spheres of cultural, linguistic, ideological, intellectual or religious influence, etc.).

As concerns the dichotomous nature of conflict, Dahrendorf's reformulation is certainly a major improvement over Marx's society-wide two-class model. However, Dahrendorf does not strike at the core of the difficulty. Reducing every conflict situation to a dualistic opposition involves straining the facts. Dahrendorf experiences the same difficulties as Marx in handling "intermediate groups." For example, he divides the "middle-class" into bureaucrats holding delegated authority, and clerical or white-collar workers who are excluded from authority; he is forced to recognize that some groups (such as staff specialists) are in an "ambiguous" position; and he acknowledges that modern enterprises have a "diffuse" authority structure resulting from functional differentiation.[16]

In short, authority, while an important dimension of conflict, is not necessarily an overriding one, nor is it logically or empirically prior to other sources of conflict. As to polarization, it is an empirical tendency rather than a necessary condition of conflict. A pluralistic model thus seems to impose itself. If one argues that dualism is intrinsic to dialectical thinking, I am prepared to abandon the term "dialectic," though not the elements thereof which are essential to a balanced view of social reality.

TOWARD A SYNTHESIS

So far we have reduced two theories that are generally considered antithetical to a minimum form. The most ambitious task that remains is to reach a synthesis between the two. The desirability of achieving a unitary approach seems obvious. It is not enough to say that two theories are complementary and can be used *ad hoc* for different purposes; one must also show that they are reconcilable. While such an endeavor is beyond that scope of this paper, I hope to show that an attempt at synthesis offers some promise by stressing four important points of convergence and overlap.

First, both approaches are holistic, i.e., look at societies as systems of interrelated parts. On first sight, this point seems to offer little comfort, because the types of interrelation on which each theory is based seem antithetical. Functionalists have adhered to a model of multiple and reciprocal causation; they have conceived of interdependence of parts as resulting mostly from functional specialization and complementarity, and as making for equilibrium. Hegelian-Marxian analysts, on the other hand, have generally leaned toward single-factor and unidirectional causation, and viewed interdependence as a conflictual relation. Furthermore, both theories can be criticized on the ground that they tend to represent societies as *more* holistic than they are in fact. Sophisticated functionalism accepts, of course, that different parts of a social system can have varying degrees of autonomy from one another, and that their relationship can be segmental. Indeed, the interdependence of differentiated parts in a system necessarily call forth the antithetical notion of relative autonomy without which the system could not be internally structured. Nevertheless, functionalists have, like Marxian theorists, tended to stress interrelationship, and, conversely, to underrate the extent of "compartmentalization" possible in a social system.

Different elements of a society can simply coexist without being significantly complementary, interdependent or in opposition to one another. For example, a subsistence economy can independently coexist with a money economy, even though the same persons participate in both, and even though they may both produce some of the same commodities. In plural societies, two or more unrelated legal systems with overlapping jurisdictions may function side by side. Persons can move back and forth from one cultural system to another, alternately assuming different values and roles. Thus anthropologists have frequently been confronted with the apparent paradox of rapid accculturation and great conservatism and cultural resilience to outside influences.[17]

The coexistence of largely autonomous and disparate elements in a plural society can be treated in a conventional functionalist framework as a limiting case of a social system. This evasion by definition is not very helpful because such plural societies do "hang together" in spite of conflict and compartmentization. These remarks suggest that social systems can consist, at least in part, of sub-systems which are functionally unrelated and structurally discrete and disparate, but which are interlocked because they share certain elements in common. For example, in a "developing" country, the labor forces engaged in two largely unrelated economic sectors (money and subsistence) typically show considerable overlap. Similarly, the same person can occupy widely different statuses in two stratification systems (e.g., a traditional caste system and an imported Western-type class system) that are juxtaposed but unrelated except through common personnel.

While both bodies of theory overstress interdependence and present an unsatisfactory model thereof, they also show enough overlap to point toward a more workable view of intra-systemic relations.[18] In three different ways the principle of interdependence contains its own dialectic. First, the functionalist notion of differentiated systems consisting of interrelated parts logically implies the opposite concept of relative autonomy. Secondly, parts can be interdependent in that they *adjust to* one another, or *react against* one another. In other words, interdependence and equilibrium are independently variable. Finally, tensions within a social system can arise from conflicting tendencies for the parts to seek more autonomy, and for the whole to maintain centralized control. This latter source of tension is characteristic, for example, of political systems stressing "mechanical" (as opposed to "organic") solidarity, such as those based on segmentary lineages.

A second major overlap concerns the dual role of both conflict and consensus. Whereas functionalism regards consensus as a major focus of stability and integration, and the dialectic views conflict as the source of disintegration and revolutionary change, each of those factors can have the opposite effect. Several authors, notably Coser, have stressed the integrative and stabilizing aspects of conflict.[19] For example, interdependent conflict groups and the crisscrossing of conflict lines can "sew the social system together" by cancelling each other out and preventing disintegration along one primary line of cleavage. Furthermore, in a number of societies, conflict is institutionalized and ritualized in ways that seem conducive to integration.[20] Gluckman goes so far as to argue that ritualized conflict evidences the absence of basic dissension. Such rituals, according to Gluckman, are most prominent in societies where there are rebels (who oppose the incumbents of social roles without rejecting social values), but not revolutionaries.[21]

Not only can conflict contribute to integration. Reciprocally, consensus can prevent adaptation to change and lead to maladjustive inertia, or precipitate the disintegration of a group. The high degree of consensus typical of "utopian" or "other-worldly" reform movements is related to their ephemeral character. Strict adherence to "impractical" norms (e.g., celibacy, or the destruction of means of subsistence in expectation of the coming of the messiah) can obviously be disastrous. This type of phenomenon is analogous at the social level to Durkheim's altruistic suicide, brought about by "excess" of social solidarity. In a different way, consensus on such norms as extreme competition and individualistic laissez-faire, or suspiciousness and treachery as reported of the Dobu,[22] or malevolence and resort to witchcraft is hardly conducive to social solidarity and integration.

At yet another level of analysis, consensus can be disintegrative. In complex and stratified societies, consensus within groups is, in part, a function of dissension between groups. In other words, in-group unity is reinforced by inter-group conflict, leading to an increasing polarization of opinion. Thus ideological polarization is a process in which growing dissension between sub-groups in a social system is intimately linked with growing consensus within the various groups. In different words, consensus is defined not only in terms of the norms of a particular group as the functionalist approach conceives of it, but also in terms of dissension with the norms of other groups. A total conception of consensus must include a dialectic of normative opposition among the constituent groups of a society.

If both conflict and consensus, as central concepts of the dialectic and functionalism, play a role opposite to that assigned to them by the respective theories, our main contention receives strong confirmation. Not only does each theory emphasize one of two aspects of social reality which are complementary and inextricably intertwined, but some of the analytical concepts are applicable to both approaches.

Thirdly, functionalism and the dialectic share an evolutionary notion of social change. For both Hegel and Marx, the dialectic process is an ascensional spiral towards progress. The functionalist concept of differentiation postulates an evolutionary growth in structural complexity and functional specificity analogous to biological evolution. Admittedly, these two evolutionary views are different, and each presents serious difficulties. We are all aware of the pitfalls of organicism, the teleological implications of "progress," and the untenability of assuming that evolution is unilinear or has an endpoint (e.g., Marx's Communism or Comte's "positive stage"). Nevertheless, the convergence of the two theories on some form of evolutionism suggests that the concept of social evolution (in the minimal sense of change in discernable directions) may be inescapable, however ridden with problems existing brands thereof might be. More specifically, the dialectical and functionalist notions of evolution, while dissimilar, have at least one important point in common: both theories hold that a given state of the social system presupposes all previous states, and, hence, contains them, if only in residual or modified form.

Finally, (and herein probably lies the major areas of *rapprochement*) both theories are fundamentally based on an equilibrium model. In the case of functionalism, this is obvious. But the dialectic sequence of thesis-antithesis-synthesis also involves a notion of equilibrium. Indeed, synthesis is the resolution of the contradiction between thesis and antithesis. The dialectic conceives of society as going through alternating phases, equilibrium and disequilibrium: the thesis is the initial equilibrated stage of the cycle; the emergence of the antithesis leads to the intermediate disequilibrated phase; finally, as the contradiction resolves itself in the synthesis, one enters the terminal, balanced stage of the cycle, which then starts anew.[23] While this model is different from the classical notion of dynamic equilibrium, the two views are not contradictory nor incompatible with a postulate of long-range tendency towards integration.

Interestingly, this theoretical convergence on equilibrium also leads to an empirical overlap in dealing with the different sources of change. Earlier, when we dealt with the inability of functionalism to account for lack of adaptation to external change and the consequences thereof, we suggested a reformulation of the dynamic equilibrium model which is very close to the dialectic. Cumulative imbalances and abrupt qualitative changes (which are dialectic notions) were found to result from lack of adjustment to exogenous change. The traditional dialectic approach is not concerned with reactions of social systems to changes from outside, and conceives of societies as being closed systems. Conversely, the problems of interrelations between systems, exogenous change, boundary-maintenance, etc., have been dealt with by functionalism. Yet, only by introducing dialectical concepts into classical functionalist theory can one satisfactorily account for systemic reactions to outside changes.

We saw that functionalism and the dialectic converge on an equilibrium model which is compatible with an assumption of long-range tendency towards integration. So far, we have used the terms "equilibrium" and "integration" interchangeably. The functionalist concept of dynamic equilibrium does imply integration, i.e., interdependence and compatibility between the parts of a system. The dialectic, while stating that incompatibilities inevitably emerge, also stresses that they resolve themselves in the synthesis. But integration and its corollaries do not exhaust the functionalist definition of dynamic equilibrium. The latter is also defined by minimization of change, a notion outwardly alien to the dialectic which treats change as axiomatic and stability as problematical.

Empirically, one can argue as strongly for the ubiquity of inertia as for that of change. Also, as we already stressed, the amount or rate of change bears no simple relation to the degree of equilibrium. However, the facts are not at issue here, but rather the way facts have been treated by the two bodies of theory under consideration. Once more, there are similarities in outlook between functionalism and the dialectic in spite of differences in emphasis. There is, for example, little in acculturation theory (an outgrowth of anthropological functionalism) to suggest minimization of change. The concept of inertia on the other hand is not alien to Marxian class analysis. Marx considers the ruling class as inherently unwilling and unable to adjust to the forces it unleashes, and views the class struggle as a fight between the "progressive" and "reactionary" elements of society. Insofar as reaction implies action, however, the bourgeoisie under capitalism is not, according to Marx, a truly inert element, but Marx considers the petty bourgeoisie and the peasantry as largely passive and inert in the class struggle.

Inertia is thus no more alien to a dialectic approach than change is to functionalism. The maintenance or reestablishment of equilibrium implies adjustive change in both bodies of thought. If one abandons the unnecessary assumption of minimization of change, as indeed many functionalists have done, there remains no fundamental difference in the dialectical and functionalist concepts of equilibrium and disequilibrium.

CONCLUSION

Because of its scope, this paper is sketchy and leaves many problems unanswered. Our central contention is that the two major approaches which have dominated much of social science present partial but complementary views of reality. Each body of theory raises difficulties which can be resolved, either by rejecting certain unnecessary postulates, or by introducing concepts borrowed from the other approach. As functionalism and the dialectic show, besides important differences, some points of convergence and overlap, there is hope of transcending *ad hoc* eclecticism and of reaching a balanced theoretical synthesis.

NOTES

1. Ralf Dahrendorf, *Class and Class Conflict in Industrial Society,* Stanford: Stanford University Press, 1959; "Toward a Theory of Social Conflict," *Journal of Conflict Resolution,* 2 (June 1958), pp. 170-183; "Out of Utopia: Toward a Reorientation of Sociological Analysis," *American Journal of Sociology,* 64 (September, 1958), pp. 115-127.
2. For a sample of titles covering the last two decades see: Bernard Barber, "Structural-Functional Analysis: Some Problems and Misunderstandings," *American Sociological Review,* 21 (April, 1956) pp. 129-135; Harry C. Bredemeier, "The Methodology of Functionalism," *American Sociological Review,* 20 (April, 1955), pp. 173-180; Walter Buckley, "Social Stratification and the Functional Theory of Social Differentiation," *American Sociological Review,* 23 (August 1958), pp. 369-375; Francesca Cancian, "Functional Analysis of Change," *American Sociological Review,* 24 (December, 1960), pp. 818-827; Kingsley Davis, "The Myth of Functional Analysis as a Special Method in Sociology and Anthropology," *American Sociological Review,* 24 (December, 1959), pp. 752-772; Kingsley Davis and Wilbert E. Moore, "Some Principles of Stratification," *American Sociological Review,* 10 (April, 1945), pp. 242-249; Ronald Philip Dore, "Function and Cause," *American Sociological Review,* 26 (December, 1961), pp. 843-853; Harold Fallding, "Functional Analysis in Sociology," *American Sociological Review,* 28 (February, 1963), pp. 5-13; Dorothy Gregg and Elgin Williams, "The Dismal Science of Functionalism," *American Anthropologist,* 50 (October-December 1948), pp. 594-611; Carl G. Hempel, "The Logic of Functional Analysis," in Llewellyn Gross (ed.), *Symposium on Sociological Theory,* Evanston, Ill.: Row, Peterson and Co., 1959, pp. 271-307; Wayne Hield, "The Study of Change in Social Science," *British Journal of Sociology,* 5 (March, 1954), pp. 1-10; David Lockwood, "Some Remarks on the 'Social System'," *British Journal of Sociology,* 7 (June 1956), pp. 134-146; Wilbert E. Moore, "But Some Are More Equal than Others," *American Sociological Review,* 28 (February, 1963), pp. 13-18; Richard L. Simpson, "A Modification of the Functional Theory of Stratification," *Social Forces,* 35 (December, 1956), pp. 132-137; Melvin Tumin, "On Inequality," *American Sociological Review,* 28 (February, 1963), pp. 19-26; Melvin Tumin, "Some Principles of Stratification: A Critical Analysis," *American Sociological Review,* 18 (August, 1953), pp. 387-394; Dennis H. Wrong, "The Functional Theory of Stratification: Some

Neglected Considerations," *American Sociological Review,* 24 (December, 1959), pp. 772-782.

3. Davis, *op. cit.*

4. Robert K. Merton, *Social Theory and Social Structure,* Glencoe, Ill.: The Free Press, 1949, Chapter I.

5. In the absence of an exact antonym for "consensus," we shall use "dissension" rather than coin "dissensus."

6. The central importance of "patterns of value-orientations" for social integration is a recurrent theme in Parsons' work. Not only must there be a substantial amount of cognitive acceptance of values by actors in a social system, but actors must internalize these values, and be motivated to act in accordance with them. Cf. Talcott Parsons, *The Social System,* Glencoe, Ill.: The Free Press, 1951, pp. 36-37, 326, 350-351; *Structure and Process in Modern Societies,* Glencoe, Ill.: The Free Press, 1960, pp. 172-176; and Max Black (ed.), *The Social Theories of Talcott Parsons,* Englewood Cliffs: Prentice-Hall, 1961, pp. 342-343.

7. Cf. A. R. Radcliffe-Brown, *Structure and Function in Primitive Society,* Glencoe, Ill.: The Free Press, 1952, p. 180.

8. See, for example, Dahrendorf's critique of Marx from the point of view of sociological theory in his *Class and Class Conflict in Industrial Society.*

9. In the following discussion, references will be mostly to his *Class and Class Conflict in Industrial Society.*

10. *Op. cit.,* pp. 136-137, 171.

11. *Op. cit.,* pp. 136-139.

12. *Op. cit.,* pp. 141-142.

13. *Op. cit.,* pp. 165, 173-174.

14. *Op. cit.,* pp. 211-239.

15. *Op. cit.,* pp. 136-137.

16. *Op. cit.,* pp. 52-56, 251, 300-303.

17. For a treatment of problems of cultural coexistence in plural societies, see J. C. Mitchell, *Tribalism and the Plural Society,* London: Oxford University Press, 1960.

18. For a detailed and useful discussion of functional autonomy and interdependence, and their relations to equilibrium, see Alvin W. Gouldner, "Reciprocity and Autonomy in Functional Theory," in Llewellyn Gross, *op. cit.,* pp. 241-270.

19. Lewis A. Coser, *The Functions of Social Conflict,* Glencoe, Ill.: The Free Press, 1956. Others have stressed that "variant" values are found side by side with "dominant" values, that these "variant" values can be integrative, and that different sub-cultures within a society adhere to different values. See Florence R. Kluckhohn and Fred L. Strodtbeck, *Variations in Value Orientations,* Evanston, Ill.: Row, Peterson, 1961; Florence R. Kluckhohn, "Dominant and Substitute Profiles of Cultural Orientations," *Social Forces,* 28 (May, 1950), pp. 376-394; Herman Turk, "Social Cohesion Through Variant Values," *American Sociological Review,* 28 (February 1963), pp. 28-37.
20. See Max Gluckman, *Custom and Conflict in Africa,* Oxford: Blackwell, 1955, and *Rituals of Rebellion in South-East Africa,* Manchester: University of Manchester Press, 1954; and Pierre L. van den Berghe, "Institutionalized Licence and Normative Stability," *Cahiers d'Etudes Africaines,* 11 (1963) pp. 413-423.
21. *Custom and Conflict in Africa,* p. 134.
22. Reo F. Fortune, *The Sorcerers of Dobu,* London: G. Routledge and Sons, 1932.
23. The term "cycle," insofar as it implies repetitiveness is, of course, somewhat misleading in reference to the dialectic process, since both Hegel and Marx conceived of social change as an ascensional spiral.

FUNCTIONALISM AND DIALECTICS

Andre Gunder Frank

The treatment by Pierre van den Berghe of "Dialectic and Functionalism: Toward a Theoretical Synthesis" provides excellent points of departure for an examination of some elementary but fundamental aspects of functional and dialectical analysis which that author did not see fit to mention and of which functionalists generally show little or no awareness in their functionalist analysis of society or in their social analysis of functionalism.

The article cited claims to find four points of convergence, overlap, or synthesis between functionalism and dialectics. These are (1) that both approaches are holistic; (2) that they converge in the role they assign to conflict and consensus, to integration and disintegration; (3) that they share an evolutionary notion of social change; and (4) that both theories are fundamentally based on an equilibrium model. Although examining functionalism and dialectics at these four points of supposed convergence cannot constitute the scientifically important step toward fruitful, balanced, theoretical analysis of social structure and social change which the cited author claims for his "synthesis," it can permit us some clarification of the theoretical assumptions, empirical basis, and policy implications of functionalism and dialectics. It can also afford us some insight into the real limitations of any attempted synthesis.

1964-65. Fernando Henrique Cardosa and Rodolfo Stavenhagen, Latin American sociologists whose life and work in underdeveloped society have been so fruitful, were helpful in the preparation of this paper. The paper was originally published as "Functionalism, Dialectics, and Synthetics," in the Spring 1966 issue of *Science & Society.*

HOLISM

Both functionalism and dialectic theory are holistic. But here the resemblance ends. Functionalist holism and dialectical holism differ from each other in at least three elementary but fundamental ways: first, in their approach to the whole; second, in the questions they ask of the whole; and third, in the whole they select for study.

The levels of abstraction of functionalist holism and dialectical holism are altogether different. Dialecticians, even bad ones, necessarily begin with a particular existing society and go on theoretically to analyze it and its transformation in its entirety. Even the best functionalists, on the other hand, almost always eschew the study of a whole society. In the few instances in which they do analyze the whole, they either leave reality aside altogether or depart from functionalist theory.

The archetype of contemporary holistic functionalist analysis of the whole is, of course, that of Talcott Parsons. But Parsons' functionalist analysis of the social system is not even intended to be an analysis of any existing social system in particular. Parsons' holism, if we can call it that at all, is an analysis of an abstract whole, or of a wholly abstract supposedly universally valid model of any and all existing or imaginary societies. Accordingly, the holistic functional interrelations he so meticulously traces out are those of a construed model and not those of any known society. Lest we be unwittingly misled into thinking otherwise by taking the abstract for the concrete, the world's other most renowned contemporary functionalist authority, Claude Levy-Strauss, goes to great pains to be explicit: he says that he works only with a functionalist *model,* and he submits that all functionalists do and must do likewise, believe it or not. Indeed, no one, to our knowledge, has ever tried to make a holistic Parsonian analysis of any really existing society, least of all of our own, and were anyone foolish enough to try, Levy-Strauss forewarns him, he must surely fail. There is no overlap or even convergence here with dialecticians who try to study our real society—and still less with the best of them who succeed.

Most functionalists, Parsonian and otherwise, who have studied reality at all, have, of course, limited their holistic attention to a part of the society of their choice and to how it is functionally related to the whole of that society. The relatively few of the better functionalists, such as Malinowski, Radcliffe-Brown, Evans-Pritchard, Meyer Fortes, Raymond Firth, Max Gluckman, Fred Eggan, or Edmund Leach, who are not Parsonians and who *have* devoted their attention to a whole existing society, have found it necessary to retreat from functionalism and to leave quite a large gap between their description of the many parts of the society's concrete social reality and their analytic demonstration that, and how, all of these parts are functionally related to each other (and not to anything else) in an equilibrated whole—a gap which, as many of their own disciples have shown, is bridged by little more than their own and their readers' functionalist faith. Still, no amount of faith has so far been enough to lend any functionalist the necessary equipment or courage to attempt such a holistic analysis of our own society or hardly even to come to grips with the relations between their favorite subjects of study and our society. Radcliffe-Brown, for instance, never did his countryman Cecil Rhodes justice. Reading the former, one would never know the latter or his work existed. A world of difference, certainly, from Marxist dialecticians.

Perhaps a still more important difference between the holism of functionalism and that of dialectics is that they do not ask the same question at all about the whole. Functionalism appeals to holism only to explain the parts, while dialectics appeals to holism to explain the whole —and thereby the parts. Even at their best, functionalists and their theory do not attempt, or even pretend, to analyze, explain, account for, understand, and least of all to predict the existence—and still less the appearance or disappearance—of a particular social system or structure. On the contrary, just like their theory, functionalists always take the existing social structure as given and for granted; and both their theoretical and apparently practical interest in it are limited to the analytic value that structure may have in explaining the existence of the particular institutional parts to which functionalists like to limit their scientific study.

More explicitly, we may note that functionalists like Merton, Davis, Durkheim, Radcliffe-Brown, and others began their holistic functionalist study of social reality in trying to account for the existence of particular social institutions (but never of the social system or structure itself) by reference to these institutions' function in the social system. After that attempt failed, they retreated to the less ambitious task of showing how these institutions function within the system.

The initial attempt of functionalists to explain or account for the existence of particular institutions by reference to their function in the social system failed, of course, because of its quite unacceptable teleological foundation, as philosopher-critics such as Hempel and Nagel analytically showed that it must and as the sophisticated debate on cross-cousin marriage between Levy-Strauss, Homans and Schneider, and the latter's critics amply confirmed empirically. Moreover, even if despite Homans and Schneider's valiant attempt and failure, it were possible to substitute a motivational or other efficient cause of an institution for the classical but unacceptable teleological final cause of social integration or pattern maintenance, the attempt to account for an institution's existence by its function would still flounder on the obstacles of its own *post hoc, ergo propter hoc* argument.

Recognition of this Archilles' heel of functionalist theory has led many functionalists to shift the battle to a front where they are less vulnerable. Instead of maintaining their efforts to account for the existence of an institution by virtue of its function, they now only seek to show how it is functionally articulated with other parts of the social system. In pursuit of this more limited end, functionalism has indeed proved to be a useful tool in expert hands. But in this sense also, Marx himself must be termed a functionalist if we recall, for example, his suggestion that "religion is the opiate of the people." Indeed, in this more limited sense and scope, the identification and analysis of social function is an integral part of Marxist or any other dialectic analysis of society. As Kingsley Davis pointed out recently, and to paraphrase John Maynard Keynes, in the long run we are all functionalists. Therefore, to attempt to synthesize functionalism and dialectics at this point is not to advance beyond but only to misrepresent Marxist dialectical and other analyses of society and their commonality with any social science. But this shift of functionalists to the examination of only the function of a particular institution, when it is not theoretically and practically linked to scientific advance on all other fronts, as it is among the better Marxists, in turn renders functionalists vulnerable in another way. For thereby they abandon holism. After all, what makes functionalism holistic is either that it deals with the whole or at least that it interprets the part in terms of the whole. But when functionalists, like economists, relegate general equilibrium theory to the first paragraph of their analysis (or more usually even forget about it altogether) and when they resort to partial equilibrium analysis to relate one part of the social system to only one or a few other parts, then they abandon even the holistic base of any possible synthetic edifice.

Thus, there is a big difference in the question that functionalism and dialectics ask of the whole. Functionalists, if they do not abandon the universally accepted scientific precept of holism altogether, only ask of the whole how it explains the part. Of the whole itself they ask no questions at all; they do not ask why it exists or how, where it came from or what is happening to it; they do not ask whether they like it or not; they simply accept the whole system as it is, gladly taking its social structure as they find it. At their best, they try to understand and, perhaps, to reform a part. In Marxism, in contrast, the *sine qua non* is precisely first to analyze and explain the origin, nature, and development of the entire social system and its structure as a whole, and then use the understanding of the whole thus gained as the necessary basis for the analysis and understanding of its parts. Therein lies its claim to holism. How wholly different then are functionalism and dialectics in this respect as well, and how spurious is any attempted synthesis.

A third sense in which the holistic similarity of functionalism and dialectics is not real and only verbal is the whole they choose to study and the criterion of selection they use to choose it. Asking the right question, as the saying goes, is more than half of getting the right answer; and asking the wrong question—such as choosing the wrong whole—assures never getting the right answer at all. As is well known and even termed a virtue by some, there is no stricture in functionalist theory or practice against choosing any old whole to work in. Family, club, community, industry, nation, free world, imaginary social systems are all fair game. And the criterion of selection among them is more often than not simply personal interest or convenience. Even when the best of functionalists wish to find and eliminate the cause of social evil, unhappiness, ignorance, crime, poverty, exploitation, underdevelopment, war, or whatever, they unabashedly try and even claim to find it in the structure of the tribal or folk community, traditional family—and, increasingly, even in the low-achievement individual. One might be led to suppose that the theoretical and empirical relevance to this task of the analysis of one social whole as against another is of no practical relevance at all. Still, we might ask why functionalists' convenience, or at least their deeply revealed preference, is to look into precisely these wholes for answers to mankind's pressing problems. Be that as it may, anyone engaged in such holistic study who can still maintain even the world perspective of his daily newspaper must surely see how empirically wrong, theoretically inadequate, and practically absurd it is to look for the causes and still less the remedies of our ills in the social structure of only a supposedly isolated community, of only one part of a supposedly dual society, of only a supposedly national society, of only a third part of a world which Wendell Willkie already rightly termed as one.

Marxists, of course, encounter the empirically and theoretically determinant whole in the single worldwide capitalist system, and the better of them in the structure of the world society which harbors not only capitalism, but now also socialism. No sensible Marxist would, in the name of historical materialism—which is not the same as economic determinism, though they are often confused—suggest that the productive structure of, or differences in access to, the means of production within the family, the community, or even only the modern state is the basic determinant of class conflict, of historical evolution, or of anything else. The reason is, of course, that the criterion of selection by Marxist dialectians of the determinant social whole for study is not determined in turn by their own convenience or desires, but rather by social reality itself. Contrary to what is so often said of them in some circles, in this respect at least, Marxists, unlike some others, do not substitute their wishes for reality. Instead, they take reality as it is, but finding it unacceptable, work to change it; and being holistic in viewing the part as it is determined by the whole, they do not seek to change the part in isolation. Unlike functionalists, they seek to promote social change, instead, by changing the social structure of the whole which is determinant of the part.

Our elementary examination of functionalism and Marxist dialectics thus shows that there are fundamental differences in the holism of the one and of the other. The first synthesis of functionalism and dialectics is entirely vitiated by the fact that they do not at all refer to the same whole, or ask the same question of it, or go about answering it in the same way.

INTEGRATION AND CONFLICT

The second proposed synthesis of functionalism and dialectics is based on their supposed convergence on social integration and social conflict. The fact is that functionalists explicitly or implicitly reject any tendency toward long-run social disintegration; and functionalist theory assures us that there is, and indeed must be, a long run tendency toward social integration in all existing social systems. But functionalist analysis does not, and due to its own short-run basis cannot, present any empirical evidence in support of the supposed fact of long run integration. Whence, then, do functionalists draw their analytical support for the supposed necessity of integration and the associated supposed impossibility of disintegration?

No less an authority than Talcott Parsons deals with this problem very succinctly and, thereby, also clarifies the real disjunction and imaginary synthesis between functionalism and the dialectical treatment of social integration. "Social Classes and Class Conflict in the Light of Recent Sociological Theory" explained that

> [Marxists] treat the socioeconomic structure of capitalist enterprise as a single indivisible entity rather than breaking it down analytically into a set of distinct variables involved in it. It is this analytical breakdown which is for present purposes the most distinctive feature of modern sociological analysis. . . . It results in a modification of the Marxian view . . . the primary structural emphasis no longer falls on . . . the theory of exploitation but rather on the structure of occupational roles.

Therefore, he continues, "conflict does not have the same order of inevitability." From this it follows, as Parsons notes several pages later, "that stratification is to an important degree an integrating structure in the social system. The ordering of relationships in this context is necessary to stability." Thus, the analytic basis of the supposed necessity for integration which functionalists pose could not be clarified more than it is by Parsons: if we start with the parts and work up to but never get to the social whole—as Parsons, other functionalists and modern sociologists in general do—then internal social conflict takes on the appearance of being integrative. Only by beginning with the social whole and breaking it down into its parts, as Marxists do, does conflict appear to be ultimately disintegrative as well. Chinese students of the problem have recently put it succinctly: Do two combine into one, or does one split into two? Which is true in fact depends on whether reality is in fact an integrated whole or only a series of isolated parts. That is, these authorities seem to agree that if in reality we face an integrated whole capitalist system, then we face its disintegration.

True to his functionalist persuasion, van den Berghe tells us in his aforementioned article, "Dialectic and Functionalism: Toward a Theoretical Synthesis," that "the usefulness of the integration or equilibrium model suggests that it must be salvaged. . . . A minimum of integration must certainly be maintained for any social system to subsist" (p. 697).

We might ask just what the model is useful for if Parsons had not already supplied the answer in no uncertain terms: "It results in a modification of the Marxian view. . . . The primary structural emphasis no longer falls on the theory of exploitation." Why integration is necessary and the model must be salvaged is made explicit on the following page: "I believe that it is correct to speak of a long-range tendency toward integration . . . rather than scrapping the model, however, we must try to modify it." Like the existing social system, the functionalist model of it must be salvaged and may not be scrapped. After all, as Talcott Parsons pointed out, it is useful for withdrawing emphasis from exploitation.

The supposed synthesis of functionalism and dialectics, which takes the analysis of conflict from dialectics and adds it to functionalism, only slights functionalists in denying their analysis of social conflict, adds nothing new to functionalist theory, and distorts Marxist dialectics and its treatment of social conflict and cohesion beyond all recognition.

Functionalists have always incorporated a part of social conflict into the very basis of structure-functionalist theory. We need only recall Simmel on conflict, Gluckman on custom and conflict, Leach on political systems, Durkheim and Merton on alienation, or even the most integralist of functionalists, Radcliffe-Brown on joking relationships or mothers' brothers. However, the function of social conflict for functionalists is only social integration. All other social conflicts—revolution and social disintegration—are off-limits for functionalist theory and practice.

Given this limitation of functionalism, something of additional value could indeed be found in Marxist dialectics. Unlike functionalism, of course, Marxist dialecticians analyze disintegrative social conflict as well as incorporate its existence and consequences into dialectic theory. Moreover, also inconsistent with functionalists but not with reality, dialecticians distinguish among kinds and degrees of social conflict instead of indiscriminately assigning it all more or less the same theoretical weight. Thus, Marxist dialecticians also can and do incorporate non-disintegrative conflict into their theory. To take only one instance, though not an unimportant one, Marxists clearly see the class relationship as socially integrative insofar as, following Durkheim's famous suggestion and Parsons' above-quoted one, the process of production is organized through the cooperation of classes in the division of labor. It is not for nothing that Marxists place so much emphasis on the social nature of production. But this recognition does not prevent Marxists or dialectic theory from also seeing the associated non-social nature of capitalist distribution of the product, the consequent interference in the productive process by the same monopoly structure which promotes it, and the resulting disintegrative class conflict. It is precisely this ability to recognize and deal with such contradiction which makes Marxist theory dialectic and fundamentally different from functionalism. Is this the aspect of dialectic theory then which is to be salvaged in and from functionalism? No! The dialectics of conflict and opposition is precluded by and excluded from functionalism altogether.

The point of the *dialectics* of conflict and opposition is the holistic interpenetration of opposite poles—the unity of opposites—within the whole which makes it two and yet one, dualist and yet holistic. Thus, Marxist dialectics sees social classes, like other opposites, as existing only in cohesive yet conflicting relation to each other, and not in mechanical addition to each other as functionalist stratification theory does. The point is then the interpenetration of integration and disintegration, of structure and change, and dynamically of the negation of the negation. In functionalism there is none of this. In the proposed "synthetic" treatment of social integration and conflict, the attempt is not so much to synthesize functionalism with dialectics as it is to salvage functionalism at any cost, even if that distorts not only dialectic theory but also denies due credit to functionalist practice.

EVOLUTION

Functionalism and dialectics also do not converge but rather diverge in the matter of evolution. As they have with social conflict, functionalists have long since incorporated social change into the very heart of functionalist analysis of society. Much of the frame of Raymond Firth, Max Gluckman, Fred Eggan, Edmund Leach, and even of the most renowned of structuralists, Malinowski and Evans-Pritchard, rests precisely on their analysis of social change. There surely was social change in Tikopia, Bantu Africa, American Indian country, Highland Burma, the Trobriands, and Nuerland. Were their functionalist students speaking dialectic prose without knowing it? The answer surely is that they were not.

These and other functionalists have long been talking about social change. But they have not been talking about evolution, and much less have they sought to subject it to dialectic analysis. As they do with social conflict—and as Raymond Firth made clear with craftsmanlike precision in his first Presidential address, entitled "Social Organization and Social

Change," to the Royal Anthropological Institute—functionalists limit their analysis of social change to that which is determined by and takes place within the existing social structure of the system. They leave out of consideration change of the social system and its structure. Indeed, they must, since in their theory the social structure is the source of change and not as in Marxist theory, change the source of the social structure. That is why quite a number of functionalists themselves, like Dahrendorf and Leach, have for some time felt that functionalist theory has a utopian yet conservative bias and that they should bring us out of it by reforming the theory—without, however, scrapping any of its structural fundamentals. Any attempt to equate the functionalists' social change within the social structure with evolutionary change both within and of the system, is certainly stretching the classical definition of evolution beyond all recognition not only of Morgan and Engels, but also of Gordon Childe, Leslie White, and Julian Steward. Though not excluding such cyclical and random or spontaneous change, evolutionary change is both quantitatively and qualitatively different. According to Marxist understanding of evolution, not only does the social structure permit or give rise to some social change as in the functionalist conception, but more importantly the ongoing process of social change determines the social structure of the moment. Social change and evolution are not seen as abstract but mechanistic succession of thesis, antithesis, and synthesis of anything, but rather as the real simultaneous existence within particular social reality of its past, present, and future. And the most important source of the most important change and evolution is the whole's dialectic division into opposites. How, then, could functionalism analyze the evolution of the social whole if, as we saw, it does not even pretend to study the whole?

EQUILIBRIUM

The sum total of functionalist holism, integration, and change within the system is that functionalist theory is an equilibrium model. As Raymond Firth also noted in the already referred to essay on social organization and social change, functionalist analysis of that change is premised on the notion of equilibrating social choice of the varying but limited alternatives set by the existing social structure and on the resulting equilibrating cyclical social change within that stable and unvarying social structure. It is quite otherwise with dialectics. Far from being only cyclical and limited by the structure, in dialectic theory not to mention reality social change is more spiral-like and transforms the structure of society. Where then, we may ask, is the covergence of functionalism and dialectics on equilibrium, and where the synthesis? The answer is on page 704 of Mr. van den Berghe's synthesis: "Functionalism and the dialectics converge on an equilibrium model which is compatible with the assumption of long-range tendency toward integration." That is, the convergence lies in the assumption of integration and the synthesis is based on the distortion of dialectics and on the ignorance or omission of its and Marxism's *sine qua non,* that social reality includes its own disequilibrating negation and that the social whole contains the disequilibrating structural seed of its own evolution and transformation.

In order to achieve "a theoretical synthesis" of functionalism and dialectics, functionalists must leave dialectics shorn of its theory and analysis of the formation, existence and transformation of the determinant social whole. They must deny the identification of this process with historical materialism as untenable, dismiss dialectical division and interpenetration of opposites as confused, and regard extra-systemic stimuli as incompatible with dialectics. Having done all this, we can only hope that functionalists will indeed do what Mr. van den Berghe declares himself "prepared to do," that is to "abandon the term 'dialectic' " (p. 701). If functionalists once abandon not only dialectics but also its name, what will there be left to synthesize? Only the fifth and final matter left pending, "modern sociological theory" itself.

CONCLUSION

The quite synthetic functionalist attempt at synthesis reviewed here is a significant example of the supposition in "modern sociological theory" that all scientists—functionalists, Marxist dialecticians, and others alike—are free to pick and choose and synthesize their methods of scientific classification and analysis precisely as it suits their personal fancy or social convenience. The resulting synthetic product is a magnificent example of the scientific fruits of this methodological liberty. But scientific, like other freedom, is limited by reality and not illimited by fancy. As both Marxist Western "materialist" and non-Marxist Oriental "idealist" philosophers have so painfully pointed out, true liberty lies in the recognition and management of reality. Though many of us, functionalists, Marxists, and others, agree that existing functionalist theory is inadequate for analyzing, let alone changing, social reality as we experience and know it, this does not give functionalists synthetic license to do with functionalist and scientific theory as they please. Where would Marxists end up if they were to leave behind the bounds that dialectic reality imposes on their choice of analytic method, or functionalists if they were to escape from the limitations that functionalists theory and reality impose on their analysis of the latter, or physicists if they left behind the universe and atom? Perhaps, like some proud metaphysicians, both ancient and modern, they would all leave our poor suffering world to others' devices and achieve the grand final synthesis of whole, integrated, evolving synthetic angels equilibrating on four or more synthetic pins.

THE FORCES OF SOCIAL CHANGE

Karl Marx and Frederich Engels

BOURGEOIS AND PROLETARIANS

The history of all hitherto existing society is the history of class struggles.

Freeman and slave, patrician and plebeian, lord and serf, guild-master and journeyman, in a word, oppressor and oppressed stood in constant opposition to one another, carried on an uninterrupted, now hidden, now open fight, a fight that each time ended, either in a revolutionary reconstitution of society at large, or in the common ruin of the contending classes.

In the earlier epochs of history, we find almost everywhere a complicated arrangement of society into various orders, a manifold gradation of social rank. In ancient Rome we have patricians, knights, plebeians, slaves; in the Middle Ages, feudal lords, vassals, guild-masters, journeymen, apprentices, serfs; in almost all of these classes, again, subordinate gradations.

The modern bourgeois society that has sprouted from the ruins of feudal society has not done away with class antagonisms. It has but established new classes, new conditions of oppression, new forms of struggle in place of the old ones.

Our epoch, the epoch of the bourgeoisie, possesses, however, this distinctive feature: it has simplified the class antagonisms. Society as a whole is more and more splitting up into two great hostile camps, into two great classes directly facing each other—bourgeoisie and proletariat.

From the serfs of the Middle Ages sprang the chartered burghers of the earliest towns. From these burghers the first elements of the bourgeoisie were developed.

The discovery of America, the rounding of the Cape, opened up fresh ground for the rising bourgeoisie. The East Indian and Chinese markets, the colonization of America, trade with the colonies, the in-

---

From T. B. Bottomore and Maximilien Rubel, *Karl Marx: Selected Readings in Sociology and Social Philosophy,* London: C. A. Watts and Co., 1961.

crease in the means of exchange and in commodities generally, gave to commerce, to navigation, to industry, an impulse never before known, and thereby, to the revolutionary element in the tottering feudal society, a rapid development.

BASIC ROLE OF THE MODE OF PRODUCTION

A. Mode of Production Determines the Social, Political and Intellectual Life Processes

In the social production of their life, men enter into definite relations that are indispensable and independent of their will, relations of production which correspond to a definite stage of development of their material productive forces. The sum total of these relations of production constitutes the economic structure of society, the real foundation, on which rises a legal and political superstructure and to which correspond definite forms of social consciousness. The mode of production of material life conditions the social, political and intellectual life process in general. It is not the consciousness of men that determines their being, but, on the contrary, their social being that determines their consciousness. At a certain stage of their development, the material productive forces of society come in conflict with the existing relations of production, or—what is but a legal expression for the same thing—with the property relations within which they have been at work hitherto. From forms of development of the productive forces these relations turn into their fetters. Then begins an epoch of social revolution. With the change of the economic foundation the entire immense superstructure is more or less rapidly transformed. In considering such transformations a distinction should always be made between the material transformation of the economic conditions of production, which can be determined with the precision of natural science, and the legal, political, religious, aesthetic or philosophic—in short, ideological forms in which men become conscious of this conflict and fight it out. Just as our opinion of an individual is not based on what he thinks of himself, so can we not judge of such a period of transformation by its own consciousness; on the contrary, this consciousness must be explained rather from the contradictions of material life, from the existing conflict between the social productive forces and the relations of production. No social order ever perishes before all the productive forces for which there is room in it have developed; and new, higher relations of production never appear before the material conditions of their existence have matured in the womb of the old society itself. Therefore mankind always sets itself only such tasks as it can solve; since, looking at the matter more closely, it will always be found that the task itself arises only when the material conditions for its solution already exist or are at least in the process of formation. In broad outlines Asiatic, ancient, feudal, and modern bourgeois modes of production can be designated as progressive epochs in the economic formation of society. The bourgeois relations of production are the last antagonistic form of the social process of production—antagonistic not in the sense of individual antagonism, but of one arising from the social conditions of life of the individuals; at the same time the productive forces developing in the womb of bourgeois society create the material conditions for the solution of that antagonism. This social formation brings, therefore, the prehistory of human society to a close.

MARX, "Preface," *A Contribution to the Critique of Political Economy* (1859), *Selected Works,* pp. 182*f.*

B. The Economic Foundation, The Superstructure, and Their Interaction

. . . The thing is easiest to grasp from the point of view of the division of labor. Society gives rise to certain common functions which it cannot dispense with. The persons selected for these functions form a new branch of the division of labor *within society.* This gives them particular interests, distinct too from the interests of those who gave them their office; they make themselves independent of the latter and—the state is in being. And now the development is the same as it was with commodity trade and later with money trade; the new independent power, while having in the main to follow the movement of production, also, owing to its inward independence, the relative independence originally transferred to it and gradually further developed, reacts in its turn upon the conditions and course of production. It is the interaction of two unequal forces: on one hand the economic movement, on the other the new political power, which strives for as much independence as possible, and which, having once been established, is also endowed with a movement of its own. . . .

C. The Class Basis of Ideology

The ideas of the ruling class are in every epoch the ruling ideas: *i.e.,* the class, which is the ruling material force of society, is at the same time its ruling intellectual force. The class which has the means of material production at its disposal, has control at the same time over the means of mental production, so that thereby, generally speaking, the ideas of those who lack the means of mental production are subject to it. The ruling ideas are nothing more than the ideal expression of the dominant material relationships, the dominant material relationships grasped as ideas; hence of the relationships which make the one class the ruling one, therefore the ideas of its dominance. The individuals composing the ruling class possess among other things consciousness, and therefore think. Insofar, therefore, as they rule as a class and determine the extent and compass of an epoch, it is self-evident that they do this in their whole range, hence among other things rule also as thinkers, as producers of ideas, and regulate the production and distribution of the ideas of their age: thus their ideas are the ruling ideas of the epoch. For instance, in an age and in a country where royal power, aristocracy and bourgeoisie are contending for mastery and where, therefore, mastery is shared, the doctrine of the separation of powers proves to be the dominant idea and is expressed as an "eternal law." The division of labor, which we saw above as one of the chief forces of history up till now, manifests itself also in the ruling class as the division of mental and material labor, so that inside this class one part appears as the thinkers of the class (its active, conceptive ideologists, who make the perfecting of the illusion of the class about itself their chief source of livelihood), while the others' attitude to these ideas and illusions is more passive and receptive, because they are in reality the active members of this class and have less time to make up illusions and ideas about themselves. Within this class this cleavage can even develop into a certain opposition and hostility between the two parts, which, however, in the case of a practical collision, in which the class itself is endangered, automatically comes to nothing, in which case there also vanishes the semblance that the ruling ideas were not the ideas of the ruling class and had a power distinct from the power of this class. The existence of revolutionary ideas in a particular period presupposes the existence of a revolutionary class. . . .

MARX'S PARADIGM FOR AN ANALYSIS OF THE STRUCTURE AND CHANGE OF WHOLE SOCIETIES

Irving Zeitling

The student of society should study first the mode of production of the society in question. This means that attention is first turned to the following four factors which are all to be regarded as causally active:

a) The direct producers in their cooperative "work-relations" and the technological know-how with which they carry on the labor process.
b) The instruments and means of production.
c) The property relations governing access to and control of the means of production and its products.
d) Nature, and the way it conditions the productive process.

Nowhere does Marx assert which of these factors is the universally decisive one determining the various forms of society and consequently, the different kinds of people within them. All that the student can be sure of, prior to investigation, is that every society will integrate, in its own distinctive way, purposive labor, its social organization, its means of production and its natural basis. It is a matter of empirical investigation which of these will be the dominant factor in any particular case. Thus to understand "present day industrial society," for example, we study the particular form of integration assumed by these factors in a number of industrial societies and construct a tentative model on that basis. To understand why any given industrial society does not conform to the model, we study its specific conditions. Moving back and forth between the general and particular, and accordingly modifying the former, we formulate generalizations about industrial society in general. With these procedural guides in mind, a checklist of the factors Marx took into account, and the approximate sequence in which he considered them,

---

can be presented. In presenting these factors, comments are made suggesting adaptations of Marx's conceptual apparatus for present-day social research.

1. Consider first the economic order and, within it, the sphere of production of the society in question. Beginning with a definite base line in time, observe the main changes taking place. Even if the student cannot keep apace of the minute, day by day changes, he can observe the main structural changes within this sphere. For example, in present-day industrial society the effects of automation, even in its early stages, can be observed in the following: (a) changing "work-relations," (b) the numerical decline of production workers, (c) the changing structure of the new middle-class, and (d) changes in the effectiveness and structure of unions. Questions such as the following would also have to constitute a central focus from this point of view. How does the new technology affect the level of production? Is unemployment rising or declining? To what extent is the change a nation-wide or merely local phenomenon? Although these questions are extremely complex, relevant data is much more timely, plentiful and refined today than in Marx's time. For this reason it is not necessary to hold the economic situation "constant" for periods as long as Marx did. Economic data are perhaps less a source of error today than a century ago.

2. Locate the main classes in the economic structure. Determine the role of each in the processes of production, distribution, and exchange. Locate also the various sub-classes or strata in the economic structure.

3. The informed observer should be able to determine the objective economic interests of the respective classes and strata. Toward this end questions such as the following could be asked: Do the direct producers own or control the tools and other means of production? If not, who does own and/or control them? Does there exist an economic surplus of material goods over and above the subsistence requirements of the producers? Who has control of the surplus? How is it used and which classes benefit most directly from it?

4. Are class-members aware of their objective position in the economic structure and the extent to which it determines their "life chances?" One indicator of this awareness is the conflict among the classes in the economic sphere. A better indicator of class consciousness is the degree to which it finds *political* expression.

5. What form does conflict take among the classes? Within the classes?

6. What is the role of the *lumpenproletariat?* How does its existence affect the other classes? Which classes exploit its existence for their own political ends?

7. Where political parties exist it is important to determine their relationship with the respective classes and to assess the degree in which the parties express the interests of the various classes.

8. Which parties are in power? What is their relationship to the respective classes? Who controls the military order, the police, or their functional equivalents?

9. What patterns, regularities or trends can be observed in the changes within and among the classes? Which classes are growing numerically? Which are diminishing? Which functions are becoming more important? Which less important? For example, in the case of automation it was seen that the role of unskilled workers is diminishing in production.

10. What is the relationship among the major institutional orders of society, e.g., the economic, political, military, legal, religious, etc.? Which of these determine the tempo and direction of change in the society? Where are the key decisions made for the society as a whole? What is the relationship between the "power elite" and the economically dominant classes?

11. How do the external relations of a society affect its development? Such problems as international relations should not be overlooked. Marx never treated a society as a closed system.

12. Locate the radical elements in the society, i.e., those classes putting forward the most radical demands for change and having an objective interest in change. What are their explicit political aims as expressed directly by them or by their political representatives? Conversely, which classes have most interest in preserving the *status quo?*

13. What representation or power do the subordinate classes have in the government? What is the political program of each party, i.e., what are its declared political aims? Contrast this with actual policies and actions.

14. Are there any coalitions, economic or political, among the classes and parties? What trends can be observed in these coalitions? Which are the conservative and which the radical elements?

15. What is the role of the "great man," or charismatic leader, in the society? For example, what Marx attempted in his *18th Brumaire* was to "demonstrate how the *class struggle* in France created circumstances and relationships that made it possible for a mediocrity to play a hero's part."[1]

16. What are some of the central ideological themes of the society? Whose interests do these themes tend to serve?
17. Consider the historical context of the society in question. For example, in studying American society in the 20th century, *generalizations* based on the period from 1914 to 1946, which included two world-wars, an economic crisis and a prolonged depression, would be quite different from those based on the period of 1946 to 1966, which included none of these.
18. The role of tradition should not be ignored. Does a revolutionary, militaristic, or any other kind of tradition prevail? "Men make their own history," said Marx, "but they do not make it just as they please; they do not make it under circumstances chosen by themselves, but under circumstances directly encountered, given and transmitted from the past. The tradition of all the dead generations weighs like a nightmare on the brain of the living."[2]
19. Consider the size and role of the state bureaucracy. Which of its administrative functions are necessary for the society as a whole? Which functions directly benefit only certain classes?
20. What is the role of the legislative body of the government? Is it an effective body or afflicted with what Marx called *parliamentary cretinism?* Is its legislation, designed to improve the conditions of the subordinate classes, enforced?

This list is intended to be merely suggestive and is far from exhaustive. It points to the various factors which Marx considered in his more concrete studies of society. This paradigm together with the general premises of his theoretical approach are what make Marx's work relevant to contemporary social-science inquiry.

NOTES

1. MESW I, p. 222.
2. *Ibid.,* p. 225.

Part 2
CLASS AND CLASS CONFLICT

INTRODUCTION

Contrary to the view espoused by conservative apologists for the status quo and sociological investigators blinded by the vision of a society moving toward a state of equilibrium, the class divisions in modern society are real and relatively unchanging. Even in countries that from the perspective of the United States appear to have made great strides toward reducing class differences, the divisions have nonetheless remained. A recent analysis of class differences in Sweden, for example, has shown that the differences between the wealthiest and the poorest members of Swedish society have been increasing in recent years despite official pronouncements by the government that it was committed to reducing discrepancies among the social classes.[1] Similarly, in societies that have followed the socialist policies of the Soviet Union, we find a growing tendency for an elite of political bureaucrats to emerge as the privileged classes. This tendency is pointed out by the article in this section by the Yugoslav sociologist Milovan Djilas.

The studies in this section provide a broad picture of social class in industrial societies. The first article is an overview of social classes in modern industrial societies by the British sociologist T. B. Bottomore. Bottomore presents a general statement which summarizes much of the available data. The article by Gabriel Kolko traces the changes, or more accurately the lack of changes, in income distribution in the United States since the 1930s. Milovan Djilas, as mentioned earlier, provides an insightful analysis of the elite groups in the Soviet Union, with the implication that the emergence of such elite groups is inevitable with the Soviet-style socialist state. This section concludes with an article by C. Wright Mills on the characteristics of the "new middle class" in American society.

NOTES

1. Perry Anderson, "Sweden: Mr. Crosland's Dreamland," *New Left Review,* Jan–Feb 1961; "Sweden II: Study in Social Democracy," *New Left Review,* May–June 1961, pp. 34-45; See also Milton Mankoff, "Power in Advanced Capitalist Society," *Social Problems,* 1970, pp. 418-430.

CLASSES IN THE INDUSTRIAL SOCIETIES

T. B. Bottomore

The two broad types of industrial society—capitalist and Soviet—present a number of similar features in their occupational structure and in the general shape of their social stratification, but they also differ widely in their political régimes and their social doctrines and policies, in the manner in which the upper social strata are constituted, and in the historical changes of social structure which they have undergone. It is desirable, therefore, to begin by examining each type of society separately, before attempting any comparison.

In the mid-nineteenth century England was generally regarded as showing most fully and clearly the typical class structure of the new capitalist society. Marx chose England as his model for studying the development of capitalism and the formation of the principal modern classes—*bourgeoisie* and proletariat—although he associated with this a model of class conflict and revolution which he derived mainly from the experiences of France. Disraeli, who was not a revolutionary, documented in *Sybil* and in other writings the formation of "two nations" within English society, warned against the dangers springing from this rift between the manufacturers and the industrial workers, and at the same time sought to turn it to advantage by enlisting the support of working men for the Tory party against the Liberals. The English class system had, however, some peculiar features which arose, according to R. H. Tawney, from "the blend of a crude plutocratic reality with the sentimental aroma of an aristocratic legend."[1] It was this set of circumstances—still to be exhaustively studied and explained by historians—which created in England the "gentleman ideal" and the public schools as agencies for consolidating and transmitting it. It produced also the snobbery of the middle classes, the "religion of inequality" as Matthew

From T. B. Bottomore, *Classes in Modern Society,* London: George Allen and Unwin, 1965.

Arnold called it, which maintained fine but strict social distinctions at which foreign observers marvelled.

What changes has this system undergone in the past century? The plutocratic reality, it may be said, has been altered by changes in the distribution of property and income, and above all by the general improvement in the levels of living. At the end of the nineteenth century severe poverty was still widespread. Charles Booth's survey of London,[2] carried out between 1887 and 1891, showed that at that time more than 30 per cent of the inhabitants were living in poverty; and similar conclusions emerged from Rowntree's study of social conditions in York,[3] begun in 1899. At the other end of the social hierarchy, in the years 1911–13, a privileged 1 per cent of the population owned 68 per cent of all private property and received 29 per cent of the total national income.

The attack upon economic inequality is of very recent date. An estate duty was first imposed towards the end of the nineteenth century, and only in 1949 did it reach the substantial rate of 80 per cent on estates above one million. Even so, these rates of taxation reduce large fortunes (and the resulting unearned incomes) very slowly, if at all, since they are counteracted by various forms of tax avoidance, and by capital gains in periods of economic expansion, which can quickly restore fortunes diminished by taxation as well as creating new ones. In 1946–7, 1 per cent of the population still owned 50 per cent of all private property, and it is unlikely that the proportion has changed very much since then. The traditional wealthy class has obviously retained most of its wealth. As Anthony Sampson has observed: "... the aristocracy are, in general, much richer than they seem. With democracy has come discretion. Their London palaces and outward show have disappeared, but the countryside is still full of millionaire peers: many of them, with the boom in property, are richer now than they have ever been."[4] The observation is probably just as true of wealthy financial or manufacturing families.

The distribution of income is affected by several factors other than the distribution of wealth—by the state of employment, collective bargaining, general social policy, and taxation. During the present century taxes upon income have been used increasingly in attempts to bring about a redistribution between rich and poor; and whereas in 1913 those with earned incomes of £10,000 a year or above paid only about 8 per cent of their income in direct taxation, in 1948 those in the same category paid 75 per cent or more in direct taxation. R. H. Tawney, in the epilogue to the 1952 edition of his *Equality,* noted that the number of incomes exceeding £6,000 a year after payment of tax had declined to a very small figure, and that whereas in 1938 the average retained income of those in the highest category (£10,000 a year and above) was twenty-eight times as great as the income of those in the lowest category (£250–£499 a year), in 1948 it was only thirteen times as great.

However, the tax returns do not provide anything like a complete picture of the distribution of income, and R. M. Titmuss, in the most thorough study of the question which has yet been made,[5] points to the influence of life assurances, super-annuation, tax-free payments on retirement, education covenants, discretionary trusts, expense accounts, and capital gains, in conserving or increasing the wealth and income of the upper class. With the present inadequate data it is impossible to arrive at a precise statement of the changes in income distribution which have occurred during the twentieth century. Most students of the problem, however, have concluded that from 1900 to 1939 there was little or no redistribution of income in favour of wage-earners, and that at the end of the period some 10 per cent of the population received almost half the national income while the other 90 per cent of the population received the other half; that between 1939 and 1949 redistribution may have transferred some 10 per cent of the national income from property owners to wage earners; but that since 1949 there has again been growing inequality. These calculations are based largely upon the income tax returns, and so they do not take account of the other sources of real income mentioned above, which benefit mainly the rich.

Both Rowntree and Booth concluded from their investigations that two of the most important causes of poverty were the lack of regular employment and the expenses of protracted ill-health. The improvement in the conditions of life for the working class in postwar Britain obviously owes much to the maintenance of full employment and to the development of the health services.[6] Full employment, besides raising the level of income of the working class and providing a degree of that economic security which the upper class has always taken for granted, has almost entirely eliminated the class of domestic servants; and this is one of the greatest gains which the working class has made in the twentieth century, in escaping from one particularly onerous form of subjection to another class.[7]

It may be argued, too, that the social services as a whole have a much greater effect in diminishing class differences than would appear from their economic consequences alone. As R. H. Tawney wrote:

> There are certain gross and crushing disabilities—conditions of life injurious to health, inferior education, economic insecurity ... which place the classes experiencing them at a permanent disadvantage with those not similarly afflicted. There are certain services by which these crucial disabilities have been greatly mitigated, and, given time and will, can be altogether removed ... The contribution to equality made by these dynamic agencies is obviously out of all proportion greater than that which would result from an annual present to every individual among the forty odd millions concerned of a sum equivalent to his quota of the total cost.[8]

The social services do not only help to create an equality in the vital conditions of life for all citizens; so far as they are used by everyone the standard of the service tends to rise. It may well be true, as some have argued, that the middle classes have benefited at least as much as the working class from the expansion of the social services, but one important consequence has been that, for example, the standards of free medical care have been vastly improved as compared with the time when such care was provided only for the poor and needy. In the field of education a similar progress is evident since the Education Act of 1944, although here class differences have proved more tenacious and difficult to overcome, while the existence of a large private sector of education has meant that there has been less vigour in the drive to improve the standard of the public service.

We must conclude that the general advance in the material conditions of the British working class, in recent decades, has been due overwhelmingly to the rapid growth of national income, which has also made possible the expansion of the social services, and not to any radical redistribution of wealth or income between classes. Moreover, even in this more affluent society a great deal of poverty remains. Its significance for the relations between classes is, however, very different from that which it had in the nineteenth century. Then, poverty was the lot of a whole class, and there was no expectation that it could be quickly alleviated within the limits of the capitalist economic system. It separated one class in society distinctly from others, and at the same time engendered a movement of revolt. In present day Britain, as in other advanced industrial countries, poverty has ceased to be of this kind; it is now less extensive, and is confined to particular groups in the population—mainly old people and workers in certain occupations or regions which have been left behind as a result of technological progress—which are too isolated or heterogeneous to form the basis of a radical social movement. These impoverished groups stand in marked contrast with the majority of the working class which enjoys a high level of living in relation both to past societies and to some middle class groups in present day society.

The thesis of *embourgeoisement,* which was briefly examined in the previous chapter, relies in the main for its factual basis upon this improvement in levels of living and the changes in the relative economic position of manual workers and some sections of white collar workers, but it also brings in the effects of social mobility in modifying the class system. Since the war, sociologists have studied social mobility much more intensively than they have studied the changes within classes themselves, and they have attributed much importance to it as a solvent of class divisions. The findings of recent studies[9] may be summarized in the following way. Social mobility has generally increased with the economic development of the industrial societies, but the increase has been due very largely to changes in the occupational structure; that is, to the expansion of white collar and professional occupations and the contraction of manual occupations. For this reason, S. M. Miller has suggested that sociologists ought to give more attention to "downward mobility," which involves a real exchange of occupational and social position between classes and may well be "... a better indicator of fluidity in a society than is upward mobility."[10]

A second important feature is that most social mobility takes place between social levels which are close together; for example, between the upper levels of the working class and the lower levels of the middle class. Movement from the working class into the upper class is very limited in any society, and notably so in Britain.[11] This characteristic can be shown more clearly by studies of recruitment to particular *élite* occupations such as the higher civil service, business management, and the older professions. In Britain, a study of the directors of large public companies reveals that more than half of them began their careers with the advantage of having business connections in the family, while another 40 per cent came from families of landowners, professional men and others of similar social position.[12] A study of higher civil servants in the administrative class shows that 30 per cent came from families of the upper and upper middle classes, and another 40 per cent from the intermediate levels of the middle class, while only 3 per cent were recruited from families of semi-skilled and unskilled manual workers.[13] Nevertheless, the same study indicates that the area of recruitment of high civil servants has been extended somewhat during the past 30 years, and the same may well be true in the case of other professions.

The main influence here has been the extension of educational opportunities; and the view that social mobility has increased substantially in postwar Britain derives very largely from the belief that educational reforms have provided vast new opportunities for upward movement. It is certainly true that before the war social mobility was restricted especially by financial and other obstacles in the way of access to secondary and higher education.[14] The Education Act of 1944 established for the first time a national system of secondary education and greatly increased the opportunities for working class children to obtain a grammar school education.[15] Also in the postwar period the access of working class children to university has been made somewhat easier by the increase of student numbers and the more lavish provision of maintenance grants. Nevertheless, Britain is still very far from having equality of opportunity in education. The existence of a private sector of school education, misleadingly called the "public schools," maintains the educational and occupational advantages of upper class families, while in the state system of education, although the opportunities for working class children have increased, it is probable that middle class families have actually made greater use of the new opportunities for grammar school and university education.[16] Even if we add to the social mobility which takes place through the educational system, that which may be assumed to occur as a result of the growth of new middle class occupations—for example, in the entertainments industry—where educational qualifications are less important, it can still not be said that the movement of individuals in the social hierarchy is very considerable or is increasing rapidly. The vast majority of people still remain in their class of origin.

It may be questioned, too, whether even a much higher rate of social mobility, involving an interchange between classes in which downward mobility was roughly equal to upward mobility, would have much effect upon the class system, in the sense of reducing the barriers or the antagonism between classes. On the contrary, in such a situation of high mobility, the working class would come to comprise those who had failed to rise in the social hierarchy in spite of the opportunities available to them, and those who had descended, through personal failure, from higher social levels; and such a class, made up of particularly embittered and frustrated individuals, might be expected to be very sharply distinguished from, and in conflict with, the rest of society. These are apparent, indeed, in Britain and in other industrial societies, some elements of such a condition among the younger generations in the population.

The most important aspect of social mobility is perhaps the impression which it makes upon the public consciousness. According to the type and degree of social mobility a society may appear to its members to be "open" and fluid, presenting manifold opportunities to talent and energy, or it may appear to be rigid and "closed." In Britain, all manner of ancient institutions and modes of behaviour—the aristocracy, the public schools, Oxbridge, differences of speech and accent, the relationships of the "old boy" network—frustrate mobility and buttress the public conception of a rigidly hierarchical society. Any increase in social mobility, even in the past two decades, has been too modest, gradual and discreet to create a new outlook. The boundaries of class may have become more blurred, chiefly at the lower levels of the social hierarchy and there may have been some expansion of opportunities, especially in the sphere of consumption, for large sections of the population. But there is no general sense of greater "classlessness," nor of great opportunities for the individual to choose and create his way of life regardless of inherited wealth or social position.

It was in the general acceptance of an egalitarian ideology, which still persists in some degree, that the USA differed most remarkably from the European societies in the nineteenth century. In America, there was no established system of feudal ranks, no historical memory of an aristocratic order of society, which could provide a model for a new social hierarchy. The American war of independence indeed was an important influence upon the European revolutions against the *ancien régime.* In the USA, in contrast with the European countries, the ownership of property was quite widely diffused in the early part of the nineteenth century, and some 80 per cent of the working population (excluding the Negro slaves) owned the means of production with which they worked. America was, predominantly, a society of small farmers, small traders, and small businessmen; the closest approach there has been to a "property-owning democracy." Of course, disparities of wealth existed, but they were not so extreme as in Europe, and they did not give rise, except in some of the southern states, to disparities of social rank comparable with those in the still aristocratic and oligarchical European societies. De Tocqueville saw in the USA the prime example of a tendency towards equality in modern societies; a society in which, as he wrote: "Great wealth tends to disappear, the number of small fortunes to increase."

The sense of belonging to a society of equals was enhanced by the possibility of easy movement in the still rudimentary hierarchy of wealth. America was the "land of opportunity," a vast, unexplored and unexploited country in which it was always possible, or seemed possible, to escape from economic want or subjection by moving to a new place, acquiring land or some other property, and adding to it by personal effort and talent.

A century and a half of economic change has destroyed most of the foundations upon which the egalitarian ideology rested. The society made up of small property owners and independent producers began to be undermined soon after the Civil War. The 1880's and 1890's, a period in which industry grew rapidly and modern communications were vastly expanded, saw the "closing of the frontier," the emergence of the first industrial and financial trusts, and a considerable growth of inequalities of wealth. Class divisions began to appear more clearly, and to resemble more closely those in the European societies, and they were more openly asserted. The conscious emergence of an upper class was signalled by the establishment of the *Social Register* (the guide to the new American "aristocracy"), and by the foundation of exclusive boarding schools and country clubs; and wealth and social position came increasingly to be transmitted through family connections. At the same time the working class became more strongly organized in trade unions and political associations, and from the 1890's to the 1930's there were numerous attempts, though without any lasting success, to bring these associations together in a broad socialist movement.

The changes in the economic system can be documented clearly from the statistics of occupations. Early in the nineteenth century 80 per cent of the employed white population were independent (self-employed) producers; by 1870 only 41 per cent were self-employed, and by 1940 only 18 per cent. In the words of C. Wright Mills:

> Over the last hundred years, the United States has been transformed from a nation of small capitalists into a nation of hired employees; but the ideology suitable for the nation of small capitalists persists, as if that small-propertied world were still a going concern.[17]

There are several reasons for the persistence of this inapt ideology, apart from the inertia which characterizes social doctrines in general. One is that the concentration of property ownership was not accompanied by any sudden expansion of the working class, or by any decline in the level of living. The industrial workers formed 28 per cent of the population in 1870, and 31 per cent in 1940; and wage-earners as a whole made up 53 per cent of the population in 1870, and 57 per cent in 1940. During the same period, however, the proportion of salaried employees in the population increased very rapidly, from 7 per cent to 25 per cent; and this expansion of the new white collar middle classes made possible a new kind of social mobility, in place of that which had been achieved earlier by the settlement of fresh lands.

Again, the concentration of wealth and income in a few hands seems never to have proceeded so far in America as in many European countries; and the gilded age of spectacular fortunes in the midst of widespread poverty lasted for a relatively short time. As in other industrial countries there has been a persistent effort to redistribute wealth and income in the USA through progressive taxation, estate duties, and taxes on capital gains. Since the war, the continued economic expansion, rising levels of living, and the steady growth of the middle classes, have had their effect upon the class structure in the same way as in other countries, but in a more conspicuous fashion. And whilst in Britain, for example, such changes have so far produced only modifications and questionings of a class system which is still extremely solid and which profoundly affects political life, in America they have brought instead confirmation of an inherited ideology of "classlessness" and have practically extinguished the tentative class consciousness which found expression in the politics of the 1930's.

This divergence is not to be explained by a higher rate of social mobility in the USA in recent times, nor by a more rapid progress in the redistribution of wealth and income. Several studies have indicated that the USA does not have a rate of mobility significantly higher than that of some other industrial societies, in which class-consciousness is nevertheless much more intense.[18] This is the case, at least, when the broad movement from manual to non-manual occupations is considered. The long-range movement from the manual strata into the *élites* does seem to be greater in the USA than in most other countries;[19] but even so, it has not been very considerable at any time during the present century. W. Miller has shown that even in the first decade of the century successful businessmen had not generally risen from the lower strata of society, but had come for the most part from old-established families in the business and professional strata.[20] Similarly, a very thorough study of social classes in Philadelphia has revealed that the leading positions in the economic system are occupied predominantly by individuals from the established upper class families.[21]

The idea that a steady reduction of income inequalities has been proceeding during the present century is strongly contested, just as a similar view is contested in Britain. In the case of the USA the contention rests largely upon the statistical studies of national income by Simon Kuznets;[22] but as Gabriel Kolko has recently pointed out[23] the relevant part of these studies deals only with the wealthiest 5 per cent of the population, and does not examine the changes which have taken place in the incomes of other groups in the population. Kolko's own calculations, based upon studies of personal incomes before taxation by the National Industrial Conference Board (for 1910–37) and by the Survey Research Center (for 1941–59) indicate that between 1910 and 1959 the share in national income of the top income-tenth declined only slightly (and has fluctuated around 30 per cent in the past decade), while the shares of the second and third income-tenths actually increased and the shares of the two poorest income-tenths declined sharply (from 8.3 per cent of national income to only 4 per cent). Kolko also observes, as Titmuss has done in his study of the same question in Britain, that calculations based upon declarations of pre-tax income necessarily leave out of account various forms of real income which benefit mainly the upper class and thus increase inequality.

It may be argued, then, that it is the traditional conception of American society as highly mobile rather than any exceptional degree of mobility at the present time, and the general increase in prosperity (though with a good deal of partially concealed poverty)[24] rather than any strong movement towards greater economic equality, which play the main part in weakening class consciousness. But there have also been other factors at work, especially in inhibiting the development of a working class movement in which the ideas of class interest, and of socialism as an alternative form of society, would have a major influence. Among these factors, the situation of the Negroes and the successive waves of immigration are particularly important. The Negroes have formed a distinctive American proletariat, with the lowest incomes, the most menial and subservient tasks, and the lowest social prestige (in part because of their slave origins) of any group in American society. The existence of this large, relatively homogeneous, easily identifiable, and exploited group, has meant that every white American, even the lowest paid labourer, possesses a certain social prestige which raises him, at least in his own view, above the level of a proletarian. Immigration has worked in the same way to raise the social position of the ordinary American worker, since many groups of immigrants (the latest being the Puerto Ricans) entered the lowest levels of the occupational hierarchy, and made it possible for those already established to advance themselves. But neither the Negroes, nor any immigrant group, have formed a proletariat in the sense that they have challenged the established order of society. And so, although the present vigorous struggle of the Negroes to gain full economic, civil and political rights may be likened to early class conflicts in Europe so far as these were concerned with the right to vote, with labour legislation and with social reform, it differs entirely from these conflicts in so far as it aims exclusively at winning acceptance in the existing society and accepts the predominant values of that society. The success of the struggles waged by Negroes and other ethnic minorities, however, would diminish the importance of ethnic divisions in American society, and one result might be the appearance of more sharply differentiated social classes and a greater awareness of class interests.

Against this development, however, there are working the same influences which we have seen in Britain: a more or less continuous rise in levels of living; a greater differentiation of the occupational structure, and so a more complex type of social stratification; a relative decline of manual occupations; and an expansion of educational opportunities which has already gone much farther in America than in other countries. These influences are at work in all the Western capitalist societies; in France, Germany and Italy, where, in the past, class divisions have been deeper and class conflicts more violent than in Britain, and equally in the Scandinavian countries, in which social welfare and equality of opportunity have advanced farther than elsewhere. The consequences are to be seen in a relative appeasement of bitter conflicts over the structure of society as a whole, and in a displacement of political interest towards new problems of technological advance, economic growth and modernization. The two cultures have replaced the two nations as a subject of political debate, at least for many Western intellectuals. Whether the changes in social conditions and attitudes have actually brought about, or will bring about, a consolidation of the present social structure in the Western countries, and what other political consequences they are likely to have, are questions which I shall consider later on.

Our immediate concern is to examine the evolution of classes in the

Soviet type of industrial society. According to Marx's view modern capitalism would be "the last antagonistic form of the process of production." As he wrote in *The Poverty of Philosophy:*

> The condition for the emancipation of the working class is the abolition of all classes ... The working class, in the course of its development, will substitute for the old civil society an association which will exclude classes and their antagonism.

The USSR, although the revolution which created it did not take place in a highly industrialized country, does nevertheless claim to be a society of the kind which Marx predicted would follow the destruction of capitalism. It claims, that is, to be a classless society, at least in the sense that there is no hierarchy of classes and no domination by one class over others. This claim is based mainly upon the fact that the private ownership of the means of production has been abolished. Social theorists in the USSR have rarely attempted to analyse the social and political foundations of a classless society, and for long periods, especially after 1930, they were at some pains to make a sharp distinction between "classlessness" and "egalitarianism." The latter was denounced as a "petty *bourgeois* deviation," and the Soviet Encyclopaedia of Stalin's time asserted that "socialism and egalitarianism have nothing in common."[25] This ideological offensive against egalitarianism coincided broadly with the change in policy of the Soviet rulers in the early 1930's, which involved increasing wage and salary differentials, and in particular offering substantial financial incentives to highly skilled workers, scientists and technicians, industrial managers and intellectuals. These policies were continued during and after the war, and as a result the range of incomes in the USSR came to be almost as great as that in the capitalist countries. It is estimated that in 1953 industrial incomes ranged between 3,500 – 5,000 roubles a year for an unskilled worker, and 80,000 – 120,000 roubles for an important factory manager. The top incomes were, therefore, some 25 – 30 times as great as those at the bottom, which is perhaps somewhat less than the difference in Britain or the USA between the income of an unskilled worker and that of a managing director. But when the effects of taxation are considered, the income range in the USSR may have been greater, for the Soviet income tax is not steeply progressive, and taxation as a whole is regressive, since the greater part of the budget income is derived from a turnover tax on food and textile goods of mass consumption. These inequalities of income have been enhanced by other factors; by the abolition of the progressive inheritance tax in 1943, and by the privileges accorded to the higher social strata in education and housing, in the use of special shops, the acquisition of cars and other scarce goods and the award of prizes, grants and annuities.

The policy of increasing income differentiation could be explained by the demands of rapid industrialization in the 1930's, and later by the needs of war and postwar reconstruction. This is not, I think, the whole explanation; but insofar as it contains some truth, we might infer that with the completion of the stage of rapid industrialization (which Rostow has called the "drive to maturity") in the USSR, there would be a slackening, or even a reversal, of the trend towards greater inequality. A recent study[26] suggests that this is in fact happening. The author observes that since 1956 a number of policy statements have emphasized the raising of minimum wages, and he quotes the programme of the 22nd Congress of the CPSU to the effect that in the next 20 years "the disparity between high and comparatively low incomes must be steadily reduced."[27] He goes on to calculate, from Soviet statistics, which have become more abundant in recent years, that wage differentials have declined considerably since 1956; for example, whereas the average earnings of engineering technical personnel exceeded those of manual workers by two and a half times in the early 1930's, they were only 50 per cent higher in 1960. He concludes: "The period since 1956 has been marked by a narrowing of skill differentials in wage rates, substantial increases in minimum wages, and the declining importance of the piece-rate system."[28]

Even at the time when the inegalitarian features of Soviet society were so blatant, it was often argued that they did not signify the growth of a new class system. A sympathetic French observer of Soviet society put the argument as follows: "Some people might be tempted to conclude on the basis of this profound wage differentiation that Soviet society has not, in reality, abolished classes . . . It seems to me that classes as they exist in Western countries have actually no true equivalent in the USSR. The prejudices based on wealth, rigid barriers, the organized opposition of one class to its enlargement from below—these no longer exist or are in process of disappearing forever in the Soviet Union. Widespread education, the encouragement profusely given by the authorities to the social advance of those elements which have been less well placed to start with—all this points towards a final result that may legitimately be termed a 'classless society' ... That is why, if anyone may argue about the presence or absence of classes in the USSR, one must in any case recognize that the upper classes are abundantly open to members of the lower classes, and that the privileged levels have nothing of crystallization, rigidity, or especially heredity about them."[29]

The high rate of social mobility, and the absence of important barriers against mobility have often been adduced in this way as evidence for the gradual disappearance of social classes in the USSR. But the argument is open to several objections. In the first place, there has been no comprehensive study of social mobility in the USSR which would permit such definite assertions about its rate, either in absolute terms or in comparison with other societies.[30] Social mobility may have been considerable in the past half century, but it can be explained by the rapid industrialization of the country, and by losses in war (that is, by the same factors as in some Western countries) rather than by any distinctive features of the social structure. Industrial development created an array of new positions in the higher levels of the social hierarchy, and while the employed population doubled between 1926 and 1937, the *intelligentsia* (officials, professional and scientific workers, managers, and clerical workers) increased nearly four times. The increase in certain occupations was even more spectacular; the numbers of engineers and architects increased nearly eight times, and the numbers of scientific workers nearly six times.[31]

The process of expansion of white collar occupations is still continuing, but in the USSR as in other industrial countries, the rate of expansion is likely to slow down as industrial maturity is reached (if we exclude, for the present, the possible effects of automation), and the degree of mobility will come to depend more directly upon social policies designed to promote the interchange of individuals between the various social strata. In the later years of Stalin's régime, there were some indications that social mobility was being restricted, while the social privileges of the upper strata were more strongly emphasized. One step in this direction was the introduction, in 1940, of fees in higher education and in the last 3 years of secondary education. This increased the existing bias in favour of the upper strata in the selection of university students, and thus of the next generation of the *intelligentsia.* The reservation of high positions for those in the upper strata was aided by the new inheritance laws and by the strengthening of family ties.[32]

Nevertheless, the upper levels of Soviet society probably remained fairly open and accessible to talented individuals from the lower strata, and in recent years there have been attempts to deal with those influences which restrict mobility, for example in the sphere of education. Such efforts have been helped by the general movement to curb privilege and to bring about a greater equality of economic condition. Even at the time when income inequalities were increasing there were other factors which made for social equality over a large part of Soviet society. There was, and is, no real "leisure class" in the USSR; and the fact that social status depends mainly upon occupation—that is, upon a definite contribution to the well-being of society (however arbitrarily the relative value of the contributions may be determined in some cases)—limits the social effects of economic differences. It seems clear from the experience of Western countries that the social distinctions based upon property ownership and inheritance are more strongly felt, and are more divisive in their effects, than those which arise from differences in earned income. Again, the divisions created in the USSR by income differences were moderated by the fact that some skilled manual workers were also highly paid, while others could improve their position through activity in the party organizations; and still more by the absence of such profound social and cultural differences between manual and non-manual workers as exist in most of the Western countries.[33]

Yet in the opinion of many sociologists the facts we have been considering do not bear directly upon the most significant aspect of the class structure in Soviet society. However "classless" social relationships may be at some levels of society, is there not, in the Soviet type of society, a governing *élite* which resembles closely the ruling classes of other societies, except that its power is more concentrated and less subject to restraint? Milovan Djilas, in *The New Class,* has argued that the Communist Party officials in these societies have come to constitute a new ruling class which, in his words, is "... made up of those who have special privileges and economic preference because of the administrative monopoly they hold."[34] Similarly, S. Ossowski, in the work quoted earlier, emphasizes the extent to which in the modern world, and especially in the Soviet countries, changes in the class structure are brought about by the decisions of political authorities; or as he says later, by compulsion or force.[35] Thus classes no longer arise spontaneously from the economic activities of individuals; instead a political *élite* imposes upon society the type of stratification to be found in a bureaucratic hierarchy.

The most comprehensive expression of this view has been given by Raymond Aron in two articles published in 1950,[36] and more recently in his book *La lutte de classes.*[37] Aron asserts that the members of the ruling group in Soviet society have

> . . . infinitely more power than the political rulers in a democratic society, because both political and economic power are concentrated in their hands . . . Politicians, trade union leaders, public officials, generals and managers all belong to one party and are part of an authoritarian organization. The unified *élite* has absolute and unbounded power.[38]

Another element in its power is the ideological monopoly which it enjoys through its control of the exposition and interpretation of an official creed—Marxism—which shapes the thoughts and opinions of the people and provides justifications for the actions of the ruling group. Aron contrasts this unified Soviet *élite* with the divided *élite,* or plurality of *élites,* in the democratic capitalist countries, and he seeks to explain the difference by the presence or absence of classes and other autonomous interest groups in the society.

These observers agree in discovering a profound division in Soviet society between the ruling *élite* and the rest of the population. Are they right in supposing that this signifies the formation of a new class system? Or is it only a temporary feature in a movement towards a genuinely classless society? Defenders of the Soviet régime have portrayed the Stalinist period—during which the privileges of the upper stratum, political dictatorship, and rule by violence, attained an extreme point—as an historical aberration, resulting from what is now termed the "cult of personality." But this is no explanation. The cult of personality has itself to be explained, and this is all the more necessary and urgent since its appearance contradicts all the expectations which Marxists had about the nature of a classless society. An explanation might be attempted by stating the social conditions which are favourable to the rise of charismatic leaders, along the lines which Max Weber first suggested. In the particular instance of the USSR we could point to such features as the sudden break with the past in the revolution, and the stresses, together with the need for authority and discipline, engendered by the rapid industrialization of an economically backward country. Or else, we may look for more general conditions which favour a unified *élite,* as Aron does when he argues that a "classless society" (in the restricted sense of a society in which all economic enterprises are publicly owned and managed) necessarily produces a great concentration of power in the hands of the political and industrial leaders; and as Ossowski does when he suggests that political power has now become so important in all the industrial countries, but especially in the Soviet countries, that the political *élite* is able to form and change the system of stratification rather than being itself a product of that system.

These ideas are at variance with Marx's conception of the relation between property ownership, social classes, and political power; and also with his account of how the class system in modern societies would develop. The great extension of the activities of government, in economic development and in the provision of social services; the growth of highly organized and powerful political parties; the influence which can be exerted through the modern media of communication; these have all worked to establish a major division in society between the governing *élite*—which may include political and military leaders, high officials, and the directors of important economic enterprises—and the mass of the population, to some extent independently of social classes based upon property ownership, or of other forms of stratification. In the USSR where this division is most firmly established—because the political rulers belong to a party, revolutionary in origin, which has an exceptionally rigorous organization, and which is further bound together by an all-embracing ideology—it is also most profoundly obscured, because the doctrine to which the ruling *élite* adheres excludes either recognition or investigation of such a phenomenon.

At least, this has been the case until recently. Now at last some fresh life appears to be stirring in the long insensible body of orthodox Marxism; and not only are Marx's ideas and theories being re-examined in a more critical spirit, but the social structure of the Soviet countries is beginning to be studied in a more realistic and objective manner. As a result, the problems of the centralization of power are now more open to rational discussion; and the attempts to combine public ownership and central planning with the creation of relatively independent local centres of decision, such as are being made in Yugoslavia through the institutions of workers' self-management, are no longer rejected out of hand as sinister deviations from orthodoxy. The Yugoslav experience, in fact, seems to many socialists (Marxist and other) to hold out the promise of an eventual classless society in which there would be neither political dictatorship nor total intellectual conformity. At the same time it illustrates very strikingly the newly tolerated diversity of institutions and doctrines within the Soviet group of countries.

The capitalist societies, as we have seen already, are also diverse in their class structure, and any comparison between the Soviet and the capitalist forms of industrial society must recognize that there is a considerable range of variation within each type of society—for example, in the nature and extent of social mobility, in the magnitude of economic inequalities, in the situation of the working class and in the degree of unification of the *élite*—which makes for a continuum of differences rather than an abrupt break between the two types. This fact, which is unpalatable to the more extreme ideologists on both sides, is given further emphasis by the common features in Soviet and capitalist societies which result mainly from three important influences upon all modern societies: the rapid progress of industrialization, the growing size of organizations, especially in the economic sphere, and the increasing part played by governments in the deliberate shaping of economic and social life.

Industrialization has sometimes been regarded by sociologists as a process which tends naturally to bring about a greater equality of condition in society. This view is supported by various arguments. The development of industry breaks down any rigid and exclusive differences of rank, by creating unprecedented opportunities for social mobility, by extending and improving education to meet the new scientific and technological needs, and by raising enormously the general level of living, thus reducing the harshness of the contrast between the conditions of the upper and lower strata of society. Furthermore, modern industry, by increasing the size of societies, as well as the amount of mobility, creates circumstances which are especially favourable to the diffusion of egalitarian ideas, as Bouglé attempted to show in a work, now much neglected, on *Les idées égalitaires;*[39] and at the same time it brings into being a large and articulate social group—the industrial workers—capable of initiating a political movement which gives a great impetus to the spread of egalitarian and democratic ideas.

This relationship between industrialization and social stratification can be seen very well in the present day developing countries. In many of them there are, or have been until recently, extremes of wealth and poverty much greater than those in the industrial countries; and the traditional upper classes have constituted a formidable obstacle to economic development, by their general resistance to change and mobility, and by their propensity to use the large share of the national income which they receive for conspicuous consumption rather than productive investment. Where industrialization gets under way successfully it is very often at the expense of upper class wealth and privileges, through confiscation or high taxation, and the opening of *élite* occupations to talented individuals from the lower social strata. Conversely, where, as in India, an extraordinarily intricate and inflexible traditional form of stratification successfully resists any radical changes, the pace of industrialization may be greatly diminished, and the whole endeavour to promote economic growth be put in jeopardy.

It would be quite wrong, however, to suppose that industrialization leads inexorably to an egalitarian society. The evidence we have already considered shows that in the Western industrial societies there has been little reduction of economic inequality in the past few decades, while in the USSR inequality actually increased between the 1930's and the 1950's, to some extent as part of a policy of incentives to induce more rapid industrialization. Moreover, the other influences at work in modern societies, mentioned earlier, tend to increase social inequality, by accentuating the distinction between *élites* and masses. The increasing size and the growing rationalization of business enterprises has had this effect, by establishing a small group of top managers, supported by expert advisers, in remote control of the routine and largely unskilled activities of large numbers of workers. Other large organizations, including the modern political parties, also display some of the same features. The increasing scope and powers of the central government is another aspect of this process in which the making of important decisions tends to be more and more concentrated in a few hands, while the powers of independent voluntary associations and of local elected bodies decline.

The principal difference between the Soviet countries and the capitalist democracies is to be found in the character of the *élites,* and its political consequences, rather than in the other aspects of social stratification. As we have seen, the range of incomes in these societies is broadly similar, and everywhere large differences of income produce distinctions between social groups in their styles of life, their opportunities and their social prestige. In the early 1950's, it appeared that economic inequalities were increasing in the Soviet societies and diminishing (though very slowly) in the capitalist societies. At the present time, both these trends seem to have been reversed, but it is difficult as yet to foresee the consequences of these changes. One fact does mark an important contrast:

namely, that in the Soviet societies, economic inequalities do not arise to any significant extent from differences in wealth, whereas the distinctions between property-owners and property-less workers, between income from property, and income from work, run all through the capitalist societies, and largely account for the strong sentiments of class position which are manifest there. This circumstance is connected with the fact that the distinctions between whole social groups are less obvious and less emphasized in the Soviet societies. Income differences produce some separation of groups, but it is probably the case that social intercourse between individuals in different occupations and income levels is a great deal easier than in the capitalist countries. One of the major divisions in Soviet society has probably been that between town and country, between urban workers and peasants. How far the gap has diminished in the USSR in recent years it is difficult to determine in the absence of serious research, but studies in other countries—notably in Yugoslavia and Poland—indicate that it is still considerable; and its full extent is shown by the problems of acculturation which arise when peasants are recruited for industrial work in the course of economic development.

The contrast between the unified ruling *élite* in the Soviet countries and the divided *élite* in the capitalist democracies, which has been so much emphasized by sociologists during the past decade, has itself to be interpreted with great care if we are to escape the absurd view that in one of these types of society there is a completely monolithic ruling party, while in the other there is no ruling group at all. The Soviet societies approach more or less closely the ideal type of a unified *élite,* which suppresses any opposition, whether political or intellectual, from other social forces, as well as any conflict within its own ranks; but it is clear that these societies have experienced in practice very serious conflicts between different interest groups, and that in recent years the opportunities for such interest groups to express criticism and to influence policy have increased.

In the capitalist societies, on the other hand, the evident division of the *élite* into divergent interest groups at one level does not preclude the existence at another level of important *common* interests and aspirations which tend to produce a uniformity of outlook and action on fundamental issues of social policy. The *élites* in these societies are recruited very largely from an upper class which has its own distinctive economic and cultural interests, and their provenance is likely to shape to a common pattern, the ends and forms of action which they adopt. Even where the association between an upper class and the *élite* groups is less strong the latter may still, by virtue of the manifold connections which are established between those who wield power in various spheres, come to act generally in concert, despite the conflicts between them on particular occasions. This is the principal argument of C. Wright Mills in *The Power Elite;* but he goes further in suggesting that the development of modern society tends to produce, by the centralization of power and the elimination or weakening of local and voluntary associations, a "mass society," the rudiments of which can be discerned everywhere, and which is gradually taking the place of the older form of industrial society with its division into social classes.[40]

However, it is not so much the homogeneity or heterogeneity of the ruling *élite* as the possibility of forming and establishing organizations which *oppose* the *élite* in power, which constitutes the principal difference between the Soviet societies and the capitalist democracies. Old-fashioned Marxists explain this disparity very easily, by observing that there are, in the Soviet societies, no exploiting or exploited classes, thus no class antagonisms, and thus no basis for political conflict; whereas in the capitalist democracies, it is precisely the existence of classes having opposed interests which engenders the major political conflicts. The second part of this statement is very generally accepted, though with many qualifications which were indicated in our earlier discussion;[41] but the first part will not bear serious examination. In many of the Soviet societies—and especially in the USSR—there have been profound social conflicts, which have erupted from time to time in large scale revolts; as for example in the resistance of the Russian peasants to collectivization in the 1930's, and in the uprising of the Hungarian people in 1956. If these conflicts have not given rise to any sustained public opposition to the ruling *élite* it is only because they have been forcibly repressed. The absence of an organized opposition is no indication at all of a state of society in which harmony and co-operation have replaced conflict when it results in this way from the persistent use of violence by the political rulers. Marx was consistent in arguing, from his premises, that with the abolition of classes the major source of political conflict in society would be eliminated, and that the need for a coercive state would then disappear. In the phrase of Saint-Simon, which Marx adopted, "the government of men is replaced by the administration of things." It is all too evident that this is not what has happened in the Soviet societies. On the contrary the repressive apparatus of the state has grown enormously;[42] and although in the USSR and other east European countries the rule of force has been moderated since the death of Stalin, government is still much more coercive than in the capitalist societies. Of late there has been more outspoken criticism; and in some spheres which do not affect very closely the political régime, a greater freedom of thought and imagination has been permitted. The official doctrines of socialist realism in art, music and literature, seem, happily, to be expiring. But there is still neither freedom of movement for the individual, nor any possibility of organized public dissent and opposition on important questions of social policy. In certain respects, as in the introduction of the death penalty for various economic offences, the coercive power of the state has been enhanced,[43] and the existence of serious conflict within the society all the more clearly demonstrated.

Two general conclusions may be drawn from this discussion. The first is that the extent of conflict, and of coercive government, in the Soviet societies, indicates either that classes and class antagonisms have survived or have been re-created in a new form in these societies; or else that there are other important sources of social conflicts besides those of class interest, and that if, through the influence of a doctrinaire creed such conflicts are denied expression, this can only be accomplished in the last resort by violence. The second conclusion is that if the main source of political and ideological conflicts in the modern capitalist societies has been the opposition between classes, and if such conflicts have helped to establish some of the vital conditions of democracy—the right of dissent and criticism, the right to create associations independently of the state—then it must be considered whether the abolition, or even the decline of social classes does not open the way for the growth of a mass society, in which the political *élite* has unbounded power, just as much as for the creation of an egalitarian and democratic society.

NOTES

1. R. H. Tawney, *Equality* (4th edn. 1952) p. 57.
2. Charles Booth, *Life and Labour of the People in London* (1902).
3. B. Seebohm Rowntree, *Poverty; A Study of Town Life* (1901).
4. Anthony Sampson, *Anatomy of Britain,* pp. 4-5.
5. R. M. Titmuss, *Income Distribution and Social Change* (1962).

6. Rowntree emphasizes the importance of these factors in his third social survey of York. See B. Seebohm Rowntree and G. R. Lavers, *Poverty and the Welfare State* (1951).
7. Marx observed in *Capital* Vol. I that the vast increase in the numbers of domestic servants, of whom there were well over a million in 1861, showed clearly the growing divergence between the classes; with wealth and luxury concentrated at one extreme, poverty and servitude at the other.
8. R. H. Tawney, *Equality* (4th edn. 1952) p. 248.
9. See especially, D. V. Glass (ed.), *Social Mobility in Britain* (1954). This comprehensive study, based mainly upon a national sample survey, has provided a model for a number of later investigations in other countries. For comparative studies which bring together much recent research see S. M. Lipset and R. Bendix, *Social Mobility in Industrial Society* (1959), and S. M. Miller, "Comparative Social Mobility," *Current Sociology,* IX (1) 1960.
10. S. M. Miller, *op. cit.* p. 59.
11. S. M. Miller, *op. cit.* p. 40.
12. G. H. Copeman, *Leaders of British Industry; A Study of the Careers of More than a Thousand Public Company Directors* (1955).
13. R. K. Kelsall, *Higher Civil Servants in Britain* (1955).
14. See data presented in L. Hogben (ed.), *Political Arithmetic* (1938).
15. D. V. Glass notes, in his introduction to *Social Mobility in Britain,* that in one region, S. W. Hertfordshire, between the 1930's and 1951, ". . . the proportion of children of manual workers in the total entry to grammar schools rose from about 15 per cent to 43 per cent." See also the material given in J. E. Floud, A. H. Halsey and F. M. Martin, *Social Class and Educational Opportunity* (1956).
16. Appendix Two (B) to the *Report on Higher Education* (Cmnd. 2154) observes that the proportion of university students coming from working class families remained almost unchanged (at about 25 per cent) between 1928–47 and 1961.
17. C. Wright Mills, *White Collar; The American Middle Classes* (1951).
18. See especially, S. M. Lipset and R. Bendix, *Social Mobility in Industrial Society* (1959).
19. S. M. Miller, *op. cit.* p. 58.
20. William Miller, "American Historians and the Business Elite," in William Miller (ed.) *Men in Business* (new edn. 1962).

21. E. Digby Baltzell, *An American Business Aristocracy* (new edn. 1962).
22. See especially his *Shares of Upper Income Groups in Income and Savings* (1953).
23. Gabriel Kolko, *Wealth and Power in America* (1962).
24. See, on the extent of poverty, Gunnar Myrdal, *Challenge to Affluence* (1963) Chapter 4, and Michael Harrington, *The Other America* (1962). The latter book makes plain that poverty is widespread, but (as in Britain) it is concentrated in particular sections of the population—here among the old, ethnic minorities, and workers in such regions as the Appalachians—and so often tends to go unrecognized.
25. An English Socialist, on the other hand, has written: "Where there is no egalitarianism there is no Socialism." Roy Jenkins, "Equality" in *New Fabian Essays* (1952).
26. Murray Yanowitch, "The Soviet Income Revolution," *Slavic Review* XXIII (4), December, 1963.
27. *op. cit.* p. 684.
28. *ibid.* p. 692.
29. Michel Gordey, *Visa to Moscow* (English trans. 1962).
30. One of the very few sources of data is the Harvard study of Soviet émigrés; see A. Inkeles and R. A. Bauer, *The Soviet Citizen: Daily Life in a Totalitarian Society* (1959). This is obviously not a study of a representative sample, but such as it is it indicates that the amount of movement from manual into non-manual occupations as a whole is not exceptionally high in the USSR when compared with some Western societies, but that movement from the manual strata into the *élites* is particularly high. (For these comparisons see S. M. Miller, *op. cit.*).
31. See S. M. Schwartz, *Labour in the Soviet Union* (1952).
32. See Alex Inkeles, "Social Stratification and Mobility in the Soviet Union," *American Sociological Review,* August, 1950.
33. The separation between manual workers and non-manual workers in the Western countries in leisure time activities is well-established by sociological research. On France, see especially P. H. Chombart de Lauwe, *L'Agglomération Parisienne* (1952); on England, T. B. Bottomore, "Social Stratification in Voluntary Organizations" in D. V. Glass (ed)., *Social Mobility in Britain* (1954). Numerous studies, from R. A. and H. M. Lynd's *Middletown* (1929) to recent investigations of voluntary associations, point to the same phenomenon in the USA. This separation is beginning to break down, perhaps, with rising levels of living, but there is little evidence as yet to show any radical change.

34. *op. cit.* p. 39.

35. S. Ossowski, *Class Structure in the Social Consciousness,* pp. 184, 186.

36. Raymond Aron, "Social Structure and the Ruling Class," *British Journal of Sociology,* I (1) March, 1950, and I (2) June, 1950.

37. Raymond Aron, *La lutte de classes* (Paris, 1964). See especially Chapters IX and X.

38. Article cit., *British Journal of Sociology,* I (2) p. 131.

39. C. Bouglé, *Les idées égalitaires: Étude sociologique* (Paris, 1925).

40. C. Wright Mills, *The Power Elite,* p. 304. ". . . we have moved a considerable distance along the road to the mass society. At the end of that road there is totalitarianism, as in Nazi Germany or in Communist Russia."

41. See above, pp. 21-3, 26-8.

42. Except in Yugoslavia, which has remained largely outside the sphere of influence of the USSR.

43. Marx himself consistently opposed the coercive power of the state, and he expressed himself forthrightly on the subject of capital punishment, in a passage which is peculiarly apposite to the present conditions in the Soviet countries: "Now, what a state of society is that which knows of no better instrument for its own defence than the hangman, and which proclaims . . . its own brutality as eternal law? . . . is there not a necessity for deeply reflecting upon an alteration of the system that breeds these crimes, instead of glorifying the hangman who executes a lot of criminals to make room only for the supply of new ones?" "Capital Punishment," *New York Daily Tribune,* February 18, 1853.

TRENDS IN THE DISTRIBUTION OF INCOME

Gabriel Kolko

The social scientist inquiring into the distribution of income in America finds his task of obtaining accurate information complicated in two significant ways by the expansion of the Federal tax system over the past two decades. Since he is seeking the same information as the tax collector, he is confronted with essentially the same barriers of deception and silence in approaching an important segment of the population, including a good number of the very wealthy. Also, he must devise ways of measuring the ingenious forms of income created by the wealthy in their efforts to minimize their taxes. Thus, he must evaluate expense-account allowances, corporate profits not paid out to stockholders, and personal earnings to be paid at a deferred date, as well as various forms of interest, dividend, and other income not appearing in existing data. In the lower-income brackets, a form of income he must take into account is home-grown food.

If, then, the social scientist is resourceful and tenacious in his research and avoids confusing illusion with reality, he will finally have revealed the unvarnished, if complicated, reality of the present-day distribution of income in the United States.

In studying the major trends in the distribution of income, we shall consider the nation's population as an aggregate of families and unattached individuals ranked according to the size of their annual income. We shall then divide them, from top to bottom, into ten groups, each containing the same number of families and unattached individuals. These will be referred to as income-tenths.

Since much of the recent research on income distribution has been done in terms of income-fifths, my departure from this approach may demand some justification. I have two major objections to discussing income distribution by fifths of the population: First, such statistics

Reprinted with permission from *Wealth and Power in America,* Gabriel Kolko, New York: Praeger, 1962.

extend back only as far as 1935–36. Second, these larger units obscure important patterns of income distribution that appear only when the population is further divided into tenths.

The conventional way of discussing income distribution is to take the whole range of personal incomes, break it down into consecutive income brackets, and then determine the percentage of families and unrelated individuals that belongs in each division. This approach was used, for instance, by a *New York Times* financial writer when he explained that "where three out of four families had incomes of less than $2,000 a year in 1939, only one out of three fell into that class ten years later."[1] As in this case, studies of income distribution based on income-size frequently ignore the role of inflation in raising dollar incomes and producing an upward shift in the distribution—those near the top of one income class are pushed into the lower levels of the next-highest class. These inflation-caused ascents in income-size distributions are absolutely unrelated to any increases in the real income—the purchasing power—of the population. For example, a family of four earning $3,000 in 1946 and earning $4,445 in 1958 had merely maintained the identical real income. From 1947 through 1958, the average American family income increased 50 per cent in dollars, but the size of this jump shrinks if one knows that 32 of these percentage points are merely the result of inflation; only 18 of the percentage points indicate greater purchasing power.[2] However, when income-size distribution figures are corrected to eliminate the inflationary content, they are well suited for the study of changes in real income.

More important, from our point of view, the changes in income-size distribution generally tell us little about the proportionate distribution of income among the population. A rise in the real income of a group does not itself indicate an increase in its percentage of the national income. In fact, an income group can enjoy a boost in real wages while simultaneously suffering a loss in its percentage of the country's income. A failure to distinguish between these two separate concepts is the basic flaw in the theory that the rising standard of living of the past few decades has been accompanied by a trend toward equalization in the percentage of the country's income earned by each tenth or fifth of the population. This failure to distinguish is illustrated in a statement by economist Henry C. Wallich of Yale University that recent changes in the income distribution "reflect both a great improvement in the over-all standard of living and also a cutting of the economic pie into servings of more nearly equal size."[3] Such a merging of two distinct issues only obscures the nature of the changes that have occurred since 1933.

A COMPARISON OF METHODS

The abundance of data on income distribution collected by different methods over the past several decades makes a comparison of their value essential. Their only common characteristic is their failure, because of understatement and nonreporting by taxpayers or interviewees, to calculate the distribution of the entire national personal money income. Studies show that the Survey Research Center data (prepared until 1959 for the Federal Reserve Board) accounted for anywhere from 77 to 95 per cent of the total, the U.S. Bureau of the Census has accounted for 74 to 81 per cent, and individual income-tax returns have accounted for 86 to 91 per cent.[4]

Census calculations of income-size distributions attempt to cover all money income except capital gains, and exclude nonmoney income-in-kind, such as home-produced food and fuel, the rental value of owner-occupied homes, wages in the form of food and services, free bank services, and certain nondeclared interest. The Office of Business Economics of the Department of Commerce, in its studies of income distribution by size and by income-fifths, includes all money income and many forms of income-in-kind, but it excludes undistributed profits, most expense-account allowances, and many forms of unreported income. The Survey Research Center data on income distribution by size and income-tenths covers money income only.

These agencies also differ in their definition of family units or households. The Survey Research Center uses a "spending unit," consisting of all related persons living in the same dwelling who pool their incomes. Husband, wife, and children under eighteen years living at home are always in the same unit. Other relatives in the household are separate units if they earn more than $15 a week and do not pool their incomes. Persons living in institutions, military reservations, hotels, or large rooming houses are excluded. The National Industrial Conference Board "recipient unit" includes all related persons who live in the same dwelling. It ignores second breadwinners, but since before 1941 their earnings were very low, this would not seriously affect the basic pattern of income distribution.[5] The Census uses the "family," defined as two or more related individuals living together, irrespective of how they treat their income, and "unrelated individuals," defined as persons who do not live with their family, but who may live with other "unrelated individuals." Only persons living in institutions or military reservations are excluded. The Office of Business Economics "consumer unit" is used to indicate either the family or unrelated individuals as defined by the Census, and also excludes only persons living in institutions or military reservations.[6]

All these methodological variations, however, are a relatively minor consideration. A much more important problem is the failure of individuals to report their total income. These omissions are so substantial that their inclusion in existing statistics would necessitate a thorough reappraisal of all previous conclusions on income distribution.

The Survey Research Center figures for income distribution by tenths, compiled from 1941 through 1959, are more reliable than either Census or Federal income-tax data, because they are obtained directly from the heads of households, who disclose information more freely in an anonymous situation to a nongovernmental agency than they do to the Federal bureaus. Consequently, the Survey figures usually account for a relatively high percentage of the national money income.[7] Prior to 1941, the best material on income distribution by tenths was compiled by the National Industrial Conference Board. Like the Survey, it excludes income-in-kind, but this, again, can be adjusted.

THE UNCHANGING PATTERN OF INEQUALITY

A radically unequal distribution of income has been characteristic of the American social structure since at least 1910, and despite minor year-to-year fluctuations in the shares of the income-tenths, no significant trend toward income equality has appeared. This, in brief, is the deduction that can be made from a study of Table 1.

Throughout the 1950's, the income of the top tenth was larger than the total for the bottom five income-tenths—about the same relationship as existed in 1910 and 1918. The income share of the richest tenth has dropped only slightly, if at all, since 1910. The average percentage of the national personal income before taxes, received by this group was about one-eighth less in 1950–59 than in 1910–41, omitting the exceptional years 1921 and 1929. This loss, however, disappears when the 1950–59 figures are corrected to allow for their exclusion of all forms of income-in-kind and the very substantial understatement of income by the

Table 1. Percentage of national personal income, before taxes, received by each income-tenth*

	Highest tenth	2nd	3rd	4th	5th	6th	7th	8th	9th	Lowest tenth
1910	33.9	12.3	10.2	8.8	8.0	7.0	6.0	5.5	4.9	3.4
1918	34.5	12.9	9.6	8.7	7.7	7.2	6.9	5.7	4.4	2.4
1921	38.2	12.8	10.5	8.9	7.4	6.5	5.9	4.6	3.2	2.0
1929	39.0	12.3	9.8	9.0	7.9	6.5	5.5	4.6	3.6	1.8
1934	33.6	13.1	11.0	9.4	8.2	7.3	6.2	5.3	3.8	2.1
1937	34.4	14.1	11.7	10.1	8.5	7.2	6.0	4.4	2.6	1.0
1941	34.0	16.0	12.0	10.0	9.0	7.0	5.0	4.0	2.0	1.0
1945	29.0	16.0	13.0	11.0	9.0	7.0	6.0	5.0	3.0	1.0
1946	32.0	15.0	12.0	10.0	9.0	7.0	6.0	5.0	3.0	1.0
1947	33.5	14.8	11.7	9.9	8.5	7.1	5.8	4.4	3.1	1.2
1948	30.9	14.7	11.9	10.1	8.8	7.5	6.3	5.0	3.3	1.4
1949	29.8	15.5	12.5	10.6	9.1	7.7	6.2	4.7	3.1	0.8
1950	28.7	15.4	12.7	10.8	9.3	7.8	6.3	4.9	3.2	0.9
1951	30.9	15.0	12.3	10.6	8.9	7.6	6.3	4.7	2.9	0.8
1952	29.5	15.3	12.4	10.6	9.1	7.7	6.4	4.9	3.1	1.0
1953	31.4	14.8	11.9	10.3	8.9	7.6	6.2	4.7	3.0	1.2
1954	29.3	15.3	12.4	10.7	9.1	7.7	6.4	4.8	3.1	1.2
1955	29.7	15.7	12.7	10.8	9.1	7.7	6.1	4.5	2.7	1.0
1956	30.6	15.3	12.3	10.5	9.0	7.6	6.1	4.5	2.8	1.3
1957	29.4	15.5	12.7	10.8	9.2	7.7	6.1	4.5	2.9	1.3
1958	27.1	16.3	13.2	11.0	9.4	7.8	6.2	4.6	3.1	1.3
1959	28.9	15.8	12.7	10.7	9.2	7.8	6.3	4.6	2.9	1.1

* In terms of "recipients" for 1910-37 and "spending units" for 1941-59.

Source: Data for 1910-37 are from National Industrial Conference Board, *Studies in Enterprise and Social Progress* (New York: National Industrial Conference Board, 1939), p. 125. Data for 1941-59 were calculated by the Survey Research Center. Figures for 1941-46 are available in rounded form only. Previously unpublished data for 1947-58 are reproduced by permission of the Board of Governors of the Federal Reserve System, and data for 1959 by permission of the Survey Research Center.

wealthy, both of which are consequences of the post-1941 expansion in income taxation.

While the income share of the richest tenth has remained large and virtually constant over the past half century, the two lowest income-tenths have experienced a sharp decline. In 1910, the combined income shares of the two poorest income-tenths were about one-quarter that of the richest tenth; by 1959, their share had dropped to one-seventh. During this same period, the percentage of the next-lowest tenth also decreased, while the fourth and fifth from the lowest tenths (the sixth- and seventh-ranking) neither gained nor lost ground appreciably. Together these five groups, which constitute the poorer half of the U.S. population, received 27 per cent of the national personal income in 1910, but only 23 per cent in 1959. Thus, for the only segments of the population in which a gain could indicate progress toward economic democracy, there has been no increase in the percentage share of the national income.

The only significant rises in income distribution have occurred in the second- and third-richest income-tenths. Their combined shares increased more than one-quarter from 1910 to 1959, and by the end of that period their combined income share was almost equal to that of the richest tenth. It should be noted, however, that their gain was made almost entirely during the Depression years of the 1930's. Further, this group is largely made up of persons in occupations such as professionals, small businessmen, top clerical workers, and lesser managers, with rising salary or wage incomes and low unemployment, and by no means was in urgent need of a greater share of the national income.

Many recent explanations of rising real and dollar incomes in the lower-income groups since 1939 or 1941, which have been utilized to prove the occurrence of a radical and purportedly permanent income redistribution, ignore the fact that these increases reflect increased employment, not an alteration in the basic distribution structure.

Prior to World War II, it was commonly assumed that the different phases of the business cycle affected the distribution of income—that relative income inequality rose when unemployment rose. However, the relationship between employment trends and income is more important in the study of real income and dollar earnings than in the study of income distribution. During an upward trend in unemployment, the *dollar earnings* of the lowest-income classes decline much more rapidly than those of the other groups, and during an upswing in employment, both the dollar earnings and real income of the lowest-income classes rise much more rapidly than those of the higher-income groups. During full employment, the rate at which the dollar income of the poorer classes increases generally keeps pace with the rate of rise for the highest classes (although occasionally falling slightly behind—as from 1948 to the early 1950's).[8]

However, even the pre-1941 data show that once common generalizations on the correlation between employment trends and income distribution did not always hold true. The income share of the highest tenth increased sharply in 1929, during a period of only moderately high employment. More important, even in the period of comparative full employment since 1941, the income shares of the poorer half of the nation have either declined or remained stable.

EXPENSE ACCOUNTS—INCOME-IN-KIND FOR CORPORATE EXECUTIVES

Material on money income must be supplemented by data on distribution of income-in-kind among income classes to arrive at more nearly accurate figures for total income and income inequality.

Extensive data show that in 1941 the total dollar value of income-in-kind for urban families was relatively insignificant, ranging from $155 for families earning less than $500, to $457 for those earning more than $10,000. For farm families, income-in-kind ranged in value from $417 for those earning less than $500, to $719 for those earning more than $3,000. Each tenth of farm consumer-units received roughly the same value in home-produced food, but the richest third received about one-half the rental value in housing.[9] Thus, except for those with extremely small earnings, income-in-kind was only a minor factor in farm incomes in 1941.

In the ensuing twenty years, the value of home-grown food has been declining consistently for the farmer, from about one-fifth of his cash income in 1941, to about one-tenth in the early postwar period. The farmer purchased 28 per cent of his total food consumption in 1923; he purchased 60 per cent in 1955. The farm population has declined radically since World War II, and its share of the national disposable income since 1945 dropped by more than half, to 3.7 per cent in 1956; and in 1957 farm food- and fuel-in-kind was equal to only 0.5 per cent of the national personal income. Clearly, the role of farm income-in-kind in the national income distribution is now of no great importance.[10]

Among urban consumers in the lowest tenths, income-in-kind has been mainly relief goods, and these have become inconsequential with the advent of full—if sporadically so—employment.

Meanwhile, as income-in-kind declined in value for farm and low-income families, it gained new prominence in the highest income-tenth, and especially the top 5 per cent of the spending units. Here it takes the form of the expense account and other executive benefits. A by-product of the steeper Federal personal and corporate tax rates instituted in 1941, the expense account is now an acknowledged form of executive remuneration. In 1959, a Harvard Business School study revealed that two-thirds of corporate executives regarded their expense accounts as tax-free compensation.

Legally, a corporation can deduct as expenses only bills incurred in the "ordinary and necessary" course of business, but the fact that a corporation in the top tax bracket is only 48 cents out of pocket for every dollar it deducts from its Federal tax bill has led to some broad interpretations of business costs. Especially at the extremes, in closely owned or very widely diffused corporations, extravagant use has been made of income-in-kind for management. The *Wall Street Journal* frequently mentions such items as $300-a-day hotel suites, $10,000-to-$25,000 parties, executive penthouses with marble walls and gold faucets. According to one *Wall Street Journal* report: "Hidden hunting lodges are one of the 'fringe benefits' awaiting officials who succeed in working their way up to the executive suite of a good many U.S. corporations. Other impressive prizes: sharing use of yachts, private planes and railroad cars, jaunts to exotic watering places and spectacular soirées—all paid for by the corporation. . . . Companies maintaining private retreats, planes and other facilities for fun or luxurious traveling generally report they are necessary to the conduct of their business. . . . This is the prime reason for some companies maintaining such facilities, though perhaps not for others. Even in the former case, executives generally manage to get considerable enjoyment from their firms' luxury properties. . . . In this way, a good many executives whose fortune-building efforts are impaired by today's high taxes still are enjoying the frills enjoyed by the Mellons, Morgans and Baruchs."[11]

Company-provided luxuries are obvious indicators of a man's position in the hierarchy. For the top corporate elite, they generally include a company car, a gas credit card, vacations, excellent medical care, country-club memberships, dining and entertainment, and the cash difference between expense allowances and actual expenditures. Lesser corporate personnel receive lesser benefits, according to their rank.

In 1954, 37 per cent of the Cadillacs registered in Manhattan and 20 per cent of those registered in Philadelphia were in the names of businesses. Some 80 per cent of the check totals of the most expensive restaurants and 30 to 40 per cent of Broadway theater tickets are covered by expense accounts. Most of the items charged to Diners' Club, American Express, and other luxury credit-card clubs by members, who numbered well over a million in 1958, are paid for by businesses.[12]

One-half of the executives in small companies and one-third of those in large companies are reimbursed for their expenses in social clubs and organizations. More than one-half of the executives in small firms and more than one-quarter of those in large companies are provided with private automobiles. One-fifth of the large corporations have their own country clubs and resorts for their executives.

Gifts received by executives—particularly those influential in purchasing—from personnel in other corporations are another type of income-in-kind. For Christmas, 1959, such giving accounted for $300 million—all tax deductible as business expenses.

Since nearly two-fifths of the top executives do not have to account to anyone for their expenses, and more than three-fifths are given no yardsticks to limit themselves, it is possible for executives to treat themselves to unusual indulgences, and from time to time some of these are revealed to the public—often in the form of advice on expense-account opportunities as suggested in the pages of business publications. One corporation president spend $17,000 of company funds on an African safari; another charged to business expenses $65,000 in jewelry, $22,000 in liquor, $35,000 in night-clubs tabs, $25,000 in gifts, and $16,000 in boat outlays.

In scope and value, the income-in-kind of the rich presents a sharp contrast to the surplus flour, corn meal, rice, and butter provided as relief goods to the poor.[13]

An unofficial Treasury Department estimate in August, 1957, placed the annual total for corporate expense-account outlays at more than $5 billion, and possibly as high as $10 billion.[14] Certainly a portion of this total was in reality income-in-kind received by members of the top income-tenth. If only one-third of this amount is considered income-in-kind for the top tenth, it would add at least 1 percentage point to this group's share of the national income in 1956.

Although existing statistics do not allow us to calculate precisely the percentage of total expense-account outlays that represent personal income-in-kind, they are sufficient to indicate that income-in-kind was an item of major consequence to the share of the top income-tenth, especially to the style of living enjoyed by many of the richest members of the economic elite.

EVASIONS AND ERRORS: $30 BILLION-PLUS

The existing data on income distribution fail to account for a significant proportion of money income because of underreporting on tax returns and nonreporting to interviewers. Since automatic payroll deductions withhold the amount of money due for Federal income taxes, persons wholly dependent on wages or salary for their incomes—and this includes the vast majority of urban low- and middle-income earners—have little reason to underreport their incomes to data collectors. Whatever payroll earnings are underreported or nonreported are probably to be found in very small companies where executives or owners are in a position to alter their required earnings statements.

However, professionals, businessmen, and others receiving cash payments for their services are in an especially advantageous position to underreport their income on tax returns. Roughly one-half of unreported entrepreneurial income represented farm income, the better part of which probably went to low-income earners.[15] The unreported half going to businessmen and professionals probably went to those already earning enough to underreport their incomes without arousing the suspicion of tax auditors. The result is ultimately indicative of an understatement of income by the upper tenths in tax and other statistics.

Refusal to report income data to interviewers also leads to an understating of income by the highest groups. Nonreporting is almost exclusively confined to the upper brackets. A 1941 Bureau of Labor Statistics study found that "the nonreporting rate tended to be higher in blocks with higher rent levels and with larger proportions of families at upper-income levels, ranging from about 1 per cent at the under $1,000 level to 35 per cent at the $10,000 and over level."[16]

Nondeclaration of income to avoid taxes is illegal, but it is so widespread that no study of income distribution can ignore it. Between 1950 and 1953, the number of Federal income-tax returns reporting high incomes *declined,* a fact that the National Bureau of Economic Research, in view of "the almost certain increase in upper bracket salaries," found "puzzling" and meriting "close investigation."[17]

In 1957, only 91 per cent of the national personal money income was reported on individual income-tax returns, somewhat more than the 86 per cent for 1944–46. The missing sum for 1957—$27.7 billion—comprised 3 per cent ($7.1 billion) of wages and salaries paid, 14 per cent ($1.6 billion) of distributed dividends, 58 per cent ($5.5 billion) of interest, and 27 per cent ($10.8 billion) of entrepreneurial income—the income of nonsalaried professionals, unincorporated businesses, and farmers.[18] About the same amount of personal income is unreported in Census and Survey Research Center data. Obviously, the omission of income of this magnitude—especially if a large segment of it belongs in any single income-tenth—could produce a crucial distortion in the resulting income-distribution figures.

In 1952, spending units earning more than $10,000 owned more than 80 per cent of the publicly held stock. So it is highly probable that spending units in the top tenth—in that year, those earning more than $7,090—received most of the unreported dividend income.[19] The Bureau of Internal Revenue's sample audit of 1948 tax returns showed that those reporting $25,000-plus in income accounted for 7.2 per cent of all returns with dividend errors and 38.4 per cent of the dollar value of all errors, and that those reporting $7,000-plus in income accounted for 40.7 per cent of all returns with dividend errors and 73.6 per cent of the dollar value of all errors.[20] Most interest-bearing savings, bonds, notes, etc., are owned by the top income-tenth, and thus a large segment of undeclared income in this category must be allocated to the economic elite. The 1948 tax audit found 52.6 per cent of the dollar value of interest errors in the returns for the $7,000-plus bracket, the top income-tenth.[21]

A good part of the existing income-distribution statistics fails to account for income earned in the corporate sector of the economy and—quite legally—not distributed to the owners of stock because of their desire to avoid high tax rates. But any nondistribution of corporate profits directly affects the income of the top income-tenth—especially of that small group within it that, as I will later show in detail, owns the vast bulk of stock. The relative importance of dividends grows with income, and above the $100,000 level, dividends are substantially larger than salary or wages. Since tax avoidance has become a primary concern of the highest income classes, especially since 1941, corporations increasingly retain dividends instead of distributing them. As Harvard economist William Crum has put it, "A group of wealthy directors owning stock in a closely held corporation may vote to retain earnings not so much because of the needs of the business as on account of the large surtaxes for which they would be personally liable were these earnings disbursed."[22] In 1923–29, corporations withheld 27 per cent of their net profits; in 1946–59 the figure was 51 per cent.[23] Had 1946–59 corporate profits been distributed at the 1923–29 rate, an average of $4.7 billion more in dividends would have been paid out annually to individuals, nearly all of them in the top income-tenth.

In this way, the economic elite can spread their dividend incomes evenly during fluctuations in the business cycle. Or they can increase the market value of their stock; then, if they sell it in the future, they will pay taxes on their profits at the much lower capital-gains rate. Corporations themselves have furthered this policy of personal tax avoidance since 1941 by sharply increased understatement and nonreporting of profits, accomplished by such devices as charging capital expenditures to current income. Thus the corporations represent vast income reserves for the economic elite.[24]

If 1950 corporate profits had been distributed at the 1923–29 rate, the top income-tenth would have received 32 per cent rather than 29 per cent of the personal income. For 1952, they would have received 30 per cent rather than 29 per cent. In any postwar year, profits undistributed after allowing for a reasonable rate of corporate savings and self-financing would have added 1 to 4 percentage points to the share of the richest tenth. The value of corporate expense-account income-in-kind would have added at least 1 percentage point. Undeclared income, very conservatively assigning only one-third to one-half of it to the top tenth, would have added an additional 3 to 5 percentage points. Thus in 1952, for example, the top income-tenth actually accounted for at least 34 per cent of all personal income rather than 29 per cent. . . .

THE DISTRIBUTION OF WEALTH

The pattern of inequality that we have seen in the distribution of income also prevails in the larger picture—the distribution of stock, real estate, savings, and all other forms of wealth. Once again, we find the heavy concentration of holdings at the top, the thin scattering at the bottom.

The arresting fact is that, as of 1953, the 9 per cent at the top of the income groupings owned more than 46 per cent of the nation's net private assets. And, in that same year, the wealthiest 11 per cent of spending units—those having a net worth of $25,000 and up—owned 60 per cent of the private assets, according to the Survey Research Center. Half of this wealthiest 11 per cent were also members of the income class earning over $7,500—a fraction that would be larger if there were not so many farmers included in the wealthiest asset group. (Farmers are not actually comparable to other wealthy spending units because of the latter's much larger and more profitable net worth in business and investment assets.)[25]

And so it is evident that a tiny minority of the American people possess both the highest income and the greatest share of private assets.

Savings

Savings are a major instrument of economic power. They are distributed much more inequitably among the income-tenths than annual personal income, and this inequality has not been lessened with rising dollar and real incomes for the lower tenths. This is a logical result of the necessity for the lower-income segments to spend all their incomes—or more—to obtain the basic essentials of life. In each postwar year, one-third of all families and unattached individuals have been spending more than they earn. The red-ink proportion for 1950, as an example, ranged from 36 per cent in the $0—$3,000 class to 13 per cent in the $7,500-plus class.[26] And even though lower- and middle-income spending units may save at some time, by the end of their earning career, they generally have accumulated very little. The expenses of raising a family and then retirement soon dissipate their savings.

There can be little dispute over which income classes have the highest savings-to-income ratio. Clearly, the higher the income the greater the savings.

The distribution of net savings by income-tenths (see Table 2) shows the impact of low income and debt. Except for 1945, when there was a backlog of unspent war wages and a scarcity of goods to purchase, the highest income-tenth has owned the bulk of savings since at least 1929. The ability to save demonstrated by this group, and especially a small elite within it, has not been reduced by so-called progressive tax laws or a purported income redistribution.[27]

Liquid assets—such as checking and savings accounts, shares in savings-and-loan associations and credit unions, and government savings bonds—are of decisive importance to low- and even middle-income families exposed to layoffs, unemployment, or medical and other emergencies. Often they represent the entire margin between security and the relief rolls.

However, since the end of World War II, an average of at least

Table 2. Percentage of total national net savings owned by each income-tenth

	1929	1935-36	1941	1945	1946	1947	1948	1949	1950
Highest	86	105	73	46	63	77	78	105	73
2nd	12	13	15	18	16	16	19	26	20
3rd	7	6	6	13	14	6	15	13	11
4th	5	2	5	8	7	6	6	8	10
5th	3	−1	5	5	4	3	6	1	4
6th	1	−2	3	4	1	4	2	*	−1
7th	*	−3	1	3	2	2	−1	−4	1
8th	0	−5	−1	3	1	−1	−3	−8	*
9th	−1	−5	−3	2	−3	−2	−5	−6	−2
Lowest	−13	−9	−4	−2	−5	−11	−17	−35	−16

* Less than one-half of 1 per cent.

Source: Data for 1929 are from Maurice Leven *et al., America's Capacity to Consume* (Washington, D.C.: Brookings Institution, 1934), p. 96; data for 1935-36, from National Resources Committee, *Consumer Expenditures in the United States* (Washington, D.C.: Government Printing Office, 1939), p. 51; data for 1941-50, from *Federal Reserve Bulletin,* August 1948, p. 923; September, 1951, p. 1067. Data for years after 1950 were never calculated. Because 1929 data exclude net savings for unattached individuals, concentration at the highest levels is slightly exaggerated.

one-quarter of American families and unattached individuals have had no liquid assets whatsoever. In early 1960, for example, 24 per cent of the spending units had no liquid assets, 27 per cent had $1 to $500, and 63 per cent had less than $1,000.[28] Because the almost identical distribution existed in 1948, when money was worth more, there obviously has been an absolute decline in the financial security of Americans.

What are the correlations to this inability to save? By income: In early 1960, 52 per cent of those in the poorest income-fifth had no liquid assets, as compared to 6 per cent in the richest fifth. By age: In virtually any year, the greatest assets were found among spending units headed by persons aged fifty-five to sixty-four; the lowest assets were found among the group needing them most, the spending units headed by persons aged sixty-five years and over.[29] By occupation: In 1960, no liquid assets were held by 51 per cent of the spending units headed by unskilled or service workers, 28 per cent of the semiskilled, and 19 per cent of the skilled—as compared to 3 per cent of the professionals.[30]

Since World War II, one-tenth of the nation has owned an average of two-thirds of all liquid assets. But liquid assets are important to the low- and middle-income classes, since they provide economic security in an insecure economy. But they are not attractive to the wealthy, who have no need to pursue security and instead are seeking profit. The wealthy, it should be remembered, put only a small proportion of their savings into liquid assets. Nevertheless, since 1950 the top income-tenth has owned more than 36 per cent of all liquid assets—roughly the same percentage as their share of the nation's total private income.[31]

Historical data on savings patterns strongly indicate that this concentration was not diminished by the New Deal. This is not a very controversial assertion among specialists on savings, for as one of them, Raymond W. Goldsmith, put it, "it is fairly clear . . . that the upper-income groups have always accounted for the major part of total personal savings. . . . This fact, of course, has been known from all investigations made of the distribution of saving."[32]

Stock Ownership

Almost all the theorists who contend there has been a redistribution of wealth in America concentrate their attention on one form of assets—stock shares in corporations. In a characteristic statement, Ernest van den Haag writes: "Corporate ownership is no longer confined to the upper classes. An increasing proportion of industry, of the productive wealth of the country, is owned by the middle- and lower-income brackets. Their money is becoming indispensable for investment, because the rich no longer can save enough to provide for all the investment needs of the economy. This shift in the ownership of wealth may be described as a peaceful, but not slow, process of socialization of the means of production.[33]

This idea of "people's capitalism"—the official and highly publicized concept of the New York Stock Exchange and the Advertising Council—is shared by too many social scientists who should know better. Popular economists, such as Adolf A. Berle, Jr., and Peter F. Drucker, have suggested that stock ownership has become very widely diffused and that there are no longer any sizable concentrations of stock held among individuals.[34] In reality, stock ownership, like every other form of wealth and assets, is very highly concentrated. This conclusion is supported by every reliable study of stock distribution in the United States.

The fact is that the concentration of stock ownership has shown no appreciable change since 1929. In that year, 51,000 individuals received one-half the value of the cash dividends received by all individual shareowners; in 1933 and 1937, this number was 45,000 and 61,000, respectively.[35] Also, in 1937, some 6.6 per cent of the population owned stock; this figure dropped to 5.1 per cent in 1956, and not until 1959 had it increased to 7.9 per cent.

Fig. 1. The distribution of common stock in publicly owned corporations in 1951

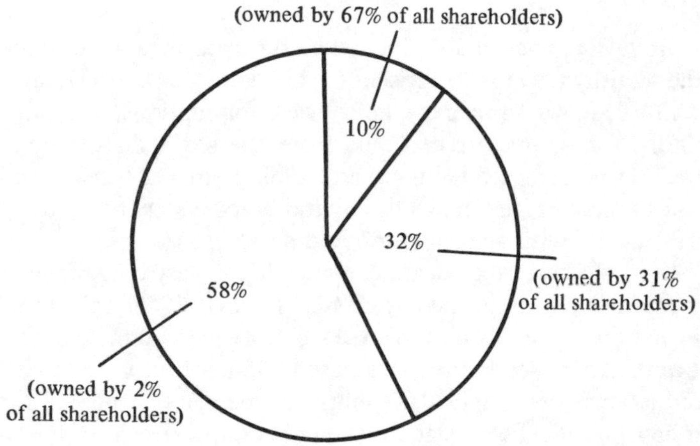

Source: Lewis H. Kimmel, *Share Ownership in the United States* (Washington, D.C.: Brookings Institution, 1952), pp. 43, 46.

Within the already small minority of the population owning stock, a very small percentage has always controlled the bulk of the stock, no matter how large the total number of stockholders. The Temporary National Economic Committee studied the distribution of shares among the 8.5 million individuals owning stock in 1,710 major companies in 1937–39. It found that 4.0 per cent of the owners of common stock held 64.9 per cent of it, and 4.5 per cent of the owners of preferred stock held 54.8 per cent of it.[36]

The Brookings Institution, in a study of 1951 stock ownership in 2,991 major corporations, discovered that only 2.1 per cent of the common-stock shareholders owned 58 per cent of the common stock and that 1.1 per cent of the preferred stockholders owned 46 per cent of the preferred stock. Thirty-one per cent of the common-stock shareholders owned 32 per cent of the shares, and two-thirds of the common-stock shareholdings accounted for a mere one-tenth of the shares.[37] J. Keith Butters, in *Effects of Taxation—Investment by Individuals* (1953), estimates that in 1949, the spending units owning $100,000 or more in marketable stocks—who made up about one-fifth of 1 per cent of the total national spending units and 2 per cent of the stockholders—owned between 65 and 71 per cent of all the marketable stock held by individuals.[38]

These data unavoidably understate the concentration of stocks held by the wealthy few, for 36 per cent of the total stock in 1937, and 33 per cent in 1951, was owned by fiduciaries, foundations, etc., and these nonindividual shares are excluded from the stock distributions given above.[39] However, even though these holdings are not listed by individuals, they remain largely controlled by top-bracket stockholders primarily interested in devising means for avoiding various taxes.

As might be predicted, stock ownership is very inequitably distributed among the various income classes. In early 1959, only 14 per cent of the nation's spending units owned stock; ownership ranged from 6 per cent in the $5,000-or-less income class to 55 per cent in the $15,000-or-more income class. The $10,000-plus income class accounted for more than half the stockholders and owned about 75 per cent of the stock in 1949 and more than 80 per cent in early 1952. In 1959, it accounted for nine-tenths of those with holdings of $25,000 and up.[40]

Despite such conclusive data on stock-ownership concentration, the public has been subjected to a widespread advertising campaign alleging that the American corporation is owned democratically. They are told that the increase in the number of shareholders, from 6.5 million in 1952 to 12.5 million in 1959, is significant, even though there were 9 to 11 million stockholders in the smaller population of 1930. The annual stockholders' meeting is portrayed as a "town meeting," the epitome of democracy—despite the irony of a town meeting in which a few participants have most of the votes. Ignored is the fact that a growing number of these affairs are stage-managed by public-relations counselors, who are prepared for all contingencies. The conclusion is inevitable that there is little "people's" in "people's capitalism."[41]

"People's capitalism" has drawn into the market persons ignorant of basic economics, many of whom have lost on their investments and have made the stock market more unstable during short-term political developments. Too many of these persons do little more than outright gambling in stocks. As a result, the Securities and Exchange Commission has been attempting since 1956 to curb the small but growing number of brokers seeking to sell nearly worthless securities to the public. Indeed, the only group consistently benefiting from the strong element of speculative mania in "people's capitalism" has been the brokers. In 1959, brokerage firms opened 203 new branch offices, compared to 73 the year before, and dozens of them moved into what the *Wall Street Journal* described as "bigger, plushier New York offices."[42]

It is suggested that the supposedly growing ownership of stocks by worker pension funds and investment companies has made 50 million Americans indirect owners in the corporate structure, and that the proportionate returns of corporate profits to these Americans will rise as the holdings of pension and similar funds rapidly increase. "The corporate system," wrote Adolf A. Berle, Jr., in 1959, "is thus in effect operating to 'socialize' American industry but without intervention of the political state."[43] Because pension funds and insurance companies supplied 10 to 15 per cent of the industrial capital during the 1950's and are expected to supply even more throughout the 1960's, Berle foresaw the possibility of the managers of these funds achieving working control over the corporate structure.

However, this theory has a basic flaw. The trustees of these pension funds are not union officals, but, as Berle admits, primarily New York banks. These banks rarely vote their pension stockholdings, and they almost never oppose existing managerial control, since in most instances the employer has the right to transfer the pension account to another bank.

In nine out of ten instances, these funds buy no stock in their own corporation, and only occasionally have the total shares held by all pension funds amounted to more than 3 per cent of the outstanding stock of any company. The pension funds are, in fact, a very long way from achieving control of the corporate system. At the end of 1959, the pension funds owned a mere 3.5 per cent of all outstanding stock listed on the New York Stock Exchange.[44] Robert Tilove, a pension-fund consultant, predicts in *Pension Funds and Economic Freedom* (1959) that by 1965, they will own no more than 6.5 per cent. As more insured workers retire, the assets of the pension funds will decline, and by 1970, their holdings will probably have become even more inconsequential.[45]

Investment companies, which owned 5.8 per cent of the stock in 1959, are too limited by law to intimidate the corporations. Anyhow, they are hardly a force for democracy, since they are owned little more equitably than private stock.

We can only conclude that there has been an enormous exaggeration of the "socializing" effect of these institutions on the American corporation. Clearly, our only realistic yardstick for measuring the extent of democracy in corporate stockholding is the distribution of private ownership.

NOTES

1. Will Lissner, in the *New York Times,* March 5, 1952, p. 1.
2. Tax Foundation, *Fiscal Facts for '58* (New York: Tax Foundation, 1958), p. 9; Selma F. Goldsmith, "Income Distribution by Size—1955–58," *Survey of Current Business,* April, 1959, p. 10.
3. Henry C. Wallich, in *People's Capitalism,* ed. David M. Potter (New York: The Advertising Council, 1957), p. 11.
4. Selma F. Goldsmith, "Appraisal of Basic Data Available for Constructing Income Size Distributions," *Studies in Income and Wealth* (New York: National Bureau of Economic Research, 1951), **XIII,** 284, 302; Selma F. Goldsmith, "The Relation of Census Income Distribution Statistics to Other Income Data," *Studies in Income and Wealth* (New York: National Bureau of Economic Research, 1958), **XXIII,** 70-75.
5. In the post-1941 period, working wives added considerably to the incomes of a large percentage of the families, and it is clear that the spending-unit calculations are the most satisfactory. In 1918–19, however, wives and children earned only 10 per cent of the total family income, and, since a number of these wives were also heads of households, it is apparent that the "recipient" definition introduces no great bias into the figures. This is especially true of our understanding of the income share of the richest tenth. In 1919, among the richest 1 per cent of the population, income-tax returns submitted by wives represented only 3.2 per cent of the total, and 5.3 per cent in 1934–36. Only 15 per cent of individual wage earners in 1935–36 were female supplementary earners. See Temporary National Economic Committee (hereafter cited as TNEC), *Concentration and Composition of Individual Incomes, 1918–1937* (Washington, D.C.: Government Printing Office, 1940), Monograph No. 4, p. 81; W. S. Woytinsky, *Earnings and Social Security in the United States* (Washington, D.C.: Social Science Research Council, 1943), pp. 50-51.
6. Definitions are taken from U.S. Senate, Committee on Banking and Currency, *Income and Housing,* Staff Report, 85th Cong., 1st Sess. (Washing-

ton, D.C.: Government Printing Office, 1957), pp. 64-72; *Federal Reserve Bulletin* (hereafter cited as FRB), July, 1959, p. 701; Bureau of the Census, *Current Population Reports,* P-60, No. 27, pp. 16-17. The Office of Business Economics data on size distributions show a substantially smaller percentage of the population in lower-income classes than do Census data, and somewhat more in the upper classes. Survey Research Center data, which are much closer to agreement with the OBE than with Census data, are utilized whenever possible, since they are far more extensive than the OBE data. Where no alternate data are available, Census data are utilized. See Goldsmith, "The Relation of Census Income Distribution . . . ," *op. cit.,* pp. 83-91.

7. National Industrial Conference Board (hereafter cited as NICB), *Studies in Enterprise and Social Progress* (New York: National Industrial Conference Board, 1939), p. 123; Don D. Lescohier, *Working Conditions* in *History of Labor in the United States,* ed. John R. Commons (New York: The Macmillan Company, 1935), **III,** 55. Independent data verifying the NICB data can be found, for 1918, in Wesley C. Mitchell *et al., Income in the United States, 1910–1918* (New York: National Bureau of Economic Research, 1921), **I,** 134-35; for 1929, in Maurice Leven *et al., America's Capacity to Consume* (Washington, D.C.: Brookings Institution, 1934), p. 96; for 1935–36, National Resources Committee, *Consumer Incomes in the United States* (Washington, D.C.: Government Printing Office, 1938), p. 95.

8. Detailed data on this trend can be found in Selma Goldsmith *et al.,* "Size Distribution of Income Since the Mid-Thirties," *Review of Economics and Statistics,* February, 1954, pp. 1-32; Jesse Burkhead, "Living Standards and Productivity," *Review of Economics and Statistics,* August, 1951, p. 247; *Monthly Labor Review,* September, 1942, p. 421.

9. Bureau of Labor Statistics, *Family Spending and Saving in Wartime* (Washington, D.C.: Government Printing Office, 1945), Bulletin No. 822, p. 94; and Nathan M. Koffsky and Jeanne E. Lear, "Size Distribution of Farm Operators' Income in 1946," *Studies in Income and Wealth* (New York: National Bureau of Economic Research, 1951), **XIII,** 243. In 1935–36, the distribution of income-in-kind among the nation's families was about equal for food; but for housing it was very much greater among the rich. See National Resources Committee, *Consumer Expenditures in the United States* (Washington, D.C.: Government Printing Office, 1939), p. 79.

10. Department of Agriculture, 1957 *Agricultural Outlook Charts* (Washington, D.C.: Government Printing Office, 1956), p. 30.

11. *Wall Street Journal,* March 18, 1958, p. 1; also p. 1 on the following dates:

October 29, November 11 and 13, 1957; February 14 and 21, March 13 and 18, 1958.

12. William H. Whyte, Jr., "The Cadillac Phenomenon," *Fortune,* February, 1955, pp. 106-11; "Expense Accounts: A $5 Billion Tax Deduction, and Growing," *U.S. News & World Report,* August 16, 1957, pp.83-88; Ernest Havemann, "The Expense Account Aristocracy," *Life,* March 9, 1953, pp. 140-42; Harvey S. Berman, "He's on an Expense Account," *Challenge,* March, 1956, pp. 55-58. For credit cards, see Robert Bendiner, "Credit Cards: The Thirty-Day Tycoons," *The Reporter,* February 5, 1959, pp. 26-30.

13. "Expense Accounts," *Harvard Business Review,* March-April, 1960, pp. 16, 172; Randolph Paul, *Taxation in the United States* (Boston: Little, Brown & Co., 1954), p. 618; *U.S. News & World Report,* August 16, 1957, p. 87; also "Expense Account Scandal," *ibid.,* January 25, 1960, pp. 50-56.

14. *Ibid.,* August 16, 1957, p. 83; and V. Henry Rothschild and Rudolf Sobernheim, "Expense Accounts for Executives," *Yale Law Journal,* July, 1958.

15. See C. Harry Kahn, "Entrepreneurial Income," *38th Annual Report, National Bureau of Economic Research, 1958,* pp. 84-85. On the other hand, Frederick D. Stocker and John C. Ellickson, "How Fully Do Farmers Report Their Incomes?" *National Tax Journal,* June, 1959, pp. 116-26, claim that tax evasion by farmers in 1952 was only 18 per cent of their income, 16 per cent in 1953, and 13 per cent in 1955—or no larger than for most occupational classes. Data given in C. Harry Kahn, "Coverage of Entrepreneurial Income on Federal Tax Returns," in U.S. House of Representatives, Committee on Ways and Means, *Tax Revision Compendium,* 86th Cong., 1st Sess. (Washington, D.C.: Government Printing Office, 1959), **II**, 1449, show that 56 per cent of the undeclared entrepreneurial income in 1957 was accounted for by the business and professional classes.

16. Robert Wasson, Abner Hurwitz, and Irving Schweiger, "Field Surveys of Consumer Income—An Appraisal," *Studies in Income and Wealth,* **XIII**, 518.

17. National Bureau of Economic Research, *The National Economic Accounts of the United States* (Washington, D.C.: Government Printing Office, 1958), p. 110.

18. Daniel M. Holland and C. Harry Kahn, "Comparison of Personal and Taxable Income," in U.S. Senate, Joint Committee on the Economic Report, *Federal Tax Policy for Economic Growth and Stability,* 84th Cong., 1st Sess. (Washington, D.C.: Government Printing Office, 1955), p. 320; Goldsmith, "Appraisal of Basic Data . . .," op. cit., p. 302; Daniel M. Holland, "Unreporting of Dividends and Interest on Tax Returns," *Tax*

Revision Compendium, **II,** 1399, 1403, 1418; Kahn, "Coverage of Entrepreneurial Income on Federal Tax Returns," *ibid.,* **II,** 1439–61.

19. George Katona *et al.,* "Stock Ownership Among American Families," *Michigan Business Review,* January, 1953, p. 14.
20. Calculated from data in Bureau of Internal Revenue, *The Audit Control Program: A Summary of Preliminary Results* (Washington, D.C.: Government Printing Office, 1951), p. 20. Holland, "Unreporting of Dividends and Interest . . .," op. cit., p. 1415, claims that the $7,000-plus returns accounted for 66 per cent of the missing dividends and 38 per cent of the interest.
21. Bureau of Internal Revenue, op. cit., p. 21. Lower-income returns generally report most of their interest receipts. See Lawrence H. Seltzer, *Interest as a Source of Personal Income and Tax Revenue* (New York: National Bureau of Economic Research, 1955), Occasional Paper 51, pp. 1257-58.
22. William Crum *et al., Fiscal Planning for Total War* (New York: National Bureau of Economic Research, 1942), p. 278.
23. Lawrence H. Seltzer, *The Nature and Tax Treatment of Capital Gains and Losses* (New York: National Bureau of Economic Research, 1951), p. 221; data for 1946–59 from *Economic Report of the President—1960,* p. 220.
24. *Montgomery's Federal Taxes* (35th ed.; New York: The Ronald Press Company, 1954), Part 5, p. 37. For corporate tax evasion, see Raymond W. Goldsmith, *A Study of Saving in the United States* (Princeton, N.J.: Princeton University Press, 1955). **I,** 969, **II,** 549-50; and William F. Hellmuth, Jr., "The Corporate Income Tax Base," *Tax Revision Compendium,* I, 283-316.
25. FRB, September, 1953, pp. 11-12 of the reprint including extra data not appearing in the regular article. The Survey Research Center study is, by admission of its authors, conservative in its estimate of the net worth of the top-income class. This is due to sampling limitations and to the exclusion from the study of insurance, trust funds, corporate bonds, state, local, and foreign bonds, annuities, pension reserves, and a considerable portion of all liquid assets. (*Ibid.,* pp. 7-8; Raymond W. Goldsmith, op. cit., **III,** 103.) Thus, the study overlooks a sizable share of the actual total assets that is heavily concentrated in the economic elite. The SRC estimate for 1953 repeated most of its errors for 1949, when it had calculated the distribution of assets on the basis of an estimated total of $613 billion. Raymond Goldsmith, the leading savings economist, more accurately fixed the total as $952 billion (*Op. cit.,* **III,** 107.)

    In a more detailed chart on the distribution of total assets and net worth in early 1950, Goldsmith shows that the top-income 5 per cent of the spending units—those earning $7,500-plus in 1949—owned 33 per cent of the net worth. (*Ibid.*, p. 126.) The top income class of 1953, however, included 9 per cent of the spending units as opposed to 5 per cent for 1950. Assuming that in 1953 the wealthiest 5 per cent of spending units owned 33 per cent of the net worth, as they did in 1950, and, conservatively, that the lower 5 per cent of spending units in the top income-tenth were only half as wealthy, the richest 9 per cent (on a pro-rata basis) owned over 46 per cent of the net worth. There is probably a margin of error in this adjusted figure, but it is very likely much smaller than that in the SRC data.

In a somewhat parallel study, using Federal estate-tax returns, Robert J. Lampman estimated that in 1953 about 1 per cent of the population owned 24 per cent of all assets of the household sector of the economy, including two-thirds of the corporate stock and four-fifths of the state and local bonds. See "The Distribution of Wealth According to Estate Tax Returns," *39th Annual Report, National Bureau of Economic Research, 1959,* pp. 40-41. Lampman's data is further developed in "Changes in the Share of Wealth Held by Top Wealth-Holders, 1922–1956," *Review of Economics and Statistics,* November, 1959, pp. 379-92. Basing his findings on estate-tax returns, Lampman ignores the problem of inaccurate reporting, the extent to which many members of the economic elite now make their property arrangements before death to avoid estate taxes, and the inaccuracies in the 1953 Survey Research Center data on wealth distribution against which he compares his results. For the liabilities of using estate-tax returns, see William L. Crum, *The Distribution of Wealth* (Boston: Harvard Business School, 1935), Research Studies No. 13.

26. *FRB,* September, 1951, p. 1063. James S. Duesenberry, *Income, Saving and the Theory of Consumer Behavior* (Cambridge, Mass.: Harvard University Press, 1949), develops this fact in a criticism of Keynes's theory of savings-investment regulation.

27. Butters, *op. cit.,* p. 28, also makes this assertion.

28. Survey Research Center, *1960 Survey of Consumer Finances* (Ann Arbor, Mich.: Survey Research Center, 1961), p. 77.

29. *Ibid.,* p. 80.

30. *Ibid.*

31. *FRB,* June, 1956, p. 572.

32. Raymond W. Goldsmith, "Trends and Structural Changes in Savings in the Twentieth Century," *Savings in the Modern Economy,* ed. Walter W. Heller *et al.* (Minneapolis, Minn.: University of Minnesota Press, 1953), p. 151.

33. Ross and Van den Haag, *op. cit.,* p. 393.

34. Adolf A. Berle, Jr., *Power Without Property* (New York: Harcourt, Brace & Company, 1959), chaps. i-iii; Peter F. Drucker, *America's Next Twenty Years* (New York: Harper & Brothers, 1957), chap. iii.
35. TNEC, *The Distribution of Ownership in the 200 Largest Nonfinancial Corporations* (Washington, D.C.: Government Printing Office, 1940), Monograph No. 29, p. 18.
36. TNEC, *Survey of Shareholdings in 1,710 Corporations with Securities Listed on a National Securities Exchange* (Washington, D.C.: Government Printing Office, 1941), Monograph No. 30, p. 241.
37. Lewis H. Kimmel, *Share Ownership in the United States* (Washington, D.C.: Brookings Institution, 1952), pp. 43, 46.
38. Butters, *op. cit.,* p. 382.
39. TNEC, Monograph **29,** p. 9; Kimmel, *Share Ownership in the United States,* p. 68.
40. Survey Research Center, *Stock Ownership Among American Families* (Ann Arbor, Mich.: Survey Research Center, June, 1960); Kimmel, *Share Ownership in the United States,* p. 95; Butters, *op. cit.,* p. 25; Katona, *op. cit.,* pp. 14ff.
41. See, for example, A. H. Raskin, " 'Town Meeting' of the Shareholders," *New York Times Magazine,* May 12, 1957, p. 15; *Wall Street Journal,* April 26, 1960, p. 4. The Stock Exchange's data were collected by a market-research agency, and were utilized as part of the advertising campaign on "people's capitalism." Given the close agreement between the SRC and Brookings studies, and the questionable reliability of the Stock Exchange data, there is no need to debate the differences between the two sets of findings. A technical criticism appears in the SRC's June, 1960, study.
42. *Wall Street Journal,* September 10, 1959, p. 1; other articles of interest in the *Wall Street Journal* appear in the issues of April 8, May 26, August 25, October 7, 1959; March 8, 1960.
43. Adolf A. Berle, Jr., "Marx Was Wrong and So Is Khrushchev," *New York Times Magazine,* November 1, 1959, p. 95; also *Power Without Property.*
44. *Wall Street Journal,* April 11, 1960, p. 2.
45. Robert Tilove, *Pension Funds and Economic Freedom* (New York: Fund for the Republic, 1959); Paul P. Harbrecht, *Pension Funds and Economic Power* (New York: Twentieth Century Fund, 1959), pp. 115-18, 244.

THE NEW CLASS IN COMMUNIST SOCIETIES

Milovan Djilas

1

Everything happened differently in the USSR and other Communist countries from what the leaders—even such prominent ones as Lenin, Stalin, Trotsky, and Bukharin—anticipated. They expected that the state would rapidly wither away, that democracy would be strengthened. The reverse happened. They expected a rapid improvement in the standard of living—there has been scarcely any change in this respect and, in the subjugated East European countries, the standard has even declined. In every instance, the standard of living has failed to rise in proportion to the rate of industrialization, which was much more rapid. It was believed that the differences between cities and villages, between intellectual and physical labour, would slowly disappear; instead these differences have increased. Communist anticipations in other areas—including their expectations for developments in the non-Communist world—have also failed to materialize.

The greatest illusion was that industrialization and collectivization in the USSR, and destruction of capitalist ownership, would result in a classless society. In 1936, when the new Constitution was promulgated, Stalin announced that the "exploiting class" had ceased to exist. The capitalist and other classes of ancient origin had in fact been destroyed, but a new class, previously unknown to history, had been formed.

It is understandable that this class, like those before it, should believe that the establishment of its power would result in happiness and freedom for all men. The only difference between this and other classes was that it treated the delay in the realization of its illusions more crudely. It thus affirmed that its power was more complete than the power of any other class before in history, and its class illusions and prejudices were proportionally greater.

Reprinted with permission from Milovan Djilas, *The New Class: An Analysis of the Communist System,* New York: Praeger, 1957.

This new class, the bureaucracy, or more accurately the political bureaucracy, has all the characteristics of earlier ones as well as some new characteristics of its own. Its origin had its special characteristics also, even though in essence it was similar to the beginnings of other classes.

Other classes, too, obtained their strength and power by the revolutionary path, destroying the political, social, and other orders they met in their way. However, almost without exception, these classes attained power *after* new economic patterns had taken shape in the old society. The case was the reverse with new classes in the Communist systems. It did not come to power to *complete* a new economic order but to *establish* its own and, in so doing, to establish its power over society.

In earlier epochs the coming to power of some class, some part of a class, or of some party, was the final event resulting from its formation and its development. The reverse was true in the USSR. There the new class was definitely formed after it attained power. Its consciousness had to develop before its economic and physical powers, because the class had not taken root in the life of the nation. This class viewed its role in relation to the world from an idealistic point of view. Its practical possibilities were not diminished by this. In spite of its illusions, it represented an objective tendency toward industrialization. Its practical bent emanated from this tendency. The promise of an ideal world increased the faith in the ranks of the new class and sowed illusions among the masses. At the same time it inspired gigantic physical undertakings.

Because this new class had not been formed as a part of the economic and social life before it came to power, it could only be created in an organization of a special type, distinguished by a special discipline based on identical philosophic and ideological views of its members. A unity of belief and iron discipline was necessary to overcome its weaknesses.

The roots of the new class were implanted in a special party, of the Bolshevik type. Lenin was right in his view that his party was an exception in the history of human society, although he did not suspect that it would be the beginning of a new class.

To be more precise, the initiators of the new class are not found in the party of the Bolshevik type as a whole but in that stratum of professional revolutionaries who made up its core even before it attained power. It was not by accident that Lenin asserted after the failure of the 1905 revolution that only professional revolutionaries—men whose sole profession was revolutionary work—could build a new party of the Bolshevik type. It was still less accidental that even Stalin, the future creator of a new class, was the most outstanding example of such a professional revolutionary. The new ruling class has been gradually developing from this very narrow stratum of revolutionaries. These revolutionaries composed its core for a long period. Trotsky noted that in pre-revolutionary professional revolutionaries was the origin of the future Stalinist bureaucrat. What he did not detect was the beginning of a new class of owners and exploiters.

This is not to say that the new party and the new class are identical. The party, however, is the core of that class, and its base. It is very difficult, perhaps impossible, to define the limits of the new class and to identify its members. The new class may be said to be made up of those who have special privileges and economic preference because of the administrative monopoly they hold.

Since administration is unavoidable in society, necessary administrative functions may be coexistent with parasitic functions in the same person. Not every member of the party is a member of the new class, any more than every artisan or member of a middle-class party is a bourgeois.

In loose terms, as the new class becomes stronger and attains a more perceptible physiognomy, the role of the party diminishes. The core and the basis of the new class is created in the party and at its top, as well as in the state political organs. The once live, compact party, full of initiative, is disappearing to become transformed into the traditional oligarchy of the new class, irresistibly drawing into its ranks those who aspire to join the new class and repressing those who have any ideals.

The party makes the class, but the class grows as a result and uses the party as a basis. The class grows stronger, while the party grows weaker; this is the inescapable fate of every Communist party in power.

If it were not materially interested in production or if it did not have within itself the potentialities for the creation of a new class, no party could act in so morally and ideologically foolhardy a fashion, let alone stay in power for long. Stalin declared, after the end of the First Five-Year Plan: "If we had not created the apparatus, we would have failed!" He should have substituted "new class" for the word "apparatus," and everything would have been clearer.

It seems unusual that a political party could be the beginning of a new class. Parties are generally the product of classes and strata which have become intellectually and economically strong. However, if one grasps the actual conditions in pre-revolutionary Russia and in other countries in which Communism prevailed over national forces, it will be clear that a party of this type is the product of specific opportunities and that there is nothing unusual or accidental in this being so. Although the roots of Bolshevism reach far back into Russian history, the party is partly the product of the unique pattern of international relationships in which Russia found itself at the end of the nineteenth and the beginning of the twentieth century. Russia was no longer able to live in the modern world as an absolute monarchy, and Russia's capitalism was too weak and too dependent on the interests of foreign powers to make it possible to have an industrial revolution. This revolution could only be implemented by a new class, or by a change in the social order. As yet, there was no such class.

In history, it is not important who implements a process, it is only important that the process be implemented. Such was the case in Russia and other countries in which Communist revolutions took place. The revolution created forces, leaders, organizations, and ideas which were necessary to it. The new class came into existence for objective reasons, and by the wish, wits, and action of its leaders.

2

The social origin of the new class lies in the proletariat just as the aristocracy arose in a peasant society, and the bourgeoisie in a commercial and artisans' society. There are exceptions, depending on national conditions, but the proletariat in economically underdeveloped countries, being backward, constitutes the raw material from which the new class arises.

There are other reasons why the new class always acts as the champion of the working class. The new class is anti-capitalistic and, consequently, logically dependent upon the working strata. The new class is supported by the proletarian struggle and the traditional faith of the proletariat in a socialist, Communist society where there is no brutal exploitation. It is vitally important for the new class to assure a normal flow of production, hence it cannot ever lose its connection with the proletariat. Most important of all, the new class cannot achieve industrialization and consolidate its power without the help of the working class. On the other hand, the working class sees in expanded industry the salvation from its poverty and despair. Over a long period of time, the interests, ideas, faith, and hope of the new class, and of parts of the working class and of the poor peasants, coincide and unite. Such mergers have occurred in the past among other widely different classes. Did not the bourgeoisie represent the peasantry in the struggle against the feudal lords?

The movement of the new class toward power comes as a result of the efforts of the proletariat and the poor. These are the masses upon which the party or the new class must lean and with which its interests are most closely allied. This is true until the new class finally establishes its power and authority. Over and above this, the new class is interested in the proletariat and the poor only to the extent necessary for developing production and for maintaining in subjugation the most aggressive and rebellious social forces.

The monopoly which the new class establishes in the name of the working class over the whole of society is, primarily, a monopoly over the working class itself. This monopoly is first intellectual, over the so-called *avant-garde* proletariat, and then over the whole proletariat. This is the biggest deception the class must accomplish, but it shows that the power and interests of the new class lie primarily in industry. Without industry the new class cannot consolidate its position or authority.

Former sons of the working class are the most steadfast members of the new class. It has always been the fate of slaves to provide for their masters the most clever and gifted representatives. In this case a new exploiting and governing class is born from the exploited class.

3

When Communist systems are being critically analysed, it is considered that their fundamental distinction lies in the fact that a bureaucracy, organized in a special stratum, rules over the people. This is generally true. However, a more detailed analysis will show that only a special stratum of bureaucrats, those who are not administrative officials, make up the core of the governing bureaucracy, or, in my terminology, of the new class. This is actually a party or political bureaucracy. Other officials are only the apparatus under the control of the new class; the apparatus may be clumsy and slow but, no matter what, it must exist in every socialist society. It is sociologically possible to draw the borderline between the different types of officials, but in practice they are practically indistinguishable. This is true not only because the Communist system by its very nature is bureaucratic, but because Communists handle the various important administrative functions. In addition, the stratum of political bureaucrats cannot enjoy their privileges if they do not give crumbs from their tables to other bureaucratic categories.

It is important to note the fundamental differences between the political bureaucracies mentioned here and those which arise with every centralization in modern economy—especially centralizations that lead to collective forms of ownership such as monopolies, companies, and state ownership. The number of white-collar workers is constantly increasing in capitalistic monopolies, and also in nationalized industries in the West. In *Human Relations in Administration,*[1] R. Dubin says that state functionaries in the economy are being transformed into a special stratum of society.

> ... Functionaries have the sense of a common destiny for all those who work together. They share the same interests, especially since there is relatively little competition insofar as promotion is in terms of seniority. In-group aggression is thus minimized and this arrangement is therefore conceived to be positively functional for the bureaucracy. However, the esprit de corps and informal social organization which typically develops in such situations often leads the personnel to defend their entrenched interests rather than to assist their clientele and elected higher officials.

While such functionaries have much in common with Communist bureaucrats, especially as regards "esprit de corps," they are not identical. Although state and other bureaucrats in non-Communist systems form a special stratum, they do not exercise authority as the Communists do. Bureaucrats in a non-Communist state have political masters, usually elected, or owners over them, while Communists have neither masters nor owners over them. The bureaucrats in a non-Communist state are officials in a modern capitalist economy, while the Communists are something different and new: a new class.

As in other owning classes, the proof that it is a special class lies in its ownership and its special relation to other classes. In the same way, the class to which a member belongs is indicated by the material and other privileges which ownership brings to him.

As defined by Roman law, property constitutes the use, enjoyment, and disposition of material goods. The Communist political bureaucracy uses, enjoys, and disposes of nationalized property.

If we assume that membership in this bureaucracy or new owning class is predicated on the use of privileges inherent in ownership—in this instance nationalized material goods—then membership in the new party class, or political bureaucracy, is reflected in a larger income in material goods and privileges than society would normally grant for such functions. In practice, the ownership privilege of the new class manifests itself as an exclusive right, as a party monopoly, for the political bureaucracy to distribute the national income, to set wages, direct economic development, and dispose of nationalized and other property. This is the way it appears to the ordinary man who considers the Communist functionary as being very rich and as a man who does not have to work.

The ownership of private property has, for many reasons, proved to be unfavourable for the establishment of the new class's authority. Besides, the destruction of private ownership was necessary for the economic transformation of nations. The new class obtains its power, privileges, ideology, and its customs from one specific form of ownership—collective ownership—which the class administers and distributes in the name of the nation and society.

The new class maintains that ownership derives from a designated social relationship. This is the relationship between the monopolists of administration, who constitute a narrow and closed stratum, and the mass of producers (farmers, workers, and intelligentsia) who have no rights. But that is not all, since the Communist bureaucracy also has complete monopolistic control over material assets.

Every substantive change in the social relationship between those who monopolize administration and those who work is inevitably reflected in the ownership relationship. Social and political relations and ownership—the totalitarianism of government and the monopoly of ownership—are being more fully brought into accord in Communism than in any other political system.

To divest Communists of their ownership rights would be to abolish them as a class. To compel them to relinquish their other social powers, so that workers may participate in sharing the profits of their work—which capitalists have had to permit as a result of strikes and parliamentary action—would mean that Communists were being deprived of their monopoly over property, ideology, and government. This would be the beginning of democracy and freedom in Communism, the end of Communist monopolism and totalitarianism. Until this happens, there can be no indication that important, fundamental changes are taking place in Communist systems, at least not in the eyes of men who think seriously about social progress.

The ownership privileges of the new class and membership in that class are the privileges of *administration.* This privilege extends from state administration and the administration of economic enterprises to that of sports and humanitarian organizations. Political, party, or so-called "general leadership" is executed by the core. This position of leadership carries privileges with it. In his *Stalin au pouvoir,* published in Paris in 1951, Orlov states that the average pay of a worker in the U.S.S.R. in 1935 was 1,800 rubles annually, while the pay and allowances of the secretary of a rayon committee amounted to 45,000 rubles annually. The situation has changed since then for both workers and party functionaries, but the essence remains the same. Other authors have arrived at the same conclusions. Discrepancies between the pay of workers and party functionaries are extreme; this could not be hidden from persons visiting the U.S.S.R. or other Communist countries in the past few years.

Other systems, too, have their professional politicians. One can think well or ill of them, but they must exist. Society cannot live without a state or a government, and therefore it cannot live without those who fight for it.

However, there are fundamental differences between professional politicians in other systems and in the Communist system. In extreme cases, politicians in other systems use the government to secure privileges for themselves and their cohorts, or to favor the economic interests of one social stratum or another. The situation is different with the Communist system where the power and the government are identical with the use, enjoyment, and disposition of almost all the nation's goods. He who grabs power grabs privileges and indirectly grabs property. Consequently, in Communism, power or politics as a profession is the ideal of those who have the desire or the prospect of living as parasites at the expense of others.

Membership in the Communist Party before the Revolution meant sacrifice. Being a professional revolutionary was one of the highest honors. Now that the party has consolidated its power, party membership means that one belongs to a privileged class. And at the core of the party are the all-powerful exploiters and masters.

For a long time the Communist revolution and the Communist system have been concealing their real nature. The emergence of the new class has been concealed under socialist phraseology and, more important, under the new collective forms of property ownership. The so-called socialist ownership is a disguise for the real ownership by the political bureaucracy. And in the beginning this bureaucracy was in a hurry to complete industrialization, and hid its class composition under that guise.

4

The development of modern Communism, and the emergence of the new class, is evident in the character and roles of those who inspired it.

The leaders and their methods, from Marx to Khrushchev, have been varied and changing. It never occurred to Marx to prevent others from voicing their ideas. Lenin tolerated free discussion in his party and did not think that party forums, let alone the party head, should regulate the expression of "proper" or "improper" ideas. Stalin abolished every type of intra-party discussion, and made the expression of ideology solely the right of the central forum—or of himself. Other Communist movements were different. For instance, Marx's International Workers' Union (the so-called First International) was not Marxist in ideology, but a union of varied groups which adopted only the resolutions on which its members agreed. Lenin's party was an *avant-garde* group combining an internal revolutionary morality and ideological monolithic structure with democracy of a kind. Under Stalin the party became a mass of ideologically disinterested men, who got their ideas from above, but were wholehearted and unanimous in the defense of a system that assured them unquestionable privileges. Marx actually never created a party; Lenin destroyed all parties except his own, including the Socialist Party. Stalin relegated even the Bolshevik Party to second rank, transforming its core into the core of the new class, and transforming the party into a privileged impersonal and colorless group.

Marx created a system of the roles of classes, and of class war in society, even though he did not discover them, and he saw that mankind is mostly made up of members of discernible classes, although he was only restating Terence's Stoic philosophy: *"Humani nihil a me alienum puto."* Lenin viewed men as sharing ideas rather than as being members of discernible classes. Stalin saw in men only obedient subjects or enemies. Marx died a poor emigrant in London, but was valued by learned men and valued in the movement; Lenin died as the leader of one of the greatest revolutions, but died as a dictator about whom a cult had already begun to form; when Stalin died, he had already transformed himself into a god.

These changes in personalities are only the reflection of changes which had already taken place and were the very soul of the Communist movement.

Although he did not realize it, Lenin started the organization of the new class. He established the party along Bolshevik lines and developed the theories of its unique and leading role in the building of a new society. This is but one aspect of his many-sided and gigantic work; it is the aspect which came about from his actions rather than his wishes. It is also the aspect which led the new class to revere him.

The real and direct originator of the new class, however, was Stalin. He was a man of quick reflexes and a tendency to coarse humor, not very educated nor a good speaker. But he was a relentless dogmatician and a great administrator, a Georgian who knew better than anyone else whither the new powers of Greater Russia were taking her. He created the new class by the use of the most barbaric means, not even sparing the class itself. It was inevitable that the new class which placed him at the top would later submit to his unbridled and brutal nature. He was the true leader of that class as long as the class was building itself up, and attaining power.

The new class was born in the revolutionary struggle in the Communist Party, but was developed in the industrial revolution. Without the revolution, without industry, the class's position would not have been secure and its power would have been limited.

While the country was being industrialized, Stalin began to introduce considerable variations in wages, at the same time allowing the development toward various privileges to proceed. He thought that industrialization would come to nothing if the new class were not made materially interested in the process, by acquisition of some property for itself. Without industrialization the new class would find it difficult to hold its position, for it would have neither historical justification nor the material resources for its continued existence.

The increase in the membership of the party, or of the bureaucracy, was closely connected with this. In 1927, on the eve of industrialization, the Soviet Communist Party had 887,233 members. In 1934, at the end of the First Five-Year Plan, the membership had increased to 1,874,488. This was a phenomenon obviously connected with industrialization: the prospects for the new class and privileges for its members were improving. What is more, the privileges and the class were expanding more rapidly than industrialization itself. It is difficult to cite any statistics on this point, but the conclusion is self-evident for anyone who bears in mind that the standard of living has not kept pace with industrial production, while the new class actually seized the lion's share of the economic and other progress earned by the sacrifices and efforts of the masses.

The establishment of the new class did not proceed smoothly. It encountered bitter opposition from existing classes and from those revolutionaries who could not reconcile reality with the ideals of their struggle. In the U.S.S.R. the opposition of revolutionaries was most evident in the Trotsky-Stalin conflict. The conflict between Trotsky and Stalin, or between oppositionists in the party and Stalin, as well as the conflict between the regime and the peasantry, became more intense as industrialization advanced and the power and authority of the new class increased.

Trotsky, an excellent speaker, brilliant stylist, and skilled polemicist, a man cultured and of excellent intelligence, was deficient in only one quality: a sense of reality. He wanted to be a revolutionary in a period when life imposed the commonplace. He wished to revive a revolutionary party which was being transformed into something completely different, into a new class unconcerned with great ideals and interested only in the everyday pleasures of life. He expected action from a mass already tired by war, hunger, and death, at a time when the new class already strongly held the reins and had begun to experience the sweetness of privilege. Trotsky's fireworks lit up the distant heavens; but he could not rekindle fires in weary men. He sharply noted the sorry aspect of the new phenomena but he did not grasp their meaning. In addition, he had never been a Bolshevik. This was his vice and his virtue. Attacking the party bureaucracy in the name of the revolution, he attacked the cult of the party and, although he was not conscious of it, the new class.

Stalin looked neither far ahead nor far behind. He had seated himself at the head of the new power which was being born—the new class, the political bureaucracy, and bureaucratism—and became its leader and organizer. He did not preach—he made decisions. He too promised a shining future, but one which bureaucracy could visualize as being real because its life was improving from day to day and its position was being strengthened. He spoke without ardor and color, but the new class was better able to understand this kind of realistic language. Trotsky wished to extend the revolution to Europe; Stalin was not opposed to the idea but this hazardous undertaking did not prevent him from worrying about Mother Russia or, specifically, about ways of strengthening the new system and increasing the power and reputation of the Russian state. Trotsky was a man of the revolution of the past; Stalin was a man of today and, thus, of the future.

In Stalin's victory Trotsky saw the Thermidoric reaction against the revolution, actually the bureaucratic corruption of the Soviet government and the revolutionary cause. Consequently, he understood and was deeply hurt by the amorality of Stalin's methods. Trotsky was the first, although he was not aware of it, who in the attempt to save the Communist movement discovered the essence of contemporary Communism. But he was not capable of seeing it through to the end. He supposed that this was only a momentary cropping up of bureaucracy, corrupting the party and the revolution, and concluded that the solution was in a change at the top, in a "palace revolution." When a palace revolution actually took place after Stalin's death, it could be seen that the essence had not changed; something deeper and more lasting was involved. The Soviet Thermidor of Stalin had not only led to the installation of a government more despotic than the previous one, but also to the installation of a class. This was the continuation of the other side of the coin, the violence of the revolution which had given birth and strength to the new class.

Stalin could, with equal if not greater right, refer to Lenin and all the revolution, just as Trotsky did. For Stalin was the lawful although wicked offspring of Lenin and the revolution.

History has no previous record of a personality like Lenin who, by his versatility and persistence, developed one of the greatest revolutions known to men. It also has no record of a personality like Stalin, who took on the enormous task of strengthening, in terms of power and property, a new class born out of one of the greatest revolutions in one of the largest of the world's countries.

Behind Lenin, who was all passion and thought, stands the dull, gray figure of Joseph Stalin, the symbol of the difficult, cruel, and unscrupulous ascent of the new class to its final power.

After Lenin and Stalin came what had to come; namely, mediocrity in the form of collective leadership. And also there came the apparently sincere, kind-hearted, non-intellectual "man of the people"—Nikita Khrushchev. The new class no longer needs the revolutionaries or dogmatists it once required; it is satisfied with simple personalities, such as Khrushchev, Malenkov, Bulganin, and Shepilov, whose every word reflects the average man. The new class itself is tired of dogmatic purges and training sessions. It would like to live quietly. It must protect itself even from its own authorized leader now that it has been adequately strengthened. Stalin remained the same as he was when the class was weak, when cruel measures were necessary against even those in its own ranks who threatened to deviate. Today this is all unnecessary. Without relinquishing anything it created under Stalin's leadership, the new class appears to be renouncing his authority for the past few years. But it is not really renouncing that authority—only Stalin's methods which, according to Khrushchev, hurt "good Communists."

Lenin's revolutionary epoch was replaced by Stalin's epoch, in which authority and ownership, and industrialization, were strengthened so that the much desired peaceful and good life of the new class could begin. Lenin's *revolutionary* Communism was replaced by Stalin's *dogmatic* communism, which in turn was replaced by *non-dogmatic* Communism, a so-called collective leadership or a group of oligarchs.

These are the three phases of development of the new class in the U.S.S.R. or of Russian Communism (or of every other type of Communism in one manner or another).

The fate of Yugoslav Communism was to unify these three phases in the single personality of Tito, along with national and personal characteristics. Tito is a great revolutionary, but without original ideas; he has attained personal power, but without Stalin's distrustfulness and dogmatism. Like Khrushchev, Tito is a representative of the people, that is, of the middle-party strata. The road which Yugoslav Communism has traveled—attaining a revolution, copying Stalinism, then renouncing Stalinism and seeking its own form—is seen most fully in the personality of Tito. Yugoslav Communism has been more consistent than other parties in preserving the substance of Communism, yet never renouncing any form which could be of value to it.

The three phases in the development of the new class—Lenin, Stalin, and "collective leadership"—are not completely divorced from each other, in substance or in ideas.

Lenin too was a dogmatist, and Stalin too was a revolutionary, just as collective leadership will resort to dogmatism and to revolutionary methods when necessary. What is more, the non-dogmatism of the collective leadership is applied only to itself, to the heads of the new class.

On the other hand, the people must be all the more persistently "educated" in the spirit of the dogma, or of Marxism-Leninism. By relaxing its dogmatic severity and exclusiveness, the new class, becoming strengthened economically, has prospects of attaining greater flexibility.

The heroic era of Communism is past. The epoch of its great leaders has ended. The epoch of practical men has set in. The new class has been created. It is at the height of its power and wealth, but it is without new ideas. It has nothing more to tell the people. The only thing that remains is for it to justify itself.

5

It would not be important to establish the fact that in contemporary Communism a new owning and exploiting class is involved and not merely a temporary dictatorship and an arbitrary bureaucracy, if some anti-Stalinist Communists including Trotsky as well as some Social Democrats had not depicted the ruling stratum as a passing bureaucratic phenomenon because of which this new ideal, classless society, still in its swaddling clothes, must suffer, just as bourgeois society had had to suffer under Cromwell's and Napoleon's despotism.

But the new class is really a new class, with a special composition and special power. By any scientific definition of a class, even the Marxist definition by which some classes are lower than others according to their specific position in production, we conclude that, in the U.S.S.R. and other Communist countries, a new class of owners and exploiters is in existence. The specific characteristic of this new class is its collective ownership. Communist theoreticians affirm, and some even believe, that Communism has arrived at collective ownership.

Collective ownership in various forms has existed in all earlier societies. All ancient Eastern despotisms were based on the pre-eminence of the state's or the king's property. In ancient Egypt after the fifteenth century B.C., arable land passed to private ownership. Before that time only homes and surrounding buildings had been privately owned. State land was handed over for cultivation while state officials administered the land and collected taxes on it. Canals and installations, as well as the most important works, were also state-owned. The state owned everything until it lost its independence in the first century of our era.

This helps to explain the deification of the Pharaohs of Egypt and of the emperors, which one encounters in all the ancient Eastern despotisms. Such ownership also explains the undertaking of gigantic tasks, such as the construction of temples, tombs, and castles of emperors, of canals, roads, and fortifications.

The Roman state treated newly conquered land as state land and owned considerable numbers of slaves. The medieval Church also had collective property.

Capitalism by its very nature was an enemy of collective ownership until the establishment of shareholders' organizations. Capitalism continued to be an enemy of collective ownership, even though it could not do anything against new encroachments by collective ownership and the enlargement of its area of operations.

The Communists did not invent collective ownership as such, but invented its all-encompassing character, more widely extended than in earlier epochs, even more extensive than in Pharaoh's Egypt. That is all that the Communists did.

The ownership of the new class, as well as its character, was formed over a period of time and was subjected to constant change during the process. At first, only a small part of the nation felt the need for all economic powers to be placed in the hands of a political party for the purpose of aiding the industrial transformation. The party, acting as the *avant-garde* of the proletariat and as the "most enlightened power of socialism," pressed for this centralization which could be attained only by a change in ownership. The change was made in fact and in form through nationalization first of large enterprises and then of smaller ones. The abolition of private ownership was a prerequisite for industrialization, and for the beginning of the new class. However, without their special role as administrators over society and as distributors of property, the Communists could not transform themselves into a new class, nor could a new class be formed and permanently established. Gradually material goods were nationalized, but in fact, through its right to use, enjoy, and distribute these goods, they became the property of a discernible stratum of the party and the bureaucracy gathered around it.

In view of the significance of ownership for its power—and also of the fruits of ownership—the party bureaucracy cannot renounce the extension of its ownership even over small-scale production facilities. Because of its totalitarianism and monopolism, the new class finds itself unavoidably at war with everything which it does not administer or handle, and must deliberately aspire to destroy or conquer it.

Stalin, said, on the eve of collectivization, that the question of "who will do what to whom" had been raised, even though the Soviet government was not meeting serious opposition from a politically and economically disunited peasantry. The new class felt insecure as long as there were any other owners except itself. It could not risk sabotage in food supplies or in agricultural raw materials. This was the direct reason for the attack on the peasantry. However, there was a second reason, a class reason: the peasants could be dangerous to the new class in an unstable situation. The new class therefore had to subordinate the peasantry to itself economically and administratively; this was done through the kolkhozes and machine-tractor stations, which required an increase proportionate to the size of the new class in the villages themselves. As a result, bureaucracy mushroomed in the villages too.

The fact that the seizure of property from other classes, especially from small owners, led to decreases in production and to chaos in the economy was of no consequence to the new class. Most important for the new class, as for every owner in history, was the attainment and consolidation of ownership. The class profited from the new property it had acquired even though the nation lost thereby. The collectivization of peasant holdings, which was economically unjustified, was unavoidable if the new class was to be securely installed in its power and its ownership.

Reliable statistics are not available, but all evidence confirms that yields per acre in the U.S.S.R. have not been increased over the yields in Czarist Russia, and that the number of livestock still does not approach the pre-revolutionary figure.

The losses in agricultural yields and in livestock can be calculated, but the losses in manpower, in the millions of peasants who were thrown into labor camps, are incalculable. Collectivization was a frightful and devastating war which resembled an insane undertaking—except for the fact that it was profitable for the new class by assuring its authority.

By various methods, such as nationalization, compulsory cooperation, high taxes, and price inequalities, private ownership was destroyed and transformed into collective ownership. The establishment of the ownership of the new class was evidenced in the changes in the psychology, the way of life, and the material position of its members, depending on the position they held on the hierarchical ladder. Country homes, the best housing, furniture, and similar things were acquired; special quarters and exclusive rest homes were established for the highest bureaucracy, for the elite of the new class. The party secretary and the chief of the secret police in some places not only became the highest authorities but obtained the best housing, automobiles, and similar evidence of privilege. Those beneath them were eligible for comparable privileges, depending upon their position in the hierarchy. The state budgets, "gifts," and the construction and reconstruction executed for the needs of the state and its representatives became the everlasting and inexhaustible sources of benefits to the political bureaucracy.

Only in cases where the new class was not capable of maintaining the ownership it had usurped, or in cases where such ownership was exorbitantly expensive or politically dangerous, were concessions made to other strata, or were other forms of ownership devised. For example, collectivization was abandoned in Yugoslavia because the peasants were resisting it and because the steady decrease in production resulting from collectivization held a latent danger for the regime. However, the new class never renounced the right in such cases to seize ownership again or to collectivize. The new class cannot renounce this right, for if it did, it would no longer be totalitarian and monopolistic.

No bureaucracy alone could be so stubborn in its purposes and aims. Only those engaged in new forms of ownership, who tread the road to new forms of production, are capable of being so persistent.

Marx foresaw that after its victory the proletariat would be exposed to danger from the deposed classes and from its own bureaucracy. When the Communists, especially those in Yugoslavia, criticize Stalin's administration and bureaucratic methods, they generally refer to what Marx anticipated. However, what is happening in Communism today has little connection with Marx and certainly no connection with this anticipation. Marx was thinking of the danger resulting from the growth of a parasitic bureaucracy, which is so prevalent in contemporary Communism. Of course, it never occurred to him to include in that category today's Communist strong men who control material assets for their own narrow caste's interests rather than for the bureaucracy as a whole. In this case, too, Marx serves as a good excuse for the Communists, where the excessive appetites of various strata of the new class or inefficient administration is under criticism.

Contemporary Communism is not only a party of a certain type, or a bureaucracy which has sprung from monopolistic ownership and excessive interference in the economy. More than anything else, the essential aspect of contemporary Communism is the new class of owners and exploiters.

6

No class is established by deliberate design, even though its ascent is accompanied by an organized and conscious struggle. This holds true for the new class in Communism, but it also embodies some special characteristics. Since the hold of the new class on economic life and on the social structure was fairly precarious, and since it was fated to arise within a specific party, it required the highest possible degree of organization, as well as a consistent effort to present a united, balanced, class-conscious front. This is why the new class is better organized and more highly class-conscious than any class in recorded history.

This proposition is true only if it is taken relatively; consciousness and organizational structure being taken in relation to the outside world and to other classes, powers, and social forces. No other class in history has been as cohesive and single-minded in defending itself and in controlling that which it holds—collective and monopolistic ownership and totalitarian authority.

On the other hand, the new class is also the most deluded and least conscious of itself. Every private capitalist or feudal lord was conscious of the fact that he belonged to a special discernible social category. He usually believed that this category was destined to make the human race happy, and that without this category chaos and general ruin would ensue. A Communist member of the new class also believes that, without his party, society would regress and founder. But he is not conscious of the fact that he belongs to a new ownership class, for he does not consider himself an owner and does not take into account the special privileges he enjoys. He thinks that he belongs to a group with prescribed ideas, aims, attitudes, and roles. That is all he sees. He cannot see that at the same time he belongs to a special social category: the *ownership* class.

Collective ownership, which acts to solidify the class, at the same times makes it unconscious of its class substance and each one of the collective owners is deluded in that he thinks he uniquely belongs to a movement which would abolish classes in society.

A comparison of other characteristics of the new class with those of other ownership classes reveals many similarities and many differences. The new class is voracious and insatiable, just as the bourgeoisie was. But it does not have the virtues of frugality and economy that the bourgeoisie had. The new class is as exclusive as the aristocracy but without aristocracy's refinement and proud chivalry.

The new class also has advantages over other classes. Because it is more compact it is better prepared for greater sacrifices and heroic exploits. The individual is completely and totally subordinated to the whole; at least, the prevailing ideal calls for such subordination even when he is out seeking to better himself. The new class is strong enough to carry out material and other ventures that no other class was ever able to do. Since it possesses the nation's goods, the new class is in a position to devote itself religiously to the aims it has set and to direct all the forces of the people to the furtherance of these aims.

The new ownership is not the same as the political government, but is created and aided by that government. The use, enjoyment, and distribution of property is the privilege of the party and the party's top men.

Party members feel that authority, that control over property, brings with it the privileges of this world. Consequently, unscrupulous ambition, duplicity, toadyism, and jealously inevitably must increase. Careerism and an ever expanding bureaucracy are the incurable diseases of Communism. Because the Communists have transformed themselves into owners, and because the road to power and to material privileges is open only through "devotion" to the party—to the class, to "socialism"—unscrupulous ambition must become one of the main ways of life and one of the main methods for the development of Communism.

In non-Communist systems, the phenomena of careerism and unscrupulous ambition are a sign that it is profitable to be a bureaucrat, or that owners have become parasites, so that the administration of property is left in the hands of employees. In Communism, careerism and unscrupulous ambition testify to the fact that there is an irresistible drive towards ownership and the privileges that accompany the administration of material goods and men.

Membership in other ownership classes is not identical with the ownership of particular property. This is still less the case in the Communist system inasmuch as ownership is collective. To be an owner or a joint owner in the Communist system means that one enters the ranks of the ruling political bureaucracy and nothing else.

In the new class, just as in other classes, some individuals constantly fall by the wayside while others go up the ladder. In private-ownership classes an individual left his property to his descendants. In the new class no one inherits anything except the aspiration to raise himself to a higher rung of the ladder. The new class is actually being created from the lowest and broadest strata of the people, and is in constant motion.

Although it is sociologically possible to prescribe who belongs to the new class, it is difficult to do so; for the new class melts into and spills over into the people, into other lower classes, and is constantly changing.

The road to the top is theoretically open to all, just as every one of Napoleon's soldiers carried a marshal's baton in his knapsack. The only thing that is required to get on the road is sincere and complete loyalty to the party or to the new class. Open at the bottom, the new class becomes increasingly and relentlessly narrower at the top. Not only is the desire necessary for the climb; also necessary is the ability to understand and develop doctrines, firmness in struggles against antagonists, exceptional dexterity and cleverness in intra-party struggles, and talent in strengthening the class. Many present themselves, but few are chosen. Although more open in some respects than other classes, the new class is also more exclusive than other classes. Since one of the new class's most important features is monopoly of authority, this exclusiveness is strengthened by bureaucratic hierarchical prejudices.

Nowhere, at any time, has the road been as wide open to the devoted and the loyal as it is in the Communist system. But the ascent to the heights has never at any time been so difficult or required so much sacrifice and so many victims. On the one hand, Communism is open and kind to all; on the other hand, it is exclusive and intolerant even of its own adherents.

7

The fact that there is a new ownership class in Communist countries does not explain everything, but it is the most important key to understanding the changes which are periodically taking place in these countries, especially in the USSR.

It goes without saying that every such change in each separate Communist country and in the Communist system as a whole must be examined separately, in order to determine the extent and significance of the change in the specific circumstances. To do this, however, the system should be understood as a whole to the fullest extent possible.

In connection with current changes in the USSR it will be profitable to point out in passing what is occurring in the kolkhozes. The establishment of kolkhozes and the Soviet government policy toward them illustrates clearly the exploiting nature of the new class.

Stalin did not and Khruschev does not consider kolkhozes as a "logical socialistic" form of ownership. In practice this means that the new class has not succeeded in completely taking over the management of the villages. Through the kolkhozes and the use of the compulsory crop-purchase system, the new class has succeeded in making vassals of the peasants and grabbing a lion's share of the peasants' income, but the new class has not become the only power of the land. Stalin was completely aware of this. Before his death, in *Economic Problems of Socialism in the U.S.S.R.,* Stalin foresaw that the kolkhozes should become state property, which is to say that the bureaucracy should become the real owner. Criticizing Stalin for his excess use of purges, Khrushchev did not however renounce Stalin's view on property in kolkhozes. The appointment by the new regime of 30,000 party workers, mostly to be presidents of kolkhozes, was only one of the measures in line with Stalin's policy.

NOTES

1. New York. Prentice-Hall, 1951.

THE NEW MIDDLE CLASS

C. Wright Mills

In the early nineteenth century, although there are no exact figures, probably four-fifths of the occupied population were self-employed enterprisers; by 1870, only about one-third, and in 1940, only about one-fifth, were still in this old middle class. Many of the remaining four-fifths of the people who now earn a living do so by working for the 2 or 3 per cent of the population who now own 40 or 50 per cent of the private property in the United States. Among these workers are the members of the new middle class, white-collar people on salary. For them, as for wage-workers, America has become a nation of employees for whom independent property is out of range. Labor markets, not control of property, determine their chances to receive income, exercise power, enjoy prestige, learn and use skills.

1. OCCUPATIONAL CHANGE

Of the three broad strata composing modern society, only the new middle class has steadily grown in proportion to the whole. Eighty years ago, there were three-quarters of a million middle-class employees; by 1940, there were over twelve and a half million. In that period the old middle class increased 135 per cent; wage-workers, 255 per cent; new middle class, 1600 per cent.*

The employees composing the new middle class do not make up one single compact stratum. They have not emerged on a single horizontal level, but have been shuffled out simultaneously on the several levels of modern society; they now form, as it were, a new pyramid within the old pyramid of society at large, rather than a horizontal layer. The great bulk of the new middle class are of the lower middle-income brackets, but

---

*In the tables in this section, figures for the intermediate years are appropriately graded; the change has been more or less steady.

The labor force	1870	1940
Old middle class	33%	20%
New middle class	6	25
Wage-workers	61	55
Total	100%	100%

regardless of how social stature is measured, types of white-collar men and women range from almost the top to almost the bottom of modern society.

The managerial stratum, subject to minor variations during these decades, has dropped slightly, from 14 to 10 per cent; the salaried professionals, displaying the same minor ups and downs, have dropped from 30 to 25 per cent of the new middle class. The major shifts in over-all composition have been in the relative decline of the sales group, occurring most sharply around 1900, from 44 to 25 per cent of the total new middle class; and the steady rise of the office workers, from 12 to 40 per cent. Today the three largest occupational groups in the white-collar stratum are schoolteachers, salespeople in and out of stores, and assorted office workers. These three form the white-collar mass.

New middle class	1870	1940
Managers	14%	10%
Salaried professionals	30	25
Salespeople	44	25
Office workers	12	40
Total	100%	100%

White-collar occupations now engage well over half the members of the American middle class as a whole. Between 1870 and 1940, white-collar workers rose from 15 to 56 per cent of the middle brackets, while the old middle class declined from 85 to 44 per cent.

Negatively, the transformation of the middle class is a shift from property to no-property; positively, it is a shift from property to a new axis of stratification, occupation. The nature and well-being of the old middle class can best be sought in the condition of entrepreneurial property; of the new middle class, in the economics and sociology of occupations. The numerical decline of the older, independent sectors of the middle class is an incident in the centralization of property; the numerical rise of the newer salaried employees is due to the industrial mechanics by which the occupations composing the new middle class have arisen.

The middle classes	1870	1940
Old middle class	*85%*	*44%*
Farmers	62	23
Businessmen	21	19
Free professionals	2	2
New middle class	*15%*	*56%*
Managers	2	6
Salaried professionals	4	14
Salespeople	7	14
Office workers	2	22
Total middle classes	100%	100%

2. INDUSTRIAL MECHANICS

In modern society, occupations are specific functions within a social division of labor, as well as skills sold for income on a labor market. Contemporary divisions of labor involve a hitherto unknown specialization of skill: from arranging abstract symbols, at $1000 an hour, to working a shovel, for $1000 a year. The major shifts in occupations since the Civil War have assumed this industrial trend: as a proportion of the labor force, fewer individuals manipulate *things,* more handle *people* and *symbols.*

This shift in needed skills is another way of describing the rise of the white-collar workers, for their characteristic skills involve the handling of paper and money and people. They are expert at dealing with people transiently and impersonally; they are masters of the commercial, professional, and technical relationship. The one thing they do not do is live by making things; rather, they live off the social machineries that organize and coordinate the people who do make things. White-collar people help turn what someone else has made into profit for still another; some of them are closer to the means of production, supervising the work of actual manufacture and recording what is done. They are the people who keep track; they man the paper routines involved in distributing what is produced. They provide technical and personal services, and they teach others the skills which they themselves practice, as well as all other skills transmitted by teaching.

As the proportion of workers needed for the extraction and production of things declines, the proportion needed for servicing, distributing, and co-ordinating rises. In 1870, over three-fourths, and in 1940, slightly less than one-half of the total employed were engaged in producing things.

By 1940, the proportion of white-collar workers of those employed in industries primarily involved in the production of things was 11 per cent; in service industries, 32 per cent; in distribution, 44 per cent; and in co-ordination, 60 per cent. The white-collar industries themselves have grown, and within each industry the white-collar occupations have grown. Three trends lie back of the fact that the white-collar ranks have thus been the most rapidly growing of modern occupations: the increasing productivity of machinery used in manufacturing; the magnification of distribution; and the increasing scale of co-ordination.

	1870	1940
Producing	77%	46%
Servicing	13	20
Distributing	7	23
Coordinating	3	11
Total employed	100%	100%

The immense productivity of mass-production technique and the increased application of technologic rationality are the first open secrets of modern occupational change: fewer men turn out more things in less time. In the middle of the nineteenth century, as J. F. Dewhurst and his associates have calculated, some 17.6 billion horsepower hours were expended in American industry, only 6 per cent by mechanical energy; by the middle of the twentieth century, 410.4 billion horsepower hours will be expended, 94 per cent by mechanical energy. This industrial revolution seems to be permanent, seems to go on through war and boom and slump; thus "a decline in production results in a more than proportional decline in employment; and an increase in production results in a less than proportional increase in employment."

Technology has thus narrowed the stratum of workers needed for given volumes of output; it has also altered the types and proportions of skill needed in the production process. Know-how, once an attribute of the mass of workers, is now in the machine and the engineering elite who design it. Machines displace unskilled workmen, make craft skills unnecessary, push up front the automatic motions of the machine-operative. Workers composing the new lower class are predominantly semi-skilled: their proportion in the urban wage-worker stratum has risen from 31 per cent in 1910 to 41 per cent in 1940.

The manpower economies brought about by machinery and the large-scale rationalization of labor forces, so apparent in production and extraction, have not, as yet, been applied so extensively in distribution—transportation, communication, finance, and trade. Yet without an elaboration of these means of distribution, the wide-flung operations of multi-plant producers could not be integrated nor their products distributed. Therefore, the proportion of people engaged in distribution has enormously increased so that today about one-fourth of the labor force is so engaged. Distribution has expanded more than production because of the lag in technological application in this field, and because of the persistence of individual and small-scale entrepreneural units at the same time that the market has been enlarged and the need to market has been deepened.

Behind this expansion of the distributive occupations lies the central problem of modern capitalism: to whom can the available goods be sold? As volume swells, the intensified search for markets draws more workers into the distributive occupations of trade, promotion, advertising. As far-flung and intricate markets come into being, and as the need to find and create even more markets becomes urgent, "middle men" who move, store, finance, promote, and sell goods are knit into a vast network of enterprises and occupations.

The physical aspect of distribution involves wide and fast transportation networks; the co-ordination of marketing involves communication; the search for markets and the selling of goods involves trade, including wholesale and retail outlets as well as financial agencies for commodity and capital markets. Each of these activities engages more people, but the manual jobs among them do not increase so fast as the white-collar tasks.

Transportation, growing rapidly after the Civil War, began to decline in point of the numbers of people involved before 1930; but this decline took place among wage-workers; the proportion of white-collar workers employed in transportation continued to rise. By 1940, some 23 per cent of the people in transportation were white-collar employees. As a new industrial segment of the U.S. economy, the communication industry has never been run by large numbers of free enterprisers; at the outset it needed large numbers of technical and other white-collar workers. By

1940, some 77 per cent of its people were in new middle-class occupations.

Trade is now the third largest segment of the occupational structure, exceeded only by farming and manufacturing. A few years after the Civil War less than 5 out of every 100 workers were engaged in trade; by 1940 almost 12 out of every 100 workers were so employed. But, while 70 per cent of those in wholesaling and retailing were free enterprisers in 1870, and less than 3 per cent were white collar, by 1940, of the people engaged in retail trade 27 per cent were free enterprisers; 41 per cent white-collar employees.

Newer methods of merchandising, such as credit financing, have resulted in an even greater percentage increase in the "financial" than in the "commercial" agents of distribution. Branch banking has lowered the status of many banking employees to the clerical level, and reduced the number of executive positions. By 1940, of all employees in finance and real estate 70 per cent were white-collar workers of the new middle class.

The organizational reason for the expansion of the white-collar occupations is the rise of big business and big government, and the consequent trend of modern social structure, the steady growth of bureaucracy. In every branch of the economy, as firms merge and corporations become dominant, free entrepreneurs become employees, and the calculations of accountant, statistician, bookkeeper, and clerk in these corporations replace the free "movement of prices" as the coordinating agent of the economic system. The rise of thousands of big and little bureaucracies and the elaborate specialization of the system as a whole create the need for many men and women to plan, coordinate, and administer new routines for others. In moving from smaller to larger and more elaborate units of economic activity, increased proportions of employees are drawn into co-ordinating and managing. Managerial and professional employees and office workers of varied sorts—floorwalkers, foremen, office managers—are needed; people to whom subordinates report, and who in turn report to superiors, are links in chains of power and obedience, co-ordinating and supervising other occupational experiences, functions, and skills. And all over the economy, the proportion of clerks of all sorts has increased: from 1 or 2 per cent in 1870 to 10 or 11 per cent of all gainful workers in 1940.

As the worlds of business undergo these changes, the increased tasks of government on all fronts draw still more people into occupations that regulate and service property and men. In response to the largeness and predatory complications of business, the crises of slump, the nationalization of the rural economy and small-town markets, the flood of immigrants, the urgencies of war and the march of technology disrupting social life, government increases its coordinating and regulating tasks. Public regulations, social services, and business taxes require more people to make mass records and to integrate people, firms, and goods, both within government and in the various segments of business and private life. All branches of government have grown, although the most startling increases are found in the executive branch of the Federal Government, where the needs for coordinating the economy have been most prevalent.

As marketable activities, occupations change (1) with shifts in the skills required, as technology and rationalization are unevenly applied across the economy; (2) with the enlargement and intensification of marketing operations in both the commodity and capital markets; and (3) with shifts in the organization of the division of work, as expanded organizations require coordination, management, and recording. The mechanics involved within and between these three trends have led to the numerical expansion of white-collar employees.

There are other less obvious ways in which the occupational structure is shaped: high agricultural tariffs, for example, delay the decline of farming as an occupation; were Argentine beef allowed to enter duty-free, the number of meat producers here might diminish. City ordinances and zoning laws abolish peddlers and affect the types of construction workers that prevail. Most states have bureaus of standards which limit entrance into professions and semi-professions; at the same time members of these occupations form associations in the attempt to control entrance into "their" market. More successful than most trade unions, such professional associations as the American Medical Association have managed for several decades to level off the proportion of physicians and surgeons. Every phase of the slump-war-boom cycle influences the numerical importance of various occupations; for instance, the movement back and forth between "construction worker" and small "contractor" is geared to slumps and booms in building.

The pressures from these loosely organized parts of the occupational world draw conscious managerial agencies into the picture. The effects of attempts to manage occupational change, directly and indirectly, are not yet great, except of course during wars, when government freezes men in their jobs or offers incentives and compulsions to remain in old occupations or shift to new ones. Yet, increasingly the class levels and occupational composition of the nation are managed; the occupational structure of the United States is being slowly reshaped as a gigantic corporate group. It is subject not only to the pulling of autonomous markets and the pushing of technology but to an "allocation of personnel" from central points of control. Occupational change thus becomes more conscious, at least to those who are coming to be in charge of it.

3. WHITE-COLLAR PYRAMIDS

Occupations, in terms of which we circumscribe the new middle class, involve several ways of ranking people. As specific activities, they entail various types and levels of *skill,* and their exercise fulfils certain *functions* within an industrial division of labor. These are the skills and functions we have been examining statistically. As sources of income, occupations are connected with *class* position; and since they normally carry an expected quota of prestige, on and off the job, they are relevant to *status* position. They also involve certain degrees of *power* over other people, directly in terms of the job, and indirectly in other social areas. Occupations are thus tied to class, status, and power as well as to skill and function; to understand the occupations composing the new middle class, we must consider them in terms of each of these dimensions.*

"Class situation" in its simplest objective sense has to do with the amount and source of income. Today, occupation rather than property is the source of income for most of those who receive any direct income: the possibilities of selling their services in the labor market, rather than of profitably buying and selling their property and its yields, now determine the life-chances of most of the middle class. All things money can buy and many that men dream about are theirs by virtue of occupational income. In new middle-class occupations men work for someone else on someone else's property. This is the clue to many differences between the old and new middle classes, as well as to the contrast between the older world of the small propertied entrepreneur and the occupational struc-

*The following pages are not intended as a detailed discussion of the class, prestige, and power of the white-collar occupations, but as preliminary and definitional.

ture of the new society. If the old middle class once fought big property structures in the name of small, free properties, the new middle class, like the wage-workers in latter-day capitalism, has been, from the beginning, dependent upon large properties for job security.

Wage-workers in the factory and on the farm are on the propertyless bottom of the occupational structure, depending upon the equipment owned by others, earning wages for the time they spend at work. In terms of property, the white-collar people are *not* "in between Capital and Labor"; they are in exactly the same property-class position as the wage-workers. They have no direct financial tie to the means of production, no prime claim upon the proceeds from property. Like factory workers —and day laborers, for that matter—they work for those who do own such means of livelihood.

Yet if bookkeepers and coal miners, insurance agents and farm laborers, doctors in a clinic and crane operators in an open pit have this condition in common, certainly their class situations are not the same. To understand their class positions, we must go beyond the common fact of source of income and consider as well the amount of income.

In 1890, the average income of white-collar occupational groups was about double that of wage-workers. Before World War I, salaries were not so adversely affected by slumps as wages were but, on the contrary, they rather steadily advanced. Since World War I, however, salaries have been reacting to turns in the economic cycles more and more like wages, although still to a lesser extent. If wars help wages more because of the greater flexibility of wages, slumps help salaries because of their greater inflexibility. Yet after each war era, salaries have never regained their previous advantage over wages. Each phase of the cycle, as well as the progressive rise of all income groups, has resulted in a narrowing of the income gap between wage-workers and white-collar employees.

In the middle 'thirties the three urban strata, entrepreneurs, white-collar, and wage-workers, formed a distinct scale with respect to median family income: the white-collar employees had a median income of $1, 896; the entrepreneurs, $1,464; the urban wage-workers, $1,175. Although the median income of white-collar workers was higher than that of the entrepreneurs, larger proportions of the entrepreneurs received both high-level and low-level incomes. The distribution of their income was spread more than that of the white collar.

The wartime boom in incomes, in fact, spread the incomes of all occupational groups, but not evenly. The spread occurred mainly among urban entrepreneurs. As an income level, the old middle class in the city is becoming less an evenly graded income group, and more a collection of different strata, with a large proportion of lumpen-bourgeoisie who receive very low incomes, and a small, prosperous bourgeoisie with very high incomes.

In the late 'forties (1948, median family income) the income of all white-collar workers was $4000, that of all urban wageworkers, $3300. These averages, however, should not obscure the overlap of specific groups within each stratum: the lower white-collar people—sales-employees and office workers—earned almost the same as skilled workers and foremen,* but more than semi-skilled urban wage-workers.

In terms of property, white-collar people are in the same position as wage-workers; in terms of occupational income, they are "somewhere in the middle." Once they were considerably above the wage-workers; they have become less so; in the middle of the century they still have an edge but the over-all rise in incomes is making the new middle class a more homogeneous income group.

As with income, so with prestige: white-collar groups are differentiated socially, perhaps more decisively than wage-workers and entrepreneurs. Wage earners certainly do form an income pyramid and a prestige gradation, as do entrepreneurs and rentiers; but the new middle class, in terms of income and prestige, is a superimposed pyramid, reaching from almost the bottom of the first to almost the top of the second.

People in white-collar occupations claim higher prestige than wage-workers, and, as a general rule, can cash in their claims with wage-workers as well as with the anonymous public. This fact has been seized upon, with much justification, as the defining characteristic of the white-collar strata, and although there are definite indications in the United States of a decline in their prestige, still, on a nation-wide basis, the majority of even the lower white-collar employees—office workers and salespeople—enjoy a middling prestige.

The historic bases of the white-collar employees' prestige, apart from superior income, have included the similarity of their place and

*It is impossible to isolate the salaried foremen from the skilled urban wage-workers in these figures. If we could do so, the income of lower white-collar workers would be closer to that of semi-skilled workers.

type of work to those of the old middle-classes' which has permitted them to borrow prestige. As their relations with entrepreneur and with esteemed customer have become more impersonal, they have borrowed prestige from the firm itself. The stylization of their appearance, in particular the fact that most white-collar jobs have permitted the wearing of street clothes on the job, has also figured in their prestige claims, as have the skills required in most white-collar jobs, and in many of them the variety of operations performed and the degree of autonomy exercised in deciding work procedures. Furthermore, the time taken to learn these skills and the way in which they have been acquired by formal education and by close contact with the higher-ups in charge has been important. White-collar employees have monopolized high school education—even in 1940 they had completed 12 grades to the 8 grades for wage-workers and entrepreneurs. They have also enjoyed status by descent: in terms of race, Negro white-collar employees exist only in isolated instances—and, more importantly, in terms of nativity, in 1930 only about 9 per cent of white-collar workers, but 16 per cent of free enterprisers and 21 per cent of wage-workers, were foreign born. Finally, as an underlying fact, the limited size of the white-collar group, compared to wage-workers, has led to successful claims to greater prestige.

The power position of groups and of individuals typically depends upon factors of class, status, and occupation, often in intricate interrelation. Given occupations involve specific powers over other people in the actual course of work; but also outside the job area, by virtue of their relations to institutions of property as well as the typical income they afford, occupations lend power. Some white-collar occupations require the direct exercise of supervision over other white-collar and wage-workers, and many more are closely attached to this managerial cadre. White-collar employees are the assistants of authority; the power they exercise is a derived power, but they do exercise it.

Moreover, within the white-collar pyramids there is a characteristic pattern of authority involving age and sex. The white-collar ranks contain a good many women: some 41 per cent of all white-collar employees, as compared with 10 per cent of free enterprisers, and 21 per cent of wage-workers, are women.* As with sex, so with age: free enterprisers

*According to our calculations, the proportions of women, 1940, in these groups are: farmers, 2.9%; businessmen, 20%; free professionals, 5.9%; managers, 7.1%; salaried professionals, 51.7%; salespeople, 27.5%; office workers, 51%; skilled workers, 3.2%; semi-skilled and unskilled, 29.8%; rural workers, 9.1%.

average (median) about 45 years of age, white-collar and wage-workers, about 34; but among free enterprisers and wage-workers, men are about 2 or 3 years older than women; among white-collar workers, there is a 6- or 7-year difference. In the white-collar pyramids, authority is roughly graded by age and sex: younger women tend to be subordinated to older men.

The occupational groups forming the white-collar pyramids, different as they may be from one another, have certain common characteristics, which are central to the character of the new middle class as a general pyramid overlapping the entrepreneurs and wage-workers. White-collar people cannot be adequately defined along any one possible dimension of stratification—skill, function, class, status, or power. They are generally in the middle ranges on each of these dimensions and on every descriptive attribute. Their position is more definable in terms of their relative differences from other strata than in any absolute terms.

On all points of definition, it must be remembered that white-collar people are not one compact horizontal stratum. They do not fulfil one central, positive *function* that can define them, although in general their functions are similar to those of the old middle class. They deal with symbols and with other people, co-ordinating, recording, and distributing; but they fulfil these functions as dependent employees, and the skills they thus employ are sometimes similar in form and required mentality to those of many wage-workers.

In terms of property, they are equal to wage-workers and different from the old middle class. Originating as propertyless dependents, they have no serious expectations of propertied independence. In terms of income, their class position is, on the average, somewhat higher than that of wage-workers. The overlap is large and the trend has been definitely toward less difference, but even today the differences are significant.

Perhaps of more psychological importance is the fact that white-collar groups have successfully claimed more prestige than wage-workers and still generally continue to do so. The bases of their prestige may not be solid today, and certainly they show no signs of being permanent; but, however vague and fragile, they continue to mark off white-collar people from wage-workers.

Members of white-collar occupations exercise a derived authority in the course of their work; moreover, compared to older hierarchies, the white-collar pyramids are youthful and feminine bureaucracies, within which youth, education, and American birth are emphasized at the wide base, where millions of office workers most clearly typify these differences between the new middle class and other occupational groups. White-collar masses, in turn, are managed by people who are more like the old middle class, having many of the social characteristics, if not the independence, of free enterprisers.

Part 3
SOME CONSEQUENCES OF SOCIAL INEQUALITY

INTRODUCTION

In one sense the central theme of the sociological enterprise is the consequences of social class—power, bureaucracy, family, deviant behavior, politics, or whatever inevitably involves us in a consideration of social class membership and its implications. Our sights in this section are limited to the question of political attitudes and social class membership. This facet of the range of possible consequences of social class is chosen because it illustrates the tie-in between contemporary social theory and empirical research. Each of the articles presented in this section takes a particular idea or set of ideas currently prevalent in social theory and tests them by surveys and observations of members of different social class positions in modern society. The studies included also provide a good illustration of how cross-cultural studies provide a fruitful testing ground for sociological insight and theory.

Each of the investigations points up the value of looking at social class membership as a determinant of political attitudes, attitudes towards revolution, involvement in radical politics, and a whole range of feelings generally associated with participation in the political process. Taken as a whole these studies lend empirical support to the contention of conflict theorists that social class position remains one of the most powerful explanatory variables at the disposal of the social theorist.

The article by Kelly and Chambliss points out how social class membership is a superior predictor of political attitudes than is either of the currently popular notions of "status inconsistency" or "status congruency." Hamilton studies the "marginal middle class" and finds evidence that they are not simply part of the "middle class" as this term is usually used. The section concludes with Zeitlin's study of the political attitudes of Cuban workers and assesses how this class responded to the socialist revolution.

STATUS CONSISTENCY AND POLITICAL ATTITUDES

K. Dennis Kelly and William J. Chambliss

In an attempt to develop a non-vertical dimension of social stratification, Lenski has suggested that the concept of status consistency is more useful in explaining political attitudes than the more conventionally used notion of social class.[1] His original findings from an investigation in Detroit indicated that low status consistency was associated with a tendency to vote Democratic and to give "liberal" responses to a series of questions pertaining to economic policies.

Kenkel's replication of Lenski's original study, however, produced contradictory results.[2] Kenkel found that respondents classified as status consistent and inconsistent did not differ with regard to political attitudes. Lenski has suggested that these different findings result from different methods used to determine status inconsistency.[3] According to Lenski, only marked differences in status inconsistency can be expected to bring about differences in political attitudes and Kenkel did not use the extreme differences that Lenski used in his original study. Whereas Lenski classified as status inconsistent those persons who scored in the lowest *quarter* of his sample, Kenkel classified as status inconsistent those persons who were in the lower *half* of his sample.

The research reported here is an attempt to resolve the discrepancy between the findings reported by Lenski and those reported by Kenkel. It may be that the relationship between status consistency and political attitudes is real, but appears only for extreme inconsistencies, as Lenski suggests, or it may be that Lenski's original findings cannot be generalized.

Dimensions of Liberalism. There are, however, other issues raised by the two studies that need to be taken into account. Lenski deals with liberalism as though it were a unidimensional concept, i.e., he assumes that a person is either liberal or conservative, presumably on a whole host of

Reprinted from *American Sociological Review,* **31,** No. 3, June, 1966.

items. It is possible, however, that persons may be liberal on some issues and conservative on others. Lipset, for example, after reviewing studies of lower class liberalism-conservatism, concluded that the lower classes are more liberal if liberalism is defined in economic terms, but that the upper classes are more liberal if liberalism is defined in non-economic terms such as support of civil liberties, internationalism, and civil rights.[4] In both the Lenski and the Kenkel studies, only issues pertaining to economic liberalism were used. If Lipset's interpretations are correct, they suggest that different results might be obtained if different dimensions of liberalism are used.

Attitudes toward Social Change. Lipset has also suggested that status inconsistent persons are prone to involvement in radical right movements such as McCarthyism and the John Birch Society.[5] This suggestion is apparently contradictory to the findings by Lenski and Kenkel, but this contradiction is obviated by the fact that Lipset is referring to a different dimension of political liberalism, namely civil liberties issues. It is possible, then, that status inconsistent persons are liberal on economic issues (as suggested by Lenski) and conservative on civil liberties issues (as suggested by Lipset and others).

Status Consistency: Perception and Fact. It is possible that status consistency has an impact on political attitudes only to the degree that the inconsistency is perceived by the actor, irrespective of the degree to which the person may in fact occupy inconsistent statuses. It is essential, therefore, that we investigate the degree to which one's perception of status inconsistency determines political attitudes as compared with the objective fact of status inconsistency.

The general issue, then, to which this research is directed concerns the relative utility of status consistency and social class as independent variables in determining political attitudes. More specifically, the following issues are joined: (1) is the failure of Kenkel's research to support Lenski's earlier findings attributable to the fact that Kenkel used a different operational definition of status inconsistency? (2) are status inconsistent persons classifiable as either liberal or conservative, as Lenski implies, or are they liberal on some matters and conservative on others, as Lipset implies? (3) do status inconsistent persons tend to be extremely conservative on civil liberties issues as Lipset and others have suggested? and (4) does status consistency vary in its impact on political attitudes depending upon the degree to which the person *perceives* that he occupies incongruent statuses? This study presents empirical data bearing on each of these questions.

METHOD

In order to obtain a heterogeneous group of respondents, a random sample of Seattle residents was drawn.[6] Since at least 200 respondents were needed in order to perform the desired analysis, mail-back questionnaires were sent to a sample of 600 persons with the hope that at least one-third would be returned. This hope turned out to be well founded as 48.5 per cent (291) of the questionnaires were returned.

Questionnaires returned in a mail-back survey would be expected to be biased toward the upper ends of the income and education hierarchies. The sample of returned questionnaires is biased in this direction. Median education for the sample is 13.2 years as compared to 12.0 for the Seattle metropolitan area; median income for the sample is $7,790 as compared to $5,194 for the population.[7] However, both income and education are well distributed over wide ranges in the sample. Thus, the sample, while not a perfect representation of the Seattle population, is nevertheless heterogeneous and heterogeneity is a most important sample characteristic for the purposes of this study.

Statuses of respondents were defined in terms of their positions in three vertical hierarchies: income, occupation, and education. Data on these statuses were obtained by the respondent's self-report. Questionnaires were sent to males only since the pressures that would be expected to result from status inconsistency among the three status factors used in this study would be expected to apply only to principal wage earners.[8] Of the 291 questionnaires returned, 246 were from principal wage earners and the analysis was limited to these respondents.

The 1963 replication of the National Opinion Research Center's study of occupational prestige was used to rank occupations.[9] A cumulative frequency distribution for employed persons in Seattle was constructed on the basis of occupational prestige. Respondents in the sample were placed according to their positions in the cumulative frequency distribution and given scores which represented the proportion of the Seattle labor force which had a less prestigeful job than they did.

Since income and education were already ranked, it was relatively easy to form cumulative frequency distributions for the Seattle labor force on these status factors using census data for the Seattle Standard

Metropolitan Statistical Area. Persons in the sample were given scores which represented the proportion of the Seattle labor force which had lower incomes and less education than they did.

The procedure used to render the three status hierarchies comparable is similar to that used by Lenski. The main difference is that in the current study respondents were ranked on their position in a cumulative frequency distribution made up of the Seattle labor force while in Lenski's study the cumulative frequency distribution was made up of the respondents in the sample only. While it can be argued that the labor force of a metropolitan area does not serve as a meaningful reference group (in a psychological sense) for residents of that area, it is certain that a randomly selected group of respondents in a sociological study is unlikely to serve as a reference group for *any* of the individuals in that group.

Status consistency scores were computed by a procedure similar to that used in a recent status consistency study by Nam and Powers.[10] This procedure consisted of summing the discrepancies between pairs of cumulative percentage ranks. The greater the score, the greater the status inconsistency. To obtain the inconsistency between any two status hierarchies by this procedure, one simply uses the absolute discrepancy between ranks in the cumulative percentage distributions.

Since the present study is using perceived status consistency as well as actual status consistency, it is necessary to construct perceived scores for each status variable for respondents. The questions on perceived status are of the type: "What percentage of the Seattle labor force do you think has a smaller income than that of the principal wage earner?" The respondent circled the appropriate percentage. Thus, the responses are already in the form of a cumulative percentage distribution.

Satisfactory Guttman scales were obtained for four dimensions of liberalism: Welfare (W), Civil Liberties (L), Internationalism (I), and Civil Rights (R), the items comprising each scale are listed below. The items on the questionnaire contained four response categories ranging from strongly agree to strongly disagree, but the scale analysis was done with dichotomized categories of agree and disagree.

Civil rights (R) scale

Item no.

33. Integrating our schools will lower the quality of education.
8. The federal government is moving too fast on the civil rights issue.

28. There are cultural differences between the races that should be reconciled before full-scale integration is attempted.
18. The Negroes should stop picketing and start showing that they can be responsible citizens and workmen.
6. Civil rights demonstrations which block construction of needed schools, houses, and other developments are justified.

Coefficient of Reproducibility (CR) = .89
Coefficient of Scalability (CS) = .63
Minimum Marginal Reproducibility (MMR) = .70

Civil liberties (L) scale
Item no.

31. All communists in the United States should be put in jail.
25. Any American who favors the communist form of government should have his citizenship revoked.
4. The law requiring that state and national employees sign loyalty oaths is necessary for the protection of democratic institutions.
20. All members of the communist party in the U.S. should be required to register their party membership annually with the federal government.

CR = .96 CS = .84 MMR = .75

Welfare (W) scale
Item no.

29. Federal aid to education is desirable if we are going to adequately meet present and future educational needs in the U.S.
32. If unemployment is high, the government should spend to create jobs.
9. A government-administered health program is necessary to insure that everyone receives adequate medical care.
12. Economic security for every man, woman and child is a goal worth striving for even if it means socialism.

CR = .90 CS = .69 MMR = .68

Internationalism (I) scale
Item no.

34. The United States should trade with Red China.
22. The United States should trade with Russia.
10. The test ban treaty should never have been agreed to by the United States.

CR = .92 CS = .78 MMR = .63

The R, L, and W scales were divided into three types so that the middle category contained persons who wanted social change to progress at about the present rate. Following popular custom, these persons were called "moderates." The "liberal" category consisted of persons who wanted social change to proceed at a faster rate than at present, while the "conservative" category wanted either no change or wanted to go back to some earlier state. The I scale was divided into only two types —liberal and conservative—because it consisted of fewer items.

FINDINGS

Status Consistency and Political Liberalism. Kenkel compared the most and least consistent *halves* of his sample and found no significant difference, while Lenski compared the most consistent *three-quarters* with the least consistent *one-quarter* of his sample and found a significant difference.

In order to consider the effect of these different cutting points, we have divided our respondents into three categories. The first category contains approximately one-half of the sample—the half with the greatest status consistency. The next two categories each contain approximately one-quarter of the sample, thus enabling us to analyze the effect of comparing the status consistent group with either the least consistent half or the least consistent quarter of the sample.

The findings of this study do *not* support the hypothesis that persons with low status consistency are more liberal than persons with high status consistency (Table 1).[11] All of the gammas are low (none is above .20), and the two largest gammas are in the *opposite* direction from that predicted by Lenski.

It can be seen that considering the least consistent half (the medium and low consistency categories combined) or quarter (the low consistents only) of the sample as the status inconsistent persons does not affect the result. Thus Lenski's suggestion that Kenkel's results stem from his use of the least consistent one-half of the sample is not supported by these data.

It should be noted that Lenski used four status factors, while Kenkel and the present study used only three. Lenski has argued that the fact that Kenkel did not use ethnicity as a status factor may explain why he

Table 1. Four dimensions of liberalism by status consistency (proportion)

	Civil rights				Civil liberties			
Status consistency	Conservative	Moderate	Liberal	Total	Conservative	Moderate	Liberal	Total
Low	.44	.42	.14	1.00 (57)	.42	.32	.26	1.00 (57)
Medium	.37	.47	.17	1.00 (64)	.44	.31	.25	1.00 (64)
High	.41	.33	.26	1.00(125)	.32	.33	.35	1.00(125)
	Gamma=−.12				Gamma=−.16			
	Welfare				Internationalism			
	Conservative	Moderate	Liberal	Total	Conservative		Liberal	Total
Low	.21	.32	.47	1.00 (57)	.53		.47	1.00 (57)
Medium	.41	.20	.39	1.00 (64)	.50		.50	1.00 (64)
High	.34	.24	.42	1.00(125)	.51		.49	1.00(125)
	Gamma=.08				Gamma=−.01			

Note: The high consistency group is the most consistent half of the sample; the medium consistency group is the next most consistent quarter; and the low consistency group is the least consistent quarter of the sample.

obtained different results.[12] This may be so, but it would lead us to conclude that the only meaningful status inconsistency is that between ethnic status and other characteristics and that ethnic status is the key to attitude formation. This also may be true, but it does not say much for the utility of status consistency as an explanatory concept.

Lenski, of course, relied solely on questions dealing with economic issues for his measure of liberalism. But even restricting the analysis to what we have termed "welfare" issues does not improve the results substantially, for the gamma for the relationship between status consistency and liberalism on welfare issues is only .08.

Radicalism and Status Consistency. Lipset's suggestion that status inconsistent persons will be more extreme (that is, less likely to fall in the middle category of a scale) than status consistent persons fares somewhat but not much better (Table 1). Status inconsistent persons (whether defined as the least consistent half or quarter of the sample) tend to be somewhat more reactionary on civil rights and civil liberties issues than do consistent persons. However, the weak relationships do not inspire great confidence.

Dimensions of Liberalism. Inspection of Table 1 makes it fairly obvious that liberalism is *not* a unidimensional phenomenon. This is even clearer when gammas are computed for each of the six possible paired relationships between our four variables: civil rights, civil liberties, internationalism, and welfare:

gamma (R, W) = .21
gamma (R, L) = .55
gamma (R, I) = .35
gamma (W, L) = .16
gamma (W, I) = .49
gamma (L, I) = .62

These gammas suggest that although liberalism on one dimension is related to liberalism on other dimensions, it certainly cannot be predicted from it. It is especially clear that a person's liberalism on civil rights and civil liberties cannot be predicted at all well from his liberalism on welfare issues.

Lipset's interpretation would thus appear to be the more reasonable; namely, liberalism on one dimension does not necessarily mean liberalism on all others.

Table 2. Four dimensions of liberalism by occupational prestige (proportion)

	Civil rights				Civil liberties			
Occupational prestige	Conservative	Moderate	Liberal	Total	Conservative	Moderate	Liberal	Total
High	.33	.33	.34	1.00 (79)	.23	.37	.41	1.00 (79)
Medium	.47	.37	.16	1.00 (86)	.43	.28	.29	1.00 (86)
Low	.42	.46	.12	1.00 (81)	.46	.32	.22	1.00 (81)
	Gamma=.20				Gamma=.27			
	Welfare				Internationalism			
	Conservative	Moderate	Liberal	Total	Conservative		Liberal	Total
High	.41	.23	.38	1.00 (79)	.42		.58	1.00 (79)
Medium	.27	.25	.49	1.00 (86)	.51		.49	1.00 (86)
Low	.35	.26	.39	1.00 (81)	.61		.39	1.00 (81)
	Gamma=−.04				Gamma=.24			

Note: The low occupational prestige group consists of persons in the lower half of the population in occupational prestige; the medium group of persons in the 50th to 80th percentile; the high group consists of persons in the upper twenty per cent.

Our findings also support the notion that social class membership relates differently to liberalism depending on the issues involved. As the data in Tables 2, 3, and 4 show, the higher the social class ranking, the greater the conservatism on welfare issues and the greater the liberalism on civil rights, civil liberties, and internationalism.

Perception of Status Consistency. The final question we raise is whether perceived status consistency is more important in determining political attitudes than actual status consistency. The data in Table 5 suggest that perceived inconsistency is not a better predictor of attitudes than actual inconsistency. The average absolute value of gamma (averaged over the four dimensions of liberalism) for each perceived status variable differs only slightly from that for the corresponding actual status variable. In five of the seven cases, the gamma for perceived status is less than that for actual status.

SUMMARY AND DISCUSSION

This investigation has attempted to answer four questions bearing on the relationship between status consistency and political attitudes. Judging from the data presented, we may conclude that:

1. Lenski's finding that status inconsistent persons are more liberal than status consistent persons is probably peculiar to his study. The results of this study support Kenkel's finding of no relationship between status consistency and political liberalism. Furthermore, this is true whether inconsistency is defined as the least consistent *half* or least consistent *quarter* of the respondents.
2. Political liberalism is *not* a unidimensional phenomenon. Persons who are liberal on some issues may be conservative on others. In general, the higher the social class standing the greater the liberalism on civil rights, civil liberties and internationalism scales, and the greater the conservatism on welfare issues.
3. Although status inconsistent persons tend to be slightly more conservative than status consistent persons, the associations are quite weak. Conservatism on civil rights and civil liberties issues is probably only very slightly more likely to characterize status inconsistent persons than is liberalism on welfare issues.
4. Whether one operationally defines status consistency by some objective criteria or in terms of respondent's perception, the results are essentially the same.

Table 3. Four dimensions of liberalism by education (proportion)

	Civil rights				Civil liberties			
Education	Conservative	Moderate	Liberal	Total	Conservative	Moderate	Liberal	Total
High	.27	.27	.45	1.00 (44)	.11	.36	.52	1.00 (44)
Medium	.41	.36	.23	1.00(103)	.40	.32	.28	1.00(103)
Low	.46	.46	.07	1.00 (99)	.46	.30	.23	1.00 (99)
	Gamma=.33				Gamma=.33			

	Welfare				Internationalism		
	Conservative	Moderate	Liberal	Total	Conservative	Liberal	Total
High	.50	.17	.34	1.00 (44)	.36	.64	1.00 (44)
Medium	.31	.31	.38	1.00(103)	.51	.49	1.00(103)
Low	.27	.22	.50	1.00 (99)	.54	.45	1.00 (99)
	Gamma=−.22				Gamma=.19		

Note: The low education group consists of persons with a high school education or less; the medium group, those who have attended college or are college graduates; the high group, those with post-graduate education.

Table 4. Four dimensions of liberalism by income (proportion)

	Civil rights				Civil liberties			
Income	Conservative	Moderate	Liberal	Total	Conservative	Moderate	Liberal	Total
High	.41	.36	.23	1.00 (91)	.35	.34	.31	1.00 (91)
Medium	.40	.39	.22	1.00(106)	.40	.30	.30	1.00(106)
Low	.43	.43	.14	1.00 (49)	.37	.33	.31	1.00 (49)
	Gamma=.05				Gamma=.02			
	Welfare				Internationalism			
	Conservative	Moderate	Liberal	Total	Conservative		Liberal	Total
High	.38	.21	.41	1.00 (91)	.45		.55	1.00 (91)
Medium	.30	.30	.40	1.00(106)	.55		.45	1.00(106)
Low	.28	.20	.51	1.00 (49)	.55		.45	1.00 (49)
	Gamma=−.11				Gamma=.14			

Note: The low income group consists of persons with incomes of less than $6,000; the medium group, $6,000 to $8,999; the high group, $9,000 and over.

Table 5. Average absolute values of gamma summarizing relationship of liberalism to actual and perceived status variables

Status variables	Average gamma for: Actual status	Perceived status
Occupational prestige	.19	.18
Education	.27	.25
Income	.08	.10
Total inconsistency	.09	.07
Education-income inconsistency	.16	.14
Education-prestige inconsistency	.18	.16
Prestige-income inconsistency	.12	.12

Note: Gammas summarizing the relationship between a given status variable (actual or perceived) and each of the four dimensions of liberalism have been averaged to produce the gamma values shown. That is, the first four values in column 1 represent averages of the gammas presented in Tables 1-4.

In general, then, it can be said that these findings raise serious doubts as to the explanatory utility of the concept of status consistency.

As a matter of fact, the results of this study indicate that social class membership and ethnic background of respondent are far more important determinants of political attitudes than the degree to which persons are status consistent or inconsistent. With respect to ethnic background, we pointed out above that Lenski's findings that status inconsistent persons were more liberal was probably attributable to the fact that ethnic background was one of the status variables he used whereas other studies have not used this variable. Thus the implication is that ethnic background, not status inconsistency, determines political attitudes.

With respect to social class, comparisons between the relative ability of social class membership and status inconsistency to predict political attitudes quite clearly demonstrate the superiority of social class as a predictor. Whether one uses education, income, or occupation as an indicator of social class membership, the correlation between social class and political attitudes is higher than the correlation between status consistency and political attitudes (compare Tables 2, 3, and 4 with Table 1). Education, it turns out, is the best predictor of political attitudes (compare Table 1 and Table 3).

When the findings of this study are combined with the results of a recent evaluation of the concept "status integration" as an explanation of suicide,[13] one is led to ponder whether these concepts are in fact contributing to the accumulation of knowledge in the social sciences. Social class membership and minority group status appear to be far superior explanatory concepts. These concepts may be time-worn and they may even smack of Marxism. But if they are in fact the kinds of sociological variables that determine the behavior of men then we should use them. Concepts like status consistency, status congruency, status crystallization, and status integration unquestionably have a more sophisticated sound to them. But if we sacrifice substantive usefulness for sophisticated appearance then our contribution to knowledge will be meager indeed.

NOTES

1. Gerhard Lenski, "Status Crystallization: A Non-Vertical Dimension of Social Status," *American Sociological Review,* 19 (August, 1954), pp. 405-413.
2. William F. Kenkel, "The Relationship Between Status Consistency and Political Economic Attitudes," *American Sociological Review,* 21 (June, 1956), pp. 365-368.
3. Gerhard Lenski, "Comment on Kenkel's Communication," *American Sociological Review,* 21 (June, 1956), pp. 368-369.
4. Seymour M. Lipset, *Political Man: The Social Bases of Politics,* Garden City, N.Y.: Doubleday, 1960, p. 92.
5. Daniel Bell (ed.), *The Radical Right,* Garden City, N.Y.: Doubleday, 1962.
6. The sample was drawn from the Seattle Telephone Directory, which is the most complete available listing of Seattle residents. The City Directory, which would supply a more complete listing in some cities, was inadequate for our purposes because in Seattle this listing is compiled from voter registration records. The bias which has typically characterized listings in telephone directories is undoubtedly much less today than in years past in view of the increasing affluence which is reflected in the proportion of the population now having telephones. According to Pacific Northwest Bell, between 90 and 95 per cent of the adult Seattle population is listed in the telephone directory.
7. U.S. Bureau of the Census, *U.S. Census of Population: 1960,* Vol. I, *Characteristics of the Population,* Part 49, Washington, D.C.: U.S. Government Printing Office, 1963, pp. 220, 399. Statistics are for males only as only males were in the sample.

8. For a discussion of the fallacies involved in the assumption that the family can be treated as the unit of evaluation, and status scores assigned to non-principal wage earners on this basis, see Walter B. Watson and Ernest A. T. Barth, "Questionable Assumptions in the Theory of Social Stratification," *Pacific Sociological Review,* 17 (Summer, 1964), pp. 21-24.
9. Robert W. Hodge, Paul M. Siegel, and Peter H. Rossi, "Occupational Prestige in the United States, 1925–1963," *American Journal of Sociology,* 70 (November, 1964), pp. 286-302.
10. Charles B. Nam and Mary G. Powers, "Variations in Socio-economic Structure by Race, Residence, and the Life Cycle," *American Sociological Review,* 30 (February, 1965), pp. 97-103.
11. For a discussion of the choice of measures of association see Herbert L. Costner, "Criteria for Measures of Association," *American Sociological Review,* 30 (June, 1965), pp. 341-353.
12. Lenski, "Comment on Kenkel's Communication," *op. cit.,* pp. 368-369.
13. William J. Chambliss and Marion F. Steele, "Status Integration and Suicide: An Assessment," *American Sociological Review,* 31 (August, 1966).

ECONOMIC INSECURITY AND THE POLITICAL ATTITUDES OF CUBAN WORKERS*

Maurice Zeitlin

Numerous students of working-class politics have noted and studied the relationship between economic insecurity and political radicalism. For example, Karl Marx argued that a major consequence of recurrent unemployment would be the workers' formation of organizations, "in order to destroy or to weaken the ruinous effects of this natural law of capitalist production in their class."[1] Karl Kautsky believed that economic insecurity would become so "intolerable for the masses of the population" that they would be "forced to seek a way out of the general misery, ... [finding] it only in socialism."[2] More recently, some social scientists have interpreted left voting as a consequence, *inter alia,* of the fact that certain central "needs" are not being met, the "need for security of income" being foremost among them.[3] A good deal of comparative research has found that the workers experiencing the most recurrent unemployment and underemployment are the ones most likely to be discontented with the existing order, to conceive of themselves as its "exploited victims," to be "class conscious," and to support the political left in their country.[4] Particularly apt to our own study is the conclusion by Zawadski and Lazarsfeld in their study of unemployed Polish workers during the de-

*Parts of this article appeared in "Political Attitudes of Cuban Workers," a paper delivered at the Annual Meetings of the American Sociological Association, 1963, and in the writer's unpublished doctoral dissertation, *Working Class Politics in Cuba: A Study in Political Sociology,* University of California, Berkeley, 1964. I am indebted to Robert Alford, Seymour Martin Lipset, Gerald Marwell, and Martin Trow for their helpful comments on various drafts of this article; to Frederick Stephan for designing the sample for this study; to the center of International Studies, Princeton University, for a grant which made this study possible; and to its director, Klaus Knorr, for his encouragement.
Reprinted by permission from *American Sociological Review,* **31,** No. 1, February 1966. This article is extracted from the larger study entitled *Revolutionary Politics and the Cuban Working Class,* (Princeton: Princeton University Press, 1967; New York: Harper and Row, 1970).

pression of the thirties, that "the experiences of unemployment are a preliminary step for the revolutionary mood, but . . . they do not lead by themselves to a readiness for mass action. Metaphorically speaking, these experiences only fertilize the ground for revolution, but do not generate it."[5]

Less than a decade before the Revolutionary Government, headed by Fidel Castro, came to power in Cuba, the International Bank for Reconstruction and Development noted that "the insecurities which result from chronic unemployment and from the instability and seasonal fluctuations of the Cuban economy, continue to keep the worker in a state of anxiety."[6] That the recurrent unemployment and underemployment and the consequent "state of anxiety" of the Cuban workers in pre-revolutionary Cuba later became a significant determinant of their support for the revolution and its leadership is the thesis of this article.

Cuba, prior to the 1959 revolution, was both misdeveloped and underdeveloped. Her economy was subject to the vagaries of export demand for sugar, and this created a "boom and bust" psychology affecting all strata of the population, not merely the working class, and inhibiting general economic growth. Chronic economic stagnation, a fluctuating, perhaps decreasing, *per capita* income,[7] and widespread unemployment and underemployment, both seasonal and structural, characterized the pre-revolutionary economy.

As early as the first decade of this century, Charles Magoon, Provisional Governor of Cuba during the United States occupation, reported that "practically all the sugar cane cutters are unemployed during six months of the year and by August find themselves without money and without means of maintaining themselves and their families."[8] A half century later this situation persisted without substantial change, and an authority of the United States Bureau of Commerce quipped that a Cuban worker might find it "easier to find a new wife than to find a new job."[9]

How correct this remark was, and how strategic an experience in the life of Cuban workers their ability to get work and keep it must have been, can be indicated by the circumstance that in the two years preceding the establishment of the Revolutionary Government, *known* average unemployment and underemployment in the labor force averaged about 20 per cent.[10] This figure for the labor force as a whole *underestimates* the extent of unemployment and underemployment *in the working class alone.* Although there are no industry-by-industry data, we do know that in the major industry of the island, sugar, the vast majority of the workers, including perhaps two-thirds of the mill workers, were unemployed most of the year. In the sugar industry, "most of the workers were employed only during the zafra," which averaged about 100 days a year.[11] The labor force estimates probably are themselves underestimates, then, since *just counting the workers in the sugar industry* (who comprised 23 per cent of the labor force, and about three-quarters of whom worked no more than five months a year) approximately 18 per cent of the labor force was unemployed seven months of the year.[12] Since the volume and value of the sugar crop profoundly affected unemployment not only in sugar but throughout the island's industries, 20 per cent is an absolute minimum estimate of pre-revolutionary average unemployment.

It scarcely seems problematic, therefore, that the severe and recurrent fluctations of the entire economy, and the consequent widespread unemployment and underemployment in the population, were of major significance in the formation of the workers' political consciousness—especially given the significant influence that revolutionary socialists (first anarchosyndicalists and then Communists) had always exerted in the Cuban working class.[13]

That Fidel Castro believed unemployment politically significant is clear. For example, in his speech at his trial for leading the abortive attack on Fort Moncada on July 26, 1953, he said that the revolutionaries had based "their chances for success on the social order, because we were assured of the people's support. . . ." Among "the people we count on in our struggle," he said, "are the seven hundred thousand unemployed Cubans, who want to earn their daily bread honorably without having to leave their country in search of sustenance; and the five hundred thousand rural workers who live in *miserable bohios* [huts], work four months of the year and spend the rest of it in hunger, sharing their misery with their children. . . ."[14]

Repeatedly in his speeches since coming to power, Castro has referred to the problem of unemployment, linking it with the meaning and the destiny of the revolution:

> A people which produces below its capacities, and, further, where an appreciable portion of what it produces is carried off by others, is not a people enjoying the economic and social conditions propitious to progress and to resolving its problems. That is why our country suffered that problem of permanent unemployment; . . . that is why there was chronic unemploy-

> ment in our country extending to several hundred thousand idle citizens; that is why the fields were worked only three or four months a year. That is the reason for the ills of the Republic, which could never have been overcome if the Republic had not adopted forms of social organization and production putting human effort in harmony with the interest of the people in progress and greater production. . . . The issue became one of the revolution having to resolve the unemployment problem and, even more difficult, to resolve it under conditions of economic aggression, embargo on spare parts, raw materials and machinery, and complete suppression of the sugar quota.[15]

That such speeches as these would appeal to the workers, and especially to the ones who had borne the brunt of unemployment and underemployment before the revolution, seems clear. In fact, whatever their own political persuasion, most serious observers of the revolution have argued that this vast reservoir of unemployed and underemployed workers inherited by the Revolutionary Government has been a major source of its popular support, although they were not the initiators of the struggle against the old regime.[16] Once the Revolutionary Government came to power, however, its social base was formed, in the words of Boris Goldenberg, by the "enormous and heterogeneous mass of the economically 'rootless', . . . the unemployed [and] underemployed . . ." throughout the population.[17]

The major hypothesis of the present article, then, is that the revolution's program and policies differentially appealed to the workers in accordance with their relative economic security before the revolution—the greater their pre-revolutionary experience of unemployment, the greater the likelihood of their support for the revolution. The correctness of this hypothesis will be examined following a description of the methods employed to obtain the data for this study.

METHODS

The data for this study are drawn from the writer's interviews with industrial workers in Cuba in the summer of 1962. What was significant about that period as far as this particular study is concerned was that the Revolutionary Government had by then clearly consolidated its power (the Bay of Pigs invasion being a year in the past); the original relatively undifferentiated popular euphoria had by then been long replaced by relatively clear lines of social cleavage generated in response to actions taken by the Revolutionary Government; it was then more than a year since Fidel Castro had declared the revolution to be "socialist"; and, therefore, a study of the differential appeals of the ideology and social content of the revolution to Cuban workers could be meaningful and valuable.[18]

Our interviews were carried out with a randomly selected sample of 210 industrial workers employed in twenty-one work centers widely scattered throughout the island's six provinces. The writer chose the work centers from a list of all mines, mills, factories and plants functioning in Cuba under the direction of the Ministry of Industries. There were approximately 200,000 industrial workers employed in the industrial work-places under the direction of the Ministry of Industries. Excluded from representation in the sample were the approximately 120,000 industrial workers employed in some 250 industrial work-places under the direction of the Department of Industrialization of the National Institute of Agrarian Reform [INRA]. Thus, sixty-two per cent of Cuba's industrial workers constituted the population from which the sample of workers interviewed for this study was drawn.

The work-places were selected by means of a self-weighting random sample in which the probability of a work-place being chosen was directly proportional to the number of workers employed in it. This sampling method tended to exclude the smaller industrial work-places (known in Cuba as "chinchales") which abounded there.[19]

In each work-place, the ten workers were selected by one of three methods: a) by visiting each department personally and selecting from a list of the jobs in that department (used in fifteen work-places); b) by selecting from a list of all workers employed in the work-place on the shift or shifts during which the interviewing was done (in five work-places); c) by selecting among the homes in the industrial community in which the workers employed in the work-place live (in one work-place).[20]

The advantage of employing method (a) for selecting the workers to be interviewed is that the writer was able to see the workers' reactions within the work-places visited—the reactions of the workers chosen to be interviewed as well as of the other workers present at that moment in the various departments. Observation of the general reactions of the workers—of reserve or suspicion, curiosity or friendliness—was an important aspect of this study. Moreover, so as to be certain that the worker selected was, indeed, the worker interviewed, this method of selection was preferable. Perhaps if Cuba had not been the center of controversy and the focus of American hostility during the period in which the study was done, this method would not have been necessary. This precautionary measure was also beneficial to the writer's research since it did provide the opportunity for direct observation of the interaction among the industrial workers themselves and between them and administrative personnel.

The interviews were carried out in Spanish by the writer and his wife, each separately interviewing five workers per work-place. All interviewing was carried out in complete privacy, in a location provided within the work-place, such as a class-room or storage room or office. Each worker interviewed, as well as anyone else concerned, was specifically told before the interviewing, in a variant of the following words, that the writer was

> . . . a correspondent, for a liberal objective American news-weekly called *The Nation,* that is published in New York City. We have permission from the Ministry of Industries, your administrator, and the union delegate to interview ten workers here. We have chosen you to be interviewed by selecting at random from a list of the jobs in this department (or all workers in this work-place). That means we do not care to know your name or to be able to identify you personally in any way. These questions are simple and do not require special knowledge. We just want your opinions about some things in your work and in Cuba in general. All your answers are between ourselves and are completely anonymous. We would very much appreciate your permission to interview you.

Every precaution was taken in the interviewing to discover and to prevent dissimulation. Dissimulation, as well as unconscious distortion, must be taken into account in the evaluation of all interview data, in whatever type of study. Internal checks for consistency as well as external checks on reliability must be built into any interview schedule, wherever possible; this was done in our study. The interviews were carried out according to a formal set of questions on a mimeographed interview schedule prepared by the writer. It was quite clear to the worker that he was being formally interviewed in accordance with pre-determined questions, and that notes on his answers were being taken throughout the interview.

Stylized probes were also employed in these interviews to make it especially difficult for the workers interviewed to give answers they did not actually feel to be true. For example, if a worker were asked: "Do you think that your children have the same opportunities, better opportunities, or worse opportunities than others to live comfortably and happily?" and he answered; "All children are equal now," he would then be asked some variant of "How is it possible for all children to be equal? Please explain what you mean." Such probes were freely used throughout the interview.

Because there were obviously some workers who were suspicious or even frightened of the purposes of the interview, every effort was made to establish rapport quickly and to put the respondent at his ease by stressing that the interview was voluntary and completely anonymous, and that the interviews were very important because they would provide the basis for information about working conditions in Cuba to Americans and other non-Cubans throughout the world. Occasionally a respondent would ask that his words not be recorded until the interview had terminated; we complied readily. The interviews ranged in length from forty-five minutes to three-and-a-half hours, averaging about one hour and a quarter, in privacy; a great effort of will would be required in that situation consistently to give answers thought to be suitable to the government and the interviewer. It would require a certain level of dramatic skill to feign enthusiasm or to manifest feelings where these did not exist. Moreover, the refusal rate was very low (eight of 210 respondents, or less than four per cent); in only a few instances did opponents of the regime evidence either hesitancy or fear in speaking their minds freely. Cubans are highly voluble, volatile and loquacious, irrespective of their political views.

The interview schedule was organized in such a way as to begin the interview with questions which were, on the surface, far removed from political questions of any kind—such as length of residence in a particular place, or length of time working in the work-place. The interviews were carried out in accordance with established canons of sociological interviewing, with especial emphasis on anonymity, on the establishment of rapport, and on special probing to ascertain the truthfulness of a response.[21]

In order to get at the workers' attitudes towards the revolution, several questions were asked of them during the interview which are believed to be more or less indicative, taken in concert, of how they viewed the revolution. Of the five chosen for combination into an index of these attitudes, two were "open-ended" questions to which the variety of responses possible was limited only by the worker's own imagination. The first of these was:

a) "Speaking in general, what are the things in Cuba that you are most proud of as a Cuban?" One hundred and fifteen workers replied to this question in terms clearly favorable to the revolution. Only such responses as could be regarded as clearly indicating or explicitly stating support of the revolution, such as mention of the revolution itself, of the "socialist government," of specific economic and social reforms of the Revolutionary Government, or of increased work security since the revolution, were counted as "favorable." All others, whether more or less "neutral" responses or "clearly hostile" ones, were classified as "not clearly favorable."

The workers could be especially blunt in their opposition, as was a young worker at a paper milling plant in Cardenas, whose answer was simply, "Of nothing, *chico* . . . I don't like Communism," or as a West Indian worker (with two teenage daughters in the militia) at the nationalized Portland Cement plant in Mariel explained (in English): "I stay only because I have two daughters who will not leave—otherwise I'd go away . . . No one bothers me, I just do not like it. Why? I can't say why. I guess I just prefer the old Cuba. . . ."

In contrast to such clearly hostile remarks were such noncommittal replies as a shoemaker's "Of our movies and our athletes," or a brewery worker's equivocal, "I am a peaceful worker. I have no passionate interest in anything. After my work, I pass my time in my house in Manacas with my little one and my wife," or a cigar-maker's witty but equally noncommittal, "Our women and our cigars."

Occasionally a revolutionary worker would wax poetic, as did a copper miner in Matahambre: "Cuba is a cup of gold to me. It is the only country in the world that is now moving forward. . . ." A sugar worker's simple statement was more typical, however: "I earn good money now. I lack nothing. . . . All of the workers are with the revolution." A Havana brewery worker said: "I am content with the revolution in general. . . . For the first time one can do what one wants without fear."

The second of these open-ended questions was (b) "What sort [*clase*] of people govern this country now?"

One hundred and twenty-five workers replied to this question in terms clearly favorable to the revolution.

Given the double meaning in Spanish of the word *clase,* which can mean "type," "sort" or "kind," as well as "class," the workers could, of course, choose to interpret the question's meaning in a number of ways. As with the preceding question, only replies which could be regarded as clearly favorable to the revolution were counted as such: "the people," "the humble," "hardworking," "good," "sincere," "moral," "honest," "defenders of the poor and humble," "the working class." Responses such as "socialists" or "revolutionaries" which did not clearly commit the worker were not regarded as favorable; neither were such equivocal replies as "Cubans," "Fidel," "Communists," nor replies which were likely meant to be hostile such as "Russians," or "Soviets," or which were undoubtedly meant to be hostile such as "shameless," or "traitors."

"To me," an opponent of the revolution working at the nationalized Texaco oil refinery in Santiago said, "they are completely Communists. All of their accomplishments have been through the work of others—including how they think. I have a sister-in-law and a brother-in-law in prison for speaking against the government—[sentenced to] seven years. . . ." Another worker opposed to the revolution said: "Socialists they say. The kids say Communists. I don't know. Listen, if somebody comes and takes that pen of yours, and you bought it, what are you going to think?"

"Well, I've never been 'political,' " a cigarette-machine operator said. "For me, they are all right." A brewery worker's reply was equally equivocal: "My experience so far is good. I don't worry about such things—neither before the revolution nor now." A skilled electrician in Santiago committed himself only so far as to say that the men in the government are "persons with socialist ideas, who though they have good intentions have committed many serious administrative errors."

"The truth is," a carpenter in a sugar central said, "that *now* those who govern here are Cubans. They are honest and hard-working men." A 67-year-old maintenance man at the Nicaro nickel plant who had been an agricultural worker until recently said: "Look, before I couldn't look a boss in the eye—I looked at my feet. Not now; now we have liberty and walk where we wish, and nothing is prohibited to us. It is a great joy to be alive now. These men [who govern us] are 100 per cent better than before. I have known governments from [Mario Garcia] Menocal [Cuban President, 1913–1921] until Batista left three years ago, and I have never seen any like this government." Equally articulate in his support of the revolution was a twenty-year-old bootmaker in a newly established factory in Guanajay: "*We* are the government, *we* run things. Go to a factory or *consolidado* anywhere, *chico,* and see: those who work govern, those who govern work, not like the capitalists who lived without working before the revolution triumphed. Now, the power of the workers and peasants has emerged."

The workers were also asked the following two questions with fixed alternatives:
c) "Do you believe that the country ought to have elections soon?"

Answer	(*N*)
No	136
Yes	52
No opinion	22

d) "Do you think the workers have more, the same, or less influence on [in] the government now than before the revolution?"

Answer	(*N*)
More influence	170
The same	17
Less	16 (includes 8 refusals)
No opinion	7

In addition, this question was included in the index as an "action criterion".
e) "Do you belong to the militia?"

Answer	(*N*)
Yes	110
No	100 (includes 8 refusals)

As is clear, the likelihood that a question would elicit a response clearly favorable to the revolution was directly related to the ease with which such a response could be given.[22] Favorable responses were distributed as follows:

Question	(*N*)
e.	110
a.	115
b.	125
c.	136
d.	170

The index of attitude toward the revolution was constructed from answers to all five questions by coding all favorable responses (militia membership included) as +1, and all others as 0 (zero):

Index Points	Definition	(N)
3-5	Favorable (4-5, very favorable, N=100; 3, moderately favorable, N=42)	142
2	Indecisive	24
0-1	Hostile	36
	Total	202

FINDINGS

Using this index to gauge the differential appeals of the revolution to the workers we interviewed, our expectation that the relative security of their employment *before* the revolution would have a significant bearing on their attitudes toward the revolution *now,* is borne out by our findings, as presented in Table 1. There is a clear relationship between the average number of months the workers worked during the year before the revolution and the probability of their support for the revolution. The workers with the least pre-revolutionary economic security are the ones who are most likely to support the revolution.

If their relative economic security before the revolution has been of significant consequence for the workers' responses to the revolution, then it should be expected that their pre-revolutionary situation significantly affected their pre-revolutionary political orientations as well. We know, for example, that a major social base of the Communists in the labor movement was among the workers in the sugar industry, i.e., in the industry which was itself most economically unstable and whose workers suffered perhaps the greatest burden of the seasonal unemployment cycle. We should, therefore, expect on both historical and comparative sociological grounds, that the workers who experienced the most unemployment and underemployment before the revolution were the ones who were most likely to support the Communists.

A simple structured question was asked of all the workers in our

Table 1. Pre-revolutionary employment status and attitude toward the revolution (per cent)

Months worked per year before revolution	Favor-able*	Indeci-sive	Hostile	(N)
6 or less	86	9	5	(63)
7–9	74	10	16	(19)
10 plus	62	13	25	(105)

Note: This and the following tables do not include workers who had not yet entered the labor force before the revolution.

* Among the workers who were employed six months or less and also among those employed 7-9 months before the revolution, 63 per cent were "very favorable" to the revolution; among those who worked 10 months or more, only 40 per cent were "very favorable."

sample in order to gauge their pre-revolutionary orientation toward the Communists:

"How would you describe your attitude toward the Communists before the revolution: hostile, indifferent, friendly, or supporter?"[23]

Answer	*(N)*
Hostile	57
Indifferent	83
Friendly	49
Supporter [*partidario*]	10
Don't know	3
Refusal	8

When we compare the workers' pre-revolutionary views of the Communists with their pre-revolutionary security of employment, the evidence indicates that the workers who experienced the most unemployment before the revolution were the ones most likely to be sympathetic to the Communists.[24]

This relationship is strengthened when we view it among only those workers in our sample who were also workers before the revolution. There has been a sizable influx of formerly salaried or self-employed persons, as well as agricultural laborers and peasants, in to the working class since the revolution—and this is reflected in our sample; these non-workers were less likely to support the Communists before the revolution than the workers. When we exclude those who were not workers before the revolution, we find that the gap between the proportions pro-Communist among the pre-revolutionary unemployed and among the employed workers becomes larger (Table 2a). There is also a slight strengthening of the relationship between pre-revolutionary employment insecurity and support for the revolution when viewed among only those who were workers before the revolution (Table 2b).

Table 2. Pre-revolutionary employment status and pre-revolutionary attitude toward the Communists (per cent)

Months worked per year before revolution	Friendly or supporter	Indifferent*	Hostile	(N)
6 or less	35	36	29	(63)
7-9	32	52	16	(19)
10 plus	26	45	29	(105)

* Includes three "don't knows."

Table 2a. Pre-revolutionary employment status and pre-revolutionary attitude toward the Communists, among workers before the revolution only (per cent)

Months worked per year before revolution	Friendly or supporter	Indifferent	Hostile	(N)
9 or less	40	32	29	(63)
10 plus	27	46	27	(89)

Table 2b. Pre-revolutionary employment status and attitude toward the revolution, among workers before the revolution only (per cent)

Months worked per year before revolution	Favorable	Indecisive	Hostile	(N)
9 or less	87	6	6	(63)
10 plus	62	13	25	(89)

To this point we have only referred to the workers' pre-revolutionary economic security, yet there has been a significant change in the economic security of many workers since the establishment of the Revolutionary Government. Among our respondents, for example, more than three quarters (79 percent) of those who had worked six months or less before the revolution, reported that they were working ten months or more on the average since the revolution, and 19 per cent said they now worked between seven and nine months a year. Thus, 98 per cent of the previously most underemployed workers said they were working more regularly than they had been before the Revolutionary Government came to power. It would seem quite likely that these changes have had consequences for their response to the revolution. In order to test the proposition that the workers whose economic security has been most enhanced since the revolution would be the most likely to support it, we would have to look simultaneously at their pre-revolutionary and present employment status.

The optimum test of the hypothesis concerning the relationship between change in employment status since the revolution and attitude toward it would require relating *decreased economic security,* as well as maintenance of *the same level* of security, to the workers' attitudes. However, as is obvious from inspection of Table 3, not all the necessary types of change in employment status are represented among the workers in our sample. We can, nevertheless, make some useful inferences concerning the consequences of relative change in economic security on the workers' attitudes by comparing the available groups of workers.

As can be seen from Table 3, our expectation is confirmed that those

Table 3. The relationship between employment status before the revolution, employment status since the revolution, and attitude toward the revolution

Months worked per year before revolution	Per cent favorable — Months worked per year since the revolution: 10+	7–9	6 or less
10+	62 (101)	(4)	(0)
7–9	78 (18)*	(1)	(0)
6 or less	86 (50)*	82 (11)*	(1)

*Of these seventy-nine workers whose economic security is greater since the revolution, 83 per cent support the revolution.

workers whose economic security is greater than it was in pre-revolutionary years are more likely than other workers to support the revolution —in this case, than those workers who were employed regularly before and have continued to be since the revolution.

RACIAL GROUP MEMBERSHIP

If it is correct, as our evidence seems to indicate, that economic insecurity conduces to revolutionary politics, then it should follow from this that a racial or ethnic group whose position is comparatively less secure economically than that of the racial or ethnic majority should also be more responsive to the revolution than the latter is. From what we know about pre-revolutionary Cuba, it is probably correct to say that Negroes and Mestizos were in general subject to greater economic insecurity than whites. (In our sample, for instance, forty-nine per cent of the Negroes and Mestizos reported that they were employed nine months or less before the revolution, compared to thirty-nine per cent of the white workers.) While Negroes were distributed throughout the occupational structure, they were disproportionately concentrated in the poorest income groups and the most menial jobs—they were, as Lowry Nelson put it, "predominantly the 'hewers of wood and drawers of water.' "[25] Apparently, there was also a tendency for Negroes working at the same jobs as whites to receive less pay,[26] although this was primarily true of the workers in the weakest unions and least organized industries. Further, in the urban slums, or *solares,* Negroes predominated; the better rooms were commonly rented only to whites. Insofar as their economic position was particularly insecure, then, it might be expected that Negro workers would be more likely to be revolutionary than white workers.

In fact, some of the most prominent left-wing leaders in Cuba were Negroes; among leaders of the Communist Party, as well as of the non-Communist labor unions, Negroes were well represented. During the revolution of the thirties, *Realengo 18,* the "soviet" of workers and peasants which withstood the military forces of Batista the longest, right into the early months of 1934, was led by a Negro Communist, Leon Alvarez. Perhaps the most revered labor leader was the martyred Jesus Menendez, the Negro head of the sugar workers' union, who was murdered in 1947 by cohorts of the notorious Eusebio Mujal. Furthermore, Oriente Province, the province with the highest concentration of Negroes in the population—perhaps twice the proportion of other provinces—was the rebel stronghold[27] during the guerrilla struggle against Batista; and Santiago, the province's capital, was the one major city in which the otherwise abortive general strike of April, 1958, was fully supported by the workers, and the entire city shut down.

However, it must also be emphasized that the social status of the Negro in pre-revolutionary Cuba differed markedly from the status of the Negro in the United States. Largely as a result of social processes characteristic of Negro slavery, and of the slaves' emancipation in Cuba—in contrast to slavery in the United States—the barriers to social intercourse between Negroes and whites, well before the revolution, were not as formidable as those in the United States. While these early developments are too complex to explore here,[28] it is important to emphasize that "Jim Crow" laws comparable to those in America have never existed in Cuba, nor were there other legal, political, and social buttresses to Negro exploitation after emancipation from slavery of the type in force in the United States. Compared to the United States, at least, the social history of Cuba involved a relatively high degree of racial integration and inter-marriage, especially in the working class. Nevertheless, racial discrimination was socially and politically enforced to a certain extent. "Before 1959, Negroes were excluded from most of the better hotels, beaches, and places of entertainment patronized by Americans and upper class Cubans."[29] While not a common practice, in some cities the public squares and parks in which Cubans congregate in the evenings had a promenade plaza reserved for whites which was a step higher than the one reserved for Negroes. As the Cuba survey of the Human Relations Areas Files states: "Opponents of Castro maintain that he invented the racial issue. It is, however, an old problem which has always become more serious in times of political crisis. . . . Many wry Negro proverbs commenting on the relations between Negroes and whites refer unmistakably to home grown attitudes of long standing: 'The black fought the war, the white enjoys the peace'; 'If you see a black and a white together, either the white man needs the black, or else the black has won a lottery.' "[30] That many Negroes recognized their social status as a problem is indicated by the fact that a Negro national federation was organized against racial discrimination.

One further element of importance in the formation of the Negroes' attitudes toward the revolution is the fact that they had a history of experience with broken promises before the revolution and, for that reason, were not likely to take too seriously mere assertions by the

Revolutionary Government that it would eliminate discrimination. "Before 1959," as the HRAF survey notes, "various political leaders gained electoral support by promising to uphold Negro rights but subsequently failed to carry out these promises. The legislative initiative gradually fell to the Communists and to the Frente Civico contra la Discrimination Racial, sponsored by the CTC [Confederation of Cuban Workers] and incorporated in Batista's patronage system. Many Negroes resented left wing efforts to capitalize on the issue, and pointed to progress made by the United States in racial matters as a commendable example. Others saw signs of a deliberate imperialist effort to weaken Cuba by depriving it of part of the resources of its population."[31]

Given this complex mix of relative Negro economic insecurity, a rebel tradition, the presence of discriminatory practices despite a relatively high level of social integration, and the probability of disillusionment with political programs, prediction of the differential response to the revolution of Negro and white workers is not without difficulty—although one would probably surmise that Negroes would be more likely than whites to support the revolution. It is particularly interesting, therefore, as Table 4 shows, that, taken as a whole, the Negro workers in our sample were no more likely than white workers to sympathize with *the Communists in pre-revolutionary Cuba,* and more likely to be hostile to them. We shall take a closer look at this relationship after discussing the differential response of Negro and white workers to the revolution.

Since the revolution, the Revolutionary Government has not only conducted a propaganda campaign in behalf of racial equity, but has also opened all hotels, beaches, and resorts (previously almost entirely privately owned and closed to the public) to all Cubans, regardless of color. "In the larger cities conspicuous desegregation was accomplished although the familiar patterns were to be observed in provincial towns in 1961."[32] Fidel Castro has sprinkled his speeches with allusions to the past exploitation and revolutionary traditions of the Negro, a typical example of which comes from a speech the writer attended at the 26th

Table 4. Racial group membership and pre-revolutionary attitude toward the Communists (per cent)

	Friendly or supporter	Indifferent	Hostile	(N)
Negroes	28	36	36	(50)
Whites	29	45	26	(152)

of July anniversary celebration in 1962 in Santiago: "In the past when voices were raised in favor of liberation for the slaves, the bourgeoisie would say 'impossible, it will ruin the country' and to instill fear, they spoke of the 'black terror.' Today they speak of the 'red terror.' In other words, in their fight against liberty they spread fear of the Negro; today they spread fear of socialism and communism."

It seems likely that the social barriers between members of the races were least among workers; consequently, the impact on them of non-discriminatory policies alone should be least, although not necessarily insignificant. Most beaches, resorts and hotels were closed to the *poor* of Cuba—white and black alike—and not just to the Negro. Thus, the Negro worker may have felt the impact of *class* more than of *racial* membership. It is unclear whether or not economic policies of the regime have benefitted Negro workers more than white workers. While it is probable that Negroes have felt that their status has improved, the complexity of events since the revolution makes the Negro workers' responses difficult to predict. Our data indicate that the Negro workers in our sample are more likely than their white fellows to support the revolution.

Table 5. Racial group membership and attitude toward the revolution (per cent)

	Favorable*	Indecisive	Hostile	(N)
Negroes	80	8	12	(50)
Whites	67	13	20	(152)

* Among Negro workers the proportion "very favorable" to the revolution is 58 per cent; among white workers the proportion "very favorable" is 47 per cent.

In the preceding discussion both economic and status variables were relevant in predicting the differential appeals of the revolution to Negro and white workers. Perhaps our finding that Negro workers are more likely than white workers to support the revolution indicates only the relatively less secure position of Negro workers as a group before the revolution, i.e., that control for pre-revolutionary employment status would eliminate the Negro-white difference. However, this reasoning is not supported by our evidence. As Table 6 indicates, both among the workers who were recurrently unemployed before the revolution and among those who were regularly employed, Negroes are more likely to support the revolution than whites. The table also shows that the original relationship between pre-revolutionary employment status and attitude toward the revolution holds among both Negro and white workers. The inference is clear that, given the persistence of the differences between Negro and white workers—even with pre-revolutionary economic security controlled—the fact of membership in the Negro racial group is in itself significant. Indeed, if we look at the effect on Negro and white workers of change in employment status since the revolution, the results are essentially the same as for pre-revolutionary employment status alone (Table 7). Both among the workers whose employment status is higher and those whose employment status is at the same level since the revolution, Negroes are more likely than whites to favor the revolution. Although employment security is not the only aspect of economic security, it is certainly among the most significant; we might infer that the social status of the Negro racial group accounts for the Negro-white differences.

Table 6. The relationship between racial group membership, pre-revolutionary employment status, and attitude toward the revolution

	Per cent favorable	
	Months worked per year before revolution	
	9 or less	10 plus
Negroes	91 (22)	73 (22)
Whites	80 (60)	59 (83)

Although the Negro unemployed are more likely to support the revolution than regularly employed Negro workers, the parallel result does not hold for *pre-revolutionary attitudes toward the Communists* (Table 8). This finding is especially interesting in the light of some recent research to be discussed below. Among white workers we observe the expected relationship that the workers who experienced the most pre-revolutionary unemployment were the most likely to support the Communists. Among Negro workers, on the other hand, there is no significant difference between the unemployed and the regularly employed in their pre-revolutionary attitudes toward the Communists.

INTERPRETATION

There are two fundamental questions about our findings:

1. Why are the pre-revolutionary unemployed and underemployed

Table 7. The relationship between racial group membership, change in employment status, and attitude toward the revolution

	Per cent favorable	
	Change in employment status	
	Same high level	higher
Negroes	71 (21)	90 (21)
Whites	60 (80)	81 (58)

workers more likely than the regularly employed to favor the revolution, and to have had pro-Communist political orientations before the revolution? Indeed, the general theoretical question of the reasons for the increased probability of political radicalism among the more economically insecure workers is at issue.

2. Why are the Negro pre-revolutionary unemployed more likely to support the revolution than their regularly employed counterparts, despite the fact that they were no more likely to be pro-Communist before the revolution?

Radical politics and "leftist voting," as Lipset has noted, are "generally interpreted as an expression of discontent, an indication that needs are not being met." He suggests, as noted above, that one such central "need" is "the need for security of income. This is quite closely related to the desire for higher income as such; however, the effect of periodic unemployment or a collapse of produce prices, for example, seems to be important in itself."[33] Positing such a "need" is not, however, a particularly fruitful formulation, especially as it stands. We know, for instance, that stable poverty, such as that of subsistence peasantry, tends to be a source of political conservatism rather than radicalism, yet their "need" for security of income is obviously not being met. One crucial factor, as Lipset himself indicates elsewhere, is whether or not individuals are exposed by their situation to possibilities for a life better than their

Table 8. The relationship between racial group membership, pre-revolutionary employment status, and pre-revolutionary attitude toward the communists

	Per cent friendly or supporter	
	Months worked per year before revolution	
	9 or less	10 plus
Negroes	27 (22)	32 (22)
Whites	37 (60)	24 (83)

present one.[34] In fact, of course, disemployed workers have had a better life and lost it.

The question remains, nonetheless, whether such an interpretation is sufficient to explain what makes unemployed workers likely to perceive a connection between their private troubles and the economic structure —and in class-conscious or politically radical terms—rather than simply to blame themselves and look inward for the source of their troubles. The answer, it is suggested, lies in the very fact of their observation that their troubles are not private but rather ones which *simultaneously affect many of their fellow workers.* Their radical response, that is, "is especially linked," in Max Weber's phrase, "to the *transparency* of the connections between the causes and the consequences" of their situation as unemployed workers. It is not only the contrast between their situation and that of employed workers, which makes them amenable to the appeals of radical politics, but also (perhaps primarily) the fact that they can so easily recognize the source of their problems to be in the "concrete economic order." "For however different life chances may be," as Weber put it, "this fact in itself, according to all experience, by no means gives birth to 'class action' . . . *The fact of being conditioned and the results of the class situation must be distinctly recognizable. For only then the contrast of life chances can be felt not as an absolutely given fact to be accepted,* but as a resultant from either (1) the given distribution of property, or (2) the structure of the concrete economic order."[35] This reasoning, which Weber applied to "the class situation of the modern proletariat," is particularly appropriate to the situation of those who are unemployed and underemployed. Especially in Cuba was the connection transparent between the "concrete economic order" and the situation of the unemployed. For it was precisely from *recurrent disemployment* that the unemployed suffered. The relationship between the seasonal nature of their unemployment, and the misdevelopment of the economy was therefore "distinctly recognizable." It is understandable that they should be more likely than employed workers to want to alter radically an economic order which is perceived as the source of their collective troubles and, therefore, be more amenable to the appeals of Communist political agitation.

This same line of interpretation applies to our contrasting findings on the Negro unemployed and their political attitudes. Let us compare, first, what John Leggett reported recently concerning his research into sources of class consciousness of Negro and white workers in Detroit.

Having found a general relationship between unemployment and class consciousness, he noted that it might be expected that "unemployed Negro workers should be more class conscious than their employed counterparts." His evidence, however, failed "to support this hypothesis. If anything, the Negro unemployed are slightly *less* class conscious than the employed, while the whites are distributed as expected. Clearly, unemployment, considered by itself, is not a source of class consciousness among Negroes."[36] He did find, however, that among *unionized* Negro workers unemployment is related to class consciousness as expected, and that unionized unemployed Negro workers are far more likely than their non-union counterparts to be militantly class conscious. His interpretation of the effects of union membership on Negro workers was, in brief, that the impact of unions is partly to make Negroes more likely "to develop and use a class frame of reference to appraise their circumstances," and "partly because of the behavior of these unions on class and race questions such as unemployment. . . ."[37]

Now, while it is true that class consciousness and left-wing political orientation are not precisely the same, they are certainly similar phenomena, and their determinants have consistently been found to be similar. There is, in fact, a parallel worth speculating about between Leggett's findings and the present ones. Leggett found that "the combination of unemployment and union membership clearly heightens class consciousness." Although on the basis of our data, it was not possible to gauge the effect of union membership on the workers' pre-revolutionary political orientations, we did find, as noted above, that the combination of unemployment and their experience since the revolution apparently heightened the probability of revolutionary political orientations among Negro workers who were unemployed before the revolution. We might speculate, then, that living through the revolution has been an experience for Negro unemployed workers equivalent in significant respects to that of union participation for unemployed Negro workers in Detroit. The revolution may have had an impact on the Negro unemployed in three relevant ways:

First, since the revolution they have been reached effectively by an ideology which stresses, as Leggett said regarding industrial unions, "a class frame of reference to appraise their circumstances."

Second, the Revolutionary Government's "behavior on class and race questions" has emphasized racial equality both in propaganda and in deed.

Third, to the extent to which revolutionary propaganda and deed have, in fact, altered the social status of the Negro racial group and of the unemployed, the connection between the racial situation and the pre-revolutionary class structure and economic order which the revolution destroyed becomes distinctly recognizable. This process may also be likened to the impact of unionization on unemployed Negroes who may recognize that their unemployment cannot now be "explained" by (be attributed to) their racial membership alone, but is also a condition affecting members of the working class regardless of race.

This third point may deserve amplification, especially since it relates to our earlier interpretation of the radicalizing effects of unemployment. Class consciousness and political radicalism may not be meaningful responses for unemployed, non-unionized Negroes, because the fact of *being Negroes* is the significant aspect of their lives, to which they probably attribute their situation as unemployed workers. They do not see the interests of organized workers as relevant to their lives because in a significant respect those interests are indeed *not* relevant to them, so long as their *racial group* does not necessarily benefit from the furthering of those interests. *Class* issues become relevant to Negro workers when, as members of the organized working class, *they* benefit as their *class* benefits. A class conscious perspective or radical political orientation can then be meaningful to them.

The same reasoning may apply to the impact of the revolution on unemployed Negroes. Their response to the revolution may have its source in the transparency of the connections between the causes and the consequences of their pre-revolutionary situation and that of unemployed white workers. The connection between the pre-revolutionary racial situation, the pre-revolutionary class structure and economic order, and the new structure of social relations formed since the revolution, may now be recognizable. To Negroes who were unemployed before the revolution, however, the connection between their situation and that of white unemployed workers was not transparent. It is, we may surmise, the revolution which has made the fact of their having been conditioned by the pre-revolutionary economic order, as well as by membership in the Negro racial group, "distinctly recognizable" to Negro workers who were unemployed before the revolution.

Particularly apt in this connection are the remarks of a Negro worker at the Nicaro nickel refinery in Oriente, when asked what he was most proud of in Cuba. Implicit in his words is the recognition of a connection between the fate of Negroes who were unemployed before the revolution and the pre-revolutionary economic order, yet with emphasis on their racial membership as the significant reason for their situation.

> I am most proud of what the revolution has done for the workers and the *campesinos*—and not only at work. For example, Negroes could not go to a beach or to a good hotel, or be *jefes* in industry, or work on the railroads or in public transportation in Santiago. This was because of their color! They could not go to school or be in political office, or have a good position in the economy either. They would wander in the streets without bread. They went out to look for work and could not get it. But now, no—all of us—we are equal: the white, the Negro, the *Mestizo* . . .

SUMMARY AND CONCLUSION

Generally, sociological studies of political behavior and of the determinants of "class consciousness" and political radicalism have been made within (relatively) stable social and political contexts. Consequently, it is difficult on the basis of the findings of such studies, to place much confidence in predictions of political behavior in times of social crisis and especially of revolutionary social change. Therefore, one important aspect of our own findings, from a theoretical point of view, is precisely and paradoxically the fact of how *expectable* they were on the basis of prior research and theory. From knowledge of a significant fact of their lives before the revolution, namely, their relative economic security, it was possible to predict more or less accurately the workers' differential responses to the ideological and social content of the revolution.

The workers who had experienced the most unemployment during pre-revolutionary years were found to be the ones who were most likely to support the revolution. Pre-revolutionary unemployment was also found to be a significant determinant of pre-revolutionary pro-Communist orientation. Change in employment status since the revolution also proved to be significant; it was found that the workers whose economic security had been enhanced since the revolution were more likely to support it than were the workers who had retained their previously high level of economic security. Negro workers were more likely than whites to support the revolution; this relationship was found to hold even with pre-revolutionary employment status and change in employment status since the revolution controlled. Among Negro and white workers, the original relationships between (a) pre-revolutionary employment status and attitude toward the revolution, and (b) change in employment status and attitude toward the revolution, also were found to hold. In contrast, it was found that while unemployed white workers were more likely to support the Communists before the revolution than their regularly employed counterparts, this was not true among Negroes. In the latter racial group, unemployed workers were no more likely before the revolution than the regularly employed to favor the Communists.

Recurrent unemployment and underemployment led to revolutionary politics among the Cuban workers in part because of their exposure to the possibilities of a better life during periods of regular employment and in part because the connection between their situation and the concrete economic order was so transparent. To the Negro unemployed before the revolution, who very likely saw their racial membership as the prime cause of their situation, a class-conscious or pro-Communist political orientation likely appeared to be meaningless. The revolution apparently made distinctly recognizable the connection between their fate and that of white members of the working class, and the pre-revolutionary economic order. Thus, the combination of their racial membership and of their pre-revolutionary unemployment now reinforced each other, making them more likely than the white pre-revolutionary unemployed to support the revolution.

NOTES

1. Karl Marx, *Capital: A Critique of Political Economy,* New York: Modern Library, 1936, p. 702.
2. Karl Kautsky, "Krisentheorien," *Die Neue Zeit,* 20 (1901–02), p. 140.
3. Seymour Martin Lipset, *Political Man: The Social Bases of Politics,* Garden City, New York: Doubleday, 1959, p. 232. The original article in which this formulation appeared was by Lipset, Paul Lazarsfeld, Allen Barton, and Juan Linz, "The Psychology of Voting: Analysis of Political Behavior," in Gardner Lindzey, ed., *Handbook of Social Psychology, Vol. 2,* Cambridge: Addison-Wesley, 1954, pp. 1124-1175.
4. See Richard Centers, *The Psychology of Social Classes,* Princeton: Princeton University Press, 1949, pp. 177-179; Herbert G. Nicholas, *The British General Election of 1950,* London: Macmillan, 1951, pp. 297-298. Lipset, *op. cit.,* pp. 113-114, 232-237, contains an excellent summary of the literature and findings on the political effects of unemployment. For the earlier literature, see Philip Eisenberg and Paul Lazarsfeld, "The Psychological Effects of Unemployment," *Psychological Bulletin,* 35 (June, 1938), pp.

358-390. O. Milton Hall, "Attitudes and Unemployment: A Comparison of the Opinions and Attitudes of Employed and Unemployed Men," *Archives of Psychology,* 165 (March, 1954), is a monograph on the effects of unemployment on the attitudes of professional engineers during the depression of the '30's. Also see John C. Leggett, "Economic Insecurity and Working Class Consciousness," *American Sociological Review,* 29 (April, 1964), pp. 226-234, and Richard F. Hamilton, "The Social Bases of French Working Class Politics," unpublished doctoral dissertation, Columbia University, 1963. General economic insecurity in any form—whether because of the fear and presence of unemployment, or being in an economically vulnerable position—apparently conduces to support of radical politics. Thus, Lipset noted in *Agrarian Socialism,* Berkeley and Los Angeles: University of California Press, 1950, pp. 10-18, that: "It was the economically and climatically *vulnerable* wheat belt that formed the backbone of all protest movements from the independent parties of the 1870's down to the contemporary C.C.F. in Canada . . . It is highly significant that the first electorally successful Socialist Party in the United States or Canada should have developed in the same Great Plains wheat belt that earlier produced the Greenbackers, the Populists, the Non-Partisans, and other agrarian upheavals." Evidence has also been adduced to show that the general insecurity of small businessmen in a large-scale corporate capitalism results in their support of *right-wing* "radicalism"; see Martin Trow, "Small Businessmen, Political Tolerance, and Support for McCarthy," *American Journal of Sociology,* 64 (November 1958), pp. 270-281.

5. Bohan Zawadski and Paul E. Lazarsfeld, "The Psychological Consequences of Unemployment," *Journal of Social Psychology,* 6 (May, 1935), p. 249.

6. *Report on Cuba,* Baltimore, Md.: Johns Hopkins Press, 1951, p. 359.

7. Real per capita income in 1903–1906 averaged $203; in 1923–26, $212; in 1943–46, $211; and in 1956–58 about $200. Data for first three periods are from Julian Alienes y Urosa, *Caracteristicas fundamentales de la economia cubana,* Havana: Banco Nacional de Cuba, 1950, p. 52. He deflated his income series by means of the old United States wholesale price index, since there was no Cuban index. Money income figures for 1956–58 were adjusted by the writer, using the same set of prices.

8. As cited in Alberto Arredondo, *Cuba: tierra indefensa,* Havana, 1945, p. 176.

9. *Investment in Cuba: Basic Information for United States Businessmen,* Washington, D.C.: U.S. Government Printing Office, 1956, p. 21, fn.

10. The 1953 Cuban census estimated 8.4 per cent of the labor force was

unemployed during the year's period of *fullest* employment, namely, at the height of the *zafra* (Oficina Nacional de los Censos Demografico y Electoral, *Censos de poblacion, viviendas y electoral,* Havana: Republica de Cuba, 1953). Systematic data on unemployment and underemployment were not collected in Cuba until 1957. In 1957, 10.8 per cent of the labor force was estimated as unemployed, on the average, during the *zafra,* with a high during the dead season of 15.1 per cent. In 1958, the average unemployment in the *zafra* and dead season was an estimated 8.4 per cent and 18 per cent respectively. Annual averages were 12.6 per cent in 1957, and 11.8 per cent in 1958. Estimated *underemployment* averaged 7.6 per cent in 1957, and 7.2 per cent in 1958, making a combined total of known average underemployment and unemployment of 20.2 per cent in 1957, and 19.0 per cent in 1958. These figures are calculated from data in the following: *Anuario de estadisticas del trabajo, 1959,* Geneva: Oficina Internacional de Trabajo, 1959, Table 10, p. 186; Oficina Nacional de los Censos Demografico y Electoral, Departamento de Econometria, "Cantidades y Indices de Empleo y Desempleo," *Empleo y desempleo en la fuerza trabajadora,* Havana: Consejo de Economia, June 3, 1958, mimeographed; *Encuesta sobre empleo, desempleo, y subempleo,* Havana, 1961 (unpublished data made available to the author). A table showing unemployment and underemployment in the Cuban labor force 1957–1958, by month, appears in the author's dissertation, *Working Class Politics in Cuba,* p. 121. "Underemployment" was defined by the Department of Economic Statistics of the Cuban Government to include "persons who work less than thirty hours a week for pay, or 'on their own account' [self-employed] and those who work without pay for a relative." Departamento de Econometria, "Informe Tecnico No. 7," *Empleo y desempleo en la fuerza trabajadora,* Julio, 1959, Havana: Consejo Nacional de Economia, October 5, 1959, p. 12 mimeographed.

11. *Investment in Cuba,* p. 24. "Only one-third of the millworkers and one-twentieth of the field workers are kept fully employed during the dead season." *Cuba: Economic and Commercial Conditions,* London: Her Majesty's Stationery Office, 1954, p. 39.

12. Cuba Economica y Financiera, *Anuario Azucarea de Cuba,* 1954, Havana, 1954; *Investment in Cuba,* p. 23. If the 1953 census categories, "Craftsmen, foremen, operatives, and kindred workers," "Laborers, except farm" and "Laborers, farm," are taken to constitute the working class, that class numbered 1,111,743 in 1952, or 56.3 per cent of the "economically active population." There were an estimated 474,053 sugar workers; thus they constituted about forty-two per cent of the manual working class, excluding private household workers, service workers, and unclassified occupations, the latter of which totalled about ten per cent of the economically active

population. Since most workers in the sugar industry were employed only during the *zafra,* this means that between one-third and two-fifths of the working class in Cuba must have been unemployed and underemployed most of the year before the establishment of the Revolutionary Government.

13. "It must be remembered that nearly all the popular education of working people on how an economic system worked and what might be done to improve it came first from the anarchosyndicalists, and most recently—and most effectively—from the Communists" *Report on Cuba,* p. 366. On the political history of the Cuban working class, see the author's dissertation, *Working Class Politics in Cuba,* Chapters 1 and 2, and the references cited therein.

14. *Pensamiento politico, economico, y social de Fidel Castro,* Havana: Editorial Lex, 1959, p. 38.

15. Speech to the workers' delegates to the Council of Technical Advisers, *El Mundo,* Havana, February 12, 1961.

16. It should be noted, however, that the rebels emphasized that workers were well-represented among them. A youthful unidentified leader of the 26th of July Movement's Labor Front told an interviewer in February, 1958, that he "was eager to dispel the notion . . . that the 26th of July Movement headed by Señor Castro was predominantly a middle class affair. He said that, although Cuban labor leaders were 'on Batista's payroll,' the rank and file sympathized with Señor Castro." (*New York Times,* February 3, 1958, p. 7.) More to the point, Javier Pazos (son of Felipe Pazos, the former head of the Cuban National Bank), who was active in the anti-Batista urban underground, but who is now in exile from Cuba, wrote recently that "of the militants in the action groups, some were students, other were *workers* who were either *unemployed* or sick of a corrupt trade union in league with Batista." *Cambridge Opinion,* No. 32, p. 21, as cited in Robin Blackburn, "Sociology of the Cuban Revolution," *New Left Review,* 21 (October, 1963), p. 80. (Italics mine.)

17. Boris Goldenberg, "El desenvolvimiento de la revolucion cubana," *Cuadernos,* 46 (January-February, 1961), Paris, p. 35. Theodore Draper cites Goldenberg's views with approval in *Castro's Revolution: Myths and Realities,* New York: Frederick Praeger, 1962, p. 53.

18. See the writer's "Labor in Cuba," *The Nation,* 195 (October 20, 1962), pp. 238-241, and "Castro and Cuba's Communists," *Ibid.,* 195 (November 3, 1962), pp. 284-287.

19. In detail, the technique utilized was the following:

a) Using a list of all industrial work-places and the number of workers employed in each, as compiled by the Ministry of Industries, the number of industrial workers was added cumulatively and the sub-totals noted. b) Twenty-one six-digit random numbers were drawn from a table of random numbers, and twenty-one factories were then selected whose cumulative sub-totals were at least as large as or larger than each of the random numbers.

In each of the work-places a predetermined fixed number of workers (because of time and resources available, ten workers per work-place) was selected at random to be interviewed. In each work-place, the probability that a worker would be selected was inversely proportional to the number of workers employed in it.

The sample consisted, then, of 210 industrial workers selected at random from a population in which each worker had a known equal probability of being selected for the sample. Eight workers refused to be interviewed, and were not replaced by others; this gave a total of 202 actual interviews as the basis of this study. As a check, the refusals were tabulated for the appropriate classification in which the refusals themselves could be construed as significant answers, viz., "hostile" to the revolution, and in all instances the relationships persisted or were strengthened. We obtained the age, sex, race, average months worked before and since the revolution, and place of work of each "refusal."

The above method of sampling may be expressed in the following formula:

$$P = m(s/N)\ (k/s) \text{—} km/N$$

where

m equals the number of industrial work-places selected to be in the sample.

s equals the number of workers employed in a given work-place for the sample.

k equals the fixed number of workers randomly selected to be interviewed in each work-place.

N equals the total number of workers employed in all work-places from which the sample was drawn.

P equals the probability that a worker in the population would be selected to be interviewed.

The method of sampling was employed to assure the inclusion in the sample of workers actually involved in industrial production using machine power and machine methods of production, rather than handicrafts methods of manufacture. In general, the larger the factor, the more likely that it was actually an industrial center. This was done for the theoretical reason that a major focus of the larger study, of which the findings reported here are a part, was to be the revolution's impact on the workers' estrangement from their work. It was, therefore, particularly necessary to interview "industrial" rather than handicraft workers. It need hardly be pointed out that this method of sampling the working class does not affect the explanatory purposes of our study. "Representativeness," as Hans Zetterberg points out "should not be confused with randomization. Randomization can be used to obtain representativeness. However, it is also used as a method of controlling irrelevant factors when testing a working hypothesis." (*On Theory and Verification in Sociology,* New York: Tressler Press, 1954, p. 57).

20. This last method was employed only in the mining town of Matahambre in Pinar del Rio. The selection was not demonstrably random. It was impossible to pull men out of the mines during their work. The attempt was made to select names from the list of workers not working during that shift, go to their homes, and interview them there. However, this proved to be impossible because there are no addresses and fewer street names in Matahambre. It was necessary, therefore, to go to neighborhoods in the community in which a high concentration of miners lived, choose a house, and inquire whether or not a miner lived there. If a miner did live there and was home, then, with the miner's consent, he was interviewed. Obviously this is not the most reliable method of assuring a random sample, yet there is no evident bias. The inadequacy here consists in our inability to know what degree of confidence to place in the randomness of the Matahambre sample.

21. The assistance of the Ministry of Industries was enlisted in the realization of this study. The theoretical and historical purposes of this study were explained to the Minister of Industries, Major Ernesto "Che" Guevara. It was his approval which made this study possible. There were no conditions attached to the writer's work and no restrictions whatsoever placed on his travel or on the kinds of question he might ask. The writer explained the purposes of his research, submitted a copy of the mimeographed interview schedule, clarified the purposes (but did not change the wording of a number of questions which appeared to the Minister to be 'loaded', and received permission to enter any mine, mill, factory or plant he wished, and to have workers taken from their work for as long as was necessary for the interviews. The writer was given credentials by the Ministry to identify him to administrators and labor union officials at the work-places visited, and was, after that, left to carry out the research at his own convenience. There was no predetermined schedule of when the writer was to arrive at any work-place, nor, it was evident, had any administrators been informed to expect the writer's visit. On several occasions, administrators or personnel chiefs telephoned to the Ministry of Industries in Havana to check the writer's credentials and his insistence that he had permission—which was apparently unbelievable to administrators trying to raise production levels —to take ten workers from their work for as long as was necessary.

22. Item analysis of the workers' answers to the five questions indicates that the latter form an acceptable Guttman scale, eighty-eight per cent of the workers giving answers exactly (67 per cent) or consistently (21 per cent) in conformity with a Guttman model of ideal classification of respondents. The coefficient of reproducibility equals 0.95. See Samuel Stouffer, et al., *Measurement and Prediction,* Princeton: Princeton University Press, 1950, p. 117.

23. It is relevant to note here that, according to this crude measure of their attitude toward the Communists before the revolution, twenty-eight per cent of the workers in our sample classified themselves as pre-revolutionary friends or supporters of the Communists; and according to the International Bank for Reconstruction and Development *Report,* written after the Communists had been officially purged from the labor movement, the Communists still had "a strong underground influence in some unions, and some authorities estimate that perhaps 25 per cent of all Cuban workers are secretly sympathetic to them." *Report on Cuba,* p. 365.

24. It may be objected that this relationship between pre-revolutionary unemployment and pro-Communism is an artifact of the circumstance that revolutionary workers are likely to "recall" a favorable attitude toward the Communists, because of their present support for the revolution. The fact that the proportion favoring the revolution exceeds the proportion who favored the Communists before the revolution by more than twice casts doubt on the validity of this objection. Moreover, when we view the relationship between pre-revolutionary employment status and pro-Communist attitudes *among revolutionary workers only,* the same relationship holds: 44 per cent of the recurrently unemployed (N=68) supported the Communists before the revolution, compared to 35 per cent of the regularly employed (N=65).

25. Lowry Nelson, *Rural Cuba,* Minneapolis, Minnesota: University of Minnesota Press, 1950, p. 157 ff. Cf. also Direccion General de Censo, *Censo de* 1943, Havana: Republica de Cuba, 1945; and *Censos de poblacion, vivienda y electoral,* Havana: Republica de Cuba, 1953.

26. Nelson, *op. cit.,* p. 156.

27. *Investment in Cuba,* p. 179. Forty per cent of the population of Oriente was estimated to be Negro or Mestizo, compared to 20 per cent or less in the other five provinces.

28. See Frank Tannenbaum, *Slave and Citizen,* New York: Alfred Knopf, 1948; and Stanley Elkins, *Slavery,* Chicago: University of Chicago Press, 1959.

29. Wyatt MacGaffey and Clifford R. Barnett, *Cuba: Its People, Its Society, Its Culture,* New Haven: Human Relations Area Files Press, 1962, p. 32. Cf. also Nelson, *op. cit.,* pp. 158-159.
30. MacGaffey and Barnett, *op. cit.,* pp. 32-33.
31. *Ibid.,* p. 282.
32. *Ibid.*
33. *Political Man,* p. 232.
34. *Ibid.,* p. 63.
35. Hans Gerth and C. Wright Mills, eds., *From Max Weber: Essays in Sociology,* New York: Oxford University Press, 1946, p. 184. Except for italicization of "transparency", italics are not in the original.
36. John C. Leggett, "Economic Insecurity and Working Class Consciousness," *American Sociological Review,* 29 (April, 1964), 230.
37. *Ibid.,* pp. 233-234.

THE MARGINAL MIDDLE CLASS: A RECONSIDERATION

Richard F. Hamilton

Most discussions of the "lower middle-class" have included the following statements as describing the basic facts of the case. For all practical purposes these and other such statements have been treated as axioms rather than as hypotheses serving to guide research.
1) "Traditionally . . . the white collar worker has thought of himself as a member of the middle class, not of the working class."[1]
2) ". . . the white collar worker has middle class values . . ."[2]
3) "Every basis on which the prestige claims of the bulk of the white-collar employees have historically rested has been declining in firmness and stability. [There has been a] leveling down of white-collar and [a] raising of wage-worker incomes . . ."[3]
4) The relative loss of status gives rise to a "status panic." Among the results of the status panic is the tendency to "seize upon minute distinctions as bases for status." These distinctions in turn "operate against any status solidarity among the mass of employees, often lead to status estrangement from work associates, and to increased status competition. The employees are thus further alienated from work . . ."[4]
5) A final prediction is that this loss of status is associated with an attempt at domination over those groups or individuals who are seen as threatening their position. Among the "threatening groups," the most frequently cited are big business, big labor, socialists and communists, and upward mobile minority groups.[5]

The aim of this paper is to test some of these claims, particularly numbers 1, 2, 3, and 5, with systematically collected survey data. The basis for this secondary analysis is the University of Michigan Survey Research Center's 1956 election study.[6] In previous work in this area those in the United States Census categories "clerical and kindred" and "sales and kindred," have been combined and treated as equivalent to

Reprinted by permission from *American Sociological Review,* **31,** No. 2, April 1966, pp. 192-199.

the "lower middle class." For present purposes we are following this convention with one change. That is, only married employed males and married women whose husbands were employed as clerical or sales employees are included here. This procedure in effect controls for a number of "non-class" factors, eliminating from the start the need to consider the male-female ratio in the occupation and more specifically the number of elderly divorced and widowed women. We will be comparing the characteristics of the employed clerical and sales men (and their wives) with equivalent skilled workers (and their wives). For reasons considered elsewhere, we have excluded foremen from the census category "craftsmen, foremen and kindred" so that, for purposes of comparison with the "upper working class," we have skilled workers only.[7]

FINDINGS

Class Identification. Our first and perhaps most important finding is that roughly *half* (52% N=124) *of the clerical and sales group identify themselves as working class.*[8] At present, therefore, the basic assumption of point one above is invalid. Theorizing about the "traditional" white-collar workers could, at best, apply only to half of those in this occupational rank. For the other half a different line of theory is necessary and different research directions are clearly in order.

One likely explanation for this seeming paradox is that working-class identifiers had manual labor origins and that, either by intent or as a result of changes in the available job offerings, they ended up in non-manual positions. We cannot test directly for this possibility since the 1956 study did not ask for father's occupation. A question asking for the perceived social class of the respondent's family when he was growing up does, however, allow an indirect test. The data show clear support for this speculation: 91% of the working-class identifiers report working-class origins as opposed to only 30% of the middle-class identifiers.[9]

The finding that about half of the clerical and sales employees identify themselves as working class indicates that, despite reports and discussion for some decades which have noted increasing "recruitment" of ex-workers and children of manual workers into the lower middle class, there has been a persistent failure to take this development into account.[10] In part, recognition of this trend was avoided by the assumption that its implications lay somewhere in the future and, in part, by the "class-centric" assumption that mobile persons would "convert"—that they all *wanted* to become middle class and would be eager to assume the signs of membership.[11]

It is reasonable to expect that any "status strains" are going to differ for the two groups because of varying training and reference groups. All other things being equal, status strain would appear most likely for the middle-class identifiers, the others having both lower levels of aspiration and consequent greater degree of achievement. There is no reason *a priori* for assuming that working-class identifiers are worried about the manual workers "catching up" or surpassing them. We might just as easily assume that, with friends and kinsmen in manual positions, they do not see the "blurring of class lines" as in any way threatening. The location in non-manual ranks, moreover, may not be willed, but rather might be the result of a "structured push" out of the manual ranks. In an effort to assess this respecification, the remainder of this article will focus on the differing attitudes and position of white-collar working-class and middle-class identifiers.

The "Middle-Class" Values. Only a very brief sampling and examination of "middle-class" values is possible at this point. One important value is the presumably greater concern with "self-help" and independence within the middle class as opposed to "collective" solutions like those implied by the so-called welfare state. This assumption, on the whole, finds only modest support. More than half of the clerical and sales

Table 1. Occupation, identification and domestic liberalism

	Occupation of head			
	Clerical, sales		Skilled	
Class identification:	Working	Middle	Working	Middle
Government should help provide jobs...				
Per cent agreeing	66	53	61	60
N=	(59)	(51)	(153)	(63)
Government should help provide low-cost medical and hospital care...				
Per cent agreeing	63	44	64	58
N=	(57)	(55)	(149)	(60)

Source: Survey Research Center, University of Michigan, 1956 Election Study (SRC 417). See footnote 6.

respondents favor government action in providing jobs and in providing medical aid for those unable to afford it.[12] (Table 1) When we separate them by identification, we find the middle-class identifiers among the clerical and sales workers to be more conservative by a fair margin.

Middle-class position, by itself, does not "make" conservatives; clerical and sales working-class identifiers do not differ from the skilled workers who make the same identification. This means that the process of mobility, for this rank at any rate, appears to involve the direct *importation* of working-class values into the middle class. Contrary to popular expectation, the persons who move down into the skilled ranks show a considerable amount of "conversion" to the working-class position on these issues, and are virtually indistinguishable from the remaining skilled.

The Leveling of Incomes. As shown elsewhere, the use of appropriate controls demonstrates that the assumption of superior earnings by the skilled workers is false.[13] When we divide the white-collar group according to class identification we come up with the additional finding that the middle-class identifiers, the "traditional" middle class, are not at all a marginal subgroup. Rather, the working-class identifiers are the ones who prove to be on the margin, the difference between the subgroup medians being more than one thousand dollars. This puts the "traditional" middle class well ahead of the skilled workers.[14]

The income data describe only one "objective" component of the position of these groups. Since these objective differences might not be appreciated by the respondents, there may not be any consequences which can be predicted *a priori.* The "status panic" thesis depends on the assumption of an intervening perception of the differences and an evaluation of them in a specified manner. The SRC study asked additional questions relevant to the financial situation which allow us to make some assessment of these subjective appreciations.

Satisfaction or panic will be a function not merely of the x dollars acquired in any given year, but also of such things as the prior earnings trends, expectations about future earnings, and learned expectations as to what one should be earning. The data in Table 2 show that the middle-class identifiers report somewhat greater income improvement in recent years than the working-class identifiers. Furthermore, the middle-class identifiers are slightly more likely than the other white-collar subgroup to expect future improvement. It should be kept in mind that they are making this estimate from a considerably higher financial level than the others. Despite these benefits, interestingly enough, the middle-class identifiers, when asked how they felt about their situation, indicated a slightly lower level of satisfaction. In fact, looking at those under age 45, we find that despite high current earnings and greater optimism, the "traditional" white-collar group shows less satisfaction than the working-class identifying clerical-sales group or either subgroup of the skilled.[15]

Table 2. Occupation, identification and perceived financial situation (per cent, of those with opinions)

	Occupation of head			
	Clerical, sales		Skilled	
Class identification:	Working	Middle	Working	Middle
During last few years, financial situation getting better...	36	47	46	48
N=	(63)	(59)	(172)	(68)
In the next few years financial situation will get better...	51	54	47	54
N=	(61)	(59)	(163)	(65)
Are "you...satisfied with... present financial situation...?" Per cent pretty well satisfied	48	44	46	44
N=	(63)	(59)	(172)	(68)

Note: For source, see Table 1.

In view of the considerable income gap between the two groups, the past trend and the expectation for the future, it appears extremely doubtful that this lesser degree of satisfaction is a result of "status anxieties" caused by the rise of groups "from below." A more likely alternative is that as a result of different training and indoctrination they have set themselves much higher expectations, the strain being between their high level of aspirations and their current level of achievement. The conventional theory, if it is to be salvaged at all, may be correct in diagnosing status strain but incorrect about the dynamics involved. It would also appear that the conventional view is wrong about the resolution of this strain. A large majority of the clerical and sales employees are under age 45, a fact which suggests that many of them may later achieve mobility into the "higher" managers and officials ranks.[16] The status problem for them, if we persist in using the conventional theory, may be a matter of the "relative rate of advance"—that is, of the rate at which others are being "left behind."

The Question of Authoritarianism. The fifth assumption of the conventional view is that the marginal middle class will be hostile to the efforts of real or assumed competitors and will attempt to block their mobility. The SRC study allows no direct evaluation of this thesis; there are, however, two questions allowing us some insight into the question.[17]

In response to the question whether the government should guarantee fair treatment in jobs and housing for Negroes, we should, following the conventional view, find the marginal clerical and sales employees to be more "conservative," that is, opposed to a government role. As it turns out, however, it is the working-class-identifying clerical and sales group, that is, the marginal group, which is the more favorably disposed of the two towards government action.[18] (Table 3) The least favorably disposed of the manual and non-manual groups happens to be the skilled who identify with the middle class. Thus, as far as this study and this question are concerned, the "authoritarianism on the margins" is a characteristic of those who see themselves as having experienced downward mobility. It is interesting to note that, paradoxically, "working-class authoritarianism" is a phenomenon of middle-class origin, to the small extent that any difference exists.

A second question, on government aid in school integration ques-

Table 3. Occupation, identification and "authoritarianism" (white respondents with opinions)

	Occupation of head			
	Clerical, sales		Skilled	
Class identification:	Working	Middle	Working	Middle
Government should help Negroes in jobs and housing...				
Per cent agreeing	74	64	69	54
N=	(51)	(53)	(137)	(61)
Government should stay out of school integration...				
Per cent *disagreeing*	39	42	40	39
N=	(54)	(55)	(144)	(64)

Note: For source, see Table 1.

tions, yields no significant differences between the manual and non-manual groups nor between the sub-groups with middle- and working-class identifications. In other words, the marginal location appears to have no effect on this attitude.[19]

A COMPARATIVE VIEW

The finding that about half the clerical and sales identify themselves with the working class is not a new one. An early (1948) comparative study found 57 per cent of the "Clerks" making the same identification.[20] (See Table 4) In seven of the nine countries studied the percentage of the "Clerks" identifying with the working class does not fall below 44. The "highs" are the United States and Great Britain (with 58 per cent). The exceptions are not "north European" countries, as has been suggested,[21] but prove to be West Germany (British Zone) and Italy. North European Norway has half of the identifiers indicating that they are working class. The West German finding is not merely the consequence of an "early" survey or as a result of studying merely the British Zone of Occupation (which included the Ruhr). This is made clear by the results of a later (1959) survey of the entire West German population. This shows only 21 per cent (N=150) of the "lower middle class" *(untere Beamte and ausführende Angestellte)* identifying themselves as working or lower class.[22]

A Trend? The SRC Study (1956) finds 52 per cent of the clerical and

Table 4. Class identification of clerks in nine countries

	Class identification (per cent)				
	Middle	Working	Upper	Don't Know	(N)
Australia	53	46	..	1	(116)
Britain	40	58	..	2	(219)
France	43	52	3	2	(189)
West Germany (British Zone)	70	25	2	3	(917)
Italy	78	22	..	..	(51)
Mexico	50	49	..	1	(303)
Netherlands	47	48	1	4	(235)
Norway	44	44	..	12	(211)
U.S.A.	39	57	1	3	(155)

Source: Data from William Buchanan and Hadley Cantril, *How Nations See Each Other*, Urbana: University of Illinois Press, 1953, Appendix D.

sales employees identifying themselves as working class. A study conducted in July, 1945, found only 35 per cent identifying themselves with the working or lower class.[23] If we assume that these are valid findings (that is, not the result of methodological differences or errors), this indicates a trend, contrary to the common expectation, of *increased* identification with the working class on the part of those marginal to the middle class. In fact, the shift in the course of the eleven years intervening between Centers' study and the SRC study amounts to seventeen percentage points.

Rather than assuming conversion, it appears likely that two factors —post-war economic expansion, and the existence of many ex-members of the armed forces (aided by the G.I. Bill)—combined to bring many sons of working-class parents into these ranks within a very short period of time. The relatively low percentage identifying themselves with the working class in Centers' study probably results from the fact that there was very little recruitment from the working class during the ten-year-long depression preceding the war.[24]

In the absence of serious and prolonged economic recessions, and with continued shifting of the occupational structure in the direction of increased non-manual jobs, we should expect continued increase in the proportion of working-class identifiers among the clerical and sales ranks in years to come.

CONCLUSIONS

The basic conclusions are the following:

1. Regardless of what the white-collar workers have done "traditionally," our finding is that one-half of them identify themselves as working class. These class identifications are closely tied in with their class of origin. Those saying that they are working class also say that their origins were working class. This high level of working-class identification, on the basis of one comparative study, is second only to Great Britain. It is similar to the level in seven other countries but stands in marked contrast to the pattern in West Germany and Italy.

2. Objectively, the middle-class identifiers among the clerical and sales workers are considerably ahead of both other clerical and sales employees and skilled workers with respect to income. In their own estimates of their condition they see themselves as having made greater economic progress in recent years and expect more in years to come than is the case with the other white-collar group and the skilled. They do

show somewhat less satisfaction with their income than the working-class identifiers or the skilled, but it would appear highly unlikely that they are suffering from a "status panic" as it has been traditionally defined.

3. The sometimes predicated tendencies toward authoritarianism or domination do not appear supported. Those objectively on the margin, the working-class identifiers, prove to be in one comparison more tolerant, in another no different from the better off traditional white-collar workers or from the skilled who identify themselves as working class.

On the basis of the limited data presented here, it is impossible to make any general claims relative to their acceptance of middle-class values. With respect to domestic economic and civil rights issues, there appears to be an importation of working-class economic values by those moving upward into the middle class and some conversion to working-class values on the part of the downward mobile. On civil rights issues, there is basically no difference between three of the subgroups such as would allow us to talk of "middle-class" or "working-class" values. The fourth group, those seeing themselves as middle class despite their skilled worker positions, are less favorably disposed toward government action in defense of Negro rights; they are the only group showing any distinctive "authoritarian" pattern.

DISCUSSION

These findings strongly suggest the inadequacy of conventional lines of theory. The major difficulty would appear to be the failure to take into account the clear evidence of increased recruitment from the working-class ranks to fill positions in the white-collar occupations. Mills escaped from this recognition by suggesting this as a future development,[25] while others have avoided consideration of these theoretical issues by assuming "conversion" to middle-class values. They have been assuming a mobility *drive* instead of recognizing that much of the observed movement is the result of a "push" rather than any "pulls."

On the basis of data allowing a limited test of the "status panic" hypothesis we find virtually no basis for acceptance of the claim that those on the margins of the middle class provide some peculiar center of "reaction" and intolerance. The data show them as reasonably well satisfied, on the basis of lower expectations and reference groups with whom they are likely to make a favorable comparison.

Our data indicate support for the thesis that "transplantation" rather than conversion processes are operating in the course of mobility. Those moving from what they sense as a working-class background into the white-collar occupations import their class identification and their economic liberalism. This would mean, contrary to the popular theorizing about the "bourgeoisification of the workers," that the actual process is one of "proletarianization" (or, more realistically for the United States, "liberalizing") of the lower middle-class ranks. This means, in turn, that rather than a "conversion of the skilled,"—making the line between skilled and semi-skilled more significant sociologically than the manual-nonmanual division—we should expect the most significant attitudinal cleavage in the United States to be between the lower and the upper middle classes.[26]

One final point has to do with the divergence between the West German and Italian experience and that of the other countries in the Buchanan-Cantril sample. In those two countries it may be the case that social controls, pressures, or other influences operate to penalize the upwardly mobile person for maintaining behavior which betrays his origins. This, in turn, would lead to a much sharper alignment between objective position and identification. It is in settings where "class" is clearly defined and of great importance that a marginal middle-class status panic would develop in periods of inflation or depression. But these conditions are not found in all times and places. In the United States there has been no strong Socialist or Communist movement which has *made* class a salient base for personal identity; instead there have been competing bases, among which religious and ethnic attachments are possibly the most important.[27] It is perhaps for these reasons that the "fundamentalist reactions" and the concern with "status politics" in the United States have not been closely linked with the marginal middle class.[28]

It has been stated with great frequency that the "open" character of American society makes the achievement of middle-class status relatively simple, given the ease of access to middle-class status symbols. It may well be that this focus on "style of life," on the bought artifacts, has obscured the fact of persisting or shifting value cleavages. On the basis of the present findings, somewhat different conclusions appear warranted, namely that the "openness" has meant that there are no penalties attached to mobility and, given the generally prevalent equalitarian ideology ("I'm just as good as anyone else"), that the working-class values could be imported into the lower middle class virtually intact, without any modification or transformation.

NOTES

1. Douglas Dowd, "The White Collar Worker," pp. 125-32 of Bert Cochran, ed., *American Labor in Midpassage,* New York: Monthly Review Press, 1959. (The quotation is from p. 129.) Another author refers to the white-collar group's "well-known desire to set itself apart from the blue-collar group." See Robert Presthus, *Men at the Top: A Study in Community Power,* New York: Oxford University Press, 1964, p. 304.

   Actually one should include marginal independent businessmen in any discussion of the "marginal middle class" or the "lower middle class." In making the separation, I am merely following a convention of long standing in American sociology which has worked with the most convenient census categories. Consideration of marginal independent businessmen is to be found in Richard F. Hamilton and Paul R. Eberts, "The Myth of Business Conservatism," paper read at the American Sociological Association convention, September 3, 1964, Montreal, Canada.

2. *Ibid.,* p. 131.
3. C. Wright Mills, *White Collar,* New York: Oxford University Press, 1951.
4. *Ibid.,* pp. 254 ff. See also Erich Fromm, *Escape from Freedom,* New York: Rinehart & Co., 1941, pp. 219 ff.
5. Fromm, *passim;* Daniel Bell, ed., *The Radical Right,* Garden City: Doubleday, 1963, *passim.*
6. For a description of the sample and a presentation of their findings see Angus Campbell, Philip E. Converse, Warren E. Miller, Donald E. Stokes, *The American Voter,* New York: John Wiley & Sons, 1960.
7. See Richard F. Hamilton, "The Income Difference between Skilled and White Collar Workers," *British Journal of Sociology,* 14 (December, 1963), pp. 363-73. See also Muzafer Sherif and Hadley Cantril, *The Psychology of Ego-Involvements,* New York: John Wiley & Sons, 1947, pp. 144 ff.
8. Four of them did not give any response. The analysis which follows deals only with those responding to the class identification question.
9. An identical split appears among the skilled workers. The data:

	Clerical, sales		Skilled	
	Working	Middle	Working	Middle
Per cent reporting working-class origins	91	30	88	32
N=	(64)	(59)	(170)	(65)

10. A study of the German experience noted this increased recruitment from working class settings over three decades ago. See Hans Speier, "The Salaried Employee in Modern Society," in his *Social Order and the Risks of War: Papers in Political Sociology,* New York: George W. Stewart, 1952, especially pp. 76 ff. (This originally appeared in *Social Research* in 1934.)
11. In the light of the assumption of conversion it is of special importance to note that only 9% of those reporting working-class origins and currently in clerical and sales occupations "convert" to the extent of assuming even the minimal verbal commitment to their new position.
12. The statements follow: "The government in Washington ought to see to it that everybody who wants to work can find a job," and "The government ought to help people get doctors and hospital care at low cost." For a more detailed consideration of the skilled workers, see Richard F. Hamilton, "The Behavior and Values of Skilled Workers," in Arthur B. Shostak and William Gomberg, eds., *Blue-Collar World,* Englewood Cliffs: Prentice-Hall, 1964.
13. See Hamilton, "The Income Difference . . ." *op. cit.,* and "Income, Class, and Reference Groups," *American Sociological Review,* 29 (August, 1964), pp. 576-79. The data from SRC 417 show the same. Taking units having a male head of household and excluding foremen from the skilled ranks, the clerical and sales median income is $5,065 as opposed to the skilled median of $4,808, a difference of $257 in favor of the white-collar group. This is the third independent source showing this finding, the others being a large N.O.R.C. probability sample of 1955, and the 1960 1/10,000 sample of the U.S. Census. The clerical and sales employees, moreover, are a relatively young group; the likelihood is that many of them move into the managers and officials ranks later in life.. Thus, the income gap noted here probably underestimates the eventual differences between the two groups by a considerable margin.
14. The medians for the four subgroups follow:

Class identification	Occupation of head			
	Clerical, sales	(N)	Skilled	(N)
Middle	$5,706	(56)	$5,344	(67)
Working	4,591	(64)	4,728	(163)

The conventional line of analysis which begins by observing "well-off workers" with middle-class characteristics and argues that they are *becoming* middle-class (i.e. changing their values), is likely to be erroneous. As we have seen, most of the well-off skilled workers who identify themselves as middle-class say that they come from middle-class families. This means they have "imported" the middle-class identification into their new milieu rather than that they have "converted."

15. The percentages for those 45 or under:

	Occupation of head			
	Clerical, sales		Skilled	
	Working	Middle	Working	Middle
In the next few years financial situation will get better...	57	66	55	59
N=	(47)	(41)	(107)	(39)
Per cent pretty well satisfied with financial situation...	50	39	47	49
N=	(48)	(41)	(112)	(39)

16. This is considered in Hamilton, "The Income Difference . . ." *op. cit.* A study by Gerald Gurin and others finds a high anxiety level among the clerical and sales workers although it does not specify its sources. See *Americans View Their Mental Health: A Nationwide Interview Survey,* New York: Basic Books, 1960, p. 225.

17. They are: "If Negroes are not getting fair treatment in jobs and housing, the government should see to it that they do." And, "The government in Washington should stay out of the question of whether white and colored children go to the same school." The choice of responses ranged from "agree strongly" to "disagree strongly."

18. This finding clearly has implications for the Lipset-Stouffer thesis that tolerance varies directly with education level—since the working-class identifiers have the lower average number of years of education. Some indications of the complexity of this relationship may be seen in Charles Herbert Stember, *Education and Attitude Change: The Effect of Schooling on Prejudice Against Minority Groups,* New York: Institute of Human Relations Press, 1961. For the original claim, see Seymour Martin Lipset, *Political Man: The Social Bases of Politics,* Garden City: Doubleday & Company, 1960, Ch. IV, "Working Class Authoritarianism," and Samuel A. Stouffer, *Communism, Conformity and Civil Liberties,* Garden City: Doubleday & Company, 1955.

19. Since there was a possibility that the result was due to a regional factor, Table 3 was repeated without Southern respondents. This did not change the results reported above.

20. William Buchanan and Hadley Cantril, *How Nations See Each Other,* Urbana: University of Illinois Press, 1953, Appendix D.

21. Lipset, *op. cit.,* pp. 241-2.

22. These results are from a probability sample of the West German population, dated 1959, and done for the *Institut für Mittelstandsforschung* under the direction of Prof. Dr. Rene König. The author wishes to thank the *Institut* and also the *Zentralerchiv für empirische Sozialforschung* and its director, Frl. Iris Brüning, for the use of these materials.

23. Richard Centers, *The Psychology of Social Classes: A Study of Class Consciousness,* Princeton: Princeton University Press, 1949, p. 86.

24. Some evidence on the impact of the depression on mobility may be found in Gerhard E. Lenski, "Trends in Inter-Generational Occupational Mobility in the United States," *American Sociological Review,* 23 (October, 1958), pp. 514-23.

25. He says, ". . . it is clear that the white-collar job market will include more wage-worker children." *Op. cit.,* p. 297.

26. For an alternative claim, see especially the works of Kurt Mayer: *Class and Society,* New York: Random House, 1955, pp. 41-42; "Recent Changes in the Class Structure of the United States," *Transactions of the Third World Congress of Sociology,* Vol. III, London: International Sociological Association, 1956, pp. 66-80; "The Changing Shape of the American Class Structure," *Social Research,* 30 (Winter 1963), pp. 458-68; and, "Diminishing Class Differentials in the United States," *Kyklos,* 12 (1959) 605-25. In this connection, see my "Affluence and the Worker: The West German Case," *American Journal of Sociology,* 71 (September, 1965), pp. 144-52.

27. Gerhard Lenski, *The Religious Factor,* Garden City: Doubleday & Company, 1961, and Will Herberg, *Protestant-Catholic-Jew,* Garden City: Doubleday & Co., 1956.

28. The John Birch Society, whose membership is by no means marginal, is the most striking case in point. See the essay by Lipset "Three Decades of the Radical Right: Coughlinites, McCarthyites, and Birchers," in Daniel Bell, *op. cit.*

Part 4
POWER
INTRODUCTION

Power, in one form or another, is the starting point for most analyses of society that begin from the conflict perspective. For the classical Marxist, power is always and inevitably in the hands of those who "control the means of production." For Mosca, Machiavelli, and Pareto, the source of power was not so clearly linked to the economic dominance of a particular class; but their theoretical perspectives nonetheless began with an emphasis on what Mosca called one of the "constant facts and tendencies that are to be found in all political organisms . . . [that] two classes of people appear—a class that rules and a class that is ruled."

Mosca also aptly located the implications of this starting point when he went on to say that it is the class that rules which is "always the less numerous, performs all political functions, monopolizes power and enjoys the advantages that power brings, whereas the second, the more numerous class, is directed and controlled by the first, in a manner that is now more or less legal, now more or less arbitrary and violent . . . ."

Following Mosca's essay, which opens the collection of readings in this section, T. B. Bottomore provides a succinct summary of the classical Marxist approach to the study of power. Gerhard Lenski's statement builds on this perspective and attempts to tie the discussion of power to the nature of all societies.

Mosca, Bottomore, and Lenski (strange bedfellows, indeed) provide the analytical framework for the study of power. The studies by C. Wright Mills and Harvey Molotch describe the location and operation of power in contemporary America. Finally, Molotch traces the operation of powerful interests and their control over government decisions.

THE RULING CLASS

Gaetano Mosca

Among the constant facts and tendencies that are to be found in all political organisms, one is so obvious that it is apparent to the most casual eye. In all societies—from societies that are very meagerly developed and have barely attained the dawnings of civilization, down to the most advanced and powerful societies—two classes of people appear—a class that rules and a class that is ruled. The first class, always the less numerous, performs all political functions, monopolizes power and enjoys the advantages that power brings, whereas the second, the more numerous class, is directed and controlled by the first, in a manner that is now more or less legal, now more or less arbitrary and violent, and supplies the first, in appearance at least, with material means of subsistence and with the instrumentalities that are essential to the vitality of the political organism.

In practical life we all recognize the existence of this ruling class (or political class, as we have elsewhere chosen to define it).[1] We all know that, in our own country, whichever it may be, the management of public affairs is in the hands of a minority of influential persons, to which management, willingly or unwillingly, the majority defer. We know that the same thing goes on in neighboring countries, and in fact we should be put to it to conceive of a real world otherwise organized—a world in which all men would be directly subject to a single person without relationships of superiority or subordination, or in which all men would share equally in the direction of political affairs. If we reason otherwise in theory, that is due partly to inveterate habits that we follow in our thinking and partly to the exaggerated importance that we attach to two political facts that loom far larger in appearance than they are in reality.

The first of these facts—and one has only to open one's eyes to see it—is that in every political organism there is one individual who is chief

---

among the leaders of the ruling class as a whole and stands, as we say, at the helm of the state. That person is not always the person who holds supreme power according to law. At times, alongside of the hereditary king or emperor there is a prime minister or a major-domo who wields an actual power that is greater than the sovereign's. At other times, in place of the elected president the influential politician who has procured the president's election will govern. Under special circumstances there may be, instead of a single person, two or three who discharge the functions of supreme control.

The second fact, too, is readily discernible. Whatever the type of political organization, pressures arising from the discontent of the masses who are governed, from the passions by which they are swayed, exert a certain amount of influence on the policies of the ruling, the political, class.

But the man who is at the head of the state would certainly not be able to govern without the support of a numerous class to enforce respect for his orders and to have them carried out; and granting that he can make one individual, or indeed many individuals, in the ruling class feel the weight of his power, he certainly cannot be at odds with the class as a whole or do away with it. Even if that were possible, he would at once be forced to create another class, without the support of which action on his part would be completely paralyzed. On the other hand, granting that the discontent of the masses might succeed in deposing a ruling class, inevitably, as we shall later show, there would have to be another organized minority within the masses themselves to discharge the functions of a ruling class. Otherwise all organization, and the whole social structure, would be destroyed.

From the point of view of scientific research the real superiority of the concept of the ruling, or political, class lies in the fact that the varying structure of ruling classes has a preponderant importance in determining the political type, and also the level of civilization, of the different peoples. According to a manner of classifying forms of government that is still in vogue, Turkey and Russia were both, up to a few years ago, absolute monarchies, England and Italy were constitutional, or limited, monarchies, and France and the United States were classed as republics. The classification was based on the fact that, in the first two countries mentioned, headship in the state was hereditary and the chief was nominally omnipotent; in the second two, his office is hereditary but his powers and prerogatives are limited; in the last two, he is elected.

That classification is obviously superficial. Absolutisms though they were, there was little in common between the manners in which Russia and Turkey were managed politically, the levels of civilization in the two countries and the organization of their ruling classes being vastly different. On the same basis, the regime in Italy, a monarchy, is much more similar to the regime in France, a republic, than it is to the regime in England, also a monarchy; and there are important differences between the political organizations of the United States and France, though both countries are republics.

As we have already suggested, ingrained habits of thinking have long stood, as they still stand, in the way of scientific progress in this matter. The classification mentioned above, which divides governments into absolute monarchies, limited monarchies and republics, was devised by Montesquieu and was intended to replace the classical categories of Aristotle, who divided governments into monarchies, aristocracies and democracies. What Aristotle called a democracy was simply an aristocracy of fairly broad membership. Aristotle himself was in a position to observe that in every Greek state, whether aristocratic or democratic, there was always one person or more who had a preponderant influence. Between the day of Polybius and the day of Montesquieu, many writers perfected Aristotle's classification by introducing into it the concept of "mixed" governments. Later on the modern democratic theory, which had its source in Rousseau, took its stand upon the concept that the majority of the citizens in any state can participate, and in fact *ought* to participate, in its political life, and the doctrine of popular sovereignty still holds sway over many minds in spite of the fact that modern scholarship is making it increasingly clear that democratic, monarchical and aristocratic principles function side by side in every political organism. We shall not stop to refute this democratic theory here, since that is the task of this work as a whole. Besides, it would be hard to destroy in a few pages a whole system of ideas that has become firmly rooted in the human mind. As Las Casas aptly wrote in his life of Christopher Columbus, it is often much harder to unlearn than to learn.

We think it may be desirable, nevertheless, to reply at this point to an objection which might very readily be made to our point of view. If it is easy to understand that a single individual cannot command a group without finding within the group a minority to support him, it is rather difficult to grant, as a constant and natural fact, that minorities rule majorities, rather than majorities minorities. But that is one of the points

—so numerous in all other sciences—where the first impression one has of things is contrary to what they are in reality. In reality the dominion of an organized minority, obeying a single impulse, over the unorganized majority is inevitable. The power of any minority is irresistible as against each single individual in the majority, who stands alone before the totality of the organized minority. At the same time, the minority is organized for the very reason that it is a minority. A hundred men acting uniformly in concert, with a common understanding, will triumph over a thousand men who are not in accord and can therefore be dealt with one by one. Meanwhile it will be easier for the former to act in concert and have a mutual understanding simply because they are a hundred and not a thousand. It follows that the larger the political community, the smaller will the proportion of the governing minority to the governed majority be, and the more difficult will it be for the majority to organize for reaction against the minority.

However, in addition to the great advantage accruing to them from the fact of being organized, ruling minorities are usually so constituted that the individuals who make them up are distinguished from the mass of the governed by qualities that give them a certain material, intellectual or even moral superiority; or else they are the heirs of individuals who possessed such qualities. In other words, members of a ruling minority regularly have some attribute, real or apparent, which is highly esteemed and very influential in the society in which they live.

In primitive societies that are still in the early stages of organization, military valor is the quality that most readily opens access to the ruling, or political, class. In societies of advanced civilization, war is the exceptional condition. It may be regarded as virtually normal in societies that are in the initial stages of their development; and the individuals who show the greatest ability in war easily gain supremacy over their fellows —the bravest become chiefs. The fact is constant, but the forms it may assume, in one set of circumstances or another, vary considerably.

As a rule the dominance of a warrior class over a peaceful multitude is attributed to a superposition of races, to the conquest of a relatively unwarlike group by an aggressive one. Sometimes that is actually the case—we have examples in India after the Aryan invasions, in the Roman Empire after the Germanic invasions and in Mexico after the Aztec conquest. But more often, under certain social conditions, we note the rise of a warlike ruling class in places where there is absolutely no trace of a foreign conquest. As long as a horde lives exclusively by the chase, all individuals can easily become warriors. There will of course be leaders who will rule over the tribe, but we will not find a warrior class rising to exploit, and at the same time to protect, another class that is devoted to peaceful pursuits. As the tribe emerges from the hunting stage and enters the agricultural and pastoral stage, then, along with an enormous increase in population and a greater stability in the means of exerting social influence, a more or less clean-cut division into two classes will take place, one class being devoted exclusively to agriculture, the other class to war. In this event, it is inevitable that the warrior class should little by little acquire such ascendancy over the other as to be able to oppress it with impunity.

Poland offers a characteristic example of the gradual metamorphosis of a warrior class into an absolutely dominant class. Originally the Poles had the same organization by rural villages as prevailed among all the Slavic peoples. There was no distinction between fighters and farmers —in other words, between nobles and peasants. But after the Poles came to settle on the broad plains that are watered by the Vistula and the Niemen, agriculture began to develop among them. However, the necessity of fighting with warlike neighbors continued, so that the tribal chiefs, or voivodes, gathered about themselves a certain number of picked men whose special occupation was the bearing of arms. These warriors were distributed among the various rural communities. They were exempt from agricultural duties, yet they received their share of the produce of the soil, along with the other members of the community. In early days their position was not considered very desirable, and country dwellers sometimes waived exemption from agricultural labor in order to avoid going to war. But gradually as this order of things grew stabilized, as one class became habituated to the practice of arms and military organization while the other hardened to the use of the plow and the spade, the warriors became nobles and masters, and the peasants, once companions and brothers, became villeins and serfs. Little by little the warrior lords increased their demands to the point where the share they took as members of the community came to include the community's whole produce minus what was absolutely necessary for subsistence on the part of the cultivators; and when the latter tried to escape such abuses they were constrained by force to stay bound to the soil, their situation taking on all the characteristics of serfdom pure and simple.

In the course of this evolution, around the year 1333, King Casimir the Great tried vainly to curb the overbearing insolence of the warriors.

When peasants came to complain of the nobles, he contented himself with asking whether they had no sticks and stones. Some generations later, in 1537, the nobility forced all tradesmen in the cities to sell such real estate as they owned, and landed property became a prerogative of nobles only. At the same time the nobility exerted pressure upon the king to open negotiations with Rome, to the end that thenceforward only nobles should be admitted to holy orders in Poland. That barred townsmen and peasants almost completely from honorific positions and stripped them of any social importance whatever.[2]

We find a parallel development in Russia. There the warriors who formed the druzhina, or escort, of the old knezes (princes descended from Rurik) also received a share in the produce of the mirs (rural peasant communities) for their livelihood. Little by little this share was increased. Since land abounded and workers were scarce, the peasants often had an eye to their advantage and moved about. At the end of the sixteenth century, accordingly, the czar Boris Godunov empowered the nobles to hold peasants to their lands by force, so establishing serfdom. However, armed forces in Russia were never composed exclusively of nobles. The muzhiks, or peasants, went to war as common soldiers under the droujina. As early as the sixteenth century, Ivan the Terrible established the order of strelitzes which amounted practically to a standing army, and which lasted until Peter the Great replaced it with regiments organized along western European lines. In those regiments members of the old druzhina, with an intermixture of foreigners, became officers, while the muzhiks provided the entire contingent of privates.[3]

Among the peoples that have recently entered the agricultural stage and are relatively civilized, it is the unvarying fact that the strictly military class is the political, or ruling, class. Sometimes the bearing of arms is reserved exclusively to that class, as happened in India and Poland. More often the members of the governed class are on occasion enrolled—always, however, as common soldiers and in the less respected divisions. So in Greece, during the war with the Medes, the citizens belonging to the richer and more influential classes formed the picked corps (the cavalry and the hoplites), the less wealthy fought as peltasts or as slingers, while the slaves, that is the laboring masses, were almost entirely barred from military service. We find analogous arrangements in republican Rome, down to the period of the Punic Wars and even as late as the day of Marius; in Latin and Germanic Europe during the Middle Ages; in Russia, as just explained, and among many other peoples. Caesar notes repeatedly that in his time the backbone of the Gallic armies was formed by cavalrymen recruited from the nobility. The Aedui, for example, could not hold out against Ariovistus after the flower of their cavalry had been killed in battle.

Everywhere—in Russia and Poland, in India and medieval Europe—the ruling warrior classes acquire almost exclusive ownership of the land. Land is the chief source of production and wealth in countries that are not very far advanced in civilization. But as civilization progresses, revenue from land increases proportionately. With the growth of population there is, at least in certain periods, an increase in rent, in the Ricardian sense of the term, largely because great centers of consumption arise—such at all times have been the great capitals and other large cities, ancient and modern. Eventually, if other circumstances permit, a very important social transformation occurs. Wealth rather than military valor comes to be the characteristic feature of the dominant class: the people who rule are the rich rather than the brave.

The condition that in the main is required for this transformation is that social organization shall have concentrated and become perfected to such an extent that the protection offered by public authority is considerably more effective than the protection offered by private force. In other words, private property must be so well protected by the practical and real efficacy of the laws as to render the power of the proprietor himself superfluous. This comes about through a series of gradual alterations in the social structure whereby a type of political organization, which we shall call the "feudal state," is transformed into an essentially different type, which we shall term the "bureaucratic state." . . .

Once this transformation has taken place, wealth produces political power just as political power has been producing wealth. In a society already somewhat mature—where, therefore, individual power is curbed by the collective power—if the powerful are as a rule the rich, to be rich is to become powerful. And, in truth, when fighting with the mailed fist is prohibited whereas fighting with pounds and pence is sanctioned, the better posts are inevitably won by those who are better supplied with pounds and pence.

There are, to be sure, states of a very high level of civilization which in theory are organized on the basis of moral principles of such a character that they seem to preclude this overbearing assertiveness on the part of wealth. But this is a case—and there are many such—where theoretical principles can have no more than a limited application in real life.

In the United States all powers flow directly or indirectly from popular elections, and suffrage is equal for all men and women in all the states of the Union. What is more, democracy prevails not only in institutions but to a certain extent also in morals. The rich ordinarily feel a certain aversion to entering public life, and the poor a certain aversion to choosing the rich for elective office. But that does not prevent a rich man from being more influential than a poor man, since he can use pressure upon the politicians who control public administration. It does not prevent elections from being carried on to the music of clinking dollars. It does not prevent whole legislatures and considerable numbers of national congressmen from feeling the influence of powerful corporations and great financiers.[4]

In China, too, down to a few years ago, though the government had not accepted the principle of popular elections, it was organized on an essentially equalitarian basis. Academic degrees gave access to public office, and degrees were conferred by examination without any apparent regard for family or wealth. According to some writers, only barbers and certain classes of boatmen, together with their children, were barred from competing for the various grades of the mandarinate.[5] But though the moneyed class in China was less numerous, less wealthy, less powerful than the moneyed class in the United States is at present, it was none the less able to modify the scrupulous application of this system to a very considerable extent. Not only was the indulgence of examiners often bought with money. The government itself sometimes sold the various academic degrees and allowed ignorant persons, often from the lowest social strata, to hold public office.[6]

In all countries of the world those other agencies for exerting social influence—personal publicity, good education, specialized training, high rank in church, public administration, and army—are always readier of access to the rich than to the poor. The rich invariably have a considerably shorter road to travel than the poor, to say nothing of the fact that the stretch of road that the rich are spared is often the roughest and most difficult.

In societies in which religious beliefs are strong and ministers of the faith form a special class a priestly aristocracy almost always arises and gains possession of a more or less important share of the wealth and the political power. Conspicuous examples of that situation would be ancient Egypt (during certain periods), Brahman India and medieval Europe. Oftentimes the priests not only perform religious functions. They possess legal and scientific knowledge and constitute the class of highest intellectual culture. Consciously or unconsciously, priestly hierarchies often show a tendency to monopolize learning and hamper the dissemination of the methods and procedures that make the acquisition of knowledge possible and easy. To that tendency may have been due, in part at least, the painfully slow diffusion of the demotic alphabet in ancient Egypt, though that alphabet was infinitely more simple than the hieroglyphic script. The Druids in Gaul were acquainted with the Greek alphabet but would not permit their rich store of sacred literature to be written down, requiring their pupils to commit it to memory at the cost of untold effort. To the same outlook may be attributed the stubborn and frequent use of dead languages that we find in ancient Chaldea, in India, and in medieval Europe. Sometimes, as was the case in India, lower classes have been explicitly forbidden to acquire knowledge of sacred books.

Specialized knowledge and really scientific culture, purged of any sacred or religious aura, become important political forces only in a highly advanced stage of civilization, and only then do they give access to membership in the ruling class to those who possess them. But in this case too, it is not so much learning in itself that has political value as the practical applications that may be made of learning to the profit of the public or the state. Sometimes all that is required is mere possession of the mechanical processes that are indispensable to the acquisition of a higher culture. This may be due to the fact that on such a basis it is easier to ascertain and measure the skill which a candidate has been able to acquire—it is easier to "mark" or grade him. So in certain periods in ancient Egypt the profession of scribe was a road to public office and power, perhaps because to have learned the hieroglyphic script was proof of long and patient study. In modern China, again, learning the numberless characters in Chinese script has formed the basis of the mandarin's education.[7] In present-day Europe and America the class that applies the findings of modern science to war, public administration, public works and public sanitation holds a fairly important position, both socially and politically, and in our western world, as in ancient Rome, an altogether privileged position is held by lawyers. They know the complicated legislation that arises in all peoples of long-standing civilization, and they become especially powerful if their knowledge of law is coupled with the type of eloquence that chances to have a strong appeal to the taste of their contemporaries.

There are examples in abundance where we see that long-standing practice in directing the military and civil organization of a community creates and develops in the higher reaches of the ruling class a real art of governing which is something better than crude empiricism and better than anything that mere individual experience could suggest. In such circumstances aristocracies of functionaries arise, such as the Roman senate, the Venetian nobility and to a certain extent the English aristocracy. Those bodies all stirred John Stuart Mill to admiration and certainly they all three developed governments that were distinguished for carefully considered policies and for great steadfastness and sagacity in carrying them out. This art of governing is not political science, though it has, at one time or another, anticipated applications of a number of the postulates of political science. However, even if the art of governing has now and again enjoyed prestige with certain classes of persons who have long held possession of political functions, knowledge of it has never served as an ordinary criterion for admitting to public offices persons who were barred from them by social station. The degree of mastery of the art of governing that a person possesses is, moreover, apart from exceptional cases, a very difficult thing to determine if the person has given no practical demonstration that he possesses it.

In some countries we find hereditary castes. In such cases the governing class is explicitly restricted to a given number of families, and birth is the one criterion that determines entry into the class or exclusion from it. Examples are exceedingly common. There is practically no country of long-standing civilization that has not had a hereditary aristocracy at one period or another in its history. We find hereditary nobilities during certain periods in China and ancient Egypt, in India, in Greece before the wars with the Medes, in ancient Rome, among the Slavs, among the Latins and Germans of the Middle Ages, in Mexico at the time of the Discovery and in Japan down to a few years ago.

In this connection two preliminary observations are in point. In the first place, all ruling classes tend to become hereditary in fact if not in law. All political forces seem to possess a quality that in physics used to be called the force of inertia. They have a tendency, that is, to remain at the point and in the state in which they find themselves. Wealth and military valor are easily maintained in certain families by moral tradition and by heredity. Qualification for important office—the habit of, and to an extent the capacity for, dealing with affairs of consequence—is much more readily acquired when one has had a certain familiarity with them from childhood. Even when academic degrees, scientific training, special aptitudes as tested by examinations and competitions, open the way to public office, there is no eliminating that special advantage in favor of certain individuals which the French call the advantage of *positions déjà prises.* In actual fact, though examinations and competitions may theoretically be open to all, the majority never have the resources for meeting the expense of long preparation, and many others are without the connections and kinships that set an individual promptly on the right road, enabling him to avoid the gropings and blunders that are inevitable when one enters an unfamiliar environment without any guidance or support.

The democratic principle of election by broad-based suffrage would seem at first glance to be in conflict with the tendency toward stability which, according to our theory, ruling classes show. But it must be noted that candidates who are successful in democratic elections are almost always the ones who possess the political forces above enumerated, which are very often hereditary. In the English, French and Italian parliaments we frequently see the sons, grandsons, brothers, nephews and sons-in-law of members and deputies, ex-members and ex-deputies.

In the second place, when we see a hereditary caste established in a country and monopolizing political power, we may be sure that such a status de jure was preceded by a similar status de facto. Before proclaiming their exclusive and hereditary right to power the families or castes in question must have held the scepter of command in a firm grasp, completely monopolizing all the political forces of that country at that period. Otherwise such a claim on their part would only have aroused the bitterest protests and provoked the bitterest struggles.

Hereditary aristocracies often come to vaunt supernatural origins, or at least origins different from, and superior to, those of the governed classes. Such claims are explained by a highly significant social fact, namely that every governing class tends to justify its actual exercise of power by resting it on some universal moral principle. This same sort of claim has come forward in our time in scientific trappings. A number of writers, developing and amplifying Darwin's theories, contend that upper classes represent a higher level in social evolution and are therefore superior to lower classes by organic structure. Gumplowicz we have already quoted. That writer goes to the point of maintaining that the divisions of populations into trade groups and professional classes in modern civilized countries are based on ethnological heterogeneousness.[8]

Now history very definitely shows the special abilities as well as the special defects—both very marked—which have been displayed by aristocracies that have either remained absolutely closed or have made entry into their circles difficult. The ancient Roman patriciate and the English and German nobilities of modern times give a ready idea of the type we refer to. Yet in dealing with this fact, and with the theories that tend to exaggerate its significance, we can always raise the same objection—that the individuals who belong to the aristocracies in question owe their special qualities not so much to the blood that flows in their veins as to their very particular upbringing, which has brought out certain intellectual and moral tendencies in them in preference to others.

Among all the factors that figure in social superiority, intellectual superiority is the one with which heredity has least to do. The children of men of highest mentality often have very mediocre talents. That is why hereditary aristocracies have never defended their rule on the basis of intellectual superiority alone, but rather on the basis of their superiorities in character and wealth.

It is argued, in rebuttal, that education and environment may serve to explain superiorities in strictly intellectual capacities but not differences of a moral order—will power, courage, pride, energy. The truth is that social position, family tradition, the habits of the class in which we live, contribute more than is commonly supposed to the greater or lesser development of the qualities mentioned. If we carefully observe individuals who have changed their social status, whether for better or for worse, and who consequently find themselves in environments different from the ones they have been accustomed to, it is apparent that their intellectual capacities are much less sensibly affected than their moral ones. Apart from a greater breadth of view that education and experience bring to anyone who is not altogether stupid, every individual, whether he remains a mere clerk or becomes a minister of state, whether he reaches the rank of sergeant or the rank of general, whether he is a millionaire or a beggar, abides inevitably on the intellectual level on which nature has placed him. And yet with changes of social status and wealth the proud man often becomes humble, servility changes to arrogance, an honest nature learns to lie, or at least to dissemble, under pressure of need, while the man who has an ingrained habit of lying and bluffing makes himself over and puts on an outward semblance at least of honesty and firmness of character. It is true, of course, that a man fallen from high estate often acquires powers of resignation, self-denial and resourcefulness, just as one who rises in the world sometimes gains in sentiments of justice and fairness. In short, whether a man change for the better or for the worse, he has to be exceptionally level-headed if he is to change his social status very appreciably and still keep his character unaltered. Mirabeau remarked that, for any man, any great climb on the social ladder produces a crisis that cures the ills he has and creates new ones that he never had before.[9]

Courage in battle, impetuousness in attack, endurance in resistance —such are the qualities that have long and often been vaunted as a monopoly of the higher classes. Certainly there may be vast natural and —if we may say so—innate differences between one individual and another in these respects; but more than anything else traditions and environmental influences are the things that keep them high, low or just average, in any large group of human beings. We generally become indifferent to danger or, perhaps better, to a given type of danger, when the persons with whom we daily live speak of it with indifference and remain cool and imperturbable before it. Many mountaineers or sailors are by nature timid men, yet they face unmoved, the ones the dangers of the precipice, the others the perils of the storm at sea. So peoples and classes that are accustomed to warfare maintain military virtues at the highest pitch.

So true is this that even peoples and social classes which are ordinarily unaccustomed to arms acquire the military virtues rapidly when the individuals who compose them are made members of organizations in which courage and daring are traditions, when—if one may venture the metaphor—they are cast into human crucibles that are heavily charged with the sentiments that are to be infused into their fiber. Mohammed II recruited his terrible Janizaries in the main from boys who had been kidnapped among the degenerate Greeks of Byzantium. The much despised Egyptian fellah, unused for long centuries to war and accustomed to remaining meek and helpless under the lash of the oppressor, became a good soldier when Mehemet Ali placed him in Turkish or Albanian regiments. The French nobility has always enjoyed a reputation for brilliant valor, but down to the end of the eighteenth century that quality was not credited in anything like the same degree to the French bourgeoisie. However, the wars of the Republic and the Empire amply proved that nature had been uniformly lavish in her endowments of courage upon all the inhabitants of France. Proletariat and bourgeoisie both furnished good soldiers and, what is more, excellent officers, though talent for command had been considered an exclusive prerogative of the nobility. Gumplowicz's theory that differentiation in social classes depends very largely on ethnological antecedents requires proof at the very least. Many facts to the contrary readily occur to one—among others the obvious fact that branches of the same family often belong to widely different social classes.

Finally, if we were to keep to the idea of those who maintain the exclusive influence of the hereditary principle in the formation of ruling classes, we should be carried to a conclusion somewhat like the one to which we were carried by the evolutionary principle: The political history of mankind ought to be much simpler than it is. If the ruling class really belonged to a different race, or if the qualities that fit it for dominion were transmitted primarily by organic heredity, it is difficult to see how, once the class was formed, it could decline and lose its power. The peculiar qualities of a race are exceedingly tenacious. Keeping to the evolutionary theory, acquired capacities in the parents are inborn in their children and, as generation succeeds generation, are progressively accentuated. The descendants of rulers, therefore, ought to become better and better fitted to rule, and the other classes ought to see their chances of challenging or supplanting them become more and more remote. Now the most commonplace experience suffices to assure one that things do not go in that way at all.

What we see is that as soon as there is a shift in the balance of political forces—when, that is, a need is felt that capacities different from the old should assert themselves in the management of the state, when the old capacities, therefore, lose some of their importance or changes in their distribution occur—then the manner in which the ruling class is constituted changes also. If a new source of wealth develops in a society, if the practical importance of knowledge grows, if an old religion declines or a new one is born, if a new current of ideas spreads, then, simultaneously, far-reaching dislocations occur in the ruling class. One might say, indeed, that the whole history of civilized mankind comes down to a conflict between the tendency of dominant elements to monopolize political power and transmit possession of it by inheritance, and the tendency toward a dislocation of old forces and an insurgence of new forces; and this conflict produces an unending ferment of endosmosis and exosmosis between the upper classes and certain portions of the lower. Ruling classes decline inevitably when they cease to find scope for the capacities through which they rose to power, when they can no longer render the social services which they once rendered, or when their talents and the services they render lose in importance in the social environment in which they live. So the Roman aristocracy declined when it was no longer the exclusive source of higher officers for the army, of administrators for the commonwealth, of governors for the provinces. So the Venetian aristocracy declined when its nobles ceased to command the galleys and no longer passed the greater part of their lives in sailing the seas and in trading and fighting.

In inorganic nature we have the example of our air, in which a tendency to immobility produced by the force of inertia is continuously in conflict with a tendency to shift about as the result of inequalities in the distribution of heat. The two tendencies, prevailing by turn in various regions on our planet, produce now calm, now wind and storm. In much the same way in human societies there prevails now the tendency that produces closed, stationary, crystallized ruling classes, now the tendency that results in a more or less rapid renovation of ruling classes.

The Oriental societies which we consider stationary have in reality not always been so, for otherwise, as we have already pointed out, they could not have made the advances in civilization of which they have left irrefutable evidence. It is much more accurate to say that we came to know them at a time when their political forces and their political classes were in a period of crystallization. The same thing occurs in what we commonly call "aging" societies, where religious beliefs, scientific knowledge, methods of producing and distributing wealth have for centuries undergone no radical alteration and have not been disturbed in their everyday course by infiltrations of foreign elements, material or intellectual. In such societies political forces are always the same, and the class that holds possession of them holds a power that is undisputed. Power is therefore perpetuated in certain families, and the inclination to immobility becomes general through all the various strata in that society.

So in India we see the caste system become thoroughly entrenched after the suppression of Buddhism. The Greeks found hereditary castes in ancient Egypt, but we know that in the periods of greatness and renaissance in Egyptian civilization political office and social status were not hereditary. We possess an Egyptian document that summarizes the life of a high army officer who lived during the period of the expulsion of the Hyksos. He had begun his career as a simple soldier. Other documents show cases in which the same individual served successively in army, civil administration and priesthood.[10]

The best-known and perhaps the most important example of a

society tending toward crystallization is the period in Roman history that used to be called the Low Empire. There, after several centuries of almost complete social immobility, a division between two classes grew sharper and sharper, the one made up of great landowners and high officials, the other made up of slaves, farmers and urban plebeians. What is even more striking, public office and social position became hereditary by custom before they became hereditary by law, and the trend was rapidly generalized during the period mentioned.[11]

On the other hand it may happen in the history of a nation that commerce with foreign peoples, forced emigrations, discoveries, wars, create new poverty and new wealth, disseminate knowledge of things that were previously unknown or cause infiltrations of new moral, intellectual and religious currents. Or again—as a result of such infiltrations or through a slow process of inner growth, or from both causes—it may happen that a new learning arises, or that certain elements of an old, long forgotten learning return to favor so that new ideas and new beliefs come to the fore and upset the intellectual habits on which the obedience of the masses has been founded. The ruling class may also be vanquished and destroyed in whole or in part by foreign invasions, or, when the circumstances just mentioned arise, it may be driven from power by the advent of new social elements who are strong in fresh political forces. Then, naturally, there comes a period of renovation, or, if one prefer, of revolution, during which individual energies have free play and certain individuals, more passionate, more energetic, more intrepid or merely shrewder than others, force their way from the bottom of the social ladder to the topmost rungs.

Once such a movement has set in, it cannot be stopped immediately. The example of individuals who have started from nowhere and reached prominent positions fires new ambitions, new greeds, new energies, and this molecular rejuvenation of the ruling class continues vigorously until a long period of social stability slows it down again. We need hardly mention examples of nations in such periods of renovation. In our age that would be superfluous. Rapid restocking of ruling classes is a frequent and very striking phenomenon in countries that have been recently colonized. When social life begins in such environments, there is no ready-made ruling class, and while such a class is in process of formation, admittance to it is gained very easily. Monopolization of land and other agencies of production is, if not quite impossible, at any rate more difficult than elsewhere. That is why, at least during a certain period, the

Greek colonies offered a wide outlet for all Greek energy and enterprise. That is why, in the United States, where the colonizing of new lands continued through the whole nineteenth century and new industries were continually springing up, examples of men who started with nothing and have attained fame and wealth are still frequent—all of which helps to foster in the people of that country the illusion that democracy is a fact.

Suppose now that a society gradually passes from its feverish state to calm. Since the human being's psychological tendencies are always the same, those who belong to the ruling class will begin to acquire a group spirit. They will become more and more exclusive and learn better and better the art of monopolizing to their advantage the qualities and capacities that are essential to acquiring power and holding it. Then, at last, the force that is essentially conservative appears—the force of habit. Many people become resigned to a lowly station, while the members of certain privileged families or classes grow convinced that they have almost an absolute right to high station and command.

A philanthropist would certainly be tempted to inquire whether mankind is happier—or less unhappy—during periods of social stability and crystallization, when everyone is almost fated to remain in the social station to which he was born, or during the directly opposite periods of renovation and revolution, which permit all to aspire to the most exalted positions and some to attain them. Such an inquiry would be difficult. The answer would have to take account of many qualifications and exceptions, and might perhaps always be influenced by the personal preferences of the observer. We shall therefore be careful not to venture on any answer of our own. Besides, even if we could reach an undebatable conclusion, it would have a very slight practical utility; for the sad fact is that what the philosophers and theologians call free will—in other words, spontaneous choice by individuals—has so far had, and will perhaps always have, little influence, if any at all, in hastening either the ending or the beginning of one of the historical periods mentioned.

THE POLITICAL FORMULA

As we have just seen, in fairly populous societies that have attained a certain level of civilization, ruling classes do not justify their power exclusively by de facto possession of it, but try to find a moral and legal basis for it, representing it as the logical and necessary consequence of doctrines and beliefs that are generally recognized and accepted. So if a society is deeply imbued with the Christian spirit the political class will govern by the will of the sovereign, who, in turn, will reign because he is God's anointed. So too in Mohammedan societies political authority is exercised directly in the name of the caliph, or vicar, of the Prophet, or in the name of someone who has received investiture, tacit or explicit, from the caliph. The Chinese mandarins ruled the state because they were supposed to be interpreters of the will of the Son of Heaven, who had received from heaven the mandate to govern paternally, and in accordance with the rules of the Confucian ethic, "the people of the hundred families." The complicated hierarchy of civil and military functionaries in the Roman Empire rested upon the will of the emperor, who, at least down to Diocletian's time, was assumed by a legal fiction to have received from the people a mandate to rule the commonwealth. The powers of all lawmakers, magistrates and government officials in the United States emanate directly or indirectly from the vote of the voters, which is held to be the expression of the sovereign will of the whole American people.

This legal and moral basis, or principle, on which the power of the political class rests, is what we have elsewhere called, and shall continue here to call, the "political formula." (Writers on the philosophy of law generally call it the "principle of sovereignty."[12]) The political formula can hardly be the same in two or more different societies; and fundamental or even notable similarities between two or more political formulas appear only where the peoples professing them have the same type of civilization (or—to use an expression which we shall shortly define—belong to the same social type). According to the level of civilization in the peoples among whom they are current, the various political formulas may be based either upon supernatural beliefs or upon concepts which, if they do not correspond to positive realities, at least appear to be rational. We shall not say that they correspond in either case to scientific truths. A conscientious observer would be obliged to confess that, if no one has ever seen the authentic document by which the Lord empowered certain privileged persons or families to rule his people on his behalf, neither can it be maintained that a popular election, however liberal the suffrage may be, is ordinarily the expression of the will of a people, or even of the will of the majority of a people.

And yet that does not mean that political formulas are mere quackeries, aptly invented to trick the masses into obedience. Anyone who viewed them in that light would fall into grave error. The truth is that they answer a real need in man's social nature; and this need, so universally felt, of governing and knowing that one is governed not on the basis of mere material or intellectual force, but on the basis of a moral principle, has beyond any doubt a practical and a real importance.

Spencer wrote that the divine right of Kings was the great superstition of past ages, and that the divine right of elected assemblies is the great superstition of our present age. The idea cannot be called wholly mistaken, but certainly it does not consider or exhaust all aspects of the question. It is further necessary to see whether a society can hold together without one of these "great superstitions"—whether a universal illusion is not a social force that contributes powerfully to consolidating political organization and unifying peoples or even whole civilizations.

Mankind is divided into social groups each of which is set apart from other groups by beliefs, sentiments, habits and interests that are peculiar to it. The individuals who belong to one such group are held together by a consciousness of common brotherhood and held apart from other groups by passions and tendencies that are more or less antagonistic and mutually repellent. As we have already indicated, the political formula must be based upon the special beliefs and the strongest sentiments of the social group in which it is current, or at least upon the beliefs and sentiments of the particular portion of that group which holds political preeminence. . . .

NOTES

1. Mosca, *Teorica dei governi e governo parlamentare,* chap. I.
2. Mickiewicz, *Les Slaves,* vol. I, leçon XXIV, pp. 376-380; *Histoire populaire de Pologne,* chaps. I-II.
3. Leroy-Beaulieu, *L'Empire des tzars et les Russes,* vol. I, pp. 338 f.
4. Jannet, *Le istituzioni politiche e sociali degli Stati Uniti d'America,* part II, chap. X f.
5. Rousset, *À travers la Chine.*
6. Mas y Sans, *La Chine et les puissances chrétiennes,* vol. II, pp. 332-334, Huc, *L'Empire chinois.*
7. This was true up to a few years ago, the examination of a mandarin covering only literary and historical studies—as the Chinese understood such studies, of course.

8. *Der Rassenkampf.* This notion transpires from Gumplowicz's whole volume. It is explicitly formulated in book II, chap. XXXIII.
9. *Correspondance entre le comte de Mirabeau et le comte de La Marck,* vol. II, p. 223.
10. Lenormant, Maspero, Brugsch.
11. Marquardt, *Manuel des antiquités romaines;* Fustel de Coulanges, *Nouvelles recherches sur quelques problèmes d'histoire.*
12. Mosca, *Teorica dei governi e governo parlamentare,* chap. I; see also Mosca, *Le constituzioni moderne.*

KARL MARX'S THEORY OF ELITES

T. B. Bottomore

Marx's theory may be stated briefly in the following propositions:
1. In every society beyond the most primitive, two categories of people may be distinguished:
a) a ruling class, and
b) one or more subject classes.
2. The dominant position of the ruling class is to be explained by its possession of the major instruments of economic production, but its political dominance is consolidated by the hold which it establishes over military force and over the production of ideas.
3. There is perpetual conflict between the ruling class and the subject class or classes; and the nature and course of such conflict is influenced primarily by the development of productive forces, i.e., by changes in technology.
4. The lines of class conflict are most sharply drawn in the modern capitalist societies, because in such societies the divergence of economic interests appears most clearly, unobscured by any personal bonds such as those of feudal society, and because the development of capitalism brings about a more radical polarization of classes than has existed in any other type of society, by its unrivalled concentration of wealth at one extreme of society and of poverty at the other, and by its gradual elimination of the intermediate and transitional social strata.
5. The class struggle within capitalist society will end with the victory of the working class, and this victory will be followed by the construction of a classless society. A number of reasons are advanced for expecting the advent of a classless society. First, the tendency of modern capitalism is to create a homogeneous working class, from which it is unlikely that new social divisions will spring in the future. Secondly, the revolutionary struggle of the workers itself engenders cooperation and a sentiment of

From *Elites and Society* by T. B. Bottomore, Basic Books, Inc., Publishers, New York, 1965. Reprinted by permission.

brotherhood, and this sentiment is strengthened by the moral and social doctrines which the revolutionary movement produces, and which have been absorbed into Marx's own thought. Thirdly, capitalism creates the material and cultural preconditions for a classless society—the material conditions by its immense productivity which renders possible the satisfaction of the basic needs of all men and removes the edge from the struggle for physical survival, and the cultural conditions by overcoming the "idiocy of rural life," promoting literacy, diffusing scientific knowledge, and engaging the mass of the people in political life.

POWER, FORCE, AND MORALITY

Gerhard Lenski

Of all the concepts used by sociologists, few are the source of more confusion and misunderstanding than power. Hence it is necessary to spell out in some detail the nature of this concept and how it functions in the distributive process.

As a starting point, [we shall assume] that survival is the chief goal of the great majority of men. If this is so, then it follows that *the ability to take life is the most effective form of power.* In other words, more men will respond more readily to the threat of the use of *force* than to any other. In effect, it constitutes the final court of appeals in human affairs; there is no appeal from force in a given situation except the exercise of superior force. Hence force stands in the same relationship to other forms of power as trumps to the other suits in the game of bridge, and those who can exercise the greatest force are like those who control trumps.

This fact has been recognized by countless observers of the human scene in every age. As Pascal put it, "Not being able to make that which is just strong, man has made that which is strong just." Cicero made the same point when he said, "Laws are dumb in the midst of arms," and Hobbes asserted that "Covenants without the sword are but words, and of no strength to secure a man at all."

This principle is also recognized by the leaders of nations, the practical men of affairs. Every sovereign state restricts, and where possible prohibits, the independent exercise of force by its subjects. States may be tolerant of many things, but never of the growth of independent military organizations within their territories. The reason is obvious: any government which cannot suppress each and every forceful challenge to its authority is overthrown. Force is the foundation of sovereignty.

On this point there is no dispute between conservatives and radicals. Their arguments are concerned only with the ends served by the state's use of force. Conservatives insist that might is employed only as the handmaiden of right, to restrain and rebuke those who put self-interest above the common good, while radicals maintain that the state employs might to suppress right, in defense of selfish interests.

If force is the foundation of political sovereignty, it is also the foundation of the distributive system in every society where there is a surplus to be divided. Where coercive power is weak, challenges inevitably occur, and the system is eventually destroyed and replaced by another based more firmly on force. Men struggling over control of the surplus of a society will not accept defeat so long as there is a higher court of appeals to which they may take their case with some likelihood of success and profit to themselves.

The principle involved here is essentially the same as the principle of escalation with which modern military men are so concerned. Small wars based on small weapons inevitably grow into more deadly wars utilizing more deadly weapons if, by advancing the level of conflict, one of the parties anticipates turning defeat into victory. Similarly, in the case of conflicts within societies, the parties involved are always motivated to take the issue to the final court of appeals so long as there is the likelihood of benefiting by it. While men will not resort to armed revolution for trivial gains, when control over the entire surplus of a society is involved, the prospect is more enticing. The attractiveness varies directly with the weakness of the current regime.

Nevertheless, as Edmund Burke, the famed English conservative, recognized, "The use of force alone is but temporary. It may subdue for a moment; but it does not remove the necessity of subduing again: and a nation is not governed, which is perpetually to be conquered." Though force is the most effective instrument for seizing power in a society, and though it always remains the foundation of any system of inequality, it is not the most effective instrument for retaining and exploiting a position of power and deriving the maximum benefits from it. Therefore, regardless of the objectives of a new regime, once organized opposition has been destroyed it is to its advantage to make increasing use of other techniques and instruments of control, and to allow force to recede into the background to be used only when other techniques fail.

If the new elite has materialistic goals and is concerned solely with self-aggrandizement, it soon discovers that the rule of might is both inefficient and costly. So long as it relies on force, much of the profit is consumed by the costs of coercion. If the population obeys only out of fear of physical violence, a large portion of the time, energy, and wealth of the elite are invariably consumed in the effort to keep it under control and separate the producers from the product of their labors. Even worse, honor, which normally ranks high in the scale of human values, is denied to those who rule by force alone.[1]

If materialistic elites have strong motives for shifting from the rule of might to the rule of right, ideologically motivated elites have even stronger. If the visions and ideals which led them to undertake the terrible risks and hardships of revolution are ever to be fulfilled, the voluntary cooperation of the population is essential, and this cannot be obtained by force. Force is, at best, the means to an end. That end, the establishment of a new social order, can never be fully attained until most members of society freely accept it as their own. The purpose of the revolution is to destroy the old elite and their institutions, which prevent the fulfillment of this dream. Once they are destroyed, an ideological elite strives to rule by persuasion. Thus *those who seize power by force find it advantageous to legitimize their rule once effective organized opposition is eliminated.* Force can no longer continue to play the role it did. It can no longer function as the private resource of a special segment of the population. Rather it must be transformed into a public resource used in the defense of law and order.

This may seem to be the equivalent of saying that those who have at great risk to themselves displaced the old elite must now give up all they have won. Actually, however, this is not at all necessary since, with a limited exercise of intelligence, force can be transformed into authority, and might into right.

There are various means by which this transformation can be effected. To begin with, by virtue of its coercive power, a new elite is in a good position to rewrite the law of the land as it sees fit. This affords them a unique opportunity, since by its very nature law is identified with justice and the rule of right. Since legal statutes are stated in general and impersonal terms, they appear to support abstract principles of justice rather than the special interests of particular men or classes of men. The fact that laws exist prior to the events to which they are applied suggests an objective impartiality which also contributes to their acceptance. Yet laws can always be written in such a way that they favor some particular segment of society. Anatole France saw this clearly when he wrote, "The law in its majestic equality forbids the rich as well as the poor to sleep under bridges, to beg in the street, and to steal bread." Edwin Sutherland provided detailed documentation of the presence of such bias, as have a host of others.[2] In short, laws may be written in such a way that they protect the interests of the elite while being couched in very general, universalistic terms.

Often a new elite finds that it does not even need to change the laws to accomplish its ends. Typically the old laws were written to serve the interests of the holders of certain key offices, and once these offices have been seized, the new elite can use them as resources to build their fortunes or attain other goals.

Institutions which shape public opinion serve as a second instrument for legitimizing the position of new elites. Through the use of a combination of inducements and threats, educational and religious institutions, together with the mass media and other molders of public opinion, can usually be transformed into instruments of propaganda for the new regime. A determined and intelligent elite working through them can usually surround itself with an aura of legitimacy within a few months or years.

The concept of "propaganda," or the manipulation of consensus, is an integral element in the synthetic theory of stratification. A recognition of this phenomenon and the special role it plays in the distributive process enables us to avoid the impasse which has driven Dahrendorf and others to despair of ever reconciling the conservative and radical traditions. Consensus and coercion are more closely related than those who preach the Janus-headed character of society would have us believe. *Coercive power can often be used to create a new consensus.*

There is probably no better example of this than the Soviet Union. Here a small minority seized control of the machinery of state in 1917 and used the coercive powers of the state to transform the educational system of the nation and the mass media into one gigantic instrument of propaganda. Within a single generation the vast majority of Russians were converted to a sincere and genuine support of most of the basic elements of the Communist Party's program.[3]

In the short run, propaganda may be used to support a great variety of programs and policies adopted by an elite. In the long run, however, its basic aim is the dissemination of an ideology which provides a moral justification for the regime's exercise of power. Gaetano Mosca put it this way:

> Ruling classes do not justify their power exclusively by *de facto* possession of it, but try to find a moral and legal basis for it, representing it as the logical and necessary consequence of doctrines and beliefs that are generally recognized and accepted.[4]

Most of the theories of political sovereignty debated by philosophers have been intellectualized versions of some popular ideology. This can be seen in the now discredited belief in the divine right of kings. In our own day, the belief in popular sovereignty serves the same justifying function. A basic element in our current American ideology is the thesis expressed by Lincoln that ours is a "government of the people, by the people, for the people." Another basic element is incorporated in Francis Scott Key's oft-sung phrase, "the land of the free." It is difficult to exaggerate the contribution of these beliefs to the political stability of our present political system and of the distributive system based on it.

Finally, the transformation of the rule of might into the rule of right is greatly facilitated by the pressures of daily life, which severely limit the political activities of the vast majority of mankind. Though the majority may become politically active in a significant way for a brief time in a revolutionary era, the necessity of securing a livelihood quickly drives most from the political arena. For better or worse, few men have the financial resources which enable them to set aside their usual economic activities for long. As a result, the affairs of state in any civilized society, and in many that are not, are directed by a small minority. The majority are largely apolitical. Even in popular democracies the vast majority do no more than cast a ballot at infrequent intervals. The formulation of public policy and the various other tasks required by the system are left in the hands of a tiny minority. This greatly facilitates the task of a new regime as it seeks to make the transition from the rule of might to the rule of right.

THE RULE OF RIGHT

On first consideration it may seem that the rule of right is merely the rule of might in a new guise, and therefore no real change can be expected in the distributive process. Such a view is as unwarranted as that which denies the role might continues to play in support of vested interests, even under the rule of right. The fact is that, as the basis of power is shifted from might to right, certain subtle but important changes occur which have far-reaching consequences.

To begin with, if the powers of the regime are to be accepted as rightful and legitimate they must be exercised in some degree, at least, in accord with the conceptions of justice and morality held by the majority—conceptions which spring from their self-interest and partisan group interests. Thus, even though the laws promulgated by a new elite may be heavily slanted to favor themselves, there are limits beyond which this cannot be carried if they wish to gain the benefits of the rule of right.

Second, after the shift to the rule of law, the interests of any single member of the elite can no longer safely be equated with the interests of the elite as a whole. For example, if a member of the new elite enters into a contractual arrangement with some member of the nonelite, and this turns out badly for him, it is to his interest to ignore the law and break the contract. However, this is not to the interest of the other members of the elite since most contractual arrangements work to their benefit. Therefore, it is to their interest to enforce the law in support of the claims of the nonelite to preserve respect for the law with all the benefits this provides them.

Vilfredo Pareto, the great Italian scholar who has contributed so much to our understanding of these problems, has pointed out a third change associated with the shift from the rule of might to the rule of right. As he observed, those who have won power by force will, under the rule of right, gradually be replaced by a new kind of person and in time these persons will form a new kind of elite. To describe the nature of this change, Pareto wrote of the passing of governmental power from "the lions" to "the foxes."[5] The lions are skilled in the use of force, the foxes in the use of cunning. In other words, the shift from the rule of might means that new skills become essential, and therefore there is a high probability that many of the elite will be displaced because they lack these skills. This displacement is greatly facilitated by the fact that the interests of the elite as a class are no longer identical with the interests of each individual member, which means that individually they become vulnerable. Even those who hang on are forced to change, so that in time the nature of the elite as a class is substantially altered, provided it is not destroyed first by a new leonine revolution or coup. Though this change means increased reliance on intelligence and less on force, as Pareto's choice of the term "fox" and his emphasis on "cunning" indicate, the shift to the rule of right is not the beginning of the millennium when lambs can lie down safely with lions—or foxes. Nor is it the end of the era in which self-interest and partisan group interests dominate human action.

As Pareto's analysis suggests, the rule of the foxes means not merely the rise and fall of individuals, but also changes in the power position of whole classes. Specifically, it means some decline in the position of the military and a corresponding rise by the commercial class and the class of professional politicians, both of which are traditionally skilled in the use of cunning. To a lesser degree, it means some improvement in the status of most of the nonmanual classes engaged in peaceful, civilian pursuits.

Fourth, and finally, the transition from the rule of might to the rule of right usually means greater decentralization of power. Under the rule of might, all power tends to be concentrated in the hands of an inner circle of the dominant elite and their agents. Independent centers of power are viewed as a threat and hence are destroyed or taken over. Under the rule of right, however, this is not the case. So long as they remain subject to the law, diverse centers of power can develop and compete side by side. This development is not inevitable, but it can, and probably will, happen once the elite no longer has to fear for the survival of the new regime. As many observers have noted, the degree of unity within a group tends to be a function of the degree to which the members perceive their existence as threatened by others.

In view of these changes, it becomes clear that shifts from the rule of might to the rule of right and vice versa constitute one of the more important sources of variation within societal types defined in technological terms. In other words, even among societies at the same level of technological development, we must expect differences along the lines indicated above, reflecting differences in their position on the might-right continuum.

THE VARIETIES OF INSTITUTIONALIZED POWER

As the foregoing makes clear, *with the shift from the rule of might to the rule of right, power continues to be the determinant of privilege, but the forms of power change.* Force is replaced by institutionalized forms of power as the most useful resource in the struggle between individuals and groups for prestige and privilege, though force still remains in the picture as the ultimate guarantee of these more genteel forms.

Institutionalized power differs from force in a number of ways which deserve note. To begin with, it is a socially acceptable form of power, which means that those who exercise it are less likely to be challenged and more likely to obtain popular support than are those who use force. Second, institutionalized power tends to be much more impersonal. Individuals claim the benefits of institutionalized power not because of their personal qualities or accomplishments, which might easily be challenged, but simply because they occupy a certain role or office or own a certain piece of property. To be sure, it is often assumed that those who enjoy the benefits of institutionalized power are entitled to them by virtue of superior accomplishments or personal qualities, but this is not the crucial issue and the beneficiary does not have to demonstrate these things. It is enough just to be the occupant of the role or office or the owner of the property. Institutionalized power insures that the benefits flow automatically to such persons without regard to their personal qualities or accomplishments. This is, of course, the chief reason why those who gain power by force strive to convert force into institutionalized power.

Institutionalized power takes many forms, but it always involves the possession of certain enforceable rights which increase one's capacity to carry out one's own will even in the face of opposition. It would be impossible to identify and discuss all these many forms here, but it is important to identify some of the more basic and show their varied nature.[6]

One of the basic distinctions within the category of institutionalized power is that between *authority* and *influence.* Authority is the enforceable right to command others. Influence, by contrast, is much more subtle. It is the ability to manipulate the social situation of others, or their perception of it, by the exercise of one's resources and rights, thereby increasing the pressures on others to act in accordance with one's own wishes.[7] Though these two forms of institutionalized power are quite distinct on the analytical level, they are often hopelessly intertwined on the empirical.

Institutionalized power varies not only in the mode of its action but also in terms of the foundations on which it rests. Here one can speak of a distinction between *the power of position* and *the power of property.* The power of position means *the power which rightfully belongs to the incumbent of any social role or organizational office possessing authority or influence.* This can be seen in the case of officers of state who enjoy great authority and influence so long as they continue to occupy their post, but who lose it when they are replaced. While this is one of the more impressive examples of the power of position, the same basic phenomenon can be seen in the case of the incumbents of a host of lesser roles. One must include under this heading not merely positions in political organizations, but also those in economic, religious, educational, and military organizations, together with age and sex roles, roles in kin groups, roles in racial and ethnic groups, and every other kind of role or office with authority or influence.

A second foundation on which institutionalized power commonly rests is the *private ownership of property.* Though property and position have often been closely linked, the connection is neither necessary nor inevitable. The ownership of property is frequently dissociated from occupancy of a particular office or role. Since property is, by definition, something in short supply and hence of value, the owner of property controls a resource which can be used to influence the actions of others. The more he owns, the greater is his capacity to influence, and thus the greater his power. In some instances, as in the ownership of slaves or of a political office which has been purchased, the power of property can take the form of authority. It also takes the form of authority to the extent that the owner is entitled to proscribe certain actions by others —that is, order them *not* to do certain things, such as trespass on his land.

Before concluding this brief introduction to institutionalized power, it may be well to take note of Simmel's observation that where the rule of law or right prevails, there is always a two-way flow of influence (and sometimes, one might add, of authority as well) between the more powerful and the less powerful.[8] This point is easily forgotten, since the very concept "power" suggests a one-directional flow. To say that there is a two-way flow does not mean that the flow is equally strong in both directions, but it does mean that one should not ignore the secondary flow or the factors responsible for it and the consequences of it.[9]

POLITICAL CYCLES

As a reading of history makes clear, there has usually been a more or less cyclical alternation in human societies between periods in which the rule of might held sway and others in which the rule of right was dominant to greater or lesser degree. These political "cycles," as I shall call them, each span the existence of a given political regime.[10] Each cycle begins with the forcible seizure of power by a new elite and involves an initial phase of violence during which organized resistance is either destroyed or suppressed. The next phase is one in which the regime strives to reduce its dependence on naked force and to increase its legitimate authority. During this phase the trend toward constitutionalism, or the rule of right, may be halted or even reversed if the power of the elite is seriously challenged by forces either at home or abroad. However, unless there is a steady succession of such challenges, the long term trend involves a reduction in the active role of force and coercion and an increase in the role of persuasion and incentive until finally the cycle comes to an end when the regime is overthrown by its successor or some foreign conqueror.

To introduce the concept of cycles into our theory is not to imply that history repeats itself or that one cycle is exactly like another. Obviously cycles differ in a number of significant ways.

To begin with, cycles do not have any uniform duration. Some are very brief, as in the case of the cycle which began in Russia with the February Revolution of 1917 and ended with the October Revolution in the same year. Others extend over centuries, as in the case of the present British cycle, which dates back to the middle of the seventeenth century.

Short cycles differ considerably from those of longer duration. Because they are so brief, the process of legitimation, or constitutionalism hardly gets started, and a new era of violence may be instituted before the last has really ended.

Even where cycles are of comparable duration, other factors inevitably influence the progress of constitutionalism, either hindering or promoting its growth. For example, the nature of the struggles which initiate the cycle can be quite important. Other things being equal, constitutionalism develops more quickly after a prolonged and bitter war to free the nation from foreign tyranny than after a revolution which sets brother against brother. The nature of the preceding regime or regimes is also likely to have some effect. Societies which have never developed a tradition of constitutional government move more slowly in this direction than those which have such a tradition. Also, it is logical to predict that the traditions of constitutionalism develop more quickly after a brief and limited palace revolution than after a prolonged and far-reaching social revolution.

The economic situation of a nation is also likely to affect the degree to which constitutionalism develops. One would predict that a high level of productivity and a rapid advance in the level of productivity would each be conducive to the development of constitutional government.

Both provide increased opportunities for men to satisfy their desires without recourse to violence.

Taking all of the foregoing together, it may be predicted that *constitutional government will be most highly developed where (1) the political cycle is of long duration, (2) the present regime was established during a war of national independence, (3) constitutional government flourished before the present cycle began, (4) there have been few, if any, serious threats to the existing regime, (5) a high level of productivity prevails, and (6) there is a period of rapid economic development.* In short, the full flowering of constitutional government depends upon a peculiar combination of circumstances which have not occurred often in human history.

Other important differences in political cycles are linked with the nature of the elite which overthrew the old regime and dominated the first phase of the new cycle. Sometimes plunder and self-aggrandizement are their sole concern; these may be called "materialistic" elites. Trujillo's regime in the Dominican Republic and the Saudi dynasty in Arabia are classic examples from recent history.

In some instances, however, elites are motivated by ideals and visions of a more equitable social order. These may be called "ideological" elites.[11] The Communist regimes which won control in Russia, Yugoslavia, and China in recent decades are examples of this type of elite.

Frequently there is some mixing of these two elements, and sometimes this mixture is highly complex. For example, a frank and honest appraisal of the American Revolution indicates that both elements were present. While some of the Founding Fathers were chiefly concerned with the attainment of the noble ideals set forth in the Declaration of Independence and the Preamble to the Constitution, others were more concerned with avoiding the payment of taxes to the British crown. The fact that materialistic and ideological elements are sometimes intermingled suggests that we must think of this distinction in variable, rather than categorical terms.

When one materialistic elite succeeds another, only minor changes are likely in the distributive system. One gang of rascals replaces another in those public offices which provide the best opportunities for plunder. These are often called "palace revolutions," since all that is involved is a turnover in personnel in the elite positions. Sometimes, if such an elite is especially vigorous and inventive, these changes in personnel may be accompanied by changes in the formal structure of government. A republic may give way to a monarchy, or vice versa. Such changes may be motivated by a desire either to make the government a more efficient instrument of plunder or to simulate social reforms and thus for a time to silence potential critics.

When ideological elements are dominant in a successful elite, much more substantial changes can be expected in both the political and the distributive systems. Along with sweeping changes in personnel, there are usually pervasive and meaningful changes in the structure of government (and often other basic institutions as well). The term "social revolution" is often employed to emphasize the difference between this type of revolution and "palace revolutions." The labels are not important, but the differences to which they direct attention are: palace revolutions affect only the few, while social revolutions affect everyone—even the Dr. Zhivagos who strive mightily to ignore them.

While the differences between political cycles should never be minimized, neither should the underlying similarities. In every society there is a natural tendency for those who seize power by force to strive to rule by constitutional means, so far as circumstances permit. Yet in the end every regime is destroyed by force or the threat of it. This is the basic theme on which there are a thousand variations.

Cyclical theories have never had a great appeal for Americans, who, because of their peculiar national experience, have inclined to more optimistic theories of history. For those chiefly familiar with American history, supplemented somewhat by an acquaintance with British history, it has been easy to interpret history as a whole, including the political component, as one more or less consistent movement from the crude, the primitive, and the tyrannical, to the efficient, the productive, and the democratic. Unfortunately, when we broaden our horizons to take account of Cuba, Paraguay, Bolivia, Argentina, Brazil, Peru, Hungary, Yugoslavia, France, Poland, Germany, Russia, Syria, Iran, India, Vietnam, China, and indeed most of the rest of the world, our faith in the progressive character of political history is badly shaken. For who would dare assert that there has been any progressive trend of long duration leading to an increase in either constitutional or democratic government in these nations?

Progressive theories of political development are likely to find wide acceptance only in those societies fortunate enough to enjoy an unusually long cycle during which the legitimation process can come to full flower. Britain and the United States have been unusually fortunate in this regard, with the former enjoying a cycle now three centuries old and the latter one which will soon be two centuries old. By contrast, in just the last half century both Poland and Cuba have each experienced the violent overthrow of no less than four regimes and the initiation of four new political cycles. Unhappily, the experiences of these nations are more nearly typical than those of Britain and the United States. This is probably the major reason why American theory in the field of stratification seems so strange and irrelevant to many foreign observers. It is adapted to a very special set of conditions which have no counterpart in most societies.

THE MIDDLE CLASSES AND THE INSTITUTIONALIZATION OF POWER

As historians and students of politics have long recognized, revolutions are the work of small minorities. Hence, when the revolution is over, the new elite is obliged to employ the services of others to achieve their objectives. Only in this way can they hope to bring the surplus of the society effectively under their control and effect its transformation into the kinds of goods and services they desire.

Fortunately for the new elite, their position of power provides them with the necessary resources for securing the help they need. The portion of the economic surplus they already control can be used to hire an army of technicians and specialists who can bring still more of the surplus under control. This can then be used to hire others to transform the raw materials into fine homes, beautiful clothes, works of art, public monuments, personal services, and the thousand and one things that men of power and privilege desire, or, in the case of an ideological elite, to staff the institutions which will transform society.

This process leads to the creation, extension, or perpetuation of a middle stratum of technicians and specialists working in the service of the elite. These include public officials, craftsmen, artists, servants, merchants, soldiers, priests, and scholars. The chief task of the officials is to locate the economic surplus and separate it from its producers. As Shaw's Caesar put it when challenged to explain his great interest in Egyptian taxes, "My friend, taxes are the chief business of a conqueror of the world." Craftsmen and artists are necessary to transform the surplus into the kinds of goods and services desired by the elite. Merchants facilitate the movement of goods to the places where they are wanted by those with the means to purchase them. Personal servants provide the innumerable services which men of rank cannot provide for themselves. Priests and scholars contribute to the maintenance of public order and, when they fail, the military can take over. In short, a complex apparatus is brought into being, the primary function of which is to insure the elite's continued control over the economic surplus and its transformation into the varied kinds of goods and services the elite desires.

As should be evident, those in the employ of the elite are rewarded in proportion to the value of their services to the elite, and the scarcity of the supply of replacements. Contrary to such functionalist theorists as Kingsley Davis and Wilbert Moore, these roles are not rewarded in proportion to their contribution to the common good.[12] It is the needs of the elite, not the needs of the total society, which determine the demand curve for such services. *The distribution of rewards in a society is a function of the distribution of power, not of system needs.* This is inevitable in such imperfect systems as human societies.

When a political cycle survives for an appreciable period of time, the nature of the middle classes and their relation to the political elite gradually changes. In eras of constitutional rule there is a tendency for these classes to arrogate to themselves certain of the powers and privileges of the elite. This is not difficult since it is their normal function to act on behalf of the elite. Powers delegated often become powers lost; once lost they are not easily recovered. Thus it appears that *the greater the degree of constitutionalism in a society, the less the middle classes function merely as agents of the elite and the greater their personal independence, autonomy, and security.* This is an important development and we shall have frequent occasion to refer to it in later pages. However, it should not be allowed to obscure the more basic relation between the middle classes and the elite which continues even in an era of constitutionalism.

NOTES

1. For a good discussion of the limitations of rule by force, see Robert Dahl and Charles Lindblom, *Politics, Economics, and Welfare* (New York: Harper & Row, 1953), pp. 107-109. See also Karl A. Wittfogel, *Oriental Despotism: A Comparative Study of Total Power* (New Haven, Conn.: Yale University Press, 1957), chap. 4.

2. Edwin Sutherland, *White Collar Crime* (New York: Holt, 1949). For a very different kind of documentation of the partiality of laws, see Philip Stern, *The Great Treasury Raid* (New York: Random House, 1964) or any of the many excellent books on political lobbying by vested interests and the benefits derived therefrom.

3. For documentation of this sweeping generalization, see Alex Inkeles and Raymond Bauer, *The Soviet Citizen* (Cambridge, Mass.: Harvard University Press, 1959). On the basis of interviews with hundreds of displaced persons from the Soviet Union immediately after World War II, these writers concluded that there was only limited questioning of the wisdom of state socialism, centralized planning, and the other major elements of Soviet domestic policy. The chief criticisms were directed at the means employed by the Party in achieving its ends—especially the use of terror. This same conclusion has been reached by most other experts on the Soviet Union.

4. Gaetano Mosca, *The Ruling Class,* translated by Hannah Kahn (New York: McGraw-Hill, 1939) p. 70.

5. See Vilfredo Pareto, *The Mind and Society,* translated by A. Bongiorno and Arthur Livingstone and edited by Livingstone (New York: Harcourt, Brace & World, 1935), vol. III, especially paragraphs 2170-2278.

6. There have been numerous attempts to classify the various forms of power, but none have been completely successful. For three of the better efforts, see Herbert Goldhamer and Edward Shils, "Types of Power and Status," *American Journal of Sociology,* 45 (1939), pp. 171-182; Harold Lasswell and Abraham Kaplan, *Power and Society: A Framework for Political Inquiry* (New Haven, Conn.: Yale University Press, 1950), chap. 5; and Robert Bierstedt, "An Analysis of Social Power," *American Sociological Review,* 15 (1950), pp. 730-738.

7. In many sociological writings the relationship between power and influence is extremely confusing. Sometimes they are treated as synonymous, other times as two distinct phenomena with no area of overlap. Influence should be treated as one special type of power. This approach is consistent both with good English usage and with the insights of some of the abler social theorists. For example, *Webster's Collegiate Dictionary* (5th ed.) defines influence as "the act or the power of producing an effect *without apparent force or direct authority*" (emphasis added).

8. Georg Simmel, *The Sociology of Georg Simmel,* edited and translated by Kurt Wolff (New York: Free Press, 1950), part 3.

9. More recently the same point was made by Robert Dahl and Charles Lindblom in their book *Politics, Economics and Welfare,* part 4, where

they point to the existence of four sociopolitical systems, two of which, price systems and polyarchical systems, involve some measure of influence by the less powerful over the more powerful.

10. I shall use the term "regime" to refer to the members of a particular political elite who come to power by force and to all their successors who come to power by legitimate means. Thus a regime governs from the time of its victory in one revolution until its defeat or overthrow in a subsequent war or revolution.

11. Pareto makes a similar distinction, though without using these labels (paragraph 2268).

12. Kingsley Davis and Wilbert Moore, "Some Principles of Stratification," *American Sociological Review,* **10,** 1945, pp. 242-249.

THE HIGHER CIRCLES

C. Wright Mills

The powers of ordinary men are circumscribed by the everyday worlds in which they live, yet even in these rounds of job, family, and neighborhood they often seem driven by forces they can neither understand nor govern. "Great changes" are beyond their control, but affect their conduct and outlook none the less. The very framework of modern society confines them to projects not their own, but from every side, such changes now press upon the men and women of the mass society, who accordingly feel that they are without purpose in an epoch in which they are without power.

But not all men are in this sense ordinary. As the means of information and of power are centralized, some men come to occupy positions in American society from which they can look down upon, so to speak, and by their decisions mightily affect, the everyday worlds of ordinary men and women. They are not made by their jobs; they set up and break down jobs for thousands of others; they are not confined by simple family responsibilities; they can escape. They may live in many hotels and houses, but they are bound by no one community. They need not merely "meet the demands of the day and hour"; in some part, they create these demands, and cause others to meet them. Whether or not they profess their power, their technical and political experience of it far transcends that of the underlying population. What Jacob Burckhardt said of "great men," most Americans might well say of their elite: "They are all that we are not."[1]

The power elite is composed of men whose positions enable them to transcend the ordinary environments of ordinary men and women; they are in positions to make decisions having major consequences. Whether they do or do not make such decisions is less important than the fact that they do occupy such pivotal positions: their failure to act, their failure to make decisions, is itself an act that is often of greater consequence than the decisions they do make. For they are in command of the major hierarchies and organizations of modern society. They rule the big corporations. They run the machinery of the state and claim its prerogatives. They direct the military establishment. They occupy the strategic command posts of the social structure, in which are now centered the effective means of the power and the wealth and the celebrity which they enjoy.

The power elite are not solitary rulers. Advisers and consultants, spokesmen and opinion-makers are often the captains of their higher thought and decision. Immediately below the elite are the professional politicians of the middle levels of power, in the Congress and in the pressure groups, as well as among the new and old upper classes of town and city and region. Mingling with them, in curious ways which we shall explore, are those professional celebrities who live by being continually displayed but are never, so long as they remain celebrities, displayed enough. If such celebrities are not at the head of any dominating hierarchy, they do often have the power to distract the attention of the public or afford sensations to the masses, or, more directly, to gain the ear of those who do occupy positions of direct power. More or less unattached, as critics of morality and technicians of power, as spokesmen of God and creators of mass sensibility, such celebrities and consultants are part of the immediate scene in which the drama of the elite is enacted. But that drama itself is centered in the command posts of the major institutional hierarchies.

1

The truth about the nature and the power of the elite is not some secret which men of affairs know but will not tell. Such men hold quite various theories about their own roles in the sequence of event and decision. Often they are uncertain about their roles, and even more often they allow their fears and their hopes to affect their assessment of their own power. No matter how great their actual power, they tend to be less acutely aware of it than of the resistances of others to its use. Moreover, most American men of affairs have learned well the rhetoric of public relations, in some cases even to the point of using it when they are alone, and thus coming to believe it. The personal awareness of the actors is only one of the several sources one must examine in order to understand the higher circles. Yet many who believe that there is no elite, or at any rate none of any consequence, rest their argument upon what men of affairs believe about themselves, or at least assert in public.

There is, however, another view: those who feel, even if vaguely, that a compact and powerful elite of great importance does now prevail in America often base that feeling upon the historical trend of our time. They have felt, for example, the domination of the military event, and from this they infer that generals and admirals, as well as other men of decision influenced by them, must be enormously powerful. They hear that the Congress has again abdicated to a handful of men decisions clearly related to the issue of war or peace. They know that the bomb was dropped over Japan in the name of the United States of America, although they were at no time consulted about the matter. They feel that they live in a time of big decisions; they know that they are not making any. Accordingly, as they consider the present as history, they infer that at its center, making decisions or failing to make them, there must be an elite of power.

On the one hand, those who share this feeling about big historical events assume that there is an elite and that its power is great. On the other hand, those who listen carefully to the reports of men apparently involved in the great decisions often do not believe that there is an elite whose powers are of decisive consequence.

Both views must be taken into account, but neither is adequate. The way to understand the power of the American elite lies neither solely in recognizing the historic scale of events nor in accepting the personal awareness reported by men of apparent decision. Behind such men and behind the events of history, linking the two, are the major institutions of modern society. These hierarchies of state and corporation and army constitute the means of power; as such they are now of a consequence not before equaled in human history—and at their summits, there are now those command posts of modern society which offer us the sociological key to an understanding of the role of the higher circles in America.

Within American society, major national power now resides in the economic, the political, and the military domains. Other institutions seem off to the side of modern history, and, on occasion, duly subordinated to these. No family is as directly powerful in national affairs as any major corporation; no church is as directly powerful in the external biographies of young men in America today as the military establishment; no college is as powerful in the shaping of momentous events as the National Security Council. Religious, educational, and family institutions are not autonomous centers of national power; on the contrary, these decentralized areas are increasingly shaped by the big three, in which developments of decisive and immediate consequence now occur.

Families and churches and schools adapt to modern life; government and armies and corporations shape it; and, as they do so, they turn these lesser institutions into means for their ends. Religious institutions provide chaplains to the armed forces where they are used as a means of increasing the effectiveness of its morale to kill. Schools select and train men for their jobs in corporations and their specialized tasks in the armed forces. The extended family has, of course, long been broken up by the industrial revolution, and now the son and the father are removed from the family, by compulsion if need be, whenever the army of the state sends out the call. And the symbols of all these lesser institutions are used to legitimate the power and the decisions of the big three.

The life-fate of the modern individual depends not only upon the family into which he was born or which he enters by marriage, but increasingly upon the corporation in which he spends the most alert hours of his best years; not only upon the school where he is educated as a child and adolescent, but also upon the state which touches him throughout his life; not only upon the church in which on occasion he hears the word of God, but also upon the army in which he is disciplined.

If the centralized state could not rely upon the inculcation of nationalist loyalties in public and private schools, its leaders would promptly seek to modify the decentralized educational system. If the bankruptcy rate among the top five hundred corporations were as high as the general divorce rate among the thirty-seven million married couples, there would be economic catastrophe on an international scale. If members of armies gave to them no more of their lives than do believers to the churches to which they belong, there would be a military crisis.

Within each of the big three, the typical institutional unit has become enlarged, has become administrative, and, in the power of its decisions, has become centralized. Behind these developments there is a fabulous technology, for as institutions, they have incorporated this technology and guide it, even as it shapes and paces their developments.

The economy—once a great scatter of small productive units in autonomous balance—has become dominated by two or three hundred giant corporations, administratively and politically interrelated, which together hold the keys to economic decisions.

The political order, once a decentralized set of several dozen states with a weak spinal cord, has become a centralized, executive establishment which has taken up into itself many powers previously scattered, and now enters into each and every crany of the social structure.

The military order, once a slim establishment in a context of distrust fed by state militia, has become the largest and most expensive feature of government, and, although well versed in smiling public relations, now has all the grim and clumsy efficiency of a sprawling bureaucratic domain.

In each of these institutional areas, the means of power at the disposal of decision makers have increased enormously; their central executive powers have been enhanced; within each of them modern administrative routines have been elaborated and tightened up.

As each of these domains becomes enlarged and centralized, the consequences of its activities become greater, and its traffic with the others increases. The decisions of a handful of corporations bear upon military and political as well as upon economic developments around the world. The decisions of the military establishment rest upon and grievously affect political life as well as the very level of economic activity. The decisions made within the political domain determine economic activities and military programs. There is no longer, on the one hand, an economy, and, on the other hand, a political order containing a military establishment unimportant to politics and to money-making. There is a political economy linked, in a thousand ways, with military institutions and decisions. On each side of the world-split running through central Europe and around the Asiatic rimlands, there is an ever-increasing interlocking of economic, military, and political structures.[2] If there is government intervention in the corporate economy, so is there corporate intervention in the governmental process. In the structural sense, this triangle of power is the source of the interlocking directorate that is most important for the historical structure of the present.

The fact of the interlocking is clearly revealed at each of the points of crisis of modern capitalist society—slump, war, and boom. In each, men of decision are led to an awareness of the interdependence of the major institutional orders. In the nineteenth century, when the scale of all institutions was smaller, their liberal integration was achieved in the automatic economy, by an autonomous play of market forces, and in the automatic political domain, by the bargain and the vote. It was then assumed that out of the imbalance and friction that followed the limited decisions then possible a new equilibrium would in due course emerge. That can no longer be assumed, and it is not assumed by the men at the top of each of the three dominant hierarchies.

For given the scope of their consequences, decisions—and indecisions—in any one of these ramify into the others, and hence top decisions tend either to become co-ordinated or to lead to a commanding indecision. It has not always been like this. When numerous small entrepreneurs made up the economy, for example, many of them could fail and the consequences still remain local; political and military authorities did not intervene. But now, given political expectations and military commitments, can they afford to allow key units of the private corporate economy to break down in slump? Increasingly, they do intervene in economic affairs, and as they do so, the controlling decisions in each order are inspected by agents of the other two, and economic, military, and political structures are interlocked.

At the pinnacle of each of the three enlarged and centralized domains, there have arisen those higher circles which make up the economic, the political, and the military elites. At the top of the economy, among the corporate rich, there are the chief executives; at the top of the political order, the members of the political directorate; at the top of the military establishment, the elite of soldier-statesmen clustered in and around the Joint Chiefs of Staff and the upper echelon. As each of these domains has coincided with the others, as decisions tend to become total in their consequence, the leading men in each of the three domains of power—the warlords, the corporation chieftains, the political directorate —tend to come together, to form the power elite of America.

2

The higher circles in and around these command posts are often thought of in terms of what their members possess: they have a greater share than other people of the things and experiences that are most highly valued. From this point of view, the elite are simply those who have the most of what there is to have, which is generally held to include money, power, and prestige—as well as all the ways of life to which these lead.[3] But the elite are not simply those who have the most, for they could not "have the most" were it not for their positions in the great institutions. For such institutions are the necessary bases of power, of wealth, and of prestige, and at the same time, the chief means of exercising power, of acquiring and retaining wealth, and of cashing in the higher claims for prestige.

By the powerful we mean, of course, those who are able to realize their will, even if others resist it. No one, accordingly, can be truly powerful unless he has access to the command of major institutions, for it is over these institutional means of power that the truly powerful are, in the first instance, powerful. Higher politicians and key officials of government command such institutional power; so do admirals and generals, and so do the major owners and executives of the larger corporations. Not all power, it is true, is anchored in and exercised by means of such institutions, but only within and through them can power be more or less continuous and important.

Wealth also is acquired and held in and through institutions. The pyramid of wealth cannot be understood merely in terms of the very rich; for the great inheriting families, as we shall see, are now supplemented by the corporate institutions of modern society: every one of the very rich families has been and is closely connected—always legally and frequently managerially as well—with one of the multi-million dollar corporations.

The modern corporation is the prime source of wealth, but, in latter-day capitalism, the political apparatus also opens and closes many avenues to wealth. The amount as well as the source of income, the power over consumer's goods as well as over productive capital, are determined by position within the political economy. If our interest in the very rich goes beyond their lavish or their miserly consumption, we must examine their relations to modern forms of corporate property as well as to the state; for such relations now determine the chances of men to secure big property and to receive high income.

Great prestige increasingly follows the major institutional units of the social structure. It is obvious that prestige depends, often quite decisively, upon access to the publicity machines that are now a central and normal feature of all the big institutions of modern America. Moreover, one feature of these hierarchies of corporation, state, and military establishment is that their top positions are increasingly interchangeable. One result of this is the accumulative nature of prestige. Claims for prestige, for example, may be initially based on military roles, then expressed in and augmented by an educational institution run by corporate executives, and cashed in, finally, in the political order, where, for General Eisenhower and those he represents, power and prestige finally meet at the very peak. Like wealth and power, prestige tends to be cumulative: the more of it you have, the more you can get. These values also tend to be translatable into one another: the wealthy find it easier than the poor to gain power; those with status find it easier than those without it to control opportunities for wealth.

If we took the one hundred most powerful men in America, the one hundred wealthiest, and the one hundred most celebrated away from the institutional positions they now occupy, away from their resources of men and women and money, away from the media of mass communication that are now focused upon them—then they would be powerless and poor and uncelebrated. For power is not of a man. Wealth does not center in the person of the wealthy. Celebrity is not inherent in any personality. To be celebrated, to be wealthy, to have power requires access to major institutions, for the institutional positions men occupy determine in large part their chances to have and to hold these valued experiences.

3

The people of the higher circles may also be conceived as members of a top social stratum, as a set of groups whose members know one another, see one another socially and at business, and so, in making decisions, take one another into account. The elite, according to this conception, feel themselves to be, and are felt by others to be, the inner circle of "the upper social classes."[4] They form a more or less compact social and psychological entity; they have become self-conscious members of a social class. People are either accepted into this class or they are not, and there is a qualitative split, rather than merely a numerical scale, separating them from those who are not elite. They are more or less aware of themselves as a social class and they behave toward one another differently from the way they do toward members of other classes. They accept one another, understand one another, marry one another, tend to work and to think if not together at least alike.

Now, we do not want by our definition to prejudge whether the elite of the command posts are conscious members of such a socially recognized class, or whether considerable proportions of the elite derive from such a clear and distinct class. These are matters to be investigated. Yet in order to be able to recognize what we intend to investigate, we must note something that all biographies and memoirs of the wealthy and the powerful and the eminent make clear: no matter what else they may be, the people of these higher circles are involved in a set of overlapping "crowds" and intricately connected "cliques." There is a kind of mutual attraction among those who "sit on the same terrace"—although this often becomes clear to them, as well as to others, only at the point at which they feel the need to draw the line; only when, in their common defense, they come to understand what they have in common, and so close their ranks against outsiders.

The idea of such ruling stratum implies that most of its members have similar social origins, that throughout their lives they maintain a network of informal connections, and that to some degree there is an interchangeability of position between the various hierarchies of money and power and celebrity. We must, of course, note at once that if such an elite stratum does exist, its social visibility and its form, for very solid historical reasons, are quite different from those of the noble cousinhoods that once ruled various European nations.

That American society has never passed through a feudal epoch is of decisive importance to the nature of the American elite, as well as to American society as a historic whole. For it means that no nobility or aristocracy, established before the capitalist era, has stood in tense opposition to the higher bourgeoisie. It means that this bourgeoisie has monopolized not only wealth but prestige and power as well. It means that no set of noble families has commanded the top positions and monopolized the values that are generally held in high esteem; and certainly that no set has done so explicitly by inherited right. It means that no high church dignitaries or court nobilities, no entrenched landlords with honorific accouterments, no monopolists of high army posts have opposed the enriched bourgeoisie and in the name of birth and prerogative successfully resisted its self-making.

But this does *not* mean that there are no upper strata in the United States. That they emerged from a "middle class" that had no recognized aristocratic superiors does not mean they remained middle class when enormous increases in wealth made their own superiority possible. Their origins and their newness may have made the upper strata less visible in America than elsewhere. But in America today there are in fact tiers and ranges of wealth and power of which people in the middle and lower ranks know very little and may not even dream. There are families who, in their well-being, are quite insulated from the economic jolts and lurches felt by the merely prosperous and those farther down the scale.

There are also men of power who in quite small groups make decisions of enormous consequence for the underlying population.

The American elite entered modern history as a virtually unopposed bourgeoisie. No national bourgeoisie, before or since, has had such opportunities and advantages. Having no military neighbors, they easily occupied an isolated continent stocked with natural resources and immensely inviting to a willing labor force. A framework of power and an ideology for its justification were already at hand. Against mercantilist restriction, they inherited the principle of *laissez-faire;* against Southern planters, they imposed the principle of industrialism. The Revolutionary War put an end to colonial pretensions to nobility, as loyalists fled the country and many estates were broken up. The Jacksonian upheaval with its status revolution put an end to pretensions to monopoly of descent by the old New England families. The Civil War broke the power, and so in due course the prestige, of the ante-bellum South's claimants for the higher esteem. The tempo of the whole capitalist development made it impossible for an inherited nobility to develop and endure in America.

No fixed ruling class, anchored in agrarian life and coming to flower in military glory, could contain in America the historic thrust of commerce and industry, or subordinate to itself the capitalist elite—as capitalists were subordinated, for example, in Germany and Japan. Nor could such a ruling class anywhere in the world contain that of the United States when industrialized violence came to decide history. Witness the fate of Germany and Japan in the two world wars of the twentieth century; and indeed the fate of Britain herself and her model ruling class, as New York became the inevitable economic, and Washington the inevitable political capital of the western capitalist world.

4

The elite who occupy the command posts may be seen as the possessors of power and wealth and celebrity; they may be seen as members of the upper stratum of a capitalistic society. They may also be defined in terms of psychological and moral criteria, as certain kinds of selected individuals. So defined, the elite, quite simply, are people of superior character and energy.

The humanist, for example, may conceive of the "elite" not as a social level or category, but as a scatter of those individuals who attempt to transcend themselves, and accordingly, are more noble, more efficient, made out of better stuff. It does not matter whether they are poor or rich, whether they hold high position or low, whether they are acclaimed or despised; they are elite because of the kind of individuals they are. The rest of the population is mass, which, according to this conception, sluggishly relaxes into uncomfortable mediocrity.[5]

This is the sort of socially unlocated conception which some American writers with conservative yearnings have recently sought to develop. But most moral and psychological conceptions of the elite are much less sophisticated, concerning themselves not with individuals but with the stratum as a whole. Such ideas, in fact, always arise in a society in which some people possess more than do others of what there is to possess. People with advantages are loath to believe that they just happen to be people with advantages. They come readily to define themselves as inherently worthy of what they possess; they come to believe themselves "naturally" elite; and, in fact, to imagine their possessions and their privileges as natural extensions of their own elite selves. In this sense, the idea of the elite as composed of men and women having a finer moral character is an ideology of the elite as a privileged ruling stratum, and this is true whether the ideology is elite-made or made up for it by others.

In eras of equalitarian rhetoric, the more intelligent or the more articulate among the lower and middle classes, as well as guilty members of the upper, may come to entertain ideas of a counter-elite. In western society, as a matter of fact, there is a long tradition and varied images of the poor, the exploited, and the oppressed as the truly virtuous, the wise, and the blessed. Stemming from Christian tradition, this moral idea of a counter-elite, composed of essentially higher types condemned to a lowly station, may be and has been used by the underlying population to justify harsh criticism of ruling elites and to celebrate utopian images of a new elite to come.

The moral conception of the elite, however, is not always merely an ideology of the overprivileged or a counter-ideology of the underprivileged. It is often a fact: having controlled experiences and select privileges, many individuals of the upper stratum do come in due course to approximate the types of character they claim to embody. Even when we give up—as we must—the idea that the elite man or woman is born with an elite character, we need not dismiss the idea that their experiences and trainings develop in them characters of a specific type.

Nowadays we must qualify the idea of elite as composed of higher types of individuals, for the men who are selected for and shaped by the top positions have many spokesmen and advisers and ghosts and make-up men who modify their self-conceptions and create their public images, as well as shape many of their decisions. There is, of course, considerable variation among the elite in this respect, but as a general rule in America today, it would be naïve to interpret any major elite group merely in terms of its ostensible personnel. The American elite often seems less a collection of persons than of corporate entities, which are in great part created and spoken for as standard types of "personality." Even the most apparently free-lance celebrity is usually a sort of synthetic production turned out each week by a disciplined staff which systematically ponders the effect of the easy ad-libbed gags the celebrity "spontaneously" echoes.

Yet, in so far as the elite flourishes as a social class or as a set of men at the command posts, it will select and form certain types of personality, and reject others. The kind of moral and psychological beings men become is in large part determined by the values they experience and the institutional roles they are allowed and expected to play. From the biographer's point of view, a man of the upper classes is formed by his relations with others like himself in a series of small intimate groupings through which he passes and to which throughout his lifetime he may return. So conceived, the elite is a set of higher circles whose members are selected, trained and certified and permitted intimate access to those who command the impersonal institutional hierarchies of modern society. If there is any one key to the *psychological* idea of the elite, it is that they combine in their persons an awareness of impersonal decision-making with intimate sensibilities shared with one another. To understand the elite as a social class we must examine a whole series of smaller face-to-face milieux, the most obvious of which, historically, has been the upper-class family, but the most important of which today are the proper secondary school and the metropolitan club.[6]

5

These several notions of the elite, when appropriately understood, are intricately bound up with one another, and we shall use them all in this examination of American success. We shall study each of several higher circles as offering candidates for the elite, and we shall do so in terms of the major institutions making up the total society of America; within and between each of these institutions, we shall trace the interrelations of wealth and power and prestige. But our main concern is with the power of those who now occupy the command posts, and with the role which they are enacting in the history of our epoch.

Such an elite may be conceived as omnipotent, and its powers thought of as a great hidden design. Thus, in vulgar Marxism, events and trends are explained by reference to "the will of the bourgeoisie"; in Nazism, by reference to "the conspiracy of the Jews"; by the petty right in America today, by reference to "the hidden force" of Communist spies. According to such notions of the omnipotent elite as historical cause, the elite is never an entirely visible agency. It is, in fact, a secular substitute for the will of God, being realized in a sort of providential design, except that usually non-elite men are thought capable of opposing it and eventually overcoming it.*

The opposite view—of the elite as impotent—is now quite popular among liberal-minded observers. Far from being omnipotent, the elites are thought to be so scattered as to lack any coherence as a historical force. Their invisibility is not the invisibility of secrecy but the invisibility of the multitude. Those who occupy the formal places of authority are so check-mated—by other elites exerting pressure, or by the public as an electorate, or by constitutional codes—that, although there may be upper classes, there is no ruling class; although there may be men of power, there is no power elite; although there may be a system of stratification, it has no effective top. In the extreme, this view of the elite, as weakened by compromise and disunited to the point of nullity, is a substitute for impersonal collective fate; for, in this view, the decisions of the visible men of the higher circles do not count in history.†

Internationally, the image of the omnipotent elite tends to prevail. All good events and pleasing happenings are quickly imputed by the opinion-makers to the leaders of their own nation; all bad events and unpleasant experiences are imputed to the enemy abroad. In both cases,

*Those who charge that Communist agents have been or are in the government, as well as those frightened by them, never raise the question: "Well, suppose there are Communists in high places, how much power do they have?" They simply assume that men in high places, or in this case even those in positions from which they might influence such men, do decide important events. Those who think Communist agents lost China to the Soviet bloc, or influenced loyal Americans to lose it, simply assume that there is a set of men who decide such matters, actively or by neglect or by stupidity. Many others, who do not believe that Communist agents were so influential, still assume that loyal American

the omnipotence of evil rulers or of virtuous leaders is assumed. Within the nation, the use of such rhetoric is rather more complicated: when men speak of the power of their own party or circle, they and their leaders are, of course, impotent; only "the people" are omnipotent. But, when they speak of the power of their opponent's party or circle, they impute to them omnipotence; "the people" are now powerlessly taken in.

More generally, American men of power tend, by convention, to deny that they are powerful. No American runs for office in order to rule or even govern, but only to serve; he does not become a bureaucrat or even an official, but a public servant. And nowadays, as I have already pointed out, such postures have become standard features of the public-relations programs of all men of power. So firm a part of the style of power-wielding have they become that conservative writers readily misinterpret them as indicating a trend toward an "amorphous power situation."

But the "power situation" of America today is less amorphous than is the perspective of those who see it as a romantic confusion. It is less a flat, momentary "situation" than a graded, durable structure. And if those who occupy its top grades are not omnipotent, neither are they impotent. It is the form and the height of the gradation of power that we must examine if we would understand the degree of power held and exercised by the elite.

If the power to decide such national issues as are decided were shared in an absolutely equal way, there would be no power elite; in fact, there would be no *gradation* of power, but only a radical homogeneity. At the opposite extreme as well, if the power to decide issues were absolutely monopolized by one small group, there would be no gradation of power; there would simply be this small group in command, and below it, the undifferentiated, dominated masses. American society today represents neither the one nor the other of these extremes, but a conception of them is none the less useful: it makes us realize more clearly the

decision-makers lost it all by themselves.

†The idea of the impotent elite . . . is mightily supported by the notion of an automatic economy in which the problem of power is solved for the economic elite by denying its existence. No one has enough power to make a real difference; events are the results of an anonymous balance. For the political elite too, the model of balance solves the problem of power. Parallel to the market-economy, there is the leaderless democracy in which no one is responsible for anything and everyone is responsible for everything; the will of men acts only through the impersonal workings of the electoral process.

question of the structure of power in the United States and the position of the power elite within it.

Within each of the most powerful institutional orders of modern society there is a gradation of power. The owner of a roadside fruit stand does not have as much power in any area of social or economic or political decision as the head of a multi-million-dollar fruit corporation; no lieutenant on the line is as powerful as the Chief of Staff in the Pentagon; no deputy sheriff carries as much authority as the President of the United States. Accordingly, the problem of defining the power elite concerns the level at which we wish to draw the line. By lowering the line, we could define the elite out of existence; by raising it, we could make the elite a very small circle indeed. In a preliminary and minimum way, we draw the line crudely, in charcoal as it were: By the power elite, we refer to those political, economic, and military circles which as an intricate set of overlapping cliques share decisions having at least national consequences. In so far as national events are decided, the power elite are those who decide them.

To say that there are obvious gradations of power and of opportunities to decide within modern society is not to say that the powerful are united, that they fully know what they do, or that they are consciously joined in conspiracy. Such issues are best faced if we concern ourselves, in the first instance, more with the structural position of the high and mighty, and with the consequences of their decisions, than with the extent of their awareness or the purity of their motives. To understand the power elite, we must attend to three major keys:

1. One, which we shall emphasize throughout our discussion of each of the higher circles, is the psychology of the several elites in their respective milieux. In so far as the power elite is composed of men of similar origin and education, in so far as their careers and their styles of life are similar, there are psychological and social bases for their unity, resting upon the fact that they are of similar social type and leading to the fact of their easy intermingling. This kind of unity reaches its frothier apex in the sharing of that prestige that is to be had in the world of the celebrity; it achieves a more solid culmination in the fact of the interchangeability of positions within and between the three dominant institutional orders.

2. Behind such psychological and social unity as we may find, are the structure and the mechanics of these institutional hierarchies over which the political directorate, the corporate rich, and the high military now preside. The greater the scale of these bureaucratic domains, the greater

the scope of their respective elite's power. How each of the major hierarchies is shaped and what relations it has with the other hierarchies determine in large part the relations of their rulers. If these hierarchies are scattered and disjointed, then their respective elites tend to be scattered and disjointed; if they have many interconnections and points of coinciding interest, then their elites tend to form a coherent kind of grouping.

The unity of the elite is not a simple reflection of the unity of institutions, but men and institutions are always related, and our conception of the power elite invites us to determine that relation. Today in America there are several important structural coincidences of interest between these institutional domains, including the development of a permanent war establishment by a privately incorporated economy inside a political vacuum.

3. The unity of the power elite, however, does not rest solely on psychological similarity and social intermingling, nor entirely on the structural coincidences of commanding positions and interests. At times it is the unity of a more explicit co-ordination. To say that these three higher circles are increasingly co-ordinated, that this is *one* basis of their unity, and that at times—as during the wars—such co-ordination is quite decisive, is not to say that the co-ordination is total or continuous, or even that it is very sure-footed. Much less is it to say that willful co-ordination is the sole or the major basis of their unity, or that the power elite has emerged as the realization of a plan. But it is to say that as the institutional mechanics of our time have opened up avenues to men pursuing their several interests, many of them have come to see that these several interests could be realized more easily if they worked together, in informal as well as in more formal ways, and accordingly they have done so.

6

It is not my thesis that for all epochs of human history and in all nations, a creative minority, a ruling class, an omnipotent elite, shape all historical events. Such statements, upon careful examination, usually turn out to be mere tautologies,[7] and even when they are not, they are so entirely general as to be useless in the attempt to understand the history of the present. The minimum definition of the power elite as those who decide whatever is decided of major consequence, does not imply that the members of this elite are always and necessarily the history-makers;

neither does it imply that they never are. We must not confuse the conception of the elite, which we wish to define, with one theory about their role: that they are the history-makers of our time. To define the elite, for example, as "those who rule America" is less to define a conception than to state one hypothesis about the role and power of that elite. No matter how we might define the elite, the extent of its members' power is subject to historical variation. If, in a dogmatic way, we try to include that variation in our generic definition, we foolishly limit the use of a needed conception. If we insist that the elite be defined as a strictly coordinated class that continually and absolutely rules, we are closing off from our view much to which the term more modestly defined might open to our observation. In short, our definition of the power elite cannot properly contain dogma concerning the degree and kind of power that ruling groups everywhere have. Much less should it permit us to smuggle into our discussion a theory of history.

During most of human history, historical change has not been visible to the people who were involved in it, or even to those enacting it. Ancient Egypt and Mesopotamia, for example, endured for some four hundred generations with but slight changes in their basic structure. That is six and a half times as long as the entire Christian era, which has only prevailed some sixty generations; it is about eighty times as long as the five generations of the United States' existence. But now the tempo of change is so rapid, and the means of observation so accessible, that the interplay of event and decision seems often to be quite historically visible, if we will only look carefully and from an adequate vantage point.

When knowledgeable journalists tell us that "events, not men, shape the big decisions," they are echoing the theory of history as Fortune, Chance, Fate, or the work of The Unseen Hand. For "events" is merely a modern word for these older ideas, all of which separate men from history-making, because all of them lead us to believe that history goes on behind men's backs. History is drift with no mastery; within it there is action but no deed; history is mere happening and the event intended by no one.[8]

The course of events in our time depends more on a series of human decisions than on any inevitable fate. The sociological meaning of "fate" is simply this: that, when the decisions are innumerable and each one is of small consequence, all of them add up in a way no man intended—to history as fate. But not all epochs are equally fateful. As the circle of those who decide is narrowed, as the means of decision are centralized and the consequences of decisions become enormous, then the course of great events often rests upon the decisions of determinable circles. This does not necessarily mean that the same circle of men follow through from one event to another in such a way that all of history is merely their plot. The power of the elite does not necessarily mean that history is not also shaped by a series of small decisions, none of which are thought out. It does not mean that a hundred small arrangements and compromises and adaptations may not be built into the going policy and the living event. The idea of the power elite implies nothing about the process of decision-making as such: it is an attempt to delimit the social areas within which that process, whatever its character, goes on. It is a conception of who is involved in the process.

The degree of foresight and control of those who are involved in decisions that count may also vary. The idea of the power elite does not mean that the estimations and calculated risks upon which decisions are made are not often wrong and that the consequences are sometimes, indeed often, not those intended. Often those who make decisions are trapped by their own inadequacies and blinded by their own errors.

Yet in our time the pivotal moment does arise, and at that moment, small circles do decide or fail to decide. In either case, they are an elite of power. The dropping of the A-bombs over Japan was such a moment; the decision on Korea was such a moment; the confusion about Quemoy and Matsu, as well as before Dienbienphu were such moments; the sequence of maneuvers which involved the United States in World War II was such a "moment." Is it not true that much of the history of our times is composed of such moments? And is not that what is meant when it is said that we live in a time of big decisions, of decisively centralized power?

Most of us do not try to make sense of our age by believing in a Greek-like, eternal recurrence, nor by a Christian belief in a salvation to come, nor by any steady march of human progress. Even though we do not reflect upon such matters, the chances are we believe with Burckhardt that we live in a mere succession of events; that sheer continuity is the only principle of history. History is merely one thing after another; history is meaningless in that it is not the realization of any determinate plot. It is true, of course, that our sense of continuity, our feeling for the history of our time, is affected by crisis. But we seldom look beyond the immediate crisis or the crisis felt to be just ahead. We believe neither in fate nor providence; and we assume, without talking about it, that "we"

—as a nation—can decisively shape the future but that "we" as individuals somehow cannot do so.

Any meaning history has, "we" shall have to give to it by our actions. Yet the fact is that although we are all of us within history we do not all possess equal powers to make history. To pretend that we do is sociological nonsense and political irresponsibility. It is nonsense because any group or any individual is limited, first of all, by the technical and institutional means of power at its command; we do not all have equal access to the means of power that now exist, nor equal influence over their use. To pretend that "we" are all history-makers is politically irresponsible because it obfuscates any attempt to locate responsibility for the consequential decisions of men who do have access to the means of power.

From even the most superficial examination of the history of the western society we learn that the power of decision-makers is first of all limited by the level of technique, by the *means* of power and violence and organization that prevail in a given society. In this connection we also learn that there is a fairly straight line running upward through the history of the West; that the means of oppression and exploitation, of violence and destruction, as well as the means of production and reconstruction, have been progressively enlarged and increasingly centralized.

As the institutional means of power and the means of communications that tie them together have become steadily more efficient, those now in command of them have come into command of instruments of rule quite unsurpassed in the history of mankind. And we are not yet at the climax of their development. We can no longer lean upon or take soft comfort from the historical ups and downs of ruling groups of previous epochs. In that sense, Hegel is correct: we learn from history that we cannot learn from it.

For every epoch and for every social structure, we must work out an answer to the question of the power of the elite. The ends of men are often merely hopes, but means are facts within some men's control. That is why all means of power tend to become ends to an elite that is in command of them. And that is why we may define the power elite in terms of the means of power—as those who occupy the command posts. The major questions about the American elite today—its composition, its unity, its power—must now be faced with due attention to the awesome means of power available to them. Caesar could do less with Rome than Napoleon with France; Napoleon less with France than Lenin with

Russia; and Lenin less with Russia than Hitler with Germany. But what was Caesar's power at its peak compared with the power of the changing inner circle of Soviet Russia or of America's temporary administrations? The men of either circle can cause great cities to be wiped out in a single night, and in a few weeks turn continents into thermonuclear wastelands. That the facilities of power are enormously enlarged and decisively centralized means that the decisions of small groups are now more consequential.

But to know that the top posts of modern social structures now permit more commanding decisions is not to know that the elite who occupy these posts are the history-makers. We might grant that the enlarged and integrated economic, military, and political structures are shaped to permit command decisions, yet still feel that, as it were, "they run themselves," that those who are on top, in short, are determined in their decisions by "necessity," which presumably means by the instituted roles that they play and the situation of these institutions in the total structure of society.

Do the elite determine the roles that they enact? Or do the roles that institutions make available to them determine the power of the elite? The general answer—and no general answer is sufficient—is that in different kinds of structures and epochs elites are quite differently related to the roles that they play: nothing in the nature of the elite or in the nature of history dictates an answer. It is also true that if most men and women take whatever roles are permitted to them and enact them as they are expected to by virtue of their position, this is precisely what the elite need *not* do, and often do not do. They may call into question the structure, their position within it, or the way in which they are to enact that position.

Nobody called for or permitted Napoleon to chase *Parlement* home on the 18 *Brumaire,* and later to transform his consulate into an emperorship.[9] Nobody called for or permitted Adolf Hitler to proclaim himself "Leader and Chancellor" the day President Hindenburg died, to abolish and usurp roles by merging the presidency and the chancellorship. Nobody called for or permitted Franklin D. Roosevelt to make the series of decisions that led to the entrance of the United States into World War II. It was no "historical necessity," but a man named Truman who, with a few other men, decided to drop a bomb over Hiroshima. It was no historical necessity, but an argument within a small circle of men that defeated Admiral Radford's proposal to bomb troops before Dienbienphu. Far from being dependent upon the structure of institutions, modern elites may smash one structure and set up another in which they then enact quite different roles. In fact, such destruction and creation of institutional structures, with all their means of power, when events seem to turn out well, is just what is involved in "great leadership," or, when they seem to turn out badly, great tyranny.

Some elite men *are,* of course, typically role-determined, but others are at times role-determining. They determine not only the role they play but today the roles of millions of other men. The creation of pivotal roles and their pivotal enactment occurs most readily when social structures are undergoing epochal transitions. It is clear that the international development of the United States to one of the two "great powers"—along with the new means of annihilation and administrative and psychic domination—have made of the United States in the middle years of the twentieth century precisely such an epochal pivot.

There is nothing about history that tells us that a power elite cannot make it. To be sure, the will of such men is always limited, but never before have the limits been so broad, for never before have the means of power been so enormous. It is this that makes our situation so precarious, and makes even more important an understanding of the powers and the limitations of the American elite. The problem of the nature and the power of this elite is now the only realistic and serious way to raise again the problem of responsible government.

7

Those who have abandoned criticism for the new American celebration take readily to the view that the elite is impotent. If they were politically serious, they ought, on the basis of their view, to say to those presumably in charge of American policy:[10]

"One day soon, you may believe that you have an opportunity to drop a bomb or a chance to exacerbate further your relations with allies or with the Russians who might also drop it. But don't be so foolish as to believe that you really have a choice. You have neither choice nor chance. The whole Complex Situation of which you are merely one balancing part is the result of Economic and Social Forces, and so will be the fateful outcome. So stand by quietly, like Tolstoy's general, and let events proceed. Even if you did act, the consequences would not be what you intended, even if you had an intention.

"But—if events come out well, talk as though you had decided. For then men have had moral choices and the power to make them and are, of course, responsible.

"If events come out badly, say that *you* didn't have the real choice, and are, of course, not accountable: *they,* the others, had the choice and they are responsible. You can get away with this even though you have at your command half the world's forces and God knows how many bombs and bombers. For you are, in fact, an impotent item in the historical fate of your times; and moral responsibility is an illusion, although it is of great use if handled in a really alert public relations manner."

The one implication that can be drawn from all such fatalisms is that if fortune or providence rules, then no elite of power can be justly considered a source of historical decisions, and the idea—much less the demand—of responsible leadership is an idle and an irresponsible notion. For clearly, an impotent elite, the plaything of history, cannot be held accountable. If the elite of our time do not have power, they cannot be held responsible; as men in a difficult position, they should engage our sympathies. The people of the United States are ruled by sovereign fortune; they, and with them their elite, are fatally overwhelmed by consequences they cannot control. If that is so, we ought all to do what many have in fact already done: withdraw entirely from political reflection and action into a materially comfortable and entirely private life.

If, on the other hand, we believe that war and peace and slump and prosperity are, precisely now, no longer matters of "fortune" or "fate," but that, precisely now more than ever, they are controllable, then we must ask—controllable by whom? The answer must be: By whom else but those who now command the enormously enlarged and decisively centralized means of decision and power? We may then ask: Why don't they, then? And for the answer to that, we must understand the context and the character of the American elite today.

There is nothing in the idea of the elite as impotent which should deter us from asking just such questions, which are now the most important questions political men can ask. The American elite is neither omnipotent nor impotent. These are abstract absolutes used publicly by spokesmen, as excuses or as boasts, but in terms of which we may seek to clarify the political issues before us, which just now are above all the issues of responsible power.

There is nothing in "the nature of history" *in our epoch* that rules out the pivotal function of small groups of decision-makers. On the contrary, the structure of the present is such as to make this not only a reasonable, but a rather compelling, view.

There is nothing in "the psychology of man," or in the social manner by which men are shaped and selected for and by the command posts of modern society, that makes unreasonable the view that they do confront choices and that the choices they make—or their failure to confront them—are history-making in their consequences.

Accordingly, political men now have every reason to hold the American power elite accountable for a decisive range of the historical events that make up the history of the present.

It is as fashionable, just now, to suppose that there is no power elite, as it was fashionable in the 'thirties to suppose a set of ruling-class villains to be the source of all social injustice and public malaise. I should be as far from supposing that some simple and unilateral ruling class could be firmly located as the prime mover of American society, as I should be from supposing that all historical change in America today is merely impersonal drift.

The view that all is blind drift is largely a fatalist projection of one's own feeling of impotence and perhaps, if one has ever been active politically in a principled way, a salve of one's guilt.

The view that all of history is due to the conspiracy of an easily located set of villains, or of heroes, is also a hurried projection from the difficult effort to understand how shifts in the structure of society open opportunities to various elites and how various elites take advantage or fail to take advantage of them. To accept either view—of all history as conspiracy or of all history as drift—is to relax the effort to understand the facts of power and the ways of the powerful.

8

In my attempt to discern the shape of the power elite of our time, and thus to give a responsible meaning to the anonymous "They," which the underlying population opposes to the anonymous "We," I shall begin by briefly examining the higher elements which most people know best: the new and the old upper classes of local society and the metropolitan 400.

I shall then outline the world of the celebrity, attempting to show that the prestige system of American society has now for the first time become truly national in scope; and that the more trivial and glamorous aspects of this national system of status tend at once to distract attention from its more authoritarian features and to justify the power that it often conceals.

In examining the very rich and the chief executives, I shall indicate how neither "America's Sixty Families" nor "The Managerial Revolution" provides an adequate idea of the transformation of the upper classes as they are organized today in the privileged stratum of the corporate rich.

After describing the American statesman as a historical type, I shall attempt to show that what observers in the Progressive Era called "the invisible government" has now become quite visible; and that what is usually taken to be the central content of politics, the pressures and the campaigns and the congressional maneuvering, has, in considerable part, now been relegated to the middle levels of power.

In discussing the military ascendancy, I shall try to make clear how it has come about that admirals and generals have assumed positions of decisive political and economic relevance, and how, in doing so, they have found many points of coinciding interests with the corporate rich and the political directorate of the visible government.

After these and other trends are made as plain as I can make them, I shall return to the master problems of the power elite, as well as take up the complementary notion of the mass society.

What I am asserting is that in this particular epoch a conjunction of historical circumstances has led to the rise of an elite of power; that the men of the circles composing this elite, severally and collectively, now make such key decisions as are made; and that, given the enlargement and the centralization of the means of power now available, the decisions that they make and fail to make carry more consequences for more people than has ever been the case in the world history of mankind.

I am also asserting that there has developed on the middle levels of power, a semi-organized stalemate, and that on the bottom level there has come into being a mass-like society which has little resemblence to the image of a society in which voluntary associations and classic publics hold the keys to power. The top of the American system of power is much more unified and much more powerful, the bottom is much more fragmented, and in truth, impotent, than is generally supposed by those who are distracted by the middling units of power which neither express such will as exists at the bottom nor determine the decisions at the top.

NOTES

1. Jacob Burckhardt, *Force and Freedom* (New York: Pantheon Books, 1943), pp. 303 ff.
2. Cf. Hans Gerth and C. Wright Mills, *Character and Social Structure* (New York: Harcourt, Brace, 1953), pp. 457 ff.
3. The statistical idea of choosing some value and calling those who have the most of it an elite derives, in modern times, from the Italian economist, Pareto, who puts the central point in this way: "Let us assume that in every branch of human activity each individual is given an index which stands as a sign of his capacity, very much the way grades are given in the various subjects in examinations in school. The highest type of lawyer, for instance, will be given 10. The man who does not get a client will be given 1—reserving zero for the man who is an out-and-out idiot. To the man who has made his millions—honestly or dishonestly as the case may be—we will give 10. To the man who has earned his thousands we will give 6; to such as just manage to keep out of the poor-house, 1, keeping zero for those who get in . . . So let us make a class of people who have the highest indices in their branch of activity, and to that class give the name of *elite.*" Vilfredo Pareto, *The Mind and Society* (New York: Harcourt, Brace, 1935), par. 2027 and 2031. Those who follow this approach end up not with one elite, but with a number corresponsing to the number of values they select. Like many rather abstract ways of reasoning, this one is useful because it forces us to think in a clear-cut way. For a skillful use of this approach, see the work of Harold D. Lasswell, in particular, *Politics: Who Gets What, When, How* (New York: McGraw-Hill, 1936); and for a more systematic use, H. D. Lasswell and Abraham Kaplan, *Power and Society* (New Haven: Yale University Press, 1950).
4. The conception of the elite as members of a top social stratum, is, of course, in line with the prevailing common-sense view of stratification. Technically, it is closer to "status group" than to "class," and has been very well stated by Joseph A. Schumpeter, "Social Classes in an Ethically Homogeneous Environment," *Imperialism and Social Classes* (New York: Augustus M. Kelley, Inc., 1951), pp. 133 ff., especially pp. 137-47. Cf. also his *Capitalism, Socialism and Democracy,* 3rd ed. (New York: Harper, 1950), Part II. For the distinction between class and status groups, see *From Max Weber: Essays in Sociology* (trans. and ed. by Gerth and Mills; New York: Oxford University Press, 1946). For an analysis of Pareto's conception of

the elite compared with Marx's conception of classes, as well as data on France, see Raymond Aron, "Social Structure and Ruling Class," *British Journal of Sociology,* vol. I, nos. 1 and 2 (1950).

5. The most popular essay in recent years which defines the elite and the mass in terms of a morally evaluated character-type is probably José Ortega y Gasset's, *The Revolt of the Masses,* 1932 (New York: New American Library, Mentor Edition, 1950), esp. pp. 91 ff.

6. "The American elite" is a confused and confusing set of images, and yet when we hear or when we use such words as Upper Class, Big Shot, Top Brass, The Millionaire Club, The High and The Mighty, we feel at least vaguely that we know what they mean, and often do. What we do not often do, however, is connect each of these images with the others; we make little effort to form a coherent picture in our minds of the elite as a whole. Even when, very occasionally, we do try to do this, we usually come to believe that it is indeed no "whole," that, like our images of it, there is no one elite, but many, and that they are not really connected with one another. What we must realize is that until we *do* try to see it as a whole, perhaps our impression that it may not be is a result merely of our lack of analytic rigor and sociological imagination.

   The first conception defines the elite in terms of the sociology of institutional position and the social structure these institutions form; the second, in terms of the statistics of selected values; the third, in terms of membership in a clique-like set of people; and the fourth, in terms of the morality of certain personality types. Or, put into inelegant shorthand: what they head up, what they have, what they belong to, who they really are.

   In this chapter . . . I have taken as generic the first view—of the elite defined in terms of institutional position—and have located the other views within it. This straight-forward conception of the elite has one practical and two theoretical advantages. The practical advantage is that it seems the easiest and the most concrete "way into" the whole problem—if only because a good deal of information is more or less readily available for sociological reflection about such circles and institutions.

   But the theoretical advantages are much more important. The institutional or structural definition, first of all, does not force us to prejudge by definition that we ought properly to leave open for investigation. The elite conceived morally, for example, as people having a certain type of character is not an ultimate definition, for apart from being rather morally arbitrary, it leads us immediately to ask *why* these people have this or that sort of character. Accordingly, we should leave open the type of characters which the members of the elite in fact turn out to have, rather than by definition select them in terms of one type or another. In a similar way, we do not want, by mere definition, to prejudge whether or not the elite are conscious members of a social class. The second theoretical advantage of defining the elite in terms of major institutions, which I hope this book as a whole makes clear, if the fact that it allows us to fit the other three conceptions of the elite into place in a systematic way: (1) The institutional positions men occupy throughout their lifetime determine their chances to get and to hold selected values. (2) The kind of psychological beings they become is in large part determined by the values they thus experience and the institutional roles they play. (3) Finally, whether or not they come to feel that they belong to a select social class, and whether or not they act according to what they hold to be its interests—these are also matters in large part determined by their institutional position, and in turn, the select values they possess and the characters they acquire.

7. As in the case, quite notably, of Gaetano Mosca, *The Ruling Class* (New York: McGraw-Hill, 1939). For a sharp analysis of Mosca, see Fritz Morstein Marx, "The Bureaucratic State," *Review of Politics,* vol. I, 1939, pp. 457 ff. Cf. also Mills, "On Intellectual Craftsmanship," April 1952, mimeographed, Columbia College, February 1955.

8. Cf. Karl Löwith, *Meaning in History* (Chicago: University of Chicago Press, 1949), pp. 125 ff. for concise and penetrating statements of several leading philosophies of history.

9. Some of these items are taken from Gerth and Mills, *Character and Social Structure,* pp. 405 ff. On role-determined and role-determining men, see also Sidney Hook's discussion, *The Hero in History* (New York: John Day, 1943).

10. I have taken the idea of the following kind of formulation from Joseph Wood Krutch's presentation of the morality of choice. See *The Measure of Man* (Indianapolis: Bobbs-Merrill, 1954), p. 52.

OIL IN SANTA BARBARA AND POWER IN AMERICA*

Harvey Molotch

More than oil leaked from Union Oil's Platform A in the Santa Barbara Channel—a bit of truth about power in America spilled out along with it. It is the thesis of this paper that this technological "accident," like all accidents, provides clues to the realities of social structure (in this instance, power arrangements) not otherwise available to the outside observer. Further, it is argued, the response of the aggrieved population (the citizenry of Santa Barbara) provides insight into the more general process which shapes disillusionment and frustration among those who come to closely examine and be injured by existing power arrangements.

A few historical details concerning the case under examination are in order. For over fifteen years, Santa Barbara's political leaders had attempted to prevent despoliation of their coastline by oil drilling on adjacent federal waters. Although they were unsuccessful in blocking eventual oil leasing (in February, 1968) of *federal* waters beyond the three-mile limit, they were able to establish a sanctuary within *state* waters (thus foregoing the extraordinary revenues which leases in such areas bring to adjacent localities—e.g., the riches of Long Beach). It was therefore a great irony that the one city which voluntarily exchanged revenue for a pure environment should find itself faced, on January 28, 1969, with a massive eruption of crude oil—an eruption which was, in the end, to cover the entire city coastline (as well as much of Ventura and Santa Barbara County coastline as well) with a thick coat of crude

---

*This paper was written as Working Paper No. 8, Community and Organization Research Institute, University of California, Santa Barbara. It was delivered at the 1969 Annual Meeting of the American Sociological Association, San Francisco. A shorter version has been published in *Ramparts,* November 1969. The author wishes to thank his wife, Linda Molotch, for her active collaboration and Robert Sollen, reporter for the *Santa Barbara News-Press,* for his cooperation and critical comments on an early draft.

Reprinted by permission from *Sociological Inquiry,* 40 (Winter), pp. 131-144.

oil. The air was soured for many hundreds of feet inland and the traditional economic base of the region (tourism) was under threat. After ten days of unsuccessful attempts, the runaway well was brought under control, only to be followed by a second eruption on February 12. This fissure was closed on March 3, but was followed by a sustained "seepage" of oil—a leakage which continues, at this writing, to pollute the sea, the air, and the famed local beaches. The oil companies had paid $603,-000,000 for their lease rights and neither they nor the federal government bear any significant legal responsibility toward the localities which these lease rights might endanger.

If the big spill had occurred almost anywhere else (e.g., Lima, Ohio; Lompoc, California), it is likely that the current research opportunity would not have developed. But Santa Barbara is different. Of its 70,000 residents, a disproportionate number are upper class and upper middle class. They are persons who, having a wide choice of where in the world they might live, have chosen Santa Barbara for its ideal climate, gentle beauty and sophisticated "culture." Thus a large number of worldly, rich, well-educated persons—individuals with resources, spare time, and contacts with national and international elites—found themselves with a commonly shared disagreeable situation: the pollution of their otherwise near-perfect environment. Santa Barbarans thus possessed none of the "problems" which otherwise are said to inhibit effective community response to external threat: they are not urban villagers (cf. Gans, 1962); they are not internally divided and parochial like the Springdalers (cf. Vidich and Bensmand 1960); nor emaciated with self-doubt and organizational naiveté as is supposed of the ghetto dwellers. With moral indignation and high self-confidence, they set out to right the wrong so obviously done to them.

Their response was immediate. The stodgy *Santa Barbara News-Press* inaugurated a series of editorials, unique in uncompromising stridency. Under the leadership of a former State Senator and a local corporate executive, a community organization was established called "GOO" (Get Oil Out!) which took a militant stand against any and all oil activity in the Channel.

In a petition to President Nixon (eventually to gain 110,000 signatures), GOO's position was clearly stated:

> . . . With the seabed filled with fissures in this area, similar disastrous oil operation accidents may be expected. And with one of the largest faults

> centered in the channel waters, one sizeable earthquake could mean possible disaster for the entire channel area . . .
>
> Therefore, we the undersigned do call upon the state of California and the Federal Government to promote conservation by:
>
> 1. Taking immediate action to have present offshore oil operations cease and desist at once.
> 2. Issuing no further leases in the Santa Barbara Channel.
> 3. Having all oil platforms and rigs removed from this area at the earliest possible date.

The same theme emerged in the hundreds of letters published by the *News-Press* in the weeks to follow and in the positions taken by virtually every local civic and government body. Both in terms of its volume (372 letters published in February alone) and the intensity of the revealed opinions, the flow of letters was hailed by the *News-Press* as "unprecedented." Rallies were held at the beach, GOO petitions were circulated at local shopping centers and sent to friends around the country; a fund-raising dramatic spoof of the oil industry was produced at a local high school. Local artists, playwrights, advertising men, retired executives and academic specialists from the local campus of the University of California (UCSB) executed special projects appropriate to their areas of expertise.

A GOO strategy emerged for a two-front attack. Local indignation, producing the petition to the President and thousands of letters to key members of Congress and the executive would lead to appropriate legislation. Legal action in the courts against the oil companies and the federal government would have the double effect of recouping some of the financial losses certain to be endured by the local tourist and fishing industries while at the same time serving notice that drilling would be a much less profitable operation than it was supposed to be. Legislation to ban drilling was introduced by Cranston in the U.S. Senate and Teague in the House of Representatives. Joint suits by the city and County of Santa Barbara (later joined by the State) for $1 billion in damages was filed against the oil companies and the federal government.

All of these activities—petitions, rallies, court action and legislative lobbying—were significant for their similarity in revealing faith in "the system." The tendency was to blame the oil companies. There was a muckraking tone to the Santa Barbara response: oil and the profit-crazy executives of Union Oil were ruining Santa Barbara—but once our national and state leaders became aware of what was going on, and were provided with the "facts" of the case, justice would be done.

Indeed, there was good reason for hope. The quick and enthusiastic responses of Teague and Cranston represented a consensus of men otherwise polar opposites in their political behavior: Democrat Cranston was a charter member of the liberal California Democratic Council; Republican Teague was a staunch fiscal and moral conservative (e.g., a strong Vietnam hawk and unrelenting harrasser of the local Center for the Study of Democratic Institutions). Their bills, for which there was great optimism, would have had the consequence of effecting a "permanent" ban on drilling in the Channel.

But from other quarters there was silence. Santa Barbara's representatives in the state legislature either said nothing or (in later stages) offered minimal support. It took several months for Senator Murphy to introduce Congressional legislation (for which he admitted to having little hope) which would have had the consequence of exchanging the oil companies' leases in the Channel for comparable leases in the under-exploited Elk Hills oil reserve in California's Kern County. Most disappointing of all to Santa Barbarans, Governor Reagan withheld support for proposals which would end the drilling.

As subsequent events unfolded, this seemingly inexplicable silence of the democratically elected representatives began to fall into place as part of a more general problem. American democracy came to be seen as a much more complicated affair than a system in which governmental officials actuate the desires of the "people who elected them" once those desires come to be known. Instead, increasing recognition came to be given to the "all-powerful oil lobby"; to legislators "in the pockets of Oil"; to academicians "bought" by Oil and to regulatory agencies which lobby for those they are supposed to regulate. In other words, Santa Barbarans became increasingly *ideological,* increasingly *sociological,* and in the words of some observers, increasingly *"radical."*[1] Writing from his lodgings in the area's most exclusive hotel (the Santa Barbara Biltmore), an irate citizen penned these words in his published letter to the *News-Press:*

> We the people can protest and protest and it means nothing because the industrial and military junta are the country. They tell us, the People, what is good for the oil companies is good for the People. To that I say, Like Hell! . . .

Profit is their language and the proof of all this is their history (*SBNP*[2], Feb. 26, 1969, p. A-6).

As time wore on, the editorials and letters continued in their bitterness.

THE EXECUTIVE BRANCH AND THE REGULATORY AGENCIES: DISILLUSIONMENT

From the start, Secretary Hickel's actions were regarded with suspicion. His publicized associations with Alaskan Oil interests did his reputation no good in Santa Barbara. When, after a halt to drilling (for "review" of procedures) immediately after the initial eruption, Hickel one day later ordered a resumption of drilling and production (even as the oil continued to gush into the channel), the government's response was seen as unbelievingly consistent with conservationists' worst fears. That he backed down within 48 hours and ordered a halt to drilling and production was taken as a response to the massive nationwide media play then being given to the Santa Barbara plight and to the citizens' mass outcry just then beginning to reach Washington.

Disenchantment with Hickel and the executive branch also came through less spectacular, less specific, but nevertheless genuine activity. First of all, Hickel's failure to support any of the legislation introduced to halt drilling was seen as an *action* favoring Oil. His remarks on the subject, while often expressing sympathy with Santa Barbarans[3] (and for a while placating local sentiment) were revealed as hypocritical in light of the action not taken. Of further note was the constant attempt by the Interior Department to minimize the extent of damage in Santa Barbara or to hint at possible "compromises" which were seen locally as near-total capitulation to the oil companies.

Volume of Oil Spillage. Many specific examples might be cited. An early (and continuing) issue in the oil spill was the *volume* of oil spilling into the Channel. The U.S. Geological Survey (administered by Interior), when queried by reporters, broke its silence on the subject with estimates which struck as incredible in Santa Barbara. One of the extraordinary attributes of the Santa Barbara locale is the presence of a technology establishment among the most sophisticated in the country. Several officials of the General Research Corporation (a local R & D firm with experience in marine technology) initiated studies of the oil outflow and announced findings of pollution volume at a "minimum" of ten fold the Interior estimate. Further, General Research provided (and the *News-Press* published) a detailed account of the methods used in making their estimate (cf. Allan, 1969). Despite repeated challenges from the press, Interior both refused to alter its estimate or to reveal its method for making estimates. Throughout the crisis, the divergence of the estimates remained at about ten fold.

The "seepage" was estimated by the Geological Survey to have been reduced from 1,260 gallons per day to about 630 gallons. General Research, however, estimated the leakage at the rate of 8,400 gallons per day at the same point in time as Interior's 630 gallon estimate. The lowest estimate of all was provided by an official of the Western Oil and Gas Association, in a letter to the *Wall Street Journal.* His estimate: "Probably less than 100 gallons a day" (*SBNP,* August 5, 1969:A-1).

Damage to Beaches. Still another point of contention was the state of the beaches at varying points in time. The oil companies, through various public relations officials, constantly minimized the actual amount of damage and maximized the effect of Union Oil's cleanup activity. What surprised (and most irritated) the locals was the fact that Interior statements implied the same goal. Thus Hickel referred at a press conference to the "recent" oil spill, providing the impression that the oil spill was over, at a time when freshly erupting oil was continuing to stain local beaches. President Nixon appeared locally to "inspect" the damage to beaches, and Interior arranged for him to land his helicopter on a city beach which had been cleaned thoroughly in the days just before, but spared him a close-up of much of the rest of the County shoreline which continued to be covered with a thick coat of crude oil. (The beach visited by Nixon has been oil stained on many occasions subsequent to the President's departure.) Secret servicemen kept the placards and shouts of several hundred demonstrators safely out of Presidential viewing or hearing distance.

Continuously, the Oil and Interior combine implied the beaches to be restored when Santa Barbarans knew that even a beach which looked clean was by no means restored. The *News-Press* through a comprehensive series of interviews with local and national experts on wildlife and geology made the following points clear:

1. As long as oil remained on the water and oil continued to leak from beneath the sands, all Santa Barbara beaches were subject to continuous doses of oil—subject only to the vagaries of wind change. Indeed, all

through the spill and up to the present point in time, a beach walk is likely to result in tar on the feet. On "bad days" the beaches are unapproachable.

2. The damage to the "ecological chain" (a concept which has become a household phrase in Santa Barbara) is of unknown proportions. Much study will be necessary to learn the extent of damage.

3. The continuous alternating natural erosion and building up of beach sands means that "clean" beaches contain layers of oil at various sublevels under the mounting sands; layers which will once again be exposed when the cycle reverses itself and erosion begins anew. Thus, it will take many years for the beaches of Santa Barbara to be completely restored, even if the present seepage is halted and no additional pollution occurs.

Damage to Wildlife. Oil on feathers is ingested by birds, continuous preening thus leads to death. In what local and national authorities called a hopeless task, two bird-cleaning centers were established to cleanse feathers and otherwise administer to damaged wild-fowl. (Oil money helped to establish and supply these centers.) Both spokesmen from Oil and the federal government then adopted these centers as sources of "data" on the extent of damage to wild-fowl. Thus, the number of dead birds due to pollution was computed on the basis of number of fatalities at the wild-fowl centers.[4] This of course is preposterous given the fact that dying birds are provided with very inefficient means of propelling themselves to such designated places. The obviousness of this dramatic understatement of fatalities was never acknowledged by either Oil or Interior—although noted in Santa Barbara.

At least those birds in the hands of local ornithologists could be confirmed as dead—and this fact could not be disputed by either Oil or Interior. Not so, however, with species whose corpses are more difficult to produce on command. Several observers at the Channel Islands (a national wildlife preserve containing one of the country's largest colonies of sea animals) reported sighting unusually large numbers of dead sea-lion pups—on the oil stained shores of one of the islands. Statement and counter-statement followed with Oil's defenders arguing that the animals were not dead at all—but only appeared inert because they were sleeping. Despite the testimony of staff experts at the local Museum of Natural History and the Museum Scientist of UCSB's Biological Sciences Department that the number of "inert" sea-lion pups was far larger than normal and that field trips had confirmed the deaths, the position of Oil, as also expressed by the Department of the Navy (which administers the stricken island) remained adamant that the sea animals were only sleeping (cf. *Life,* June 13, 1969; July 4, 1969). The dramatic beaching of an unusually large number of dead whales on the beaches of Northern California—whales which had just completed their migration through the Santa Barbara Channel—was acknowledged, but held not to be caused by oil pollution. No direct linkage (or non-linkage) with oil could be demonstrated by investigating scientists (cf. *San Francisco Chronicle,* March 12, 1969:1-3).

In the end, it was not simply Interior, its U.S. Geological Survey and the President which either supported or tacitly accepted Oil's public relations tactics. The regulatory agencies at both national and state level, by action, inaction and implication had the consequence of defending Oil at virtually every turn. Thus at the outset of the first big blow, as the ocean churned with bubbling oil and gas, the U.S. Coast Guard (which patrols Channel waters regularly) failed to notify local officials of the pollution threat because, in the words of the local commander, "the seriousness of the situation was not apparent until late in the day Tuesday and it was difficult to reach officials after business hours" (*SBNP,* January 30, 1969: A-1, 4). Officials ended up hearing of the spill from the *News-Press.*

The Army Corps of Engineers must approve all structures placed on the ocean floor and thus had the discretion to hold public hearings on each application for a permit to build a drilling platform. With the exception of a single *pro forma* ceremony held on a platform erected in 1967, requests for such hearings were never granted. In its most recent handling of these matters (at a point long after the initial eruption and as oil still leaks into the ocean) the Corps changed its criteria for public hearings by restricting written objections to new drilling to "the effects of the proposed exploratory drilling on *navigation or national defense*" (*SBNP,* August 17, 1969:A-1, 4). Prior to the spill, effects on *fish and wildlife* were specified by the Army as possible grounds for objection, but at that time such objections, when raised, were more easily dismissed as unfounded.

The Federal Water Pollution Control Administration consistently attempted to understate the amount of damage done to waterfowl by quoting the "hospital dead" as though a reasonable assessment of the net damage. State agencies followed the same pattern. The charge of "Industry domination" of state conservation boards was levelled by the State

Deputy Attorney General, Charles O'Brien (*SBNP,* February 9, 1969:A-6). Thomas Gaines, a Union Oil executive, actually sits as a member on the state Agency Board most directly connected with the control of pollution in Channel waters. In correspondence with complaining citizens, N. B. Livermore, Jr., of the Resources Agency of California refers to the continuing oil spill as "minor seepage" with "no major long-term effect on the marine ecology." The letter adopts the perspective of Interior and Oil, even though the state was in no way being held culpable for the spill (letter, undated to Joseph Keefe, citizen, University of California, Santa Barbara Library, on file).

With these details under their belts, Santa Barbarans were in a position to understand the sweeping condemnation of the regulatory system as contained in a *News-Press* front page, banner-headlined interview with Rep. Richard D. Ottenger (D-NY), quoted as follows: "And so on down the line. Each agency has a tendency to become the captive of the industry that it is to regulate" (*SBNP,* March 1, 1969:A-1).

THE CONGRESS: DISILLUSIONMENT

Irritations with Interior were paralleled by frustrations encountered in dealing with the Congressional establishment which had the responsibility of holding hearings on ameliorative legislation. A delegation of Santa Barbarans was scheduled to testify in Washington on the Cranston bill. From the questions which Congressmen asked of them, and the manner in which they were "handled," the delegation could only conclude that the Committee was "in the pockets of Oil." As one of the returning delegates put it, the presentation bespoke of "total futility."

At this writing, six months after their introduction, both the Cranston and Teague bills lie buried in committee with little prospect of surfacing. Cranston has softened his bill significantly—requiring only that new drilling be suspended until Congress is convinced that sufficient technological safeguards exist. But to no avail.

SCIENCE AND TECHNOLOGY: DISILLUSIONMENT

From the start, part of the shock of the oil spill was that such a thing could happen in a country with such sophisticated technology. The much overworked phrase, "If we can send a man to the moon . . ." was even more overworked in Santa Barbara. When, in years previous, Santa

Barbara's elected officials had attempted to halt the original sale of leases, "assurances" were given from Interior that such an "accident" could not occur, given the highly developed state of the art. Not only did it occur, but the original gusher of oil spewed forth completely out of control for ten days and the continuing "seepage" which followed it remains uncontrolled to the present moment, seven months later. That the government would embark upon so massive a drilling program with such unsophisticated technologies was striking indeed.

Further, not only were the technologies inadequate and the plans for stopping a leak, should it occur, nonexistent, but the area in which the drilling took place was known to be ultra-hazardous from the outset. That is, drilling was occurring on an ocean bottom known for its extraordinary geological circumstances—porous sands lacking a bedrock "ceiling" capable of containing runaway oil and gas. Thus the continuing leakage through the sands at various points above the oil reservoir is unstoppable, and could have been anticipated with the data *known to all parties involved.*

Another peculiarity of the Channel is the fact that it is located in the heart of earthquake activity in that region of the country which, among all regions, is among the very most earthquake prone.[5] Santa Barbarans are now asking what might occur in an earthquake: if pipes on the ocean floor and casings through the ocean bottom should be sheared, the damage done by the Channel's *thousands* of potential producing wells would be devastating to the entire coast of Southern California.[6]

Recurrent attempts have been made to ameliorate the continuing seep by placing floating booms around an area of leakage and then having workboats skim off the leakage from within the demarcated area.[7] Chemical dispersants, of various varieties, have also been tried. But the oil bounces over the sea booms in the choppy waters; the work boats suck up only a drop in the bucket and the dispersants are effective only when used in quantities which constitute a graver pollution threat than the oil they are designed to eliminate. Cement is poured into suspected fissures in an attempt to seal them up. Oil on beaches is periodically cleaned by dumping straw over the sands and then raking up the straw along with the oil it absorbs.

This striking contrast between the sophistication of the means used to locate and extract oil compared to the primitiveness of the means to control and clean it up was widely noted in Santa Barbara. It is the result of a system which promotes research and development which leads to strategic profitability rather than to social utility. The common sight of men throwing straw on miles of beaches within sight of complex drilling rigs capable of exploiting resources thousands of feet below the ocean's surface, made the point clear.

The futility of the clean-up and control efforts was widely noted in Santa Barbara. Secretary Hickel's announcement that the Interior Department was generating new "tough" regulations to control off-shore drilling was thus met with great skepticism. The Santa Barbara County Board of Supervisors was invited to "review" these new regulations—and refused to do so in the belief that such participation would be used to provide the fraudulent impression of democratic responsiveness—when, in fact, the relevant decisions had been already made. In previous years when they were fighting against the leasing of the Channel, the Supervisors had been assured of technological safeguards; now, as the emergency continued, they could witness for themselves the dearth of any means for ending the leakage in the Channel. They had also heard the testimony of a high-ranking Interior engineer who, when asked if such safeguards could positively prevent future spills, explained that "no prudent engineer would ever make such a claim" (*SBNP,* February 19, 1969:A-1). They also had the testimony of Donald Solanas, a regional supervisor of Interior's U.S. Geological Survey, who had said about the Union Platform eruption:

> I could have had an engineer on that platform 24 hours a day, 7 days a week and he couldn't have prevented the accident.

His "explanation" of the cause of the "accident": "Mother earth broke down on us" (*SBNP,* February 28, 1969: C-12).

Given these facts, as contained in the remarks of Interior's own spokesmen, combined with testimony and information received from non-Interior personnel, Interior's new regulations and the invitation to the County to participate in making them, could only be a ruse to preface a resumption of drilling. In initiating the County's policy of not responding to Interior's "invitation," a County Supervisor explained: "I think we may be falling into a trap" (*SBNP,* April 1, 1969).

The very next day, the Supervisors' suspicions were confirmed. Interior announced a selective resumption of drilling "to relieve pressures." (*News-Press* letter writers asked if the "pressure" was geological or political.") The new tough regulations were themselves seriously flawed by the fact that most of their provisions specified those measures, such as buoyant booms around platforms, availability of chemical dispersants, etc., which had proven almost totally useless in the current emergency. They fell far short of minimum safety requirements as enumerated by UC Santa Barbara geologist Robert Curry who citicized a previous version of the same regulations as "relatively trivial" and "toothless"[8] (*SBNP,* March 5, 1969:C-9).

On the other hand, the new regulations did specify that oil companies would henceforth be financially responsible for damages resulting from pollution mishaps. (This had been the *de facto* reality in the Union case; the company had assumed responsibility for the clean-up, and advised stockholders that such costs were covered by "more than adequate" insurance.[9]) The liability requirement has been vociferously condemned by the oil companies—particularly by those firms which have failed to make significant strikes on their Channel leases (*SBNP,* March 14, 1969). Several of these companies have now entered suit (supported by the ACLU) against the federal government charging that the arbitrary changing of lease conditions renders Channel exploitation "economically and practically impossible," thus depriving them of rights of due process (*SBNP,* April 10, 1969:A-1).

The weaknesses of the new regulations came not as a surprise to people who had already adapted to thinking of Oil and the Interior Department as the same source. There was much less preparation for the results of the Presidential Committee of "distinguished" scientists and engineers (the DuBridge Panel) which was to recommend means of eliminating the seepage under Platform A. Given the half-hearted, inexpensive and primitive attempts by Union Oil to deal with the seepage, feeling ran high that at last the technological sophistication of the nation would be harnessed to solve this particular vexing problem. Instead, the panel—after a two-day session and after hearing testimony from no one not connected with either Oil or Interior—recommended the "solution" of drilling an additional 50 wells under Platform A in order to pump the area dry as quickly as possible. The process would require ten to twenty years, one member of the panel estimated.[10]

The recommendation was severely terse, requiring no more than one and a half pages of type. Despite an immediate local clamor, Interior refused to make public the data or the reasoning behind the recommendations. The information on Channel geological conditions was provided by the oil companies; the Geological Survey routinely depends upon the oil industry for the data upon which it makes its "regulatory" decisions. The data, being proprietary, could thus not be released. Totally inexplicable, in light of this "explanation," is Interior's continuing refusal to immediately provide the information given a recent clearance by Union Oil for public release of all the data. Santa Barbara's local experts have thus been thwarted by the counter-arguments of Oil-Interior that "if you had the information we have, you would agree with us."

Science was also having its non-neutral consequences on the other battlefront being waged by Santa Barbarans. The Chief Deputy Attorney General of California, in his April 7 speech to the blue-ribbon Channel City Club of Santa Barbara, complained that the oil industry

> is preventing oil drilling experts from aiding the Attorney General's office in its lawsuits over the Santa Barbara oil spill (*SBNP,* Aug. 8, 1969).

Complaining that his office has been unable to get assistance from petroleum experts at California universities, the Deputy Attorney General further stated:

> The university experts all seem to be working on grants from the oil industry. There is an atmosphere of fear. The experts are afraid that if they assist us in our case on behalf of the people of California, they will lose their oil industry grants.

At the Santa Barbara Campus of the University, there is little Oil money in evidence and few, if any, faculty members have entered into proprietary research arrangements with Oil. Petroleum geology and engineering is simply not a local specialty. Yet it is a fact that Oil interests did contact several Santa Barbara faculty members with offers of funds for studies of the ecological effects of the oil spill, with publication rights stipulated by Oil.[11] It is also the case that the Federal Water Pollution Control Administration explicitly requested a UC Santa Barbara botanist to withhold the findings of his study, funded by that Agency, on the ecological consequences of the spill (*SBNP,* July 29, 1969:A-3).

Except for the Deputy Attorney General's complaint, none of these revelations received any publicity outside of Santa Barbara. But the Attorney's allegation became something of a state-wide issue. A professor at the Berkeley campus, in his attempt to refute the allegation, actually confirmed it. Wilbur H. Somerton, Professor of petroleum engineering, indicated he could not testify against Oil

> because my work depends on good relations with the petroleum industry. My interest is serving the petroleum industry. I view my obligation to the community as supplying it with well-trained petroleum engineers. We train the industry's engineers and they help us. (*SBNP,* April 12, 1969, as quoted from a *San Francisco Chronicle* interview.)

Santa Barbara's leaders were incredulous about the whole affair. The question—one which is more often asked by the downtrodden sectors of the society—was asked: "Whose University is this, anyway?" A local executive and GOO leader asked, "If the truth isn't in the universities, where is it?" A conservative member of the State Legislature, in a move reminiscent of SDS demands, went so far as to ask an end to all faculty "moonlighting" for industry. In Santa Barbara, the only place where all of this publicity was occurring, there was thus an opportunity for insight into the linkages between knowledge, the University, government and Oil and the resultant non-neutrality of science. The backgrounds of many members of the DuBridge Panel were linked publicly to the oil industry. In a line of reasoning usually the handiwork of groups like SDS, a *News-Press* letter writer labeled Dr. DuBridge as a servant of Oil interests because, as a past President of Cal Tech, he would have had to defer to Oil in generating the massive funding which that institution requires. In fact, the relationship was quite direct. Not only has Union Oil been a contributor to Cal Tech, but Fred Hartley (Union's President) is a Cal Tech trustee. The impropriety of such a man as DuBridge serving as the key "scientist" in determining the Santa Barbara outcome seemed more and more obvious.

TAXATION AND PATRIOTISM: DISILLUSIONMENT

From Engler's detailed study of the politics of Oil, we learn that the oil companies combat local resistance with arguments that hurt: taxation and patriotism (cf. Engler, 1961). They threaten to take their operations elsewhere, thus depriving the locality of taxes and jobs. The more grandiose argument is made that oil is necessary for the national defense; hence, any weakening of "incentives" to discover and produce oil plays into the hands of the enemy.

Santa Barbara, needing money less than most locales and valuing environment more, learned enough to know better. Santa Barbara wanted oil to leave, but oil would not. Because the oil is produced in federal waters, only a tiny proportion of Santa Barbara County's budget indirectly comes from oil, and virtually none of the city of Santa Barbara's budget comes from oil. *News-Press* letters and articles disposed of the defense argument with these points: (1) oil companies deliberately limit oil production under geographical quota restrictions designed to maintain the high price of oil by regulating supply; (2) the federal oil import quota (also sponsored by the oil industry) which restricts imports from abroad, weakens the country's defense posture by forcing the nation to exhaust its own finite supply while the Soviets rely on the Middle East; (3) most oil imported into the U.S. comes from relatively dependable sources in South America which foreign wars would not endanger; (4) the next major war will be a nuclear holocaust with possible oil shortages a very low level problem.

Just as an attempt to answer the national defense argument led to conclusions the very opposite of Oil's position, so did a closer examination of the tax argument. For not only did Oil not pay very much in local taxes, Oil also paid very little in *federal* taxes. In another of its front-page editorials the *News-Press* made the facts clear. The combination of the output restrictions, extraordinary tax write-off privileges for drilling expenses, the import quota, and the 27.5 per cent depletion allowance, all created an artificially high price of U.S. oil—a price almost double the world market price for the comparable product delivered to comparable U.S. destinations.[12] The combination of incentives available creates a situation where some oil companies pay no taxes whatever during extraordinarily profitable years. In the years 1962–1966, Standard of New Jersey paid less than 4 per cent of profits in taxes, Standard of California, less than 3 per cent, and 22 of the largest oil companies paid slightly more than 6 per cent (*SBNP,* February 16, 1969:A-1). It was pointed out, again and again to Santa Barbarans, that it was this system of subsidy which made the relatively high cost deep-sea exploration and drilling in the Channel profitable in the first place. Thus, the citizens of Santa Barbara, as federal taxpayers and fleeced consumers were subsidizing their own demise. The consequence of such a revelation can only be *infuriating.*

THE MOBILIZATION OF BIAS

The actions of Oil and Interior and the contexts in which such actions took place can be re-examined in terms of their function in diffusing local opposition, disorienting dissenters, and otherwise limiting the scope of issues which are potentially part of public controversies. E. E. Schattschneider (1960:71) has noted:

> All forms of political organization have a bias in favor of the exploitation of some kinds of conflict and the suppression of others because *organization is the mobilization of bias.* Some issues are organized into politics while others are organized out.

Expanding the notion slightly, certain techniques shaping the "mobilization of bias" can be said to have been revealed by the present case study.

1. *The pseudo-event.* Boorstin (1962) has described the use of the pseudo-event in a large variety of task accomplishment situations. A pseudo-event occurs when men arrange conditions to simulate a certain kind of event, such that certain prearranged consequences follow as though the actual event had taken place. Several pseudo-events may be cited. *Local participation in decision making.* From the outset, it was obvious that national actions vis-à-vis Oil in Santa Barbara had as their strategy the freezing out of any local participation in decisions affecting the Channel. Thus, when in 1968 the federal government first called for bids on a Channel lease, local officials were not even informed. When subsequently queried about the matter, federal officials indicated that the lease which was advertised for bid was just a corrective measure to prevent drainage of a "little old oil pool" on federal property adjacent to a slate lease producing for Standard and Humble. This "little old pool" was to draw a high bonus bid of $21,189,000 from a syndicate headed by Phillips (*SBNP,* February 9, 1969:A-17). Further, local officials were not notified by any government agency in the case of the original oil spill, nor (except after the spill was already widely known) in the case of any of the previous or subsequent more "minor" spills. Perhaps the thrust of the federal government's colonialist attitude toward the local community was contained in an Interior Department engineer's memo written to J. Cordell Moore, Assistant Secretary of Interior, explaining the policy of refusing public hearings prefatory to drilling: "We preferred not to stir up the natives any more than possible."[13] (The memo was released by Senator Cranston and excerpted on page 1 of the *News-Press.*)

Given this known history, the Santa Barbara County Board of Supervisors refused the call for "participation" in drawing up new "tougher" drilling regulations, precisely because they knew the government had no intention of creating "safe" drilling regulations. They refused to take part in the pseudo-event and thus refused to let the consequences (in this case the appearance of democratic decision-making and local assent) of a pseudo-event occur.

Other attempts at the staging of pseudo-events may be cited. Nixon's "inspection" of the Santa Barbara beachfront was an obvious one. Another series of pseudo-events were the Congressional hearings staged by legislators who were, in the words of a local well-to-do lady leader of GOO, "kept men." The locals blew off steam—but the hearing of arguments and the proposing of appropriate legislation based on those arguments (the presumed essence of the Congressional hearing as a formal event) certainly did not come off. Many Santa Barbarans had a similar impression of the court hearings regarding the various legal maneuvers against oil drilling; legal proceedings came to be similarly seen as ceremonious arrangements for the accomplishing of tasks not revealed by their formally-stated properties.

2. *The creeping event.* A creeping event is, in a sense, the opposite of a pseudo-event. It occurs when something *is* actually taking place, but when the manifest signs of the event are arranged to occur at an inconspicuously gradual and piece-meal pace, thus eliminating some of the consequences which would otherwise follow from the event if it were to be perceived all-at-once to be occurring. Two major creeping events were arranged for the Santa Barbara Channel. Although the great bulk of the bidding for leases in the Channel occurred simultaneously, the first lease was, as was made clear earlier, advertised for bid prior to the others and prior to any public announcement of the leasing of the Channel. The federal waters' virginity was thus ended with only a whimper. A more salient example of the creeping event is the resumption of production and drilling after Hickel's second moratorium. Authorization to resume *production* on different specific groups of wells occurred on these dates in 1969: February 17; February 21; February 22; and March 3. Authorization to resume *drilling* of various groups of new wells was announced by Interior on these dates in 1969: April 1, June 12, July 2, August 2, and August 16. (This is being written on August 20.) Each time, the resumption was announced as a safety precaution to relieve pressures, until finally on the most recent resumption date, the word "deplete" was used for the first time as the reason for granting permission to drill. There is thus no *particular* point in time in which production and drilling was re-authorized for the Channel—and full resumption has still not been officially authorized.

A creeping event has the consequences of diffusing resistance to the event by holding back what journalists call a "time peg" on which to hang "the story." Even if the aggrieved party should get wind that "something is going on," strenuous reaction is inhibited. Non-routine activity has as its prerequisite the crossing of a certain threshold point of input; the dribbling out of an event has the consequence of making each of the revealed inputs fall below the threshold level necessary for non-routine activity. By the time it becomes quite clear that "something *is* going on" both the aggrieved and the sponsors of the creeping event can ask why there should be a response *"now"* when there was none previously to the very same kind of stimulus. In such manner, the aggrieved has resort only to frustration and a gnawing feeling that "events" are sweeping him by.

3. *The "neutrality" of science and the "knowledge" producers.* I have already dealt at some length with the disillusionment of Santa Barbarans with the "experts" and the University. After learning for themselves of the collusion between government and Oil and the use of secret science as a prop to that collusion, Santa Barbarans found themselves in the unenviable position of having to demonstrate that science and knowledge were, in fact, not neutral arbiters. They had to demonstrate, by themselves, that continued drilling was not safe, that the "experts" who said it was safe were the hirelings directly or indirectly of Oil interests and that the report of the DuBridge Panel recommending massive drilling was a fraudulent document. They had to document that the University *petroleum* geologists were themselves in league with their adversaries and that knowledge unfavorable to the Oil interests was systematically withheld by virtue of the very structure of the knowledge industry. As the SDS has learned in other contexts, this is no small task. It is a long story to tell, a complicated story to tell, and one which pits lay persons (and a few academic renagades) against a profession and patrons of a profession. An illustration of the difficulties involved may be drawn from very recent history. Seventeen Santa Barbara plaintiffs, represented by the ACLU, sought a temporary injunction against additional Channel drilling at least until the information utilized by the DuBridge Panel was made public and a hearing could be held. The injunction was not granted and, in the end, the presiding federal judge ruled in favor of what he termed the "expert" opinions available to the Secretary of the Interior. It was a function of limited time for rebuttal, the disorienting confusions of courtroom procedures, and also perhaps the desire to not offend the Court, that the ACLU lawyer could not make his subtle, complex and

highly controversial case that the "experts" were partisans and that their scientific "findings" follow from that partisanship.

4. *Constraints of communication media.* Just as the courtroom setting was not amenable to a full reproduction of the details surrounding the basis for the ACLU case, so the media in general—through restrictions of time and style—prevent a full airing of the details of the case. A more cynical analysis of the media's inability to make known the Santa Barbara "problem" in its full fidelity might hinge on an allegation that the media are constrained by fear of "pressures" from Oil and its allies; Metromedia, for example, sent a team to Santa Barbara which spent several days documenting, interviewing and filming for an hour-long program—only to suddenly drop the whole matter due to what is reported by locals in touch with the network to have been "pressures" from Oil. Such blatant interventions aside, however, the problem of full reproduction of the Santa Barbara "news" would remain problematic nonetheless.

News media are notorious for the anecdotal nature of their reporting; even so-called "think-pieces" rarely go beyond a stringing together of proximate "events." There are no analyses of the "mobilization of bias" or linkages of men's actions and their pecuniary interests. Science and learning are assumed to be neutral; regulatory agencies are assumed to function as "watch-dogs" for the public. Information to the contrary of these assumptions is treated as exotic exception; in the manner of Drew Pearson columns, exception piles upon exception without intellectual combination, analysis or ideological synthesis. The complexity of the situation to be reported, the wealth of details needed to support such analyses require more time and effort than journalists have at their command. Their recitation would produce long stories not consistent with space requirements and make-up preferences of newspapers and analogous constraints of the other media. A full telling of the whole story would tax the reader/viewer and would risk boring him.

For these reasons, the rather extensive media coverage of the oil spill centered on a few dramatic moments in its history (e.g., the initial gusher of oil) and a few simple-to-tell "human interest" aspects such as the pathetic deaths of the sea birds struggling along the oil-covered sands. With increasing temporal and geographical distance from the initial spill, national coverage became increasingly rare and increasingly sloppy. Interior statements on the state of the "crisis" were reported without local rejoinders as the newsmen who would have gathered them began leaving the scene. It is to be kept in mind that, relative to other local events, the Santa Barbara spill received extraordinarily extensive national coverage.[14] The point is that this coverage is nevertheless inadequate in both its quality and quantity to adequately inform the American public.

5. *The routinization of evil.* An oft quoted American cliché is that the news media cover only the "bad" things; the everyday world of people going about their business in conformity with American ideals loses out to the coverage of student and ghetto "riots," wars and crime, corruption and sin. The grain of truth in this cliché should not obfuscate the fact that there are *certain kinds of evil* which, partially for reasons cited in the preceding paragraphs, also lose their place in the public media and the public mind. Pollution of the Santa Barbara Channel is now routine; the issue is not whether or not the Channel is polluted, but *how much* it is polluted. A recent oil slick discovered off a Phillips Platform in the Channel was dismissed by an oil company official as a "routine" drilling by-product which was not viewed as "obnoxious." That "about half" of the current oil seeping into the Channel is allegedly being recovered is taken as an improvement sufficient to preclude the "outrage" that a big national story would require.

Similarly, the pollution of the "moral environment" becomes routine; politicians are, of course, on the take, in the pockets of Oil, etc. The depletion allowance issue becomes not whether or not such special benefits should exist at all, but rather whether it should be at the level of 20 or 27.5 per cent. "Compromises" emerge such as the 24 per cent depletion allowance and the new "tough" drilling regulations, which are already being hailed as "victories" for the reformers (cf. *Los Angeles Times,* July 14, 1969:17). Like the oil spill itself, the depletion allowance debate becomes buried in its own disorienting detail, its ceremonious pseudo-events and in the triviality of the "solutions" which ultimately come to be considered as the "real" options. Evil is both banal and complicated; both of these attributes contribute to its durability.[15]

THE STRUGGLE FOR THE MEANS TO POWER

It should (although it does not) go without saying that the parties competing to shape decision-making on oil in Santa Barbara do not have equal access to the means of "mobilizing bias" which this paper has discussed. The same social structural characteristics which Michels has asserted make for an "iron law of oligarchy" make for, in this case, a series of extraordinary advantages for the Oil-government combine. The ability to create pseudo-events such as Nixon's Santa Barbara inspection or controls necessary to bring off well-timed creeping events are not evenly distributed throughout the social structure. Lacking such ready access to media, lacking the ability to stage events at will, lacking a well-integrated system of arrangements for goal attainment (at least in comparison to their adversaries) Santa Barbara's leaders have met with repeated frustrations.

Their response to their relative powerlessness has been analogous to other groups and individuals who, from a similar vantage point, come to see the system up close. They become willing to expand their repertoire of means of influence as their cynicism and bitterness increase concomitantly. Letter writing gives way to demonstrations, demonstrations to civil disobedience. People refuse to participate in "democratic procedures" which are a part of the opposition's event-management strategy. Confrontation politics arise as a means of countering with "events" of one's own, thus providing the media with "stories" which can be simply and energetically told. The lesson is learned that "the power to make a reportable event is . . . the power to make experience" (Boorstin, 1962:10).

Rallies were held at local beaches; Congressmen and state and national officials were greeted by demonstrations. (Fred Hartley, of Union Oil, inadvertently landed his plane in the midst of one such demonstration, causing a rather ugly name-calling scene to ensue.) A "sail-in" was held one Sunday with a flotilla of local pleasure boats forming a circle around Platform A, each craft bearing large anti-oil banners. (Months earlier boats coming near the platforms were sprayed by oil personnel with fire hoses.) City-hall meetings were packed with citizens reciting "demands" for immediate and forceful local action.

A City Council election in the midst of the crisis resulted in the landslide election of the Council's bitterest critic and the defeat of a veteran Councilman suspected of having "oil interests." In a rare action, the *News-Press* condemned the local Chamber of Commerce for accepting oil money for a fraudulent tourist advertising campaign which touted Santa Barbara (including its beaches) as restored to its former beauty. (In the end, references to the beaches were removed from subsequent advertisements, but thc oil-financed campaign continued briefly.)

In the meantime, as a *Wall Street Journal* reporter was to observe, "a current of gloom and despair" ran through the ranks of Santa Barbara's militants. The president of Sloan Instruments Corporation, an international R & D firm with headquarters in Santa Barbara, came to comment:

> We are so God-damned frustrated. The whole democratic process seems to be falling apart. Nobody responds to us, and we end up doing things progressively less reasonable. This town is going to blow up if there isn't some reasonable attitude expressed by the Federal Government—nothing seems to happen except that we lose.

Similarly, a well-to-do widow, during a legal proceeding in Federal District Court in which Santa Barbara was once again "losing," whispered in the author's ear:

> Now I understand why those young people at the University go around throwing things. . . . The individual has no rights at all.

One possible grand strategy for Santa Barbara was outlined by a local public relations man and GOO worker:

> We've got to run the oil men out. The city owns the wharf and the harbor that the company has to use. The city has got to deny its facilities to oil traffic, service boats, cranes and the like. If the city contravenes some federal navigation laws (which such actions would unquestionably involve), to hell with it.
>
> The only hope to save Santa Barbara is to awaken the nation to the ravishment. That will take public officials who are willing to block oil traffic with their bodies and with police hoses, if necessary. Then federal marshals or federal troops would have to come in. This would pull in the national news media (*SBNP,* July 6, 1969, p. 7).

This scenario has thus far not occurred in Santa Barbara, although the use of the wharf by the oil industries has led to certain militant actions. A picket was maintained at the wharf for two weeks, protesting the conversion of the pier from a recreation and tourist facility to a heavy industrial plant for the use of the oil companies.[16] A boycott of other wharf businesses (e.g., two restaurants) was urged. The picket line was led by white, middle-class adults—one of whom had almost won the mayorality of Santa Barbara in a previous election. Hardly a "radical" or a "militant," this same man was several months later representing his neighborhood protective association in its opposition to the presence of a "Free School" described by this man (somewhat ambivalently) as a "hippie hotel."

Prior to the picketing, a dramatic Easter Sunday confrontation (involving approximatively 500 persons) took place between demonstrators and city police. Unexpectedly, as a wharf rally was breaking up, an oil service truck began driving up the pier to make delivery of casing supplies for oil drilling. There was a spontaneous sit-down in front of the truck. For the first time since the Ku Klux Klan folded in the 1930's, a group of Santa Barbarans (some young, some "hippie," but many hard-working middle-class adults), was publicly taking the law into its own hands. After much lengthy discussion between police, the truck driver and the demonstrators, the truck was ordered away and the demonstrators remained to rejoice in their victory. The following day's *News-Press* editorial, while not supportive of such tactics, found much to excuse—noteworthy given the paper's long standing *bitter* opposition to similar tactics when exercised by dissident Northern blacks or student radicals.

A companion demonstration on the water failed to materialize; a group of Santa Barbarans was to sail to the Union platform and "take it"; choppy seas, however, precluded a landing, causing the would-be conquerors to return to port in failure.

It would be difficult to speculate at this writing what forms Santa Barbara's resistance might take in the future. The veteran *News-Press* reporter who has covered the important oil stories has publicly stated that if the government fails to eliminate both the pollution and its causes "there will, at best be civil disobedience in Santa Barbara and at worst, violence." In fact, talk of "blowing up" the ugly platforms has been recurrent—and is heard in all social circles.

But just as this kind of talk is not completely serious, it is difficult to know the degree to which the other kinds of militant statements are serious. Despite frequent observations of the "radicalization"[17] of Santa Barbara, it is difficult to determine the extent to which the authentic grievances against Oil have generalized to a radical analysis of American society. Certainly an SDS membership campaign among Santa Barbara adults would be a dismal failure. But that is too severe a test. People, especially basically contented people, change their world-view only very slowly, if at all. Most Santa Barbarans go about their comfortable lives in the ways they always did; they may even help Ronald Reagan to another term in the statehouse. But I do conclude that large numbers of persons have been moved, and that they have been moved in the directions of the radical left. They have gained insights into the structure of power in America not possessed by similarly situated persons in other parts of the country. The claim is thus that some Santa Barbarans, especially those with most interest and most information about the oil spill and its surrounding circumstances, have come to view power in America more intellectually, more analytically, more sociologically—more *radically*—than they did before.

I hold this to be a general sociological response to a series of concomitant circumstances, which can be simply enumerated (*again!*) as follows:

1. *Injustice.* The powerful are operating in a manner inconsistent with the normatively sanctioned expectations of an aggrieved population. The aggrieved population is deprived of certain felt needs as a result.
2. *Information.* Those who are unjustly treated are provided with rather complete information regarding this disparity between expectations and actual performances of the powerful. In the present case, that information has been provided to Santa Barbarans (and only to Santa Barbarans) by virtue of their own observations of local physical conditions and by virtue of the unrelenting coverage of the city's newspaper. Hardly a day has gone by since the initial spill that the front page has not carried an oil story; everything the paper can get its hands on is printed. It carries analyses; it makes the connections. As an appropriate result, Oil officials have condemned the paper as a "lousy" and "distorted" publication of "lies."[18]
3. *Literacy and Leisure.* In order for the information relevant to the injustice to be assimilated in all its infuriating complexity, the aggrieved parties must be, in the larger sense of the terms, literate and leisured. They must have the ability and the time to read, to ponder and to get upset.

My perspective thus differs from those who would regard the radical response as appropriate to some form or another of social or psychological freak. Radicalism is not a subtle form of mental illness (cf. recent statements of such as Bettelheim) caused by "rapid technological change," or increasing "impersonality" in the modern world; radicals are neither "immature," "underdisciplined," nor "anti-intellectual." Quite the reverse. They are persons who most clearly live under the conditions specified above and who make the most rational (and moral) response, given those circumstances. Thus radical movements draw their membership disproportionately from the most leisured, intelligent and informed of the white youth (cf. Flacks, 1967), and from the young blacks whose situations are most analogous to these white counterparts.

NOTES

1. See the report of Morton Mintz in the June 29, 1969 *Washington Post.* The conjunction of these three attributes is not, in my opinion, coincidental.
2. *SBNP* will be used to denote Santa Barbara News Press throughout this paper.
3. Hickel publicly stated and wrote (personal communication) that the original leasing was a mistake and that he was doing all within discretionary power to solve the problem.
4. In a February 7 letter to Union Oil shareholders, Fred Hartley informed them that the bird refuge centers had been "very successful in their efforts." In fact, by April 30, 1969, only 150 birds (of thousands treated) had been returned to the natural habitat as "fully recovered" and the survival rate of birds treated was estimated as a miraculously high (in light of previous experience) 20 per cent (cf. *SBNP,* April 30, 1969, F-3).
5. Cf. "Damaging Earthquakes of the United States through 1966," Fig. 2, National Earthquake Information Center, Environmental Science Services Administration, Coast and Geodetic Survey.
6. See Interview with Donald Weaver, Professor of Geology, UCSB, *SBNP,* Feb. 21, 1969, p. A-1, 6. (Also, remarks by Professor Donald Runnells, UCSB geologist, *SBNP,* Feb. 23, 1969, p. B-2.) Both stress the dangers of faults in the Channel, and potential earthquakes.
7. More recently, plastic tents have been placed on the ocean floor to trap seeping oil; it is being claimed that half the runaway oil is now being trapped in these tents.
8. Curry's criticism is as follows:

   These new regulations make no mention at all about in-pipe safety valves to prevent blowouts, or to shut off the flow of oil deep in the well should the oil and gas escape from the drill hole region into a natural fissure at some depth below the wellhead blowout preventers. There is also no requirement for a backup valve in case the required preventer fails to work. Remember, the runaway well on Union Platform A was equipped with a wellhead blowout preventer. The blowout occurred some 200 feet below that device.

Only one of the new guidelines seems to recognize the possible calamitous results of earthquakes which are inevitable on the western offshore leases. None of the regulations require the minimization of pollution hazards during drilling that may result from a moderate-magnitude, near-by shallow-focus earthquake, seismic sea wave (tsunami) or submarine landslide which could shear off wells below the surface.

None of the regulations state anything at all about onshore oil and gas storage facilities liable to release their contents into the oceans upon rupture due to an earthquake or seismic seawave.

None of the new regulations stipulate that wells must be cased to below a level of geologic hazard, or below a depth of possible open fissures or porous sands, and, as such, none of these changes would have helped the present situation in the Santa Barbara Channel or the almost continuous blowout that has been going on since last year in the Bass Straits off Tasmania, where one also finds porous sands extending all the way up to the sea floor in a tectonically active region—exactly the situation we have here.

9. Letter from Fred Hartly, President of Union Oil, to "all shareholders," dated February 7, 1969.

10. Robert Curry of the geography department of the University of California, Santa Barbara, warned that such a tactic might in fact accelerate leakage. If, as he thought, the oil reservoirs under the Channel are linked, accelerated development of one such reservoir would, through erosion of subterranean linkage channels, accelerate the flow of oil into the reservoir under Platform A, thus adding to the uncontrolled flow of oil through the sands and into the ocean. Curry was not asked to testify by the DuBridge Panel.

11. Verbal communication from one of the faculty members involved. The kind of "studies" which oil enjoys is typified by a research conclusion by Professor Wheeler J. North of Cal Tech, who after performing a one week study of the Channel ecology under Western Oil and Gas Association sponsorship, determined that it was the California winter floods which caused most of the evident disturbance and that (as quoted from the Association Journal) "Santa Barbara beaches and marine life should be back to normal by summer with no adverse impact on tourism." Summer came with oil on the beaches, birds unreturned, and beach motels with unprecedented vacancies.

12. Cf. Walter J. Mead, "The Economics of Depletion Allowance," testimony presented to Assembly Revenue and Taxation Committee, California Legislature, June 10, 1969, mimeo; "The System of Government Subsidies to the Oil Industry," testimony presented to the U.S. Senate Subcommittee on Antitrust and Monopoly, March 11, 1969. The ostensible purpose of the

depletion allowance is to encourage oil companies to explore for new oil reserves. A report to the Treasury Department by Consad Research Corp. concluded that *elimination* of the depletion allowance would decrease oil reserves by only 3 per cent. The report advised that more efficient means could be found than a system which causes the government to pay $10 for every $1 in oil added to reserves. (Cf. Leo Rennert, "Oil Industry's Favors," *SBNP,* April 27, 1969, pp. A-14, 15 as reprinted from the *Sacramento Bee.*)

13. Cranston publicly confronted the staff engineer, Eugene Standley, who stated that he could neither confirm or deny writing the memo. (Cf. *SBNP,* March 11, 1969, p. A-1.)

14. Major magazine coverage occurred in these (and other) national publications: *Time* (Feb. 14, 1969); *Newsweek* (March 3, 1969); *Life* (June 13, 1969); *Saturday Review* (May 10, 1969); *Sierra Club Bulletin; Sports Illustrated* (April 10, 1969). The last three articles cited were written by Santa Barbarans.

15. The notion of the banality of evil is adapted from the usage of Arendt, 1963.

16. As a result of local opposition, Union Oil was to subsequently move its operations from the Santa Barbara wharf to a more distant port in Ventura County.

17. Cf. Morton Mintz, "Oil Spill 'Radicalizes' a Conservative West Coast City," *Washington Post,* June 29, 1969, pp. C-1, 5.

18. Union Oil's public relations director stated: "In all my long career, I have never seen such distorted coverage of a news event as the *Santa Barbara News-Press* has foisted on its readers. It's a lousy newspaper." (*SBNP,* May 28, 1969, p. A-1.)

Part 5
BUREAUCRATISM

INTRODUCTION

In the rhetoric of modern radicals, "bureaucracy" ranks alongside "the establishment" as one of the most despicable aspects of contemporary society. Pointing the finger in protest and attempting to stop the machinery is an appealing outlet for the frustrations and hostilities experienced in day-to-day encounters with "officials," "representatives," "agents," and bureaucrats." It is not, however, an adequate substitute for an understanding of why bureaucracies emerge and persist; why they have the shape they do; and why they create the kind of world that modern man faces.

Sociologists have long recognized the importance and the dire consequences of bureaucratic organization for the lives of men. Max Weber saw bureaucratism as the lip of the tidal wave that would destroy everything of value in society.[1] Karl Marx also pointed to the understanding of the emergent bureaucratic form as critical for an understanding of contemporary society:

> . . . In addition to classes, sub-classes and parties the problem of bureaucracy became increasingly important in Marx's analysis. . . . He definitely anticipated the role of bureaucratic organization in inhibiting the growth of democracy to which Weber and afterwards Michels gave so much attention.[2]

Similarly, Frederich Engels made much of the role of bureaucracy in his introduction to *Civil War in France:*

> Society had created its own organs to look after its common interests, originally through simple divisions of labor, but these organs, at whose head was the State power, had in the course of time, in pursuance of their own special interests, transformed themselves from servants of society into masters of society.[3]

The opening article in this section is the classical statement of bureaucracy by Max Weber. Weber's astute perceptions of the role of bureaucracy in modern society are the foundation upon which most inquiries into bureaucracy are built. Gouldner's criticism of the neo-Weberian investigations of bureaucracy is a perceptive statement of how a promising beginning can go awry when the study of the real animal is replaced by a fetish for the logic of the animal's "true meaning." The section's final article, by Chambliss, analyzes the relationship between vice, corruption, bureaucratic organizations of law enforcement agencies and the prevailing power structure of American communities.

These papers provide a framework within which much that is obviously missing in the life of modern man is linked to power as it is wielded through bureaucratic organizations. As such, these papers provide a perspective within which bureaucracies can be analyzed, understood, and changed.

NOTES

1. See Robert Nisbet, *The Sociological Tradition,* Basic Books, 1966.
2. Irving Zeitlin, *Marxism: A Re-Examination,* Van Norstrand, 1967, p. 151.
3. Frederich Engels, *Civil War In France,* New York: International Publishers, 1968.

BUREAUCRACY

Max Weber

CHARACTERISTICS OF BUREAUCRACY

Modern officialdom functions in the following specific manner:

I. There is the principle of fixed and official jurisdictional areas, which are generally ordered by rules, that is, by laws or administrative regulations.

1. The regular activities required for the purposes of the bureaucratically governed structure are distributed in a fixed way as official duties.
2. The authority to give the commands required for the discharge of these duties is distributed in a stable way and is strictly delimited by rules concerning the coercive means, physical, sacerdotal, or otherwise, which may be placed at the disposal of officials.
3. Methodical provision is made for the regular and continuous fulfilment of these duties and for the execution of the corresponding rights; only persons who have the generally regulated qualifications to serve are employed.

In public and lawful government these three elements constitute "bureaucratic authority." In private economic domination, they constitute bureaucratic "management." Bureaucracy, thus understood, is fully developed in political and ecclesiastical communities only in the modern state, and, in the private economy, only in the most advanced institutions of capitalism. Permanent and public office authority, with fixed jurisdiction, is not the historical rule but rather the exception. This is so even in large political structures such as those of the ancient Orient, the Germanic and Mongolian empires of conquest, or of many feudal structures of state. In all these cases, the ruler executes the most important measures through personal trustees, table-companions, or court-serv-

---

ants. Their commissions and authority are not precisely delimited and are temporarily called into being for each case.

II. The principles of office hierarchy and of levels of graded authority mean a firmly ordered system of super- and subordination in which there is a supervision of the lower offices by the higher ones. Such a system offers the governed the possibility of appealing the decision of a lower office to its higher authority, in a definitely regulated manner. With the full development of the bureaucratic type, the office hierarchy is monocratically organized. The principle of hierarchical office authority is found in all bureaucratic structures: in state and ecclesiastical structures as well as in large party organizations and private enterprises. It does not matter for the character of bureaucracy whether its authority is called "private" or "public."

When the principle of jurisdictional "competency" is fully carried through, hierarchical subordination—at least in public office—does not mean that the "higher" authority is simply authorized to take over the business of the "lower." Indeed, the opposite is the rule. Once established and having fulfilled its task, an office tends to continue in existence and be held by another incumbent.

III. The management of the modern office is based upon written documents ("the files"), which are preserved in their original or draught form. There is, therefore, a staff of subaltern officials and scribes of all sorts. The body of officials actively engaged in a "public" office, along with the respective apparatus of material implements and the files, make up a "bureau." In private enterprise, "the bureau" is often called "the office."

In principle, the modern organization of the civil service separates the bureau from the private domicile of the official, and, in general, bureaucracy segregates official activity as something distinct from the sphere of private life. Public monies and equipment are divorced from the private property of the official. This condition is everywhere the product of a long development. Nowadays, it is found in public as well as in private enterprises; in the latter, the principle extends even to the leading entrepreneur. In principle, the executive office is separated from the household, business from private correspondence, and business assets from private fortunes. The more consistently the modern type of business management has been carried through the more are these separations the case. The beginnings of this process are to be found as early as the Middle Ages.

It is the peculiarity of the modern entrepreneur that he conducts himself as the "first official" of his enterprise, in the very same way in which the ruler of a specifically modern bureaucratic state spoke of himself as "the first servant" of the state.* The idea that the bureau activities of the state are intrinsically different in character from the management of private economic offices is a continental European notion and, by way of contrast, is totally foreign to the American way.

IV. Office management, at least all specialized office management—and such management is distinctly modern—usually presupposes thorough and expert training. This increasingly holds for the modern executive and employee of private enterprises, in the same manner as it holds for the state official.

V. When the office is fully developed, official activity demands the full working capacity of the official, irrespective of the fact that his obligatory time in the bureau may be firmly delimited. In the normal case, this is only the product of a long development, in the public as well as in the private office. Formerly, in all cases, the normal state of affairs was reversed: official business was discharged as a secondary activity.

VI. The management of the office follows general rules, which are more or less stable, more or less exhaustive, and which can be learned. Knowledge of these rules represents a special technical learning which the officials possess. It involves jurisprudence, or administrative or business management.

The reduction of modern office management to rules is deeply embedded in its very nature. The theory of modern public administration, for instance, assumes that the authority to order certain matters by decree—which has been legally granted to public authorities—does not entitle the bureau to regulate the matter by commands given for each case, but only to regulate the matter abstractly. This stands in extreme contrast to the regulation of all relationships through individual privileges and bestowals of favor, which is absolutely dominant in patrimonialism, at least insofar as such relationships are not fixed by sacred tradition.

THE POSITION OF THE OFFICIAL

All this results in the following for the internal and external position of the official:

I. Office holding is a "vocation." This is shown, first, in the requirement

*Frederick II of Prussia.

of a firmly prescribed course of training, which demands the entire capacity for work for a long period of time, and in the generally prescribed and special examinations which are prerequisites of employment. Furthermore, the position of the official is in the nature of a duty. This determines the internal structure of his relations, in the following manner: Legally and actually, office holding is not considered a source to be exploited for rents or emoluments, as was normally the case during the Middle Ages and frequently up to the threshold of recent times. Nor is office holding considered a usual exchange of services for equivalents, as is the case with free labor contracts. Entrance into an office, including one in the private economy, is considered an acceptance of a specific obligation of faithful management in return for a secure existence. It is decisive for the specific nature of modern loyalty to an office that, in the pure type, it does not establish a relationship to a *person,* like the vassal's or disciple's faith in feudal or in patrimonial relations of authority. Modern loyalty is devoted to impersonal and functional purposes. Behind the functional purposes, of course, "ideas of culture values" usually stand. These are *ersatz* for the earthly or supra-mundane personal master: ideas such as "state," "church," "community," "party," or "enterprise" are thought of as being realized in a community; they provide an ideological halo for the master.

The political official—at least in the fully developed modern state—is not considered the personal servant of a ruler. Today, the bishop, the priest, and the preacher are in fact no longer, as in early Christian times, holders of purely personal charisma. The supra-mundane and sacred values which they offer are given to everybody who seems to be worthy of them and who asks for them. In former times, such leaders acted upon the personal command of their master; in principle, they were responsible only to him. Nowadays, in spite of the partial survival of the old theory, such religious leaders are officials in the service of a functional purpose, which in the present-day "church" has become routinized and, in turn, ideologically hallowed.

THE LEVELING OF SOCIAL DIFFERENCES

Bureaucratic organization has usually come into power on the basis of a leveling of economic and social differences. This leveling has been at least relative, and has concerned the significance of social and economic differences for the assumption of administrative functions.

Bureaucracy inevitably accompanies modern *mass democracy* in contrast to the democratic self-government of small homogeneous units. This results from the characteristic principle of bureaucracy: the abstract regularity of the execution of authority, which is a result of the demand for "equality before the law" in the personal and functional sense—hence, of the horror of "privilege," and the principled rejection of doing business "from case to case." Such regularity also follows from the social preconditions of the origin of bureaucracies. The non-bureaucratic administration of any large social structure rests in some way upon the fact that existing social, material, or honorific preferences and ranks are connected with administrative functions and duties. This usually means that a direct or indirect economic exploitation or a "social" exploitation of position, which every sort of administrative activity gives to its bearers, is equivalent to the assumption of administrative functions.

Bureaucratization and democratization within the administration of the state therefore signify and increase the cash expenditures of the public treasury. And this is the case in spite of the fact that bureaucratic administration is usually more "economical" in character than other forms of administration. Until recent times—at least from the point of view of the treasury—the cheapest way of satisfying the need for administration was to leave almost the entire local administration and lower judicature to the landlords of Eastern Prussia. The same fact applies to the administration of sheriffs in England. Mass democracy makes a clean sweep of the feudal, patrimonial, and—at least in intent—the plutocratic privileges in administration. Unavoidably it puts paid professional labor in place of the historically inherited avocational administration by notables.

This not only applies to structures of the state. For it is no accident that in their own organizations, the democratic mass parties have completely broken with traditional notable rule based upon personal relationships and personal esteem. Yet such personal structures frequently continue among the old conservative as well as the old liberal parties. Democratic mass parties are bureaucratically organized under the leadership of party officials, professional party and trade union secretaries, et cetera. In Germany, for instance, this has happened in the Social Democratic party and in the agrarian mass-movement; and in England, for the first time, in the caucus democracy of Gladstone-Chamberlain, which was originally organized in Birmingham and since the 1870's has spread. In the United States, both parties since Jackson's administration have developed bureaucratically. In France, however, attempts to organize disciplined political parties on the basis of an election system that would compel bureaucratic organization have repeatedly failed. The resistance of local circles of notables against the ultimately unavoidable bureaucratization of the parties, which would encompass the entire country and break their influence, could not be overcome. Every advance of the simple election techniques, for instance the system of proportional elections, which calculates with figures, means a strict and interlocal bureaucratic organization of the parties and therewith an increasing domination of party bureaucracy and discipline, as well as the elimination of the local circles of notables—at least this holds for great states.

The progress of bureaucratization in the state administration itself is a parallel phenomenon of democracy, as is quite obvious in France, North America, and now in England. Of course one must always remember that the term "democratization" can be misleading. The *demos* itself, in the sense of an inarticulate mass, never "governs" larger associations; rather, it is governed, and its existence only changes the way in which the executive leaders are selected and the measure of influence which the *demos,* or better, which social circles from its midst are able to exert upon the content and the direction of administrative activities by supplementing what is called "public opinion." "Democratization," in the sense here intended, does not necessarily mean an increasingly active share of the governed in the authority of the social structure. This may be a result of democratization, but it is not necessarily the case.

We must expressly recall at this point that the political concept of democracy, deduced from the "equal rights" of the governed, includes these postulates: (1) prevention of the development of a closed status group of officials in the interest of a universal accessibility of office, and (2) minimization of the authority of officialdom in the interest of expanding the sphere of influence of "public opinion" as far as practicable. Hence, wherever possible, political democracy strives to shorten the term of office by election and recall and by not binding the candidate to a special expertness. Thereby democracy inevitably comes into conflict with the bureaucratic tendencies which, by its fight against notable rule, democracy has produced. The generally loose term "democratization" cannot be used here, insofar as it is understood to mean the minimization of the civil servants' ruling power in favor of the greatest possible "direct" rule of the *demos,* which in practice means the respective party leaders of the *demos.* The most decisive thing here—indeed it is rather exclusively so—is the *leveling of the governed* in opposition to the ruling and bureaucratically articulated group, which in its turn may occupy a quite autocratic position, both in fact and in form.

In Russia, the destruction of the position of the old landed nobility through the regulation of the Mjeshtshitelstvo (rank order) and the permeation of the old nobility by an office nobility were characteristic transitional phenomena in the development of bureaucracy. In China, the estimation of rank and the qualification for office according to the number of examinations passed mean something similar, but they have had consequences which, in theory at least, are still sharper. In France, the Revolution and still more Bonapartism have made the bureaucracy all-powerful. In the Catholic Church, first the feudal and then all independent local intermediary powers were eliminated. This was begun by Gregory VII and continued through the Council of Trent, the Vatican Council, and it was completed by the edicts of Pius X. The transformation of these local powers into pure functionaries of the central authority were connected with the constant increase in the factual significance of the formally quite dependent chaplains, a process which above all was based on the political party organization of Catholicism. Hence this process meant an advance of bureaucracy and at the same time of "passive democratization," as it were, that is, the leveling of the governed. The substitution of the bureaucratic army for the self-equipped army of notables is everywhere a process of "passive" democratization, in the sense in which every establishment of an absolute military monarchy in the place of a feudal estate or of a republic of notables is. This has held, in principle, even for the development of the state in Egypt in spite of all the peculiarities involved. Under the Roman principate the bureaucratization of the provincial administration in the field of tax collection, for instance, went hand in hand with the elimination of the plutocracy of a capitalist class, which, under the Republic, had been all-powerful. Ancient capitalism itself was finally eliminated with this stroke.

It is obvious that almost always economic conditions of some sort play their part in such "democratizing" developments. Very frequently we meet with the influence of an economically determined origin of new classes, whether plutocratic, petty bourgeois, or proletarian in character. Such classes may call on the aid of, or they may only call to life or recall to life, a political power, no matter whether it is of legitimate or of Caesarist stamp. They may do so in order to attain economic or social advantages by political assistance. On the other hand, there are equally possible and historically documented cases in which initiative came "from on high" and was of a purely political nature and drew advantages from political constellations, especially in foreign affairs. Such leadership exploited economic and social antagonisms as well as class interests merely as a means for their own purpose of gaining purely political power. For this reason, political authority has thrown the antagonistic classes out of their almost always unstable equilibrium and called their latent interest conflicts into battle. It seems hardly possible to give a general statement of this.

The extent and direction of the course along which economic influences have moved, as well as the nature in which political power relations exert influence, vary widely. In Hellenic Antiquity, the transition to disciplined combat by Hoplites, and in Athens, the increasing importance of the navy laid the foundation for the conquest of political power by the strata on whose shoulders the military burden rested. In Rome, however, the same development shook the rule of the office nobility only temporarily and seemingly. Although the modern mass army has everywhere been a means of breaking the power of notables, by itself it has in no way served as a leverage for active, but rather for merely passive, democratization. One contributing factor, however, has been the fact that the ancient citizen army rested economically upon self-equipment, whereas the modern army rests upon the bureaucratic procurement of requirements.

The advance of the bureaucratic structure rests upon "technical" superiority. This fact leads here, as in the whole field of technique, to the following: the advance has been realized most slowly where older structural forms have been technically well developed and functionally adjusted to the requirements at hand. This was the case, for instance, in the administration of notables in England and hence England was the slowest of all countries to succumb to bureaucratization or, indeed, is still only partly in the process of doing so. The same general phenomenon exists when highly developed systems of gaslight or of steam railroads with large and fixed capital offer stronger obstacles to electrification than in completely new areas which are opened up for electrification.

THE PERMANENT CHARACTER OF THE BUREAUCRATIC MACHINE

Once it is fully established, bureaucracy is among those social structures which are the hardest to destroy. Bureaucracy is *the* means of carrying "community action" over into rationally ordered "societal action." Therefore, as an instrument for "societalizing" relations of power, bureaucracy has been and is a power instrument of the first order—for the one who controls the bureaucratic apparatus.

Under otherwise equal conditions, a "societal action," which is methodically ordered and led, is superior to every resistance of "mass" or even of "communal action." And where the bureaucratization of administration has been completely carried through, a form of power relation is established that is practically unshatterable.

The individual bureaucrat cannot squirm out of the apparatus in which he is harnessed. In contrast to the honorific or avocational "notable," the professional bureaucrat is chained to his activity by his entire material and ideal existence. In the great majority of cases, he is only a single cog in an ever-moving mechanism which prescribes to him an essentially fixed route of march. The official is entrusted with specialized tasks and normally the mechanism cannot be put into motion or arrested by him, but only from the very top. The individual bureaucrat is thus forged to the community of all the functionaries who are integrated into the mechanism. They have a common interest in seeing that the mechanism continues its functions and that the societally exercised authority carries on.

The ruled, for their part, cannot dispense with or replace the bureaucratic apparatus of authority once it exists. For this bureaucracy rests upon expert training, a functional specialization of work, and an attitude set for habitual and virtuoso-like mastery of single yet methodically integrated functions. If the official stops working, or if his work is forcefully interrupted, chaos results, and it is difficult to improvise replacements from among the governed who are fit to master such chaos. This holds for public administration as well as for private economic management. More and more the material fate of the masses depends upon the steady and correct functioning of the increasingly bureaucratic organizations of private capitalism. The idea of eliminating these organizations becomes more and more utopian.

The discipline of officialdom refers to the attitude-set of the official for precise obedience within his *habitual* activity, in public as well as in private organizations. This discipline increasingly becomes the basis of all order, however great the practical importance of administration on the basis of the filed documents may be. The naïve idea of Bakuninism of destroying the basis of "acquired rights" and "domination" by destroying public documents overlooks the settled orientation of *man* for keeping to the habitual rules and regulations that continue to exist independently of the documents. Every reorganization of beaten or dissolved troops, as well as the restoration of administrative orders destroyed by revolt, panic, or other catastrophes, is realized by appealing to the trained orientation of obedient compliance to such orders. Such compliance has been conditioned into the officials, on the one hand, and, on the other hand, into the governed. If such an appeal is successful it brings, as it were, the disturbed mechanism into gear again.

The objective indispensability of the once-existing apparatus, with its peculiar, "impersonal" character, means that the mechanism—in contrast to feudal orders based upon personal piety—is easily made to work for anybody who knows how to gain control over it. A rationally ordered system of officials continues to function smoothly after the enemy has occupied the area; he merely needs to change the top officials. This body of officials continues to operate because it is to the vital interest of everyone concerned, including above all the enemy.

During the course of his long years in power, Bismarck brought his ministerial colleagues into unconditional bureaucratic dependence by eliminating all independent statesmen. Upon his retirement, he saw to his surprise that they continued to manage their offices unconcerned and undismayed, as if he had not been the master mind and creator of these creatures, but rather as if some single figure had been exchanged for some other figure in the bureaucratic machine. With all the changes of masters in France since the time of the First Empire, the power machine has remained essentially the same. Such a machine makes "revolution," in the sense of the forceful creation of entirely new formations of authority, technically more and more impossible, especially when the apparatus controls the modern means of communication (telegraph, et cetera) and also by virtue of its internal rationalized structure. In classic fashion, France has demonstrated how this process has substituted *coups d'état* for "revolutions": all successful transformations in France have amounted to *coups d'état.*

METAPHYSICAL PATHOS AND THE THEORY OF BUREAUCRACY

Alvin W. Gouldner

The conduct of a polemic focusses attention on the differences between two points of view to the neglect of their continuity and convergences. No modern polemic better exemplifies this than the controversy between the proponents of capitalism and of socialism. Each tends to define itself as the antithesis of the other; even the uncommitted bystander, rare though he be, is likely to think of the two as if they were utterly alien systems.

There have always been some, however, who have taken exception to this sharp contrast between socialism and capitalism and who have insisted that there are significant similarities between the two. One of these, the French sociologist Emile Durkheim, maintained that socialism like capitalism involved an overbearing preoccupation with economic interests. In both socialist and capitalist societies, Durkheim argued, economic concerns were at the center of attention. In Durkheim's view, neither capitalism nor socialism deemed it necessary to bridle materialistic ends; neither society subordinated pecuniary interests to some higher, governing moral norms. Therefore, "from Durkheim's point of view," writes Talcott Parsons, "socialism and laissez-faire individualism are of the same piece."[1]

Bertrand Russell came to similar conclusions on the basis of a trip to the then newly established Soviet Republic: ". . . the practical difference between socialism and capitalism is not so great as politicians on both sides suppose. Certain features will appear in the early stages of individualism under either system; and under either system certain other features will appear in its later stages."[2]

Without doubt, though, the most sophisticated formulation of this view was that conceived by the German sociologist, Max Weber. To

From *American Political Science Review,* Vol. 49, (1955), pp. 496-507. Reprinted by permission.

Weber, the distinguishing characteristic of modern capitalism was the "rational organization of free labor." The pursuit of private gain, noted Weber, was well known in many earlier societies; what distinguishes present-day capitalism, he held, is the peculiar organization of the production unit, an organization that is essentially bureaucratic. This conception of capitalism, writes Parsons, "has one important concrete result; in contradistinction to Marx and most 'liberal' theories, it strongly minimizes the differences between capitalism and socialism, emphasizing rather their continuity. Not only would socialistic organization leave the central fact of bureaucracy untouched, it would greatly accentuate its importance."[3]

While Marx had dwelt largely on the interrelations *among* production units, that is, their market ties, Weber focussed on the social relations *within* the industrial unit. If social relations inside of socialist and capitalist factories are fundamentally alike, in that they are both bureaucratic, then, asked Weber, does a socialist revolution yield very much of an improvement for the capitalist proletarian?

If Marx argued that the workers of the world had nothing to *lose* by revolting, Weber contended that they really had nothing to *gain.* "For the time being," he declared, "the dictatorship of the official and not that of the worker is on the march." Capitalism and socialism are thus placed under the same conceptual umbrella—bureaucracy—with the important practical result that the problem of choosing between them loses much of its point.

It is for this reason that the discussions of bureaucratic organization which are heir to the Weberian analysis must be understood as being, in part, a displacement of the controversy over socialism. Weber made it clear that questions of economic choice could no longer be treated in isolation from questions of administration. From Weber's time forward, administrative and economic choices were seen to be but two facets of the same hard problem. This has been recognized even by socialists, at least when they have been unencumbered by Communist party orthodoxy. For example, Oskar Lange once remarked, with a frankness that we hope he will never be compelled to regret, ". . . the real danger of socialism is that of bureaucratic organization of economic life. . . ."[4]

It is sometimes assumed today that the Weberian outlook is at bottom anti-socialist. In effect, the argument runs, Weber's viewpoint devitalizes the myth-like appeal of socialism, draining off its ability to muster immense enthusiasms. Weber's theses are therefore held to be an "ideology" serviceable for the survival of capitalism, while Weber himself is characterized as the "Marx of the bourgeoisie."

Now all this may be true, but it is only a partial truth; for, in actuality, Weber's theories cut two ways, not one. If it is correct that his theory of bureaucracy saps the fervor of the socialist offensive, it also undermines the stamina of the capitalist bastions. If socialism and capitalism are similar in being bureaucratic, then not only is there little *profit* in substituting one for the other, but there is also little *loss.*

Considered only from the standpoint of its political consequences then, the Weberian outlook is not anti-socialist alone, nor anti-capitalist alone, it is both. In the final analysis its political slogan becomes "a plague on both your houses." If Weber is to be regarded as an "ideologist," he is an ideologist not of counter-revolution but of quiescence and neutralism. For many intellectuals who have erected a theory of group organization on Weberian foundations, the world has been emptied of choice, leaving them disoriented and despairing.

That gifted historian of ideas, Arthur O. Lovejoy, astutely observed that every theory is associated with, or generates, a set of sentiments which those subscribing to the theory could only dimly sense. Lovejoy called this the "metaphysical pathos" of ideas, a pathos which is "exemplified in any description of the nature of things, any characterization of the world to which one belongs, in terms which, like the words of a poem, evoke through their associations and through a sort of empathy which they engender, a congenial mood or tone of feeling."[5]

As a result, a commitment to a theory often occurs by a process other than the one which its proponents believe and it is usually more consequential than they realize. A commitment to a theory may be made because the theory is congruent with the mood or deep-lying sentiments of its adherents, rather than merely because it has been cerebrally inspected and found valid. This is as true for the rigorous prose of social science as it is for the more lucid metaphor of creative literature, for each has its own silent appeal and its own metaphysical pathos.

Furthermore, those who have committed themselves to a theory always get more than they have bargained for. We do not make a commercial contract with a theory in which we agree to accept only the consignment of intellectual goods which has been expressly ordered; usually we take also the metaphysical pathos in which the theory comes packaged. In the end, the theory reinforces or induces in the adherent a subtle alteration in the structure of sentiments through which he views the world.

So too is it with the theory of organization. Paradoxically enough, some of the very theories which promise to make man's own work more intelligible to himself and more amenable to his intelligence are infused with an intangible metaphysical pathos which insinuates, in the very midst of new discoveries, that all is lost. For the metaphysical pathos of much of the modern theory of group organization is that of pessimism and fatalism.

I. EXPLANATION OF BUREAUCRACY

Nowhere does the fatalism of the theory of organization become more articulate than in its efforts to account for the development of bureaucratic behavior. One of the less challenging explanations, for example, premises a supposedly invariant human nature. Thus in an otherwise illuminating analysis, one political scientist remarks: "Civil servants are ordinary mortals; they have the defects and weaknesses typical of human nature. Each loves, as Shakespeare said, 'his brief moment of authority.' "

This, however, is difficult to reconcile with recurrent complaints, from civic leaders or business managers, that it is often hard to persuade people either to run for political office or to accept positions as foremen. Apparently there are some people who do not hanker after their brief moment of authority.[6]

In any event, it does not seem possible to account for bureaucracy in any of its forms as an outgrowth of "human nature." This explanation cannot cope with the rudimentary fact that in some times and in some places there is much bureaucracy, but in other times and places there is little. Leaving aside the question of the validity of the argument, its practical results are again all too evident. For if bureaucracy is rooted in human nature then all hope for a remedy must be abandoned.

Much more serious as goads to pessimism are theories explaining bureaucracy as the end-product of increased size and complexity in organizations. This is by far the most popular of the interpretations. Marshall Dimock and Howard Hyde, for example, in their report to the Temporary National Economic Committee (TNEC), state: "The broadest structural cause of bureaucracy, whether in business or in government, is the tremendous size of the organization. Thus with capital or appropriations measured in hundreds of millions and in billions of dollars and personnel in tens and hundreds of thousands, it is difficult to avoid the obtrusion of the objectionable features of bureaucracy."[7]

While suggesting varied causes for the development of bureaucracy, Max Weber also interpreted it as a consequence of large size. For example, in discussing the ubiquity of bureaucratic forms Weber adds: "The same [bureaucratic] phenomena are found in the large-scale capitalistic enterprise; and the larger it is, the greater their role."[8] He underscores the role of size by emphasizing that "only by reversion in every field—political, religious, economic, etc.—to small-scale organization would it be possible to escape its influence."[9] Despite his consideration of other possible sources of bureaucracy, these comments suggest that Weber regarded organizational size as the controlling factor in the development of bureaucracy.

Weber's emphasis on size as the crucial determinant of bureaucratic development is unsatisfactory for several reasons. First, there are historic examples of human efforts carried out on an enormous scale which were not bureaucratic in any serious sense of the term.[10] The building of the Egyptian pyramids is an obvious example. Second, Weber never considers the possibility that it is not "large size" as such that disposes to bureaucracy; large size may be important only because it generates other social forces which, in their turn, generate bureaucratic patterns.

Of course, in every analysis there are always intervening variables —the unknown "x"—which stand between any cause and effect. Scientific progress depends, in part, on moving away from the gross causes and coming closer to those which are more invariably connected with the object of interest. The point is that when a social scientist accepts "size" as an explanatory factor, instead of going on to ask what there is *about size* that makes for bureaucracy, he is making an analytic *decision.* It is not a formulation unavoidably dictated by the nature of the data itself.

Significantly, though, it is a decision that leads once again to bleak pessimism. For to inform members of our society that the only way out of the bureaucratic impasse is to return to the historical past and to trade in large- for small-scale organizations, is, in effect, to announce the practical impossibility of coping with bureaucracy. Moreover, many people in our society believe that "bigness" symbolizes progress; to tell them that it also creates bureaucracy is to place them on the horns of a dilemma which gores no matter which way they turn. In such a position the most painless response is inaction.

Underlying this conception of the matter there is a Hegelian dialectic in which "good" and "bad" are viewed as inseparably connected opposites; bureaucracy, "the bad thing," is represented as the inescapable price that has to be paid for the good things, the efficiency and abundance of modern life. One social scientist clearly puts it this way: "Assembly line techniques offer marked advantages over those of custom craftsmanship. They also have their price. They entail the imposition of an order of progression, the fixing of a rate or rhythm of operation, and the discipline of a regular routine. Set order, fixed pace, and adherence to routine—these are the very stuff of which red tape is made. Yet they are of the essence of system, too."[11] However true or false, there can be little doubt that this is an outlook which is convenient and comfortable for bureaucrats—if not for many others.

II. THE STRUCTURAL-FUNCTIONALISTS

The fuller ramifications of this approach to bureaucracy can best be explained by turning to the analyses of industrial organization made by some of the "structural-functionalists." This is a comparatively new and vigorous school of American sociologists, which has grown directly out of the theories of Durkheim, Weber, and others, and whose most elaborate expression is to be found in the work of Talcott Parsons.

Parsons' recent analyses of industrial bureaucracy are of sufficient importance to be quoted in full. "Though with many individual exceptions [which he does not examine], *technological advance* almost always leads to increasingly *elaborate division of labor* and the concomitant requirement of increasingly elaborate organization." He continues:

> The fundamental reason for this is, of course, that with elaborate differentiation of functions the need for *minute coordination* of the different functions develops at the same time. . . . There must be a *complex organization of supervision* to make quite sure that exactly the right thing is done. . . . Feeding the various parts into the process, in such a way that a modern assembly line can operate smoothly, requires very *complex organization* to see that they are available in just the right quantities at the right times and places. . . . One of the most important phases of this process of change is concerned with the necessity for *formalization* when certain points of complexity are reached . . .

> Smaller and simpler organizations are typically managed with a high degree of particularism (i.e., personal consideration) in the relations of persons in authority to their own subordinates. But when the "distance" between points of decision and of operation increases, and the number of operating units affected by decisions with it, uniformity and coordination can be attained only by a high degree of formalization . . .[12]

Surprisingly enough, this is an atavistic recurrence of technological determinism in which characteristic bureaucratic traits—such as an elaborate division of labor, complex organization, and formalization—are held to stem directly from technological advance. This is a form of *technological* determinism because bureaucracy is seen as the result of technological change, without inquiring into the motives and meanings which these changes have for the people involved, and without wondering whether technological change would have a different impact on the formal organization of a group that had a high motivation to produce and therefore did not require close supervision. This is a form of technological *determinism,* because no alternative solutions are appraised or deemed possible and coordination is seen as attainable "*only* by a high degree of formalization . . ."

Here once again we are invited to draw the conclusion that those who want modern technology must be prepared to pay for it with a minute and even stultifying division of labor.

All this, though, is a theoretical tapestry devoid of even the plainest empirical trimmings. Even on logical grounds, however, it is tenuous indeed. For it is evident that organizational patterns, such as a high division of labor, are found in spheres where modern technology has made comparatively little headway. This, in fact, is a point that Weber was at pains to insist upon. And if, as he maintained, bureaucratic forms are also found in charitable, political, or religious organizations—and not solely in industry—then they certainly cannot be explained as a consequence of modern machine technology.

Beyond these logical considerations, there are also some *empirical* grounds for questioning the adequacy of Parsons' analysis. Peter Drucker, for example, became extremely doubtful about the necessity of a minute division of labor while observing large-scale American industry during World War II. (This is crucial for Parsons' argument, because he holds that it is through increased specialization that technology evokes the other elements of bureaucratic organization.) Drucker comments that "we have learned that it is neither necessary nor always efficient to organize all mass production in such a manner as to have the majority of workers confine themselves to doing one and only one of the elementary manipulations . . . It was impossible [because of wartime shortages of skilled labor] to 'lay out' the job in the usual assembly-line fashion in which one unskilled operation done by one unskilled man is followed by the next unskilled man. The operation was broken down into its unskilled components like any assembly-line job. *But then the unskilled components were put together again with the result that an unskilled worker actually performed the job of a highly skilled mechanic*—and did it as reliably and efficiently as had been done by skilled men."[13]

In short, lower degrees of specialization than those normally found in large-scale industry are not necessarily forbidden by modern technology. Drucker's observations must, at the very least, raise the question as to how much of the minute division of labor is attributable to technological causes. Parsons, though, gives no consideration to other factors contributing to an extreme division of labor. However, Carl Dreyfuss, a German industrial sociologist, has advanced an array of keen observations and hypotheses which meet this question directly. He writes: "the artificial complication of the rank order . . . permits numerous employees to feel that they hold high positions and are to a certain extent independent." Moreover, he notes that a complicated division of labor is "with its unwarranted differentiations, telescoped positions, and ramifications, diametrically opposed to efforts of rationalization."[14] In other words, Dreyfuss suggests that much of the complex division of labor today is not to be explained by technological requirements, but rather in terms of the prestige satisfactions, the "psychic income," that it presumably provides workers.

In Dreyfuss' view, the "minute division of labor" also stems from management's need to *control* workers and to make themselves independent of any specific individual or group of workers. A high division of labor, said Dreyfuss, means that "individual workers and employees can be exchanged and replaced at any time."[15] Through its use, "dependence of the employee upon the employer is greatly increased. It is much more difficult for today's employee, trained in only one particular function, to find reemployment than it was for his predecessor, a many-sided, well-instructed business man, able and fitted to fill a variety of positions."[16]

A similar view is advanced in the more recent studies of industrial organization of Yankee City, which were made by W. L. Warner and J. O. Low. "While machine processes were adopted by shoe factories primarily to reduce costs and to speed the processing, the machine has other great advantages over the human worker from the managerial point of view," comment Warner and Low.

> Control problems are simplified . . . on two counts through mechanization: (1) machines are easier to control than human beings, and (2) mechanization tends to disrupt the social solidarity of the workers, who thereby become easier to control than they would if they were able to maintain close social relations during working hours . . . these factors tend to increase the subordination of the individual worker to management; from the management's viewpoint they are valuable means of social control over workers . . . The routinization of jobs also simplifies control of workers in another way. The individual operative today does not have the feeling of security that the oldtime craftsman derived from his special technical abilities. In most cases, today's operative is aware that only a comparatively brief training period protects him in his job from a large number of untrained individuals. The members of the supervisory hierarchy are also well aware of this fact. The psychological effect of this result of the division of labor is to intensify the subordinate position of the individual operative and to make him submit the more readily to the limitations on his behavior required by the supervisory group.[17]

It is unnecessary for our purpose here to resolve this disparity between Warner and Dreyfuss, on the one hand, and Parsons, on the other. What may be suggested, however, is that there is considerable reason for holding Parsons' position to be both logically and empirically inadequate and to recognize that it has, without compelling scientific warrant, accommodated itself to the metaphysical pathos of organizational theory, which sees no escape from bureaucracy.

III. THE TRADITION OF MICHELS

There is another offshoot among the structural-functionalists which is distinguished by its concern for the problems bequeathed by Robert Michels and, as such, it is even more morosely pessimistic than others in the school. Michels, it will be remembered, focussed his empirical studies on the Social Democratic parties of pre-World War I Europe. He chose these, quite deliberately, because he wanted to see whether groups which stood for greater freedom and democracy, and were hostile to authoritarianism, were not themselves afflicted by the very organizational deformity to which they were opposed.

Michel's conclusions were, of course, formulated in his "iron law of oligarchy," in which he maintained that always and everywhere a "system of leadership is incompatible with the most essential postulates of democracy."[18] Oligarchy, said Michels, "derives from the tactical and technical necessities which result from the consolidation of every disciplined political aggregate . . .[19] It is the outcome of organic necessity, and consequently affects every organization, be it socialist or even anarchist."[20]

In concluding his study, Michels remarks with a flourish of defensive pathos, ". . . it seemed necessary to lay considerable stress upon the pessimist aspect of democracy which is forced upon us by historical study . . ."[21] "The democratic currents of history resemble successive waves. They break ever on the same shoals . . . It is probable that this cruel game will continue without end."[22]

Focussing, as Michels did, on an apparently democratic group, Philip Selznick examined the TVA, which many Americans had long believed to be an advanced expression of democratic values. Like Michels, Selznick assumes that "wherever there is organization, whether formally democratic or not, there is a split between the leader and the led, between the agent and the initiator. The phenomenon of abdication to bureaucratic directives in corporations, in trade unions, in parties, and in cooperatives is so widespread that it indicates a fundamental weakness of democracy."[23]

Selznick's study concludes that the TVA's emphasis on "decentralization" is to be best understood as a result of that agency's needs to adapt to suspicious local communities and to survive in competition with older governmental agencies based in Washington. "Decentralization" is viewed as a "halo that becomes especially useful in countries which prize the symbols of democracy."[24] In its turn, the TVA's emphasis on "participation" is explained as a catchword, satisfying the agency's needs to transform "an unorganized citizenry into a reliable instrument for the achievement of administrative goals . . ."[25]

Selznick, like Michels, is impressed with the similarity in the organizational devices employed by different groups, whether they are democratic or authoritarian in ideology. He asserts ". . . there seems to be a continuum between the voluntary associations set up by the democratic (mass) state—such as committees of farmers to boost or control agricultural production—and the citizens' associations of the totalitarian (mass) state. Indeed the devices of corporatism emerge as relatively effective responses to the need to deal with the mass, and in time of war the administrative techniques of avowedly democratic countries and avowedly totalitarian countries tend to converge."[26]

In Selznick's analysis human action involves a commitment to two sets of interests: first to the goals intended, and second to the organizational instruments through which these goals are pursued. These tools are, however, recalcitrant; they generate "needs" which cannot be neglected. Hence if men persist in their ends, they are forced to satisfy the needs of their organizational instruments. They are, therefore, as much committed to their tools as to their ends, and "these commitments may lead to unanticipated consequences resulting in a deflection of original ends."[27]

For these reasons, organizational behavior must be interpreted not so much in terms of the *ends* that administrators deliberately seek, as in terms of the organizational "needs" which their pursuit engenders. "The needs in question are organizational, not individual, and include the security of the organization as a whole in relation to social forces in its environment; the stability of the lines of authority and communication; the stability of informal relations within the organization; the continuity of policy and of the sources of its determination; a homogeneity of outlook with respect to the means and role of the organization."[28]

"In general," writes Selznick, "we have been concerned to formulate some of the underlying tendencies which are likely to inhibit the democratic process. Like all conservative or pessimistic criticism, such a statement of inherent problems seems to cast doubt upon the possibility of complete democratic achievement. It does cast such a doubt. The alternative, however, is the transformation of democracy into a utopian notion which, unaware of its internal dangers, is unarmed to meet them."[29] This, however, is an argument that rests upon assumptions which are not transparently self-evident and are acceptable without dispute only by those who are susceptible to its metaphysical pathos. Despite demagogic appeals to democratic symbols, there seem to be few places in either the Eastern or Western worlds in which there is a real and present danger of the "transformation of democracy into a utopian notion." Surely this is not to be expected among the class conscious working classes of Europe, the laborite masses of England, the untutored peasants of China, or among the confused and often apathetic American electorate to whom politics is something of a dirty game, to be periodically enlivened with scandals and investigations. And if this appraisal is correct, then just who is there to be "armed" with this knowledge of the internal dangers of democracy?

For some reason Selznick has chosen—and this was not forced upon him by the data—to focus on the things which harry and impede democratic aspirations, rather than on those which strengthen and energize it. It is for this reason perhaps that he is led to reiterate Michel's apologia: "Attention being focussed on the structural conditions which influence behavior, we are directed to emphasize constraints, the limitations of alternatives imposed by the system upon its participants. This will tend to give pessimistic overtones to the analysis, since such factors as good will and intelligence will be de-emphasized."[30]

Selznick chose to focus on those social constraints that *thwart* democratic aspirations, but neglected to consider the constraints that enable them to be *realized,* and that foster and encourage "good will" and "intelligence." Are these, however, random occurrences, mere historic butterflies which flit through events with only ephemeral beauty? Or are they, as much as anything else, often the unanticipated products of our "commitments"? Why is it that "unanticipated consequences" are always tacitly assumed to be destructive of democratic values and "bad"; why can't they sometimes be "good"? Are there no constraints which *force* men to adhere valorously to their democratic beliefs, which *compel* them to be intelligent rather than blind, which leave them *no choice* but to be men of good will rather than predators? The neglect of these possibilities suggests the presence of a distorting pathos.

It is the pathos of pessimism, rather than the compulsions of rigorous analysis, that lead to the assumption that organizational constraints have stacked the deck against democracy. For on the face of it there is every reason to assume that "the underlying tendencies which are likely to inhibit the democratic process" are just as likely to impair authoritarian rule. It is only in the light of such a pessimistic pathos that the defeat of democratic values can be assumed to be probable, while their victory is seen as a slender thing, delicately constituted and precariously balanced.

When, for example, Michels spoke of the "iron law of oligarchy," he attended solely to the ways in which organizational needs inhibit democratic possibilities. But the very same evidence to which he called attention could enable us to formulate the very opposite theorem—the "iron law of democracy." Even as Michels himself saw, if oligarchical waves repeatedly wash away the bridges of democracy, this eternal recurrence can happen only because men doggedly rebuild them after each inundation. Michels chose to dwell on only one aspect of this process, neglecting to consider this other side. There cannot be an iron law of oligarchy, however, unless there is an iron law of democracy.

Much the same may be said for Selznick. He posits certain organizational needs: a need for the security of the organization, for *stable* lines of authority and communication, for stable informal relationships. But for each of the organizational needs which Selznick postulates, a set of contrary needs can also be posited, and the satisfaction of these would seem to be just as necessary for the survival of an organization. If, as Selznick says, an organization must have security in its environment, then certainly Toynbee's observation that too much security can be stultifying and corrosive is at least as well taken. To Selznick's security need, a Toynbee might counterpose a need for a moderate challenge or threat.

A similar analysis might also be made of Selznick's postulated need for *homogeneity* of outlook concerning the means and role of the organization. For unless there is some heterogeneity of outlook, then where is an organization to find the tools and flexibility to cope with changes in its environment? Underlying Selznick's need for homogeneity in outlook, is there not another "need," *a need that consent of the governed be given—at least in some measure—to their governors?* Indeed, this would seem to be at the very core of Selznick's empirical analysis, though it is obscured in his high-level theoretical statement of the needs of organizations. And if all organizations must adjust to such a need for consent, is there not built into the very marrow or organization a large element of what we mean by democracy? This would appear to be an organizational constraint that makes oligarchies, and all separation of leaders from those led, no less inherently unstable than democratic organization.[31]

These contrary needs are just as real and just as consequential for organizational behavior as those proposed by Selznick. But they point in a different direction. They are oriented to problems of change, of growth, of challenging contingencies, of provoking and unsettling encounters. Selznick's analysis seems almost to imply that survival is possible only in an icy stasis, in which "security," "continuity," and "stability" are the key terms. If anything, the opposite seems more likely to be true, and organizational survival is impossible in such a state.

Wrapping themselves in the shrouds of nineteenth-century political economy, some social scientists appear to be bent on resurrecting a dismal science. For the iron law of wages, which maintained that workers could never improve their material standards of life, some sociologists have substituted the iron law of oligarchy, which declares that men cannot improve their political standards of life. Woven to a great extent out of theoretical whole cloth, much of the discussion of bureaucracy and of organizational needs seems to have provided a screen onto which some intellectuals have projected their own despair and pessimism, reinforcing the despair of others.

Perhaps the situation can be illuminated with an analogy. For many years now infantile paralysis has killed and maimed scores of people. For many years also doctors, biologists, and chemists have been searching for the causes and cure of this disease. Consider the public reaction if, instead of reporting on their newest vaccines, these scientists had issued the following announcement: "We have not reached any conclusions concerning the causes of the disease, nor has our research investigated defenses against it. The public seems to have perfectionist aspirations of flawless health, they have 'utopian' illusions concerning the possibilities of immortality and it is this—not the disease—that is the danger against which the public needs to be armed. We must remember that the human animal is not immortal and that for definite reasons his lifespan is finite." It is likely, of course, that such scientists would be castigated for having usurped the prerogatives and functions of clergymen.

This, however, seems to parallel the way in which some social scientists have approached the study of organizational pathology. Instead of telling men how bureaucracy might be mitigated, they insist that it is inevitable. Instead of explaining how democratic patterns may, to some extent, be fortified and extended, they warn us that democracy cannot be perfect. Instead of controlling the disease, they suggest that we are deluded, or more politely, incurably romantic, for hoping to control it. Instead of assuming responsibilities as realistic clinicians, striving to further democratic potentialities wherever they can, many social scientists have become morticians, all too eager to bury men's hopes.[32]

NOTES

1. Talcott Parsons, *The Structure of Social Action* (New York, 1937), p. 341. For Durkheim's own statement, see his *Le Socialisme* (Paris, 1908), especially Ch. 2. The present writer is preparing an English translation of this volume.

2. Bertrand and Dora Russell, *Prospects of Industrial Civilization* (New York, 1923), p. 14. Compare this with the discussion of Stalinist Communism by a postwar Russian refugee. G. F. Achminow, *Die Macht im Hintergrund: Totengraber des Kommunismus* (Ulm, 1950), which is discussed in Hans Gerth and C. Wright Mills, *Character and Social Structure* (New York, 1953), p. 477.
3. Parsons, p. 509. See also the provocative fuller development of this argument as it applies to industrial organization: George C. Homans, "Industrial Harmony as a Goal," in *Industrial Conflict,* eds. Kornhauser, Dubin, and Ross (New York, 1954).
4. Oskar Lange and Fred M. Taylor, *On the Economic Theory of Socialism,* ed. Lippincott (Minneapolis, 1948), p. 109.
5. Arthur O. Lovejoy, *The Great Chain of Being* (Cambridge, Mass., 1948), p. 11.
6. John A. Vieg, "Bureaucracy—Fact and Fiction," in *Elements of Public Administration,* ed. Fritz Morstein Marx (New York, 1946), p. 52.
7. Monograph # 11, Temporary National Economic Committee, *Bureaucracy and Trusteeship in Large Corporations* (Washington, D.C., 1940), p. 36.
8. Max Weber: *The Theory of Social and Economic Organization,* translated and edited by A. M. Henderson and Talcott Parsons (New York, 1947), p. 334.
9. *Ibid.,* p. 338.
10. See Reinhard Bendix, "Bureaucracy: The Problem and Its Setting," *American Sociological Review,* Vol. 12, pp. 502-7 (Oct., 1947). On the other hand, there are theoretically significant cases of small organizations which are highly bureaucratized, for example, the Boulton and Watt factory in 1775–1805. This "case illustrates the fact that the bureaucratization of industry is not synonymous with the recent growth in the size of business enterprises." Reinhard Bendix, "Bureaucratization in Industry," in *Industrial Conflict,* p. 166.
11. Vieg, pp. 5-6.
12. Talcott Parsons, *The Social System* (Glencoe, Illinois, 1951), pp. 507-8. Emphasis added.
13. Peter Drucker, *Concept of the Corporation* (New York, 1946), pp. 183-184.
14. Carl Dreyfuss, *Occupation and Ideology of the Salaried Employee,* trans. Eva Abramovitch (New York, 1938), p. 17.

15. *Ibid.,* p. 75.
16. *Ibid.,* p. 77.
17. W. Lloyd Warner and J. O. Low, *The Social System of the Modern Factory* (New Haven, 1947), pp. 78, 80, 174.
18. Robert Michels, *Political Parties* (Glencoe, Ill., 1949), p. 400. Michel's work was first published in 1915.
19. *Ibid.,* p. 401.
20. *Ibid.,* p. 402.
21. *Ibid.,* p. 405.
22. *Ibid.,* p. 408.
23. Philip Selznick, *TVA and the Grass Roots* (Berkeley and Los Angeles, 1949), p. 9.
24. *Ibid.,* p. 220.
25. *Loc. cit.*
26. *Loc. cit.*
27. *Ibid.,* p. 259.
28. *Ibid.,* p. 252.
29. *Ibid.,* p. 265.
30. *Ibid.,* p. 252.
31. See Arthur Schweitzer, "Ideological Groups," *American Sociological Review,* Vol. 9, pp. 415-427 (Aug., 1944), particularly his discussion of factors inhibiting oligarchy. For example, "A leadership concentrating all power in its hands creates indifference among the functionaries and sympathizers as well as decline in membership of the organization. This process of shrinkage, endangering the position of the leaders, is the best protection against the supposedly inevitable iron law of oligarchy" (p. 419). Much of the research deriving from the Lewinian tradition would seem to lend credence to this inference.
32. We have sought to develop the positive implications of this approach to bureaucratic organization in *Patterns of Industrial Bureaucracy* (Glencoe, Ill., 1954).

VICE, CORRUPTION, BUREAUCRACY, AND POWER

William J. Chambliss

At the turn of the century Lincoln Steffens made a career and helped make a president by exposing corruption in American cities.[1] In more recent years the task of exposure has fallen into the generally less daring hands of social scientists who, unlike their journalistic predecessors, have gathered their information from police departments, attorney generals' offices, and grand jury records.[2] This difference in the source of the information has probably distorted the descriptions of organized crime. It may well have led to a premature acceptance of the justice department's long-espoused view that there is a national criminal organization.[3] It most certainly has led to an overemphasis on the *criminal* in organized crime and a de-emphasis on *corruption* as an institutionalized part of America's legal-political system.[4] Concomitantly it has led to a failure to see the degree to which the structure of America's law and politics creates and perpetuates syndicates that supply the vices in our major cities.

Getting into the bowels of the city rather than the records and IBM cards of the bureaucracies brings the role of corruption into sharp relief. It also makes it clear that "organized crime" is not something that exists outside the law and government, but is instead a creation of them or perhaps more accurately, a hidden but nonetheless integral part of the governmental structure. The people who are most likely to be exposed by public inquiries (whether conducted by the FBI, a grand jury or the Internal Revenue Service) may be officially outside of government, but the cabal of which they are a part is organized around, run by, and created in the interests of economic, legal, and political elites.

The study of Rainfall West (a pseudonymn), which is the basis of the analysis of the relationship between vice and the political and eco-

I am grateful to W. G. O. Carson, Terence Morris, Paul Rock, Charles Michener, Patrick Douglas, Donald Cressey, and Robert Seidman for helpful comments on earlier versions of this paper.

nomic system which follows, makes it quite clear that the business of vice in the city is an integral part of the political and economic structure of the community. The cabal that manages the vices is composed of leading businessmen, law-enforcement officers, political leaders, and a member of a leading local trade union. Working for, and with, this cabal of "respectable" community members is a staff who coordinate the daily activities of prostitution, gambling, bookmaking, the sale and distribution of drugs, and other vices. Representatives from each of these groups, which comprise the political and economic power centers of the community, meet regularly to distribute the profits, discuss problems, and make the necessary organizational and policy decisions which maintain a profitable, trouble-free business.

DATA COLLECTION

The data reported in this paper were gathered over a period of seven years, from 1962–1969. Most of the data came from interviews with persons who were members of either the vice syndicate, law-enforcement agencies, or both. The interviews ranged in intensity from casual conversations to extended interviews (complete with tape recording) at frequent intervals over the full seven years of the study. In addition, I participated in many, though not all, of the vices that comprise the cornerstone upon which the corruption of the law-enforcement agencies is laid.

There is of course considerable latitude for discretion on my part as to what, ultimately, I believe to characterize the situation. Obviously not everyone told the same story, nor did I give equal credibility to everyone who gave me information. The story that emerges is one that fits most closely with my own observations and with otherwise inexplicable facts. I am confident that the data are accurate, valid, and reliable. But this cannot be demonstrated by pointing to unbiased sampling, objective measures, and the like for alas, in this type of research such procedures are impossible.

THE SETTING: RAINFALL WEST

Rainfall West is practically indistinguishable from any other city of a million inhabitants. The conspicuous bulk of the population that is the middle class shares with its contemporaries everywhere a smug complacency and a firm belief in the intrinsic worth of the area and the city. The smugness may be exaggerated here due to the relative freedom from "urban blight" that is the fate of larger cities. This, plus the fact that Rainfall West's natural surroundings attract tourists thereby provide the citizenry with confirmation of their faith that this is indeed a "chosen land!"[5]

There is of course an invisible, although fairly large, minority of the population that does not think they live in the promised land. These are the inhabitants of the slums and ghettos that make up the invisible center of the city. The invisible center is kept so by urban renewal programs which ring the slums with brick buildings and skyscrapers. Yet it requires only a very slight effort to get past the brick and mortar and into the not-so-enthusiastic city center (as contrasted with the wildly bubbling "civic center" which is located less than a mile away). Despite the ease of access, few of the residents who live in the suburbs and work in the area surrounding the slums take the time to go "where the action is." Those who do go for specific reasons: to bet on a football game, to find a prostitute, to see a "dirty movie," or to obtain a personal loan that would be unavailable from conventional financial institutions.

BUREAUCRATIC CORRUPTION AND ORGANIZED CRIME: A STUDY IN SYMBIOSIS

Laws prohibiting gambling, prostitution, pornography, drug use, and high interest rates on personal loans are laws about which there is a conspicuous lack of consensus. Even among persons who agree that such things are improper and should be controlled by law, there is considerable disagreement as to what the proper legal action should be. Should persons found guilty of committing such acts be imprisoned or counseled? Reflecting this dissension is the fact that there are large groups of people, some with considerable political power, who insist on their right to enjoy the pleasures of vice without interference from the law.

In Rainfall West those involved in providing gambling and other vices enjoyed pointing out that such services were profitable because of the demand for them by members of the "respectable" community. Prostitutes work in apartments which are on the fringes of the lower-class area of the city precisely because they must have an appearance of ecological respectability to avoid "contaminating" their clients. Although the prostitutes may exaggerate somewhat out of professional pride, their verbal reports are always to the effect that "all" of their clients are "very important people." My own observations of the comings and goings in several apartment houses where prostitutes work generally verified the girls' claims. Of some fifty persons seen going to prostitutes' rooms in apartment houses, only one was dressed in anything less casual than a suit.

Observations of "panorama," i.e., pornographic films shown in the back rooms of restaurants and "game rooms," confirmed the impression that the principal users of vice are middle- and upper-class clientele. During several weeks of observations over seventy percent of the consumers of these pornographic vignettes were well-dressed, single-minded visitors to the slums who came for fifteen or twenty minutes of viewing and left as inconspicuously as possible. The remaining thirty percent of those who viewed the panoramas were poorly-dressed, older men who lived in the area.

Information on gambling and bookmaking in the permanently established or floating games is a little less readily available. Bookmakers reported that the bulk of their "real business" came from "doctors, lawyers, and dentists" in the city:

> It's the big boys—your professionals—who do the betting down here. Of course, they don't come down themselves; they either send someone or they call up. Most of them call up, cause I know them or they know Mr. [one of the key figures in the gambling operation].
>
> *Q.* How 'bout the guys who walk in off the street and bet?
>
> *A.* Yeh; well, they're important. They do place bets and they sit around here and wait for the results. But that's mostly small stuff. I'd be out of business if I had to depend on them guys.

The poker and card games that are held throughout the city are of two types: the small, daily game that caters almost exclusively to local residents of the area or working-class men who drop in for a hand or two while they are driving their delivery route or on their lunch hour; and the "action game," which takes place twenty-four hours a day in the city and is located in more obscure places such as a downtown hotel suite. (The hotel and these games are, like the prostitutes, located on the fringes of the lower-class areas.) The "action games" were the playground of well-dressed men who were by manner, finances, and dress clearly well-to-do businessmen.

Then of course there are the games, movies, and gambling nights at the private clubs—country clubs, Elks, Lions, and Masons clubs—

where gambling is a mainstay. Gambling nights at the different clubs varied in frequency. The largest and most exclusive country club in Rainfall West has a "funtime" once a month at which one can find every conceivable variety of gambling and a limited, but fairly sophisticated, selection of pornography. The admission is presumably limited to members of the club, but it is relatively easy to gain entrance simply by "joining" with a temporary membership and paying a two-dollar fee at the door. Other clubs, such as the local fraternal organizations, have pinball machines present at all times, and in some there are also slot machines. Many of these clubs have on-going poker and other gambling card games which are run by people who work for the crime cabal. In all of these cases, the vices are of course catering exclusively to middle- and upper-class clients.

Not all the business and professional men in Rainfall West partake of the vices. Some of the leading citizens sincerely oppose the presence of vice in their city. Even larger numbers of the middle and working classes are adamant in their opposition to vice of all kinds. On occasion, they make their views forcefully known to the politicians and law-enforcement officers, thus making it necessary for these public officials to express their own opposition. The law enforcers must appear to be snuffing out vice by enforcing the law.

Into this situation must be added the fact that there are very large, tax-free profits to be had by those willing to supply the vices under these circumstances, that is, where a demand by people with money exists; where the profits from supplying the demand are high and the risks of punishment minimal, then it is a certainty that there will be people willing to provide the services demanded.

The law-enforcement system is thus placed squarely in the middle of two essentially conflicting demands—on the one hand it is their job to "enforce the law," albeit with discretion. At the same time there is considerable disagreement as to whether or not some acts should really be against the law. The conflict is heightened by the fact that there are some persons of influence in the community who insist that all laws be rigorously enforced while other influential persons demand that some laws not be enforced, at least not against themselves.

Faced with such a dilemma and such an ambivalent situation, the law enforcers do what any well-managed bureaucracy would do under similar circumstances—they follow the line of least resistance. They use the discretion that is inherent in their positions to resolve the problem by establishing procedures which minimize organizational strains and which provide the greatest promise of rewards for the organization and the individuals involved. Typically, this means that the law enforcers adopt a "tolerance policy" toward the vices and selectively enforce these laws only when it is to their advantage to do so. Since the persons demanding enforcement are generally middle-class persons who rarely go into the less prosperous sections of the city, the enforcers by controlling the ecological location of the vices, can control their visibility and minimize complaints. The law enforcers can, then, control the visibility of such things as sexual deviance, gambling, and prostitution and thereby appease those persons who demand the enforcement of the applicable laws. At the same time, since controlling visibility does not eliminate access for persons sufficiently interested to ferret out the tolerated vice areas, those who demand these services are also appeased.

Another advantage deriving from such a policy is that the legal system is in a position to exercise considerable control over potential sources of "real trouble." Violence which may accompany gambling can be controlled by having the cooperation of the gamblers. Since gambling and prostitution are profitable, there will be competition among persons who want to provide these services. This competition is likely to become violent, for if the legal system is not in control of who is running the vices, competing groups may well go to war to obtain dominance over the rackets. If, however, the legal system cooperates with one group, there is sufficient concentration of power to avoid these uprisings. Prostitution can be kept "clean" if the law enforcers cooperate with the prostitutes; the law can minimize the chance, for example, that a prostitute will steal money from a customer. In these and many other ways, then, the law-enforcement system maximizes its visible effectiveness by creating and supporting a shadow government that manages the vices.

Initially this may necessitate bringing in people from other cities to help set up the necessary organization. Or it may mean recruiting and training local talent or simply co-opting, coercing, and purchasing the knowledge and skills of entrepreneurs who are at the moment engaged in vice operations. When this move is made it often involves considerable strain, since some of those being brought in may not initially cooperate. Whatever the particulars, the ultimate result is the same: there emerges a syndicate composed of politicans, law enforcers, and citizens capable of supplying and controlling the vices in the city. The most efficient cabal is one that has representatives of all the leading centers of power. Businessmen must be involved because of their political influence and their ability to control the mass media. The latter note for business was illustrated when a fledgling magazine published an article intimating that some leading politicans were corrupt. Immediately the major advertisers cancelled their advertisements in the magazine. One large chain store refused to sell that issue of the magazine in any of its stores. And when one of the leading cabal members was accused of accepting bribes, a number of the community's most prominent businessmen sponsored a large advertisement declaring their unfailing support for and confidence in the integrity of this "outstanding public servant."

The cabal must also have the cooperation of businessmen in procuring loans, loans which enable them individually and collectively to purchase legitimate businesses as well as to expand the vice enterprises. For this a member of the banking community is a considerable asset. In Rainfall West the vice-president of one of the local banks (who was an investigator for a federal law-enforcement agency before he entered banking) is a willing and knowing member of the relationships necessary. Not only does he serve on the board of directors of a loan agency controlled by the cabal, he also advises cabal members on how to keep their earnings a secret. He sometimes serves as a go-between, passing investment tips from the cabal on to other businessmen in the community. In this way the cabal serves the economic interests of businessmen indirectly as well as directly.

The political influence of the cabal is obtained more directly. The huge, tax-free profits make it possible for the cabal to generously support political candidates of its choice. Often the cabal supports both candidates in a race, thus assuring influence regardless of who wins. Usually there is a favorite, ultracooperative candidate who receives the greater proportion of the contributions, but everyone is likely to receive something.

THE BUREAUCRACY

Contrary to the prevailing myths that universal rules govern bureaucracies, the fact is that in day-to-day operations the rules can and must be applied selectively. As a consequence, the possibility and in the end the certainty, of some degree of corruption is built into the structure of bureaucratic organizations.

The starting point for understanding this structural invitation to corruption in bureaucracies is the observation that there is inevitably a high degree of discretion possible in the application of all the rules and procedures which are the foundation of the organization. Rules can specify what should be done only when the actions being considered fall clearly into unambiguously specifiable categories. But "unambiguously specifiable categories" about which there can be no reasonable grounds for disagreement or conflicting interpretation are a virtual impossibiltiy given the inherently ambiguous nature of language. Most events therefore fall in the penumbra of the bureaucratic rules where the discretion of office-holders must hold sway.

Furthermore, since discretion must be applied for most decisions this means that it may be applied for any decision the office-holder chooses. If one has a reason to look for it, vagueness and ambiguity can be found in any rule, no matter how carefully it has been stipulated. In addition, if ambiguity and vagueness are not sufficient to justify particularistic criteria being applied, contradictory rules or implications of rules can be readily located which have the same effect of justifying the decisions which, for whatever reason the office-holder wishes, he can use his position to enforce.

Finally, since it is characteristic of organizations to develop their own set of common practices which take on the status of rules (whether written or unwritten), the entire process of applying rules becomes totally dependent on the discretion of the office-holder. The bureaucracy thus has a set of "precedents" which can be invoked whenever the articulated rules do not match up very well with the decision desired by the office-holder.

This amounts, then, to a situation in which the office-holder in effect has a license to apply "rules" from a practically limitless set of choices, thus forcing persons to depend on their ability to ingratiate themselves to office-holders at all levels in order to see that the rules most useful to them get applied. It is not, as prevailing myths would have it, a rational system with universal standards. It is instead, irrational and particularistic. The bureaucracy is a type of organization in which the organization's reason for being is displaced by a set of goals that often create effects which are exactly opposite of the organization's presumed purpose. This is precisely the consequence of the organizational response to the dilemma created by laws prohibiting the vices. It is the bureaucratic nature of law enforcement and political organization which makes possible the corruption of the legal-political bureaucracy.

In Rainfall West and most other American cities, the goal of maintaining a smoothly functioning organization takes precedence over all other goals of law as an institution. Where conflict arises between the long-range goals of "the law" and the short-range goal of sustaining the organization, the long-range goals lose out even at the expense of undermining the socially agreed-upon purposes for which the organization presumably exists.

But note that the law-enforcement agencies' tendency to follow "the line of least resistance" of maintaining organizational goals in the face of conflicting demands is in fact a choice of whose demands will be granted. The bureaucracies are not equally susceptible to all "interests" in the society. They do not fear castigation, interference, and disruption from the alcoholics on skid row or the cafe-owners in the slums. Although some residents of the black ghetto in Rainfall West and of other lower-class areas of the city have been campaigning for years to rid their communities of the gambling casinos, whore houses, pornography stalls, and bookmaking operations, their pleas continue to fall on deaf ears. Their pleas are literally limited to the letters they write and the committees they form which receive no publicity and create no stir in the smoothly functioning organizations that occupy the political and legal offices of the city. On the other hand, when the president of a large corporation in the city objected to the "slanderous lies" being spread about one of the leading members of the crime cabal in Rainfall West, the magazine carrying these "lies" was removed from newsstand sale, and the editors lost many of their most profitable advertisers. Similarly, when any question of the honesty or integrity of the policemen, prosecuting attorneys, or judges involved in the cabal is raised publicly, it is either squelched before it can be aired (the editor of the leading daily newspaper in Rainfall West is a long-time "friend" of one of the cabal's leading members), or it arouses the denial of influential members of the banking community (especially those banks which loan money to cabal members) as well as leading politicans, law-enforcement officers, and the like.

In short, the bureaucracies are susceptible to differential influence according to the economic and political power of the groups trying to influence them. Cabal links with the most powerful economic groups in the city make it virtually impossible to expose the ongoing relationships, since every facet of politics and the mass media is subject to reprisals by cabal members and their friends.

The fact that the bureaucrats must listen to the economic elites of the city and not the have-nots is, then, one important element that stimulates the growth and maintenance of a crime cabal. But the links between the elites and the cabal are more than merely spiritual. It is not simply that the economic elite of the city plays golf with the political and legal elite. There are in fact important economic ties between the two groups.

Most obvious is the fact that the political and legal elites are strongly influenced by campaign contributions from the economic elite. We need not dwell on this here; it is well documented in innumerable other studies. What is not well recognized is that the crime cabal is itself an important source of revenue for the economic elite. In at least one instance the leading bankers and industrialists of the city were a part of a multi-million dollar stock swindle which was engineered and manipulated by the crime cabal with the assistance of confidence-men from another state. This entire case was surrounded with such secrecy that the eastern newspapers were calling people at the University of Rainfall West to find out why news about the scandal was not forthcoming from local wire services. When the scandal was exposed the fact that industrialists and cabal members were heavily financing the operation (and taking the profits) was conveniently ignored in the newspapers and the courts; the "evil-doers" were limited to the "outsiders" who were in reality the front men for the entire confidence operation.

In a broader sense, key members of the economic elite in the community are also members of the cabal. The day-to-day, week-to-week operations of the cabal are determined by the criminal-political-legal elite, but the economic elite benefits mightily from the cabal. Not surprisingly, any threat to the cabal is quickly squelched by the economic elite under the name of "concerned citizens"; indeed they are.

The crime cabal is thus an inevitable outgrowth of the political economy of American cities. The ruling elites from every sphere benefit economically and socially from the presence of a smooth-running cabal. The bureaucracies that are the law-enforcement agencies and government function best when a cabal is part of the governmental structure. And the general public is satisfied when the control of the vices gives an appearance of respectability, but a reality of availability.

VICE IN RAINFALL WEST

The vices available in Rainfall West are varied and tantalizing. Gambling ranges from bookmaking (at practically every street corner in the center of the city) to open poker games, bingo parlors, off-track betting, casinos, roulette and dice games (concentrated in a few locations and also floating out into the suburban country clubs and fraternal organizations), and innumerable two- and five-dollar stud-poker games scattered liberally throughout the city.

The most conspicuous card games take place from about ten in the morning (it varies slightly from one "fun house" to the next) until midnight. But there are a number of other twenty-four hour games that run continuously. In the more public games the limit ranges from one to five dollars for each bet; in the more select games that run twenty-four hours a day, there is a "pot limit" or "no limit" rule. These games are reported to have betting as high as twenty and thirty thousand dollars. I have seen a bet made and called for a thousand dollars in one of these games. During this game, which was the highest-stakes game I witnessed in the seven years of the study, the police lieutenant in charge of the vice squad was called in to supervise the game—not, need I add, to break up the game or make any arrests, but only to insure against violence.

Prostitution covers the usual range of ethnic group, age, shape, and size of female. It is also found in houses with madams *à la* New Orleans stereotype, on the street through pimps, or in suburban apartment buildings and hotels. Prices range from five dollars for a short time with a street walker to two-hundred dollars for a night with a lady who has her own apartment (which she usually shares with her boyfriend, who is discreetly absent during business operations).

High-interest loans are easy to arrange through stores that advertise "your signature is worth $5,000." It is really worth considerably more; it may in fact be worth your life. The interest rates vary from a low of twenty percent for three months to as high as one-hundred percent for varying periods. Repayment is demanded not through the courts but through the help of "The Gaspipe Gang" who call on recalcitrant debtors and use physical force to bring about payment. The "interest only" repayment is the most popular alternative practiced by borrowers and is preferred by the loan sharks as well. The longer repayment can be prolonged, the more advantageous it is to the loan agents.

Pinball machines are readily available throughout the city, and most of them pay off in cash.

The gambling, prostitution, drug distribution, pornography, and usury (high-interest loans) which flourish in the lower-class center of the city do so with the compliance, encouragement, and cooperation of the major political and law-enforcement officials in the city. There is in fact a symbiotic relationship between the law enforcement-political organizations of the city and a group of *local* (as distinct from national) men who control the distribution of vices.

CORRUPTION IN RAINFALL WEST

One spring a businessman whom I shall call Mr. Van Meter sold his resturant and was looking for a new investment when he noticed an advertisement in the paper: "Excellent investment opportunity for someone with $30,000 cash to purchase the good will and equipment of a long-established restaurant in downtown area . . ." Mr. Van Meter made the necessary inquiries, inspected the business and its potential, and purchased it. In addition to the restaurant, the business consisted of a "card room" which was legally licensed by the city, operating under a publicly acknowledged "tolerance policy" which allowed card games, including poker, to be played. These games were limited by the "tolerance policy" to a maximum of $1.00 limit for each bet.

Mr. Van Meter had purchased a resturant with a built-in criminal enterprise. It was never clear whether at the time of purchasing the business he was fully aware of the criminal nature of the card room. Certainly the "official tolerance policy" was bound to create confusion over the illegality of gambling in the licensed card rooms. The full extent to which this purchase involved Mr. Van Meter in illegal activities began to be clear immediately upon purchase of the property.

> We had just completed taking the inventory of [the restaurant]. I was then handed the $60,000 keys of the premises by Mr. Bataglia, and he approached me and said, "Up until now, I have never discussed with you the fact that we run a bookmaking operation here and that we did not sell this to you; however, if you wish to have this operation continue here, you must place another $5,000 with us, and we will count you in. Now, if you do not buy it, we will put out this bookmaking operation, and you will go broke. In other words," Mr. Bataglia continued, "we will use you, and you need us." I told Mr. Bataglia that I did not come to this town to bookmake or to operate any form of rackets, and I assumed that I had purchased a legitimate business. Mr. Bataglia said, "You have purchased a legitimate business; however, you must have the bookmaking operation in order to survive." I promptly kicked him out of the place.[6]

The question of the "legitimacy" of the business Mr. Van Meter had purchased was not as simple as he thought. It was, to be sure, a licensed operation; there was a license to operate the restaurant, a license to operate the card room attached to the restaurant, and a license to operate the cigar stand (where much of the bookmaking operation had taken place before Mr. Van Meter purchased the place). These licenses, although providing a "legitimate business," also had the effect of making the owner of the business continually in violation of the law, for the laws were so constructed that no one could possibly operate a "legitimate" business "legally." Thus anyone operating the business was vulnerable to being continually harassed and even closed by the authorities if he failed to cooperate with law-enforcement personnel.

The card room attached to the business was the most conspicuous example of a legitimate enterprise that was necessarily run illegally. Rainfall West had adopted by city ordinance a "tolerance policy" toward gambling. This "tolerance policy" consisted of allowing card rooms to be licensed by the city, pinball machines that paid off money to winners, and "panorama" shows. The resturant purchased by Mr. Van Meter had a "card room" attached to it. The city ordinance required that there be a maximum one dollar bet at the card table.

This ordinance was in clear and open violation of the state law. The attorney general had said publicly that the tolerance policy of the city was illegal; that there was only one policy for the state, and that policy was that all gambling was illegal. Despite these rulings from higher state officials, the tolerance policy continued and flourished in the city, although it did so illegally.

This general illegality of the card room was not, however, easily enforceable against any *one* person running a card room without enforcement against *all* persons running card rooms. There were, however, wrinkles in the tolerance policy ordinance that made it possible to discriminately close down one card room without taking action against all of them. This was accomplished in part by the limit of one dollar on a bet. The card room was allowed to take a certain percentage of the pot from each game. But the number of people playing and the amount of percentage permitted did not allow one to make a profit if the table limit was left at one dollar. Furthermore, since most people gambling wanted to bet more, they would not patronize a card room that insisted on the one-dollar limit. Mr. Van Meter, like all other card-room operators, allowed a two- to five-dollar limit. The ordinance was written in such a way that everyone would be in violation of it; it was therefore possible for the police to harass or close down whatever card rooms they chose at their own discretion.

The health and fire regulations of the city were also written in such a way that no one could comply with all the ordinances. It was impossible to serve meals and live up to the health standards required. Thus when the health or fire department chose to enforce the rules, they could do so selectively.

The same set of circumstances governed the cabaret licenses in the city. The city ordinances required that a resturant be attached to every cabaret; the restaurant, the ordinance stated, had to have at least seventy-five percent of the total floor space of the cabaret and restaurant combined. Furthermore, these restaurants had to be extremely large in order to comprise seventy-five percent of the total floor space of the cabaret and restaurant combined. For example, a one-hundred square foot cabaret would require a three-hundred square foot restaurant. Since there was a much higher demand for cabarets than for restaurants in the central section of the city, cabaret owners who complied with the law would necessarily lose money. Another burden on the cabaret owners was an ordinance governing the use of entertainers in the cabaret. The ordinance required that any entertainer had to be at least twenty-five feet from the nearest customer during her act. This imposed a tremendous burden on the cabaret owner, since it meant that the cabaret had to be absolutely gigantic to accommodate any customers outside the twenty-five foot buffer zone. When combined with the requirement for a restaurant three times the size of the cabaret, the ordinance simply made it impossible to run a cabaret legally.

The effect of these ordinances, like those governing card rooms and restaurants generally, was to give the police and the prosecuting attorney complete discretion to choose who should operate gambling rooms, cabarets, and restaurants. This discretion was used to ensure payoffs to the police and cooperation with the criminal syndicate. Mr. Van Meter discovered the payoff system fairly early in his venture:

> I found shortages that were occurring in the bar and asked an employee to explain them, which he did in this manner: "The money is saved to pay the 'juice' of the place." I asked him what the "juice" was. He said in this city you must "pay to stay." Mr. Davis said, "You pay for the beat-man (from the police department) $250.00 per month. That takes care of the various

> shifts, and you must pay the upper brass, also $200.00 each month. A beat-man collects around the first of each month, and another man collects for the upper brass. You get the privilege to stay in business. That is true; however, you must remember that it is not what they will do for you, but what they will to *to* you, if you don't make these payoffs as are ordered." "If I refuse, what then?" I asked. "The *least* that could happen to you is you will lose your business."

During the next three months, Mr. Van Meter made the payoffs required. He refused, however, to allow the bookmaking operation back into the building. He also refused to hire persons to run the card room and bar whom members of the organized crime syndicate and the police recommended to him for the job. He fired one employee whom he found taking bets while tending bar. Then in August of the same year a man whom Mr. Van Meter had known prior to buying the restaurant met him in his office:

> Mr. Danielski met with me in my office, and he came prepared to offer me $500 per month—in cash deductions—of my remaining balance of the contract owing against *the restaurant* if I would give him the bookmaking operation, and he would guarantee me another $800 a month more business. He warned that if he wanted to give my establishment trouble, he would go to a certain faction of the police department; if he wanted me open, he would go to another faction. "So do some thinking on the subject, and I will be in on Monday for your answer." Monday, I gave Mr. Danielski his answer. The answer was no.

> In June of 19 . . ., a man by the name of Joe Link, who I found later was a second-string gang member of Mr. Bataglia's, made application to me to operate my card room. I did give him the opportunity to operate the card room because I had known him some 20 years ago when he was attending the same high school that I was. After I had refused the offer of Mr. Danielski, Mr. Joe Link had received orders from Mr. Danielski and Mr. Bataglia to run my customers out and in any way he could, cripple my operation to bring me to terms. I terminated Mr. Link on November 6, 19 . . ., and shortly after, after I had removed Mr. Link, police officer Herb C. conferred with me in my office, and Officer Herb C. said that I had better reappoint Mr. Link in my card room; that his superiors were not happy with me. If I did not return Mr. Link to his former position, then it would be necessary to clear anyone that I wanted to replace Mr. Link with. Officer C. felt that no one else would be acceptable. He further stated I had better make a decision soon, because he would not allow the card room to run without an approved boss. I informed Officer C. that I would employ

> anyone I chose in my card room or in any other department. Officer C. said, "Mr. Van Meter, you, I think, do not realize how a powerful a force you will be fighting or how deep in City Hall this reaches. Even I am not let know all the bosses or where the money goes." I did not return Mr. Link, as I was ordered by Officer C., and I did select my own card room bosses.
>
> On November 7, 19 . . ., I received a phone call stating that I soon would have a visitor who was going to shoot me between the eyes if I did not comply with the demands to return Mr. Link to his former position.

The crime cabal in Rainfall West (including police officers, politicians, and members of the organized criminal syndicate), like the criminal law which underpins it, relies on the threat of coercion to maintain order. But the threat is not an empty one. Although Mr. Van Meter was not "shot between the eyes" as threatened, others who crossed the cabal were not so fortunate. It has never been established that any of the suspicious deaths that have taken place involving members of crime cabal were murder; the evidence, nonetheless, points rather strongly in that direction.

Eric Tandlin, former county auditor for Rainfall West, is but one of thirteen similar cases which occurred from 1955–1969. Eric Tandlin had been county auditor for seventeen years. He had kept his nose clean, done the bidding of the right politicians, and received a special gift every Christmas for his cooperation. He had also, in the course of doing business with the politicians and criminals, developed an extensive knowledge of the operations. Suddenly, without warning or expectation on his part, Eric was not supported for reelection to auditor by his party. He lost the nomination to the brother-in-law of the chief of police. It was a shock from which Eric did not soon recover. He began drinking heavily, frequenting the gambling houses, and he also began talking a great deal. He made friends with a reporter who promised to put him in touch with someone from the attorney general's office. This was on Friday evening. Saturday night at 6:30, just as the card rooms were being prepared for the evening, word spread through the grapevine along First Street that Eric had been done in: "Danielski took Eric for a walk down by the bay."

> The Sunday morning paper carried a small front-page story telling that "Eric Tandlin, aged forty-seven, was found drowned in back bay yesterday at around 5:00 P.M. The coroner's office listed the cause of death as possible suicide. Friends said Mr. Tandlin, who had been county auditor for many

> years until his defeat in the primaries last fall, had been despondent over his failure to be reelected."

The coroner, who was the brother-in-law of the chief of police, put the probable cause of death as "suicide." The people of Miriam Street knew better, and they knew that this was also a warning not to talk to reporters, sociologists, or anyone else "nosing around."

Drowning is a favorite method of eliminating "troublemakers" because it is difficult to ascertain whether or not the person accidentally fell from a boat, was held under water by someone else, or committed suicide.[7]

In the last few years the cabal has been responsible for the deaths of several of its members. L. S., who was in charge of some of the pinball operations but who came into disfavor with the cabal, was found drowned at the edge of a lake near his home. J. B., an assistant police chief who had been a minor membeı of the cabal for years, drowned while on a fishing trip aboard one of the yachts owned by a leading member of the cabal. In both instances the coroner, who was the brother-in-law of one of the leading cabal members, diagnosed the deaths as "accidental drownings." Over the years he has often made that diagnosis when cabal members or workers in the organization have met with misfortune.

Other deaths have been arranged in more traditional ways; at least one man was shot in an argument in a bar. The offender was tried before a judge who has consistently shown great compassion for any crimes committed by members of the cabal (although he has compensated for this leniency with cabal members by being unusually harsh in judgments against blacks who appear before him), and the case was "thrown out of court," for lack of evidence.

Murder, however, is not the preferred method of handling uncooperative people. Far better, in the strategy of the crime cabal, is the time-honored technique of blackmail and co-optation. If the person can be purchased for a reasonable amount (as they tried to purchase Mr. Van Meter), this is the easiest and safest solution. If this fails, then some form of blackmail or relatively minor coercion may be in order.

Sheriff McCallister was strongly supported by the cabal in his bid for office. Generous campaign contributions were provided, since McCallister was running against a local lawyer who was familiar with the goings-on of the cabal and who had vowed to cause them trouble.

McCallister won the election (cabal candidates almost never lose local elections) but had a strong change of heart after election. He announced in very clear tones that he would not permit the operation of gambling houses in the county. He was not intending to do anything about the operations within the city limits, since that was not his jurisdiction, but the county, he insisted, would be kept clean.

The cabal was as annoyed as it was surprised. The county operations were only a small portion of the total enterprise, but they were nonetheless important, and no one wanted to give up the territory. Further, the prospect of closing down the "lay-off" center was no small matter. The lay-off center is crucial to the entire operation. It is here that the results of horse races and other sports events come directly to the bookmakers. It is also here that the cabal protects itself against potential bankruptcy. When the betting is particularly heavy in one direction, the bets are "laid off" by wiring Las Vegas, where the national betting pattern always takes care of local variations. Clearly something had to be done about McCallister.

No man is entirely pure, and McCallister was less pure than many. He had only two major weaknesses—gambling and young girls. One weekend shortly after he took office, a good friend of his asked if he would like to go to Las Vegas for the weekend. He jumped at the opportunity. The weekend went well in some respects, but McCallister was unlucky at cards. He left $14,000 worth of I.O.Us in Las Vegas when he flew back to Rainfall West Sunday night. Monday morning one of the cabal chiefs visited McCallister in his office.

> "Say, Mac, I understand you was down in Vegas over the weekend."
>
> "Yeah."
>
> "Hear you lost a little bit at the tables, Mac."
>
> "Uuh-huh."
>
> "Well, the boys wanted me to tell you not to worry about those pieces of paper you left. We got them back for you."
>
> "I don't . . . "
>
> "Also, Mac, we thought you might like to have a momento of your trip, so we brought you these pictures . . . "

The "momentos" were pictures of McCallister in a hotel room with several young girls.

Thereafter things returned to normal in the county.

Lest one think the cabal is exploitative, it should be noted that McCallister was not kept in line by the threat of exposure alone. He was, in fact, subsequently placed on the payroll in the amount of $1000 a month. When his term as sheriff was over, an appointment was arranged for him to the State Parole Board. He was thus able to continue serving the cabal in a variety of ways for the rest of his life. Cooperation paid off much better than exposure would have. Even a reform sheriff is fortunate if he is reelected more than once, and his life is always hanging rather tenuously on the edge of hostility from those he is opposing.

Threats from outside the organization are more rare than are threats from within. Nonetheless, they occur and must be dealt with in the best possible way. No set strategy exists, but each incident is handled in its own way. During Robert Kennedy's days as attorney general, the federal attorney for the state began a campaign to rid the state of cabal members. People who held political office were generally immune, but some of the higher-ups in the operational section of the cabal were indicted. Ultimately five members of the cabal were sentenced to prison, including a high-ranking member of the local Teamsters' union. It was a scandalous thing; politicians whose lives depended on the cabal fought the entire nasty businesss with all their power. They were able to protect the major leaders of the cabal and to avert having any of the cabal politicians exposed. Some blood ran, however, and it was a sad day for those five men who had to go to prison. The organization, however, was kept intact and indeed, the five men who went to prison continued to receive their full share of profits from the cabal enterprises. Corruption was unabated. The net effect on organized crime in the state was nil.

One reason that Mr. Van Meter escaped being "shot between the eyes" was that although he was not fully cooperative, he was nonetheless paying into the cabal $450.00 a month in "juice." Eventually he cut down on these payments. When this happened, Mr. Van Meter became a serious problem for the cabal, and something more than mere threats was called for.

> No extortion was paid by me directly to them, but it involved a third party. Some time shortly after the first of each month, the sum of $250.00 was paid to Officer C. [mentioned earlier], which he presumably divided up with other patrolmen of the beat. Two-hundred dollars each month was given to [another bagman] for what the boys termed as "going to the upper braid." The $200.00 per month was paid each month from June 19 . . . , with payment of $200.00 being made in January 19 . . . After that I refused

> to make further payments . . . After some wrangling back and forth, I just told them that I would not pay any more. They said, "Well, we will take $100.00 per month on a temporary basis." I paid $100.00 per month for the next twelve months. Early the next year I had planned to cut off all payments to the patrolmen . . . About the 8th of July the explosion occurred. Police officers Merrill and Lynch conducted a scare program—jerked patrons off stools, ran others out of my establishment; Patrolman Lynch ordered my card room floorman into the rest room and ordered my card room closed. When my floorman came out of the rest room, he left white and shaking and was never to be seen in the city again.

Following this incident, Mr. Van Meter met with his attorney, the chief of police, and a former mayor. The meeting was cordial, but he was told they could do nothing unless he could produce affidavits substantiating his claims. He did so, but quickly became enmeshed in requests and demands for more affidavits and the resistance of the prosecuting attorney's office to cooperate.

The refusal of cooperation from the prosecuting attorney was not surprising. What Mr. Van Meter did not realize was that the prosecuting attorney was the key political figure behind the corruption of the legal and political machinery. He was also the political boss of the county and had very great influence on state politics, as he came from the most populous area of the state. Over the years his influence had been used to place men in key positions throughout the various government bureaucracies, including the police department, the judiciary, the city council, and relevant governmental agencies such as the tax office and the licensing bureau.

There was, however, a shift in emphasis for a short time in the cabal's dealings with Mr. Van Meter. They offered to buy his business at the price he had paid for it. When he refused, the pace of harassment increased. Longshoremen came into his restaurant and started fights. Police stood around the card room day and night "observing." The city health officials would come to inspect the cooking area during mealtimes and thereby delay service to customers; the fire department made frequent visits to inspect the fire precautions. Mr. Van Meter was cited on several occasions for violating health and safety standards.

Finally, he was called before the city council to answer an adverse police report stating that he allowed drunks and brawling in his establishment. At the hearing he was warned that he would lose all of his licenses if a drunk were ever again found in his restaurant.

Within six months after the hearing before the city council, Johnny Van Meter was forced out of business and out of the city. During this period the pressure on him continued at an ever-increasing rate. Longshoremen came into the restaurant and card room and picked fights with customers, employees, and Mr. Van Meter himself. Several days running the health department chose 5 P.M. to inspect the health facilities of the establishment. The fire inspector came at the lunch hour to inspect the fire equipment and write up every minor infraction he could find. Toward the end of Mr. Van Meter's attempt to fight the combine of government, police force, and criminal syndicate, he had innumerable threats to his life. Bricks and stones were thrown through the windows of his building. Ultimately he sold his business back to the previous owner at a loss of $30,000.

The affair caused considerable consternation among the legal-political-criminal cabal which controlled and profited from the rackets in Rainfall West. In the "good old days" the problem would have been quickly solved, one informant remarked, "by a bullet through the fat slob's head." But the ready resort to murder as a solution to problems was clearly frowned upon by the powers that operated organized crime in Rainfall West. Although many murders over the past ten years were the work of the syndicate, these murders were limited to trouble-makers *within* the syndicate. As nearly as could be determined, there had not been a murder of an "outsider" for a number of years.

Overall, the gambling, bookmaking, pinball, and usury operations grossed at least twenty-five million dollars a year in the city alone. It was literally the case that drunks would be arrested on the street for "public intoxication," while gamblers were making thousands of dollars and policemen were accepting bribes five feet away.

Payoffs, bribes, and associated corruption were not limited to illegal activities. To obtain a license for tow-truck operations one had to pay $10,000 to the licensing bureau; a license for a taxi franchise cost $15,000. In addition, taxi drivers who either sold "bootleg" liquor (standard-brand liquors sold after hours or on Sunday) or steered customers to prostitutes or gambling places paid the beat policeman and the sergeant of the vice squad. Tow-truck operators also paid the policeman who called the company when an accident occurred.

Informant: When I would go out on a call from a policeman, I would always carry matchbooks with three dollars tucked behind the covers. I would hand this to the cops when I came to the scene of the accident.

Q. Did every policeman accept these bribes?

Informant: No. Once in a while you would run into a cop who would say he wasn't interested. But that was rare. Almost all of them would take it.

Most of the cabarets, topless bars, and taverns were owned either directly or indirectly by members of the organized crime syndicate. Thus the syndicate controlled not only the gambling enterprises but also the "legitimate" businesses associated with "night life." In addition, several of the hotels and restaurants were owned by the syndicate. The true ownership of these establishments was disguised in several ways, such as formally placing them in the name of a corporation with a board of directors whose members were really front-men for the syndicate, or placing them in the names of relatives of syndicate members. It must be underlined that official ownership by "the syndicate" must be interpreted to mean all those who were simultaneously in the political or legal bureaucracies and the syndicate, as well as those who were involved solely in the day-to-day operations of the vice syndicate.

The governing board of the syndicate consisted of seven men, four of whom held high positions in the government and three of whom were responsible for the operation of the various enterprises. The profits were split among these seven men. We are *not,* then, talking about a syndicate that paid off officials; we are talking about a syndicate that is part and parcel of the government, although not subject to election.

OTHER STUDIES

There is an abundance of data indicating that what is true in Rainfall West is true in virtually every other city in the United States and has been true since at least the 1900s. Writing at the turn of the century, Lincoln Steffens observed that "the spirit of graft and of lawlessness is the American spirit." He went on to describe the results of his inquiries:

> In the very first study—St. Louis—the startling truth lay bare that corruption was not merely political; it was financial, commercial, social; the ramifications of boodle were so complex, various and far-reaching, that our mind could hardly grasp them . . . St. Louis exemplified boodle; Minneapolis, police graft; Pittsburg, a political and industrial machine; Philadelphia, general civic corruption.[8]

In 1931, when the National Commission on Law Observance and Enforcement completed an inquiry into the police, it concluded:

> Nearly all of the large cities suffer from an alliance between politicians and criminals. For example, Los Angeles was controlled by a few gamblers for a number of years. San Francisco suffered similarly some years ago and at one period in its history was so completely dominated by the gamblers that three prominent gamblers who were in control of the politics of the city and who quarrelled about the appointment of the police chief settled their quarrel by shaking dice to determine who would name the chief for the first two years, who for the second two years, and who for the third.
>
> Recently the gamblers were driven out of Detroit by the commissioner. These gamblers were strong enough politically to oust this commissioner from office despite the fact that he was recognized by police chiefs as one of the strongest and ablest police executives in America. For a number of years Kansas City, Mo., was controlled by a vice ring and no interference with their enterprises was tolerated. Chicago, *despite its unenviable reputation,* is but one of numerous cities where the people have frequently been betrayed by their elected officials.[9]

Frank Tannenbaum observed:

> It is clear from the evidence at hand, that a considerable measure of the crime in the community is made possible and perhaps inevitable by the peculiar connection that exists between the political organizations of our large cities and the criminal activities of various gangs that are permitted and even encouraged to operate.[10]

The Kefauver Commission summed up the results of their extensive investigation into organized crime in 1951:

> 1) There is a nationwide crime syndicate known as the Mafia, whose tentacles are found in many large cities. It has international ramifications which appear most clearly in connection with the narcotics traffic.
> 2) Its leaders are usually found in control of the most lucrative rackets in their cities.
> 3) There are indications of centralized direction and control of these rackets, but leadership appears to be in a group rather than in a single individual.[11]

And in 1969, Donald R. Cressey, using data gathered from the U.S. Attorney General and local crime commissions summed up the state of organized crime in the U.S.:

> In the United States, criminals have managed to put together an organization which is at once a nationwide illicit cartel and a nationwide confederation. This organization is dedicated to amassing millions of dollars by means of extortion, and from usury, the illicit sale of lottery tickets, chances on the outcome of horse races and athletic events, narcotics and untaxed liquor.[12]

The same general conclusion is apparent from the frequency with which cities have major scandals linking organized criminals with major political and legal figures. Detroit, Chicago, Denver, Reading, (Pennsylvania), Columbus (Ohio), Cleveland (Ohio), Miami, New York, Boston, and a horde of other cities have been scandalized and cleaned up innumerable times.[13] Yet organized crime persists and in fact thrives. Despite periodic forays, exposures, and reform movements prompted by journalists, sociologists, and politicians, organized crime has become an institution in the United States and many other parts of the world as well.

Once established, the effect of organized crime on the entire legal and political system is profound. To maintain order in such an organization requires the use of extralegal procedures, since obviously the law cannot always be relied on to serve the interests of the crime cabal. The law can harass uncooperative people—it can even be used to send persons to prison on real or faked charges. But to make discipline and obedience certain, it is necessary to enforce the rules of the syndicate in extralegal ways. To avoid detection of these procedures the police, prosecuting attorney's office, and judiciary must be organized in ways that make them incapable of discovering events that the cabal does not want disclosed. In actual practice it means that policemen, prosecutors, and judges who are *not* members of the cabal must not be in a position to investigate those things that the syndicate does not want investigated. The military chain of command of the police is, of course, well suited to such a purpose. So, in fact, is the availability of sanctions that are subtle but nonetheless important, such as relegating uncooperative policemen to undesirable positions in the department. Conversely, cooperative policemen are rewarded with promotions, prestigious positions on the force, and of course "a piece of the action."

Another consequence is a widespread acceptance of petty graft. The matchbox fee of the accident officers is but one illustration. Free meals, free cigarettes, bottles of whiskey at Christmas, and the like are practically universal in the police department. Television sets, cases of expensive whiskey, and on occasion new automobiles or "inside information" on investments are commonplace in the prosecuting attorney's office.

Significantly, the symbiotic relationship between organized crime and the legal system not only negates the law-enforcement function of the law vis-à-vis these types of crimes, but actually serves to increase crime in a number of ways. Most important, perhaps, is the gradual commitment to maintaining the secrecy of the relationship which in turn necessitates the commission of crimes other than those involved in the vices per se. At times, it becomes necessary to murder recalcitrant members of the syndicate or to intimidate through physical punishment those who do not pay their debts to the loan sharks. Calculating the extent of such activities is risky business. A conservative estimate of the number of persons killed by the syndicate from 1955 to 1969 in Rainfall West is fifteen. Estimates range as high as "hundreds." Such information is impossible to verify in a manner that creates confidence. It is a virtual certainty that some murders were perpetrated by the syndicate in order to protect the secrecy of their operations. It is also certain that the local law-enforcement officials, politicians, and businessmen involved with the syndicate cooperated in these murders.

The location of the vices in the ghettos and slums of the city may well contribute to a host of other types of criminality. It is not solely their own experiences with injustice and police harassment that lead ghetto residents to disdain the law and law enforcers. It is also their day-to-day observations that criminal syndicates operate openly and freely in their areas with complete immunity from punishment while persons standing on a corner or playing cards in an apartment are subject to arrest. We do not know that such observations undermine respect for and willingness to comply with the law, but it seems likely that they do.

CONCLUSION

It is no accident that whenever the presence of vice and organizations that provide the vices is exposed to public view by the politicians, it is always couched in terms of "organized crime." The question of "corruption" is conveniently left in the shade and is never exposed to daylight. Similarly, it is no accident that "organized crime" is inevitably seen as consisting of an organization of "criminals" with names like Valachi, Genovese, and Joe Bonanna. Yet the data from the study of Rainfall

West as well as earlier studies of vice make it abundantly clear that both of these characteristics are misleading.

I have argued, and I think the data show quite clearly, that the people who run the organizations which supply the vices in American cities are members of the business, political, and law-enforcement communities, not simply members of the "criminal" society. Furthermore, it is also clear from this study that corruption of political-legal organizations is a critical part of the life-blood of the crime cabal. The study of "organized crime" is thus a misnomer: the study should be of corruption, bureaucracy and power.[14] By relying on governmental agencies for their information on vice and the rackets, social scientists and lawyers have inadvertently contributed to the miscasting of the issue in terms that are descriptively biased and theoretically sterile. They have been diverted from the sociologically interesting and important issues raised by the persistence of crime cabals. As a consequence the real significance of the existence of syndicates that supply the vices has been overlooked; for instead of seeing these social entities as intimately tied to and in symbiosis with the legal and political bureaucracies of the state, they have emphasized the criminality of only a portion of those involved. Such a view contributes little to our knowledge of crime and even less to attempts at crime control.

NOTES

1. L. Steffens, *The Shame of the Cities,* New York: Sagamore Press, 1957. See also Lincoln Steffens, *The Autobiography of Lincoln Steffens,* New York: Harcourt Brace, 1931.
2. D. Cressey, *Theft of the Nation,* New York: Harper and Row, 1969; John Gardiner, "Wincanton: The Politics of Corruption" in William J. Chambliss, *Crime and the Legal Process,* New York: McGraw-Hill, 1969, pp. 103-135.
3. The view of organized crime as controlled by a national syndicate is criticized by Norval Morris and G. Hawkins in *The Honest Politician's Guide to Crime Control,* Chicago: University of Chicago Press, 1970.
4. Most recent examples of this are Donald Cressey, *op. cit.;* N. Morris and G. Hawkins, *op. cit.;* R. W. Thrower, "Introduction to Symposium on Organized Crime," *Journal of Public Law,* **20,** 1971, p. 33; Gus Tyler, "Sociodynamics of Organized Crime," *Journal of Public Law,* **20,** 1971, p. 33; W. S. Lynch and J. W. Phillips, "Organized Crime: Violence and

Corruption," *Journal of Public Law,* **20,** 1971, p. 59; T. Schelling, "What is the Business of Organized Crime?" *Journal of Public Law,* **20,** 1971, p. 71; R. King "Wild Shots in the War on Crime," *Journal of Public Law,* **20,** 1971, p. 83; T. J. Mckeon "The Incursion by Organized Crime into Legitimate Business," *Journal of Public Law,* **20,** 1971 p. 117. For a discussion of the importance of studying corruption, see E. L. Mckitrick, "The Study of Corruption," *Political Science Quarterly,* **72,** 1957, p. 502; William J. Chambliss, *Crime and the Legal Process, op. cit.,* p. 89; William J. Chambliss and Robert B. Seidman, *Law, Order and Power,* Reading, Mass.: Addison-Wesley Publishing Company 1971, pp. 484-502.

5. Thinking of one's own residence as a "chosen land" need not, of course, be connected with any objectively verifiable evidence. A small Indian farm town where the standard of living is scarcely ever above the poverty level has painted signs on sidewalks which read "Isn't God good to Indians?" Any outside observer knowing something of the hardships and disadvantages that derive from living in this town might well answer an unequivocal no. Most members of this community nevertheless answer affirmatively.
6. All quotations are from taped interviews. The names of persons and places are fictitious.
7. According to one informant, "Murder is the easiest crime of all to get away with. There are 101 ways to commit murder that are guaranteed to let you get away with it." He might have added that this was especially true when the coroner, the prosecuting attorney, and key police officials were cooperating with the murderers.
8. L. Steffens, *Shame of the Cities, op. cit.,* p. 151.
9. A. Vollmer, D. G. Monroe, and E. W. Garrett, "Police Conditions in the United States." *National Commission on Law Observance and Enforcement Report on Police,* Report No. 14, Washington, D.C., 45, 1937.
10. F. Tannenbaum, *Crime and the Community,* New York: Columbia University Press, 1938, p. 128.
11. *The Challenge of Crime in a Free Society,* Washington, D.C.: U.S. Government Printing Office, 1967, p. 7.
12. D. Cressey, *op. cit.* See also D. Bell, *End of Ideology,* New York: The Free Press, 1960.
13. A. Wilson, "The Police and their Problems: A Theory," *Public Policy,* **12,** 1963.
14. See U. McMullen, "A Theory of Corruption," *Sociological Review,* 9, 1961, p. 181.

Part 6
THE SOCIOLOGY OF DEVELOPMENT

What social science needs is less use of elaborate techniques and more courage to tackle, rather than dodge, the central issues. But to demand that is to ignore the social reasons that have made social science what it is.

J. D. BERNAL, *Science in History*

INTRODUCTION

Just as it aids our understanding to divide a particular society into those groups or classes that rule and those that are ruled, so it is theoretically useful to divide the world into those nations that rule and those that are ruled. The division of the world into a dominant "metropolis" and subservient "satellites" has its historical roots in the commercial development which began in Italian cities in the fifteenth century.[1] From commercial centers such as Venice and later Spanish, Portuguese, and northwestern European towns, a commercial network emerged which effectively brought large parts of the world bordering the Mediterranean Sea, including North Africa, under the domination of a few commercial centers. During the fifteenth century this network expanded to include some of the sub-Saharan African countries, as well as the islands off the coast of Africa and in the Atlantic. Spain and England expanded the commercial links further by "discovering" and exploiting the West Indies and America in the late fifteenth and sixteenth centuries. Africa was "opened up" by the European commercial centers during the sixteenth, seventeenth, and eighteenth centuries. In addition to commercial links, the metropolis centers began the intensive exploitation of the natural resources of these satellite nations which continues today. Africa also supplied slaves, who were taken to the less populated lands of the West Indies and America and used as a resource for development. During this time Asia, Oceania, and Eastern Europe were also conquered by the leading European commercial cities "until the entire face of the globe had been incorporated into a single organic mercantilist or mercantile capitalist and later also industrial and financial capitalist system whose metropolitan center developed in Western Europe and then North America and whose peripheral satellites underdeveloped on all the remaining continents."[2]

In recent years much has been made of the fact that most former colonies have gained their independence. It is noteworthy that there are some very important exceptions to this generalization. In January 1971, Portugal still maintained colonies in three large African nations: Guinea, Mozambique, and Angola. South Africa, Rhodesia, and Southwest Africa—all former colonies—have maintained the colonial system of government with only a formal break in the ties to the nations that were the original colonizers. Most nations that have gained their independence remain so completely dependent upon the former colonizing countries that "independence" is a gross misnomer. It is more accurate, in fact, to characterize the contemporary period as a neocolonial era rather than one of independence. At the present time the economic dependence of the nonindustrialized nations on the industrialized is virtually total. Africa, Latin America, and most of Asia remain satellites of the industrialized western nations. Furthermore, political influence and control of these "independent" nations by western powers such as the United States, France, and England is exceedingly strong if not complete. As this book goes to press, France is fighting a war in Chad to support a neocolonial regime sympathetic to French interests; England is arming South Africa and Rhodesia to suppress the black majority in those countries (although the arming is being done ostensibly to provide a bulwark against the Russian "threat" in the Indian Ocean and the Chinese "peril" in East Africa); the United States, through NATO, is supplying arms to Portugal which are used by that country to fight a war against Africans trying to abolish Portuguese colonial rule in Mozambique, Angola, and Guinea; the United States is fighting a war in Vietnam and suppressing populist movements across the globe.

In these and hundreds of other instances the power and influence of the industrialized nations in the affairs of the nonindustrialized world is made dramatically clear.

Paul Baran provides a useful theoretical perspective for understanding the ongoing relationship between nonindustrialized and industrialized societies. Andre Gunder Frank follows Baran's analysis with an application of the model to the facts of economic development in Latin America.

The article by Kwame Nkrumah traces some of the subtle and not-so-subtle influences exerted by the industrial nations in their efforts to make former colonies neocolonial satellites of the western metropolis.

NOTES

1. This summary comes from Andre Gunder Frank, *Capitalism and Underdevelopment in Latin America: Historical Studies of Chile and Brazil, Monthly Review Press,* 1967, pp. 14-15.
2. *Ibid.*

THE POLITICAL ECONOMY OF GROWTH

Paul Baran

I

The question why social and economic development has recently moved into the forefront of economic discussion—particularly in the United States—may appear to be a recondite and tedious issue in the history of knowledge only tenuously related to the subject matter itself. This is not quite the case. The history of thought reveals also here the thought of history, and an examination of the circumstances that have brought about the present burst of interest in social and economic change may shed valuable light on the nature and significance of the current debate, as well as on the substance of the problem itself.

It will be recalled that a strong interest in economic development is by no means an unprecedented novelty in the realm of political economy. In fact, economic growth was the central theme of classical economics. This much is indicated by the title and contents of Adam Smith's pathbreaking work, and many a generation of economic thinkers, regardless of the names that they gave their writings, were concerned with analyzing the forces that made for economic progress. Their concern with the conditions necessary for economic development grew out of their keen observation and study of the society in which they lived, and resulted in their firm conviction that the political, social, and economic relations prevailing at the time greatly impeded and retarded the development of productive resources. Whether they referred to the fallacies of the mercantilist foreign trade theory or to the rigidities of the guild system, or whether the issue was related to the functions of the state in economic life or to the role played by the landowning class, the classical economists had no trouble in showing that economic progress was predicated upon the removal of outdated political, social, and economic institutions, upon the creation of conditions of free competition under which individual enterprise and initiative would be given ample opportunity for unhampered performance.

Not that they confined themselves to a critique of the then existing society without making an attempt to provide a *positive* analysis of the working principles of the rising capitalist order. On the contrary, it was precisely this positive effort that furnished us with much of what we know today about the functioning of the capitalist system. What matters in the present context, however, is that the chief impetus to their prodigious scientific and publicistic endeavors was supplied by the strongly felt necessity to convince the public of the urgency of liberation from feudal and semi-feudal shackles. In this sense, if in no other, it is wholly appropriate to relate the classical school of economics to the rise and development of capitalism, to the triumph of the modern bourgeoisie. In the words of Professor Lionel Robbins:

> The System of Economic Freedom was not just a detached recommendation not to interfere: It was an urgent demand that what were thought to be hampering and anti-social impediments should be removed and that the immense potential of free pioneering individual initiative should be released. And, of course, it was in this spirit that in the world of practice its proponents addressed themselves to agitation against the main forms of these impediments: against the privileges of regulated companies and corporations, against the law of apprenticeship, against restriction on movement, against restraints on importation. The sense of a crusade which emerged in the free trade movement is typical of the atmosphere of the general movement for freeing spontaneous enterprise and energies, of which, without doubt, the classical economists were the intellectual spearhead.[1]

Yet, as soon as capitalism became fully established, and the bourgeois social and economic order firmly entrenched, this order was "consciously and unconsciously" accepted as history's "terminal station," and the discussion of social and economic change all but ceased. Like the Boston lady, who, in reply to an inquiry whether she had traveled much, observed that she had no need to travel since she had been fortunate enough to be born right in Boston, the neoclassical economists, in contrast to their classical predecessors, were much less concerned with problems of traveling and much more with the question how best to explore and to furnish the house in which they were born. To be sure, to some of them that house did not appear altogether perfect. They all thought of it, however, as sufficiently comfortable and sufficiently spacious to permit of various improvements. But such improvements—desirable as they may have seemed—were to be undertaken slowly, cautiously, and circumspectly, lest harm be done to the foundations and the pillars of the structure. Merely marginal adjustments were deemed practicable and advisable—nothing drastic, nothing radical could hope for approval on the part of economic science.[2] *Natura non facit saltum* suggests clearly that no moving was contemplated; it is certainly not the motto of economic development.

For economic development implies precisely the opposite of what Marshall placed on the title page of his *Principles.* It implies the crude but crucial fact—often, if not always, overlooked—that economic development has historically always meant a far-reaching transformation of society's economic, social, and political structure, of the dominant organization of production, distribution, and consumption. Economic development has always been propelled by classes and groups interested in a new economic and social order, has always been opposed and obstructed by those interested in the preservation of the *status quo,* rooted in and deriving innumerable benefits and habits of thought from the existing fabric of society, the prevailing mores, customs, and institutions. It has always been marked by more or less violent clashes, has proceeded by starts and spurts, suffered setbacks and gained new terrain—it has never been a smooth, harmonious process unfolding placidly over time and space.

However, this historical generalization—probably one of the best established that we have—was quickly lost sight of in bourgeois economics. In fact, having started as advocacy of capitalism, having grown to be its most sophisticated and perhaps most influential rationalization, it had to share the fate of all the other branches of bourgeois thought. As long as reason and the lessons to be learned from history were manifestly on the side of the bourgeoisie in its struggle against the obscurantist ideologies and institutions of feudalism, both reason and history were confidently invoked as the supreme arbiters in the fateful contest. There are no more magnificent witnesses to this grand alliance of the ascending bourgeoisie with reason and historical thinking than the great Encyclopedists of the eighteenth century, than the great realists of the nascent bourgeois literature.

But when reason and the study of history began revealing the irrationality, the limitations, and the merely transitory nature of the capitalist order, bourgeois ideology as a whole and with it bourgeois economics began abandoning both reason and history. Whether this abandonment assumed the form of a rationalism driven to its own self-destruction and turning into the agnosticism of modern positivism, or whether it appeared frankly in the form of some existentialist philosophy contemptuously rejecting all search for and all reliance upon a rational comprehension of history, the result was that bourgeois thought (and economics as a part of it) turned ever more into a neatly packed kit of assorted ideological gadgets required for the functioning and the preservation of the existing social order.

In its beginnings, economics was a revolutionary intellectual effort to seek out and to establish the working principles of an economic system best able to advance the cause of mankind. In its later days it has turned upon its own past, becoming a mere attempt at an explanation and justification of the *status quo*—condemning and suppressing at the same time all endeavors to judge the existing economic order by standards of reason, or to comprehend the origins of the prevailing conditions and the developmental potentialities that they contain. As Marx remarked: "The economists explain to us the process of production under given conditions; what they do not explain to us, however, is how these conditions themselves are being produced, i.e., the historical movement that brings them into being."[3]

Thus the concern with economic and social change was left to a "heretical" school of economics and social science. Marx and Engels accepted in essence the insistence of the classical economists on capitalism's giant contribution to economic development. Yet, not wedded to the now dominant capitalist class, and neither "consciously nor unconsciously" compelled to regard capitalism as the "natural" form of society and as the ultimate fulfillment of human aspirations, they were able to perceive the limits and barriers to progress inherent in the capitalist system. Indeed, their approach to the matter was radically different from that of bourgeois economics. While the latter was (and is) interested in economic development only to the extent that it has led to the establishment, and is conducive to the stabilization, of the capitalist order, Marx and Engels considered the capitalist order itself as likely to survive only as long as it did not become a fetter on further economic and social progress. Overcoming the limitations of bourgeois thought, they were able to comprehend the era of capitalism as merely creating the prerequisites for a development of humanity that would lead far beyond the confines of the capitalist order. Once more: the *critical* efforts of Marx and his followers yielded most important *positive* results. They destroyed the veil of harmony with which bourgeois economics obscured the view of the capitalist system, and laid bare the conflict-laden, irrational nature of the capitalist order. Much if not all that we know about the complex mechanism responsible for the development (and stagnation) of productive forces, and for the rise and decay of social organizations, is the result of the analytical work undertaken by Marx and by those whom he inspired.

Such might have remained the situation, with economic development relegated to the "underworld" of economic and social thought, were it not for historical processes that in the course of a few decades have drastically changed our entire social, political, and intellectual landscape. Indeed, while the neoclassical economists were busy with further refinements of static equilibrium analysis and with the elaboration of additional arguments proving the viability and intrinsic harmony of the capitalist system, capitalism itself was going through far-reaching transformations.

Towards the end of the nineteenth century, the first phase of the industrialization of the Western world was nearing its completion. The economic consequence of the thorough exploitation of the then available technology—based primarily on coal and steam—was not merely a tremendous expansion of heavy industry, a vast increase of output, and a revolution in the means of transportation and communication; it was also a momentous change in the structure of the capitalist economies. Concentration and centralization of capital made giant strides, and large-scale enterprise moved into the center of the economic scene, displacing and absorbing the small firm. Shattering the competitive mechanism which regulated, for better or worse, the functioning of the economic system, large-scale enterprise became the basis of monopoly and oligopoly—the characteristic features of modern capitalism. The world of neoclassical economics was rapidly disintegrating. Neither the slow (but steady) growth, nor relatively painless continuous adjustments on the margin were to be expected under conditions of ubiquitous indivisibilities and discontinuities, of increasing returns to scale, and of narrowing investment opportunities. The harmonious movement of capital from the advanced to the less developed countries that was expected to be propelled by the profit motive assumed in reality the form of embittered struggles for investment outlets, markets, and sources of raw materials. Western penetration of backward and colonial areas, that was supposed to spread the blessings of Western civilization into every nook and corner of the globe, spelled in actual fact ruthless oppression and exploitation of the subjugated nations.

The powerful tendencies towards stagnation, imperialist conflagrations, and severe political crises discerned by Marx as early as the middle of the nineteenth century, and later observed and analyzed by Hobson, Lenin, Hilferding, Rosa Luxemburg, and others, expressed themselves so manifestly as to give cause for alarm to all but the most complacent. A frantic armaments race among the Great Powers began absorbing growing parts of their national outputs and became the most important single factor in determining the level of their economic activity. In quick succession the Sino-Japanese War, the Spanish-American War, the Boer War, the bloody suppression of the Boxer Rebellion, the Russo-Japanese War, the Russian Revolution in 1905, the Chinese Revolution in 1911—1912, and finally the First World War ushered in the present epoch in the development of capitalism—the epoch of imperialism, wars, national and social revolutions.[4]

The Marxian theoretic challenge has become eminently practical: The "Indian summer" of stability, prosperity, and confidence in the future of capitalism—following the First World War—lasted less than one decade. The dream of "organized capitalism," of a "Ford-versus-Marx" solution of all economic and social ills, and of "economic democracy" assuring justice and welfare to all became the shortest-lived utopia on the historical record. The Great Depression with its manifold and protracted repercussions rendered the continuation of the "conspiracy of optimism" about economic growth and social progress under capitalism increasingly difficult to maintain. The time-honored "scientific" and "objective" finding of economics that socialism is impossible was dramatically refuted by the success of the industrialization effort in the USSR.

Tardily and reluctantly, economics began taking cognizance of the new situation. Although inspired by the immediate problem of counteracting depression and unemployment, and consequently addressing itself primarily to the issues of the short run, the "New Economics" of John Maynard Keynes carried implications that transcended by far its original scope. In an attempt at clarification of the determinants of short-run changes in the levels of output, employment, and income, Keynesian economics found itself face to face with the entire irrationality, the glaring discrepancy between the productive potentialities and the productive performance characteristic of the capitalist order. At the risk of grossly exaggerating the intellectual performance of Keynes, it might be said that what Hegel accomplished with respect to German classical philosophy, Keynes achieved with regard to neoclassical economics. Operating with the customary tools of conventional theory, remaining well within the confines of "pure economics," faithfully refraining from considering the socioeconomic process as a whole, the Keynesian analysis advanced to the very limits of bourgeois economic theorizing, and exploded its entire structure. Indeed, it amounted to an "official" admission on the part of the "Holy See" of conventional economics that instability, a strong tendency towards stagnation, chronic underutilization of human and material resources, are inherent in the capitalist system. It implicitly repudiated the zealously guarded "purity" of academic economics by revealing the paramount importance for the comprehension of the economic process of the structure of society, the relations of classes, the distribution of income, the role of the state, and other "exogenous" factors.

Yet this unintentionally undertaken revival of the inquiry into the "nature and causes of the wealth of nations" had nothing in common with the youthful, revolutionary enthusiasm of the early crusade for *laissez faire.* Although contributing greatly to the understanding of the mechanics of the capitalist economy, the New Economics was unable to rise to a full theoretic grasp of the general crisis of capitalism, and remained merely a supreme effort on the part of bourgeois economic thought to discover a way of saving the capitalist system in spite of the manifest symptoms of its disintegration and decay. Thus the "Keynesian Revolution" has never become associated with a vigorous movement for the abolition of an outlived and destructive social order, for economic development and social progress. Again, not unlike the philosophy of Hegel, in its "Leftist" interpretation, it supplied intellectual ammunition to a reform movement which expected once more to solve the contradictions of capitalism by changing the prevailing distribution of income, and by having a benevolent state provide henceforth for steady economic expansion and increasing standards of living. But the logic of monopoly capitalism proved to be much stronger than ever realized by Keynes and his radical followers. It turned their theoretic accomplishments to purposes quite alien to their intentions. The "Welfare State," guided by the canons of Keynesian economics and the precepts of "functional finance," has remained essentially on paper. It was fascist Germany that thus far has made the most extensive use of Keynesian insights in building an economic machine that enabled it to unleash the Second World War.

The war and the years of the postwar boom suspended all Keynesian concern with the excess accumulation of capital, with the shortage of effective demand. The requirements for the reconstruction of war damage in some countries, the satisfaction of postponed demand on the part of businesses and consumers in others, the urge to turn to productive purposes the technological innovations developed during (and frequently in connection with) the war—all combined to create a huge market for the output of capitalist enterprise.

Economists who only unwillingly and only under irresistible pressure of incontrovertible facts had "swallowed" the anti-capitalist implications of the Keynesian doctrine returned with conspicuous alacrity to the customary panegyrics of capitalist harmony. Remaining "close to observable facts," they cheerfully began to discuss inflation as the main threat to the continuous equilibrium of capitalist economics, and declared once more that oversaving, excess capacity, and depressions were relics of a remote and backward past. Extolling the virtues of the market mechanism, glorifying monopoly and "big business," economics all but canceled whatever advance was reached as a result of the Keynesian Revolution, and returned to the complacency of the "merry twenties."

To be sure, this regression will probably be no more than shortlived; it has in fact not even affected the entire profession. Not only behind some recent writings on problems of economic growth, but even behind the more down-to-earth discussions of current business conditions and short-run economic prospects, lurks a gnawing uncertainty about the future of capitalism and a painful awareness that the impediments to economic progress that are inherent in the capitalist system are bound to reappear with renewed force and increased obstinacy as soon as the extraordinary hothouse situation of the postwar period has ceased to exist.

II

But if the ability of the economy of the United States (and of other highly developed capitalist countries) is giving rise to much concern and provides a stimulus to thinking about the basic problems of economic growth and development, the processes unfolding in the world at large cannot fail to lend these meditations the utmost urgency.

For the Second World War and the events that constituted its sequel were a major earthquake that shattered the structure of the capitalist world even more violently than the First World War and the Russian Revolution. Indeed, the First World War led "merely" to the loss of Russia to the capitalist system. The Second World War, however, has been followed not only by the Chinese Revolution, but by a nearly universal awakening of the vast multitudes inhabiting the world's dependent and colonial areas. Aroused by the staggering irrationality and oppressiveness of their social and economic order, weary of the continuous exploitation by their foreign and domestic masters, the peoples of the underdeveloped countries have begun to manifest a mounting determination to overthrow a social and political system that is perpetuating their squalor, misery, and stagnation.

The momentous movement to do away with the entire edifice of imperialism, to put an end to the backwardness and prostration of the overwhelming majority of the human race, would by itself have created considerable consternation in the ruling class of the United States and other capitalist countries sitting on top of the imperialist pyramid. What has transformed this consternation into a state of near-panic, however, is the historic confluence of the restiveness in the underdeveloped countries with the spectacular advance and expansion of the world's socialist camp. The military performance of the Soviet Union during the war and the rapid recovery of its war-ravaged economy provided the final proof of the strength and viability of a socialist society. There can no longer remain any doubt that a socioeconomic system based on comprehensive economic planning can function, grow, and withstand the most trying historical tests—without the benefits of private enterprise and without the institution of private property in the means of production. What is more, a large number of dependent countries went through a social revolution after the war, and thus entered the road to rapid economic and social progress. Eastern and Southeastern Europe, and even more importantly China, dropped out of the orbit of world capitalism and became sources of encouragement and inspiration to all other colonial and dependent countries.

As a result of these developments, the issue of economic and social progress not merely returns to the center of the historical stage but relates—as two or three centuries ago—to the very essence of the widening and sharpening struggle between two antagonistic social orders. What has changed is perhaps not so much the nature and the plot of the drama as the leading dramatis personae. If in the seventeenth and eighteenth centuries the struggle for progress was tantamount to the struggle against the outlived institutions of the feudal age, similarly current efforts to bring about conditions indispensable for economic development in advanced and backward capitalist countries alike come continuously into conflict with the economic and political order of capitalism and imperialism. Thus to ruling opinion in the United States (but also in some other parts of the capitalist world), the world-wide drive for economic progress inevitably appears as profoundly subversive of the existing social order and of the prevailing system of international domination—as a revolutionary movement that has to be bribed, blocked, and if possible, broken, if the capitalist system is at all to be preserved.

It is needless to say that approaching economic development from this standpoint amounts to its repudiation. As far as *advanced* capitalist countries are concerned, the incompatibility of sustained economic growth with the capitalist system has been brought into sharp relief by some of the recent writings on economic growth. The mere specification of the conditions that need to be fulfilled for output to increase at rates that would be attainable with the available human and material resources—presented in different forms by Domar, Harrod, Colm, and others—shows with utmost clarity that such rates of increase are impossible under capitalism. Indeed, both consumption and private investment are rather narrowly circumscribed by the requirements of profit maximization under conditions of monopoly and oligopoly, and the nature and volume of government spending are no less rigidly determined by the social basis and function of the state in a capitalist society. Consequently neither maximum output, rationally allocated as between investment and consumption, nor some predetermined level of output combined with a lessening of the burden of work, are to be expected in the capitalist system. What appears to be more probable is the continuous re-emergence of the grim dilemma between war-induced bursts of output and depression-induced floods of unemployment.

Yet, although demonstrating, and indeed greatly clarifying, the vicious and portentous nature of this impasse, none of the writers just mentioned has stated what is an inescapable conclusion of their own investigations—that socialist economic planning represents the only rational solution of the problem. To be sure, it may be held that there is no need for explicit statements of what necessarily emerges from the logic of a rigorous argument. However, even self-evident truths must be communicated if they are to be recognized as such by those whom they may otherwise escape. Nothing is perhaps more characteristic of the intellectual atmosphere surrounding the present discussion of economic growth—a discussion in which truisms and trivia abound—than that it is *this* self-evident truth that is strictly taboo even to the most enlightened writers on the subject.

Matters are still worse when it comes to economic development in *underdeveloped* countries. There a maze of pretense, hypocrisy, and make-believe confuse the discussion, and a major effort is required to penetrate the smoke screen obscuring the main issue. What is decisive is that economic development in underdeveloped countries is profoundly inimical to the dominant interests in the advanced capitalist countries. Supplying many important raw materials to the industrialized countries, providing their corporations with vast profits and investment outlets, the backward world has always represented the indispensable hinterland of the highly developed capitalist West. Thus the ruling class in the United States (and elsewhere) is bitterly opposed to the industrialization of the so-called "source-countries" and to the emergence of integrated processing economies in the colonial and semi-colonial areas. This opposition appears regardless of the nature of the regime in the underdeveloped country that seeks to reduce the foreign grip on its economy and to provide for a measure of independent development. Whether it is a democratically elected government in Venezuela, in Guatemala, or in British Guiana, an indigenous popular movement (as in Kenya, in the Philippines, or in Indo-China), a nationalist administration (as in Iran, Egypt, or Argentina) that undertakes to oppose the foreign domination of its country—all leverages of diplomatic intrigue, economic pressure, and political subversion are set into motion to overthrow the recalcitrant national government and to replace it with politicians who are willing to serve the interests of the capitalist countries.

The resistance of imperialist powers to economic and social development in colonial and dependent territories becomes even more desperate when the popular aspirations to national and social liberation express themselves in a revolutionary movement that, internationally connected and supported, threatens to overthrow the entire economic and social order of capitalism and imperialism. Under such circumstances, the resistance hardens into a counter-revolutionary alliance of all imperialist countries (and their reliable retainers) and assumes the form of a systematic crusade against national and social revolutions.

The requirements of this crusade have molded decisively the attitude toward the development of underdeveloped countries prevailing at the present time in the Western world. As the Prussian Junkers presented the continuation of serfdom on their estates as indispensable for the defense of Christianity against the onslaught of liberal godlessness, so the drive of the Western ruling classes to maintain the economic, social, and political *status quo* in underdeveloped countries is proclaimed as the defense of democracy and freedom. As the Prussian Junkers' interest in high tariffs on grains was announced to be dictated solely by their deep concern with the preservation of German food supplies under conditions of war, so the anxiety of dominant Western corporations to safeguard their investments abroad and to remain assured of the accustomed flow of raw materials from the backward world is publicized as patriotic solicitude for the "free world's" supply of indispensable strategic materials.

The arsenal of "united action" against the independent development of underdeveloped countries comprises an entire gamut of political and ideological stratagems. There are in the first place the widely broadcast statements of Western statesmen that appear to *favor* economic development in the underdeveloped world. Indeed, much is being made at the present time of the advanced countries' aid and support for the economic advancement of the backward areas. This advancement is conceived of as a slow, gradual improvement of the living standards of the native populations, and it is expected to *lessen* popular pressure for industrialization, to *weaken* the movement for economic and social progress.

However, this scheme of "bribing" the peoples of the underdeveloped countries to refrain from overthrowing the existing system and from entering the road to rapid economic growth is beset by a host of insuperable contradictions. The logic of economic growth is such that a slow and gradual improvement of living standards in little-developed countries is an extremely difficult if not altogether impossible project. Whatever small increases in national output might be attained with the help of such Western investment and charity as may be forthcoming are swamped by the rapid growth of the population, by the corruption of the local governments, by squandering of resources by the underdeveloped countries' ruling classes, and by profit withdrawals on the part of foreign investors.

For, where far-reaching structural changes in the economy are required if the economic development of a country is to shift into high gear and is to outstrip the growth of population, where technological indivisibilities render growth dependent on large investments and long-run planning, where tradition-bound patterns of thought and work obstruct the introduction of new methods and means of production—then only a sweeping reorganization of society, only an all-out mobilization of all its creative potentialities, can move the economy off dead center. As mentioned before, the mere notions of "development" and "growth" suggest a transition to something that is new from something that is old, that has outlived itself. It can only be achieved through a determined struggle against the conservative, retrograde forces, through a change in the social, political, and economic structure of a backward, stagnant society. Since a social organization, however inadequate, never disappears by itself, since a ruling class, however parasitic, never yields power unless compelled to do so by overwhelming pressure, development and progress can only be attained if all the energies and abilities of a people that was politically, socially, and economically disfranchised under the old system are thrown into battle against the fortresses of the *ancien régime.*

But the crusade against national and social revolutions conducted at the present time by the Western powers relies upon a mobilization of altogether different social strata. It cements an international entente of precisely those social groups and economic interests that are, and are bound to be, bitterly antagonistic to genuine economic and social progress, and it subordinates considerations of economic development to the purpose of strengthening this alliance. It provides economic and military aid to regimes in underdeveloped countries that are manifestly inimical to economic development, and it maintains in power governments that would have been otherwise swept aside by the popular drive for a more rational and more progressive economic and social order.

It is a part of the same effort to bribe the peoples of the underdeveloped countries while avoiding the appearance of old-fashioned imperialism that political independence has been recently granted to a number of dependent nations and that native politicians have been allowed to rise to high offices. There is hardly any need to stress that such independence and autonomy are little more than sham as long as the countries in question remain economic appendages of the advanced capitalist countries and as long as their governments depend for survival on the pleasure of their foreign patrons.

What is more, the attainment of political independence by colonial peoples yields results under the conditions of imperialism that are frequently quite different from those hoped for by these peoples themselves. Their newly won political independence often precipitates merely a change in their Western masters, with the younger, more enterprising, more resourceful imperialist power seizing the controls that have slipped out of the hands of the old, now weakened imperialist countries. Thus where it is politically no longer possible to operate through the medium of the old-fashioned and compromised colonial administrations and to impose its control merely by means of economic infiltration, American imperialism sponsors (or tolerates) political independence of colonial countries, becoming subsequently the dominant power in the newly "liberated" regions. Both methods of expansion of American influence can be studied in Africa, Southeast Asia, and the Near East.

III

A considerable ideological campaign is being undertaken in order to "sell" to the public this modern, more subtle and less transparent policy of imperialism. As an astute economist recently remarked, " 'development' as compared with 'civilization' ... [has become] an intellectual *quid pro quo* for international domination by a major country."[5] And social sciences provide, as usual, the requisite rationalization for the systematic effort of the ruling class of the advanced capitalist countries to prevent, or at least to retard, the political and economic liberation of the colonial and dependent nations. Stimulated by lavish support on the part of various government agencies and private foundations, economists, anthropologists, social psychologists, and other social scientists in the West have been directing an ever-increasing amount of attention to the development of underdeveloped countries.

In the field of economic research, much energy is now given to an attempt to demonstrate that the advanced countries themselves have reached their present level of development by a process of spontaneous, slow growth—within the framework of the capitalist order and without major shocks and revolutionary upheavals. It is argued that it was, in fact, the relative absence of political disturbance and the continuity and stability of social institutions that provided the "climate" essential for the emergence and prosperity of the capitalist entrepreneur, who in turn is credited with having played a decisive role in promoting economic progress. Accordingly, large resources are being devoted to an extensive campaign of rewriting the history of capitalism. Its purpose is the rehabilitation of the "robber baron" and his glorification as the hero and prime mover of economic and social progress, and its related task is the minimization of the suffering and privations that were associated with the beginning and the growth of capitalist enterprise.

Thus the historically minded members of the economics profession seek to prove that by relying on the forces of the free market and of private initiative economic development was achieved in the past without excessive sacrifices—with the obvious moral that this method still represents the most commendable avenue to economic progress. Little mention, if any, is accorded by these historians to the role that the exploitation of the now underdeveloped countries has played in the evolution of Western capitalism; little attention, if any, is given to the fact that the colonial and dependent countries today have no recourse to such sources of primary accumulation of capital as were available to the now advanced capitalist countries, that economic development in the age of monopoly capitalism and imperialism faces obstacles that have little in common with those encountered two or three hundred years ago, and that what was possible in a certain historical setting is unrealistic in another.

The more theoretically inclined economists follow a different tack. Dwelling on the technical aspects of economic development, they discover a host of insuperable difficulties preventing the formulation of a coherent theory of economic and social change. They list with obvious relish all and sundry matters more or less germane to the problem of economic development about which "we do not know enough," they stress the lack of unambiguous criteria for a rational allocation of resources under dynamic conditions, they elaborate on the obstacles to industrialization stemming from the character of the labor force in underdeveloped countries, from the scarcity of native managerial talent, from likely balance-of-payments disequilibria—with the result that all efforts at rapid development appear as adventures on uncharted seas, as gross violations of all accepted economic reasoning.

These endeavors to discredit implicitly or explicitly the drive for rapid development of underdeveloped countries, to present it as the manifestation of a deplorable impatience and irrationality of unenlightened mobs devilishly manipulated by sinister, power-greedy politicians—these are assisted by the neo-Malthusians who explain the backwardness of the backward countries as the inevitable result of their "excessive" population growth, and who therefore denounce all attempts at economic development in these areas as utopian so long as the population increase has not been brought to a halt. However, since a reduction of the population growth—assuming for the sake of argument that such a reduction is necessary—can only be achieved as a *result* of an all-round development of the backward societies, the neo-Malthusian position renders economic development a hopeless task, made insolvable by the very nature of the human animal.

A similar impact on opinion is exercised by most anthropological and quasi-philosophical writing related to the problem of economic development of underdeveloped countries. Here it has become fashionable to question the "absolute desirability" of economic development, to deride as unscientific its identification with progress, to accuse its protagonists in the West of "ethnocentrism," of hypostatization of their own culture, and of insufficient respect for the mores and values of more primitive peoples. In keeping with the general relativism and agnosticism of contemporary bourgeois thought, this strand of social science denies the possibility of a rational judgment on the usefulness, let alone urgency, of economic and social change in colonial and dependent areas, and counsels utmost caution in disturbing the continuity of the backward societies. While not explicitly endorsing the "white man's burden" concept of imperialist domination, this approach comes very close to it by pointing to the "cultural heterogeneity" of backward nations, by stressing the incomparability of value systems, and by suggesting that colonial and dependent peoples may actually "prefer" their present state to economic development and to national and social liberation. Small wonder that such a doctrine provides a poor background for the comprehension of the unprecedented popular movements that are at the present time revolutionizing and rejuvenating the greater part of the human race; small wonder that it supplies aid and comfort not to the peoples in the colonial and dependent countries struggling for freedom but to their masters seeking to preserve the *status quo*.

This political and ideological setting of the current discussion of economic development explains the highly unsatisfactory nature of what has been accomplished thus far. Robert Lynd's challenging question, "Knowledge for What?" bears not only on the fruitfulness of an intellectual effort in terms of the ends that it is designed to serve; it also necessarily relates to the conduct and the contents of the effort itself. Thus, motivated by the overriding preoccupation with the requirements of the counter-revolutionary crusade, muzzled by the fear of antagonizing the dominant interests determined to obstruct at all cost economic and social progress in the colonial and dependent countries, research and writing on economic development eschew as much as possible reference to what is in the very center of the problem. They make no reference to the irrationalities of monopoly capitalism and imperialism that block economic development in advanced capitalist countries, and they give no attention to the system of internal and foreign domination that prevents or distorts economic growth in the underdeveloped world. Correspondingly little emphasis is placed on the study of the unique experience in rapid development gathered in the USSR and in other countries of the socialist sector of the world—as if that experience was of interest only to Military Intelligence. And yet there can be no doubt that efforts at economic development could all derive immeasurable profit from fully comprehending the process of economic growth that has taken place in the Soviet Union and in other socialist countries.

IV

In speaking thus far about economic development, I have confined myself to rather broad allusions to this complex term. It is time to buckle down to a somewhat more detailed examination of this process, and it may be convenient to begin by deciding on a definition of economic growth. Not that it is my objective to present here a formula that would exclude any other, nor do I wish to suggest that other definitions might not be superior for other purposes. All I propose to do is to organize my categories in such a way as to be able to approach the subject matter by what appears to me to be a simple and useful method—a method which I plan to explore further in the course of subsequent chapters.

Let economic growth (or development) be defined as increase over time in *per capita* output of material goods.[6] It may be permissible in the present context to neglect the difficulty of comparing outputs over time, a difficulty arising whenever the outputs to be compared consist of more than one product, whenever, therefore, changes in output may affect its components unequally, and whenever certain products appear in the output of one period without appearing in the output of the other. This familiar index number problem, disturbing as it is even with regard to slow, gradual growth, becomes particularly vexing when what is considered is more or less rapid economic growth, the outstanding characteristic of which is profound change not only in the magnitude but also in the composition of output. Indeed, intertemporal comparisons threaten to be outright misleading when the periods to be compared are separated by changes in economic and social organization, by big spurts in urbanization, by decreases or increases of the "marketed share" of output, and so forth. Especially troublesome is the services sector, the expansion of which would cause an increase in Gross National Product (as conventionally defined) suggesting thus "economic growth"—although in most countries it would be considered to be a retrograde step rather than one in the direction of economic progress.[7] Pigou's famous gentleman marrying his cook and thus reducing national income comes readily to mind. Equally easily can one imagine a tremendous expansion of national income caused by the introduction of compulsory payments to wives for services rendered.

But we shall assume that increases of aggregate output over time can somehow be measured, and shall ask ourselves how such increases come about. They can be the result of one of the following developments (or a combination of them): (1) The aggregate resource utilization may expand *without changes in organization and/or technology,* i.e. previously unutilized resources (manpower, land) may be brought into the productive process; (2) The productivity per unit of resources at work may rise as a result of *organizational measures,* i.e. by transfer of workers from less productive or unproductive occupations to more productive pursuits, by a lengthening of the working day, by an improvement in nutrition and strengthening of incentives available to workers, by rationalization of methods of production and more economic utilization of fuel, raw materials, and so forth; (3) *Society's "technical arm" may become stronger,* i.e. (a) worn-out or obsolete plant and equipment may be replaced by more efficient facilities, and/or (b) new (technologically improved or unchanged) productive facilities may be added to the previously existing stock.

The first three routes to expansion of output—(1), (2) and (3) (a)—are typically not associated with *net* investment. Although it is probably impossible to impute to each of these four processes a proper share of the increase of output that has actually taken place, there can be little doubt that the economic application of increasing technical knowledge and net investment in additional productive facilities have been the most important sources of economic growth.

To be sure, in actual fact some net investment may be needed for all of them: previously unused resources may be unusable without some outlays on equipment, soil improvements, and the like; organizational changes may be predicated upon the installation of conveyor belts or similar devices; technological progress yielding improved machinery to be added to or substituted for worn-out equipment may be forthcoming only under conditions of large net investment. "If . . . technique largely depends on the state of science, science depends far more still on the *state* and the requirements of technique. If society has a technical need, that helps science forward more than ten universities. The whole of hydrostatics (Torricelli, etc.) was called forth by the necessity for regulating the mountain streams of Italy in the sixteenth and seventeenth centuries. We have only known anything reasonable about electricity since its technical applicability was discovered."[8]

On the other hand, plowing back amortization allowances—without any *net* investment—*on a higher technological plane* may per se support a significant expansion of output. Therefore where the capital intensity of the productive process is already large—in other words, where depreciation allowance constitutes an important part of the cost of the product—there is continuously available a source of capital for financing technological improvements without any need for *net* investment. While this aggravates the instability of the advanced capitalist economies by increasing the amount of currently generated surplus that has to be disposed of by investment, it also gives the advanced countries a major advantage over the underdeveloped countries where the annual amortization allowances necessarily amount to little.[9]

Net investment in any case can take place only if society's total output *exceeds* what is used for its current consumption and for making good the wear and tear on its productive facilities employed during the period in question. The volume and the nature of net investment taking place in a society at any given time depends, therefore, on the *size* and the *mode of utilization* of the currently generated *economic surplus.*

Both, as we shall see later, are essentially determined by the degree to which society's productive resources have been developed, and by the social structure within which the productive process unfolds. The understanding of the factors responsible for the size and the mode of utilization of the economic surplus is one of the foremost tasks of a theory of economic development. It is not even approached in the realm of "pure" economics. We have to look for it in the political economy of growth.

NOTES

1. Lionel Robbins, *The Theory of Economic Policy in English Classical Political Economy* (London, 1952), p. 19. It is strange, therefore, to read on the next page of Professor Robbins' book: ". . . I find it hard to understand how anyone who has given serious attention to the actual works of these men . . . can question their integrity and their transparent devotion to the general good . . . It has become fashionable to dismiss them and their ideas not on grounds of logic and assumptions, but on the grounds of alleged class interest. On this view the classical economists are the spokesmen of business, and *consciously or unconsciously* the apologists of the dominant class." (Italics added.) Yet "consciously or unconsciously" is precisely the issue. No serious writer to my knowledge has asserted that the classical economists—at least the great and important ones—were *consciously* servile scribes of a dominant or rising bourgeois class. In that case they would have hardly been worth the paper they were printed on, let alone the paper they are being reprinted on. The crux of the matter is that they were—*probably most unconsciously*—the spokesmen of a rising bourgeoisie whose interests they *objectively* served. Professor Robbins himself has clearly seen the distinction between subjective awareness of interests and their objective contents in his *The Economic Basis of Class Conflict* (London, 1939) (p. 4). In general it may well be said that for the appraisal of a group's or an individual's role in the historical process, subjective motivations (conscious or unconscious) are much less important than objective performances. In case of doubt, it is always useful to ask in all such matters: *cui bono?* The answer may not always be conclusive—it is never irrelevant.
2. Thus it is by no means fortuitous that the marginal utility theory, the static character of which is one of its outstanding features, has become the heart of neoclassical economics.
3. Marx, *The Poverty of Philosophy* (Stuttgart-Berlin, 1921). p. 86.
4. "The record of the main European wars . . . is shown by the following index series (combining size of the fighting force, number of casualties, number of countries involved, and proportions of combatants to total population):

Century:	12th	13th	14th	15th	16th	17th	18th	19th	20th
Index:	18	24	60	100	180	500	370	120	3080

For details see Pitirim Sorokin, *Social and Cultural Dynamics,* Vol. 3, 1937, and Quincy Wright, *A Study of War,* Vol. 1, Chap. 9 and Appendixes, 1942; cited in Harold D. Lasswell, *World Politics Faces Economics* (New York and London, 1945), p. 7.

5. H. G. Johnson, *Economic Journal* (June 1955), p. 303.
6. Colin Clark suggests a different definition: "Economic progress can be defined simply as an improvement in economic welfare. Economic welfare, following Pigou, can be defined in the first instance as an abundance of all those goods and services which are customarily exchanged for money. Leisure is an element in economic welfare, and more precisely we can define economic progress as the attaining of an increasing output of those goods and services for a minimum expenditure of effort, and of other scarce resources, both natural and artificial." *The Conditions of Economic Progress* (London, 1940), p. 1. This definition appears to me unsatisfactory for a number of reasons: (1) the identification of economic growth with increase in welfare leaves out of account a considerable share of total output that bears no relation to welfare, however the latter may be conceived: currently produced investment goods, armaments, net exports, and the like belong in this group; (2) Regarding an increase of output of "all these goods and services which are customarily exchanged for money" as identical with "improvement in economic welfare" is untenable. Economic welfare may be greatly improved by an increased supply of goods and services that are customarily *not* exchanged for money (schools, hospitals, roads, or bridges) while on the other hand a great number of goods and services that *are* customarily exchanged for money make no contribution whatever to human welfare (patent medicines and beauty parlors, narcotics, and items of conspicuous display, etc.); (3) Economic welfare can be improved without any *increase* of output—by a change in its *structure* and *distribution;* (4) While it is obviously *desirable* to secure any given output with a minimum of input, even an inefficiently secured increase in output might still constitute economic growth. It would seem to be preferable, therefore, to consider economic growth as an increase in output of goods regardless of whether they make a contribution to welfare, to the available stock of producers' goods, or to armaments—leaving to a related but nevertheless separate examination the factors determining the composition of this output and the purposes to which it is put.
7. This was noted in the United Nations' *Economic Survey of Europe Since the War* (1953): "In the eastern European countries services not directly connected with the production and transport of goods are not regarded as productive and their value is thus excluded from national income. For a poor country which is trying to develop its industry and to reduce the underemployment common in service trades, the Marxist definition of national income has some obvious advantages over the more inclusive concept suited to wealthy industrialized economies and now commonly adopted in under-developed countries." (p. 25.)

8. F. Engels, "Letter to H. Starkenburg," in Marx and Engels, *Selected Works* (Moscow, 1949–1950), Vol. II, p. 457. On the interesting relation between economic development on one hand and the progress of science and technology on the other, cf. B. Hessen, *The Social and Economic Roots of Newton's Principia* (Sydney, 1946), as well as J. D. Bernal, *Science in History* (London, 1954).
9. Cf. Marx, *Theories of Surplus Value* (London, 1951), pp. 354 ff., where this point is stressed.

LATIN AMERICAN ECONOMIC INTEGRATION

Andre Gunder Frank

Recent years have witnessed the birth and development of two Latin American free trade zones, one in South America and one in Central America. Any superficial resemblance these may have to the European Common Market should not lead us to expect the current steps toward economic integration in Latin America to reproduce the European results. Even apart from the fact that a free trade zone is a much weaker form of integration than a common market, the circumstances in Latin America are quite different, especially as regards the area's low degree of economic development and high degree of imperialist economic dependence.

For the time being, there is virtually no intra-regional trade in South America, to say nothing of Central America. Therefore, the most important, if not only, significance of a free trade zone, customs union, or similar arrangement is the creation of a potential market large enough to attract and justify investment in Latin American industrialization. The free trade zone is thus defended by many of its proponents, who recall Adam Smith's dictum that the division of labor depends on the extent of the market. But history shows that the extent of the market, in turn, depends less on its territorial extension than on the income of its consumers. Hence increasing the breadth rather than the depth of the market is at best only a minor step in the right direction and at worst, as will be argued here, a premature step which will impede the larger and more necessary step. What is really needed is to solve the problem of poverty and low productivity, especially in agriculture. Even if we leave aside for the moment the human needs and welfare of the people and consider only effective demand and supply in the industrial sector, history still provides ample evidence for the primary importance of solving the problem of agriculture. The successful industrialization of Western

Europe was evidently dependent on the revolution in European agriculture as well as, of course, on the colonization of the now underdeveloped continents of the world. But the priority of depth over breadth of the market, of solving the problem of agricultural productivity, is attested to equally by the failure to date of attempts to industrialize such countries as Brazil and Mexico. Brazil already has a market of continental proportions. It has built in Sao Paulo the largest industrial complex in Latin America. But having failed even to attack its agricultural problem, notoriously one of the world's most serious, Brazil remains a very underdeveloped and non-industrialized country. Mexico, whose revolution fifty years ago produced what was before Cuba the most far-reaching agricultural reform in Latin America, stopped her land reform short and failed to release large parts of the potential productivity and energy of her rural people. As a result, Mexico's industrialization and economic development drive has also stopped short. The truth is that to foster industry and economic development, Latin America must transform its agriculture; and to do that it must in turn radically alter its entire internal and external political, economic, and social structure. Economic integration, especially integration of the present economic structures of its various countries with each other, will not solve the problem.

What, then, *will* integration do—and what will it prevent? It will, notwithstanding "provisions" to the contrary, attract capital to the centers that are already most industrialized and not to those that are least so. Indeed, to the extent that the capital will come from inside Latin America, integration will draw capital out of the poorer and into the richer regions, just as has already happened in the development of Brazil. It will widen also the gap between country and city, and it will certainly not benefit the large mass of peasants. It will, in short, make the rich richer and the poor poorer, relatively, certainly, and absolutely as well, if Latin American developments in the past ten years, even without a common market, are any guide. The thesis that a free market equalizes incomes, or even prices, among its sectors is a myth that was invented by the rich while they were exploiting the poor.

Nor is this all. Given the present economic structure of Latin America, local capital is scarce; given the present political structure, foreign capital is "welcome." The industrial capital that the economic integration is supposed to attract would therefore in large part, and in Central America obviously almost wholly, have to come from abroad, especially the United States. But the principal aim of investment capital is of course to benefit the investors. And it does. According to U.S. Department of Commerce calculations, during the 1950's the total amount of money sent from Latin America to the United States as "earnings" on U.S. investments in the region was double the value of the investments. Latin American calculations show an even higher rate of return. For example, the Joint Brazil-U.S. Economic Commission estimated that withdrawals to the United States between 1939 and 1951 came to sixty-one (yes, 61) times the amount of long-term investment. Thus economic integration of Latin America under present circumstances will not only draw capital from the poor to the rich in Latin America itself. It will also make the poor Latin Americans poorer and the rich North Americans richer.

Matters are still worse. Economic integration carries with it special privileges for firms inside the integrated region. They receive tariff protection, often tax and credit privileges, and in Central America virtually total monopoly positions. In many if not all cases the quality of their products will be poorer and their prices higher than those of comparable imported goods. The Latin American consumer will therefore lose by the arrangement. Such short-term losses from infant-industry protection are justified and even welcome if the sacrifices involved will bring or at least contribute to long-term benefits. But, as we have already seen, the long-term effects of integration in Latin America are likely to be unfavorable. Thus current steps toward integration involve short-term sacrifices to be followed by greater long-term sacrifices.

The truth is that countries which have successfully industrialized in the past have done so without foreign investment and "aid." Outstanding examples are Japan and the Soviet Union, not to speak of the countries of Western Europe. The countries that have been the recipients of heavy foreign investment have remained non-industrialized and underdeveloped. The only apparent exceptions are the United States, the British Dominions, and Israel. But in all these cases foreign immigration accompanied the foreign capital, and all the benefits went to the immigrants and none to the natives. The exceptions thus seem to prove the rule. It will be interesting to see if foreign aid to a *socialist* country, such as Yugoslavia, Cuba, or Eastern Europe, will result in economic development. It has been suggested that, because a socialist country can control its economy and thus can channel the aid into development-producing industrial projects, foreign capital can aid a socialist country to develop where it fails to do so in a capitalist country. If this argument is well taken, then economic integration will also benefit Latin America only if it comes *after* the respective countries' conversion to socialism, and not before.

If Latin American economic integration will not make a positive contribution, will it serve to *prevent* economic development? The political implications of the move to integration suggest that it will, to the extent that it proceeds before rather than after fundamental change. The United States used to oppose the Latin American Free Trade Zone project. The Kennedy administration is supporting it. Why? United States involvement in Latin America used to be based principally on the client relation maintained with the commercial bourgeoisie in each country, while the latter maintains a similar client relation with its own landowning class. This triple alliance long served the interests of all the partners and permitted the U.S. to follow a divide-and-rule policy in which it maintained a bilateral relation with each country separately. Integration threatened the stability of this arrangement. Now, underlying economic, social, and political developments are increasingly threatening the stability of this form of alliance anyway. The growth of national, mostly light, industry and the concomitant development of a national industrial bourgeoisie in some countries, along with a relative shift of interest of American capital from extractive to secondary and tertiary industries in Latin America have altered the economic relations. This, along with social mobility and the growth of middle classes, which have become the pivots of the electoral process, as well as the declining relative power of the landowner, have changed national political alignments. For these reasons, American policy, as the Alliance for Progress makes amply clear, has been to shift its reliance away from the "feudal" landowner toward strengthening of ties with the newer groups interested in maintaining the status quo. Economic integration measures strengthen the hand of these new groups relative to that of the landowners while tying (through American investment and "aid") these groups increasingly to the United States. At the same time, of course, integration opens the doors to that same American investment in secondary and tertiary industry. Above all, in the context of a continent in flux, the Latin American Free Trade Zone contributes to political stability. It strengthens existing groups, excepting the "feudals," and creates others with an interest in preserving the status quo. Thus, the Free Trade Zone has, from the American point of view, become desirable: the more successful this project, the less desirable and necessary are alliances with military dictators like Trujillo, Duvalier, and Stroessner. Less desirable because their very dictatorial power affords them, domestically, a certain degree of independence from U.S. management; and less necessary because the political weight of the new domestic forces created by integration affords political stability and an opportunity for the U.S. to play one group off against another. "Divide and rule" no longer operates by dividing one country from another as much as by dividing one class and interest group from another. But U.S. domination remains the same.

If economic integration contributes to class division, will it also in the long run contribute to progress by increasing class struggle? To the extent that integration does foster industry even if not industrialization, it adds to the growth of the industrial working class. That class, it might be argued, will then ultimately destroy the alliance which keeps Latin America underdeveloped. The evidence in Latin America so far, however, is that industrial workers, especially organized industrial workers, far from being a progressive force, have been a conservative element. They too have been a relatively privileged group, an aristocracy of the proletariat, which derives its privileges from the present economic structure and thus has an interest in preserving it. Except in special cases, only the peasants in Latin America have a large and independent revolutionary potential. And economic integration will indeed intensify their exploitation. Thus, in the last as in the first analysis, it is in destroying the existing agricultural structure, and not in integrating the present industrial structure, that the key to Latin America's future lies. Only that step can and will lead to genuine industrialization.

BEFORE INDEPENDENCE

Kwame Nkrumah

In the year 1482, three small Portuguese ships set out from Elmina in Ghana. Their mission was to find a route round Africa which would outflank the Arab States which controlled North Africa. The Portuguese hoped to reach the legendary kingdom of that supposed great African Christian monarch, Prester John. This fleet, commanded by Diogo Cam, never rounded the tip of Africa but it did discover the ancient kingdom of the Congo, and the long history of European intervention in Central Africa had begun.

The Portuguese were already established in a number of forts along the African West Coast, of which the Fort of St. George at Elmina (1481), from which the expedition started, was the largest and best equipped. The African States of this coast and hinterland were well organised politically, militarily and economically. They controlled the produce of the interior and sold it on their own terms. They did not need to enter any military or economic alliance with the Portuguese, who were tolerated solely as traders.

In the Congo, however, it was different. The King of the Congo, the Mani Congo, was in reality only a feudal overlord and he was engaged, as had been the Portuguese monarchy eighty years before, in a life and death struggle with his nominal vassals. The Portuguese therefore were welcomed by the Mani Congo as potential allies. The Portuguese on their side saw the opportunity of establishing a Christian State as a bastion against Islamic intrusion and as a link with the Kingdom of Prester John. The first consignment of technical aid, consisting of priests and skilled craftsmen with the tools of their trade and a variety of religious objects, arrived in 1490.

From then onwards there was a small but steady flow of European

---

Reprinted by permission of Kwame Nkrumah and Panaf Books Limited, 89 Fleet Street, London E.C.4., from *Challenge of the Congo,* first published in London in 1967.

technicians, who included, in 1492, two German printers. Considering that printing had been established in England only fifteen years before and had not yet been established in Spain, the provision of printers is a remarkable tribute to the level of civilisation reached in the Congo. The Portuguese, with the support of the Mani Congo, set out on a systematic policy of westernisation in the Congo. At this point emerged the contradiction that has haunted European and African relations ever since.

The Congolese wanted to secure, through trade with Europe, foreign exchange in the form of gold and silver, capital equipment like merchant ships and printing presses, and above all European specialists in medicine, teaching, shipbuilding and navigation. The Portuguese on the other hand were determined to exploit the economic superiority which they had derived from their specialised naval knowledge, their large merchant fleet and their command of the sea. This command of the sea involved alliances with those who controlled the approaches to the Congo and beyond. Such an alliance was fatal to any real partnership between the Congo and Portugal. The centre of Portuguese naval power in the Central and South Atlantic was the island of São Tome, originally colonised as a Portuguese penal settlement in the very year the first group of priests and technicians were sent to the Congo. It was ruled by a Lord Proprietor, whose goodwill the Portuguese had to maintain at all costs.

The Lord Proprietor of São Tome had one overriding interest—the slave trade. Once Portugal began to develop Brazil she became herself dependent on the slaves sold through the São Tome slaving organisations.

The development of all this was in the future. At the time, it appeared on paper that Portugal and the Congo treated each other as equal states. The Mani Congo, who ascended the Ivory Throne in 1506, became a Christian as part of a concerted policy of westernisation. Much of the correspondence of this remarkable king, Dom Affonso, with the Kings of Portugal has survived and it is clear that he looked on the Portuguese alliance as the most effective method of modernising his kingdom. Before we condemn his lack of realism in this regard, it is necessary to remember that there are African rulers today who are pursuing a similar policy. What subsequently happened in the Congo should be an object lesson to them.

In much the same way as modern colonialist powers provided their colonial territories with model constitutions, so King Manoel of Portugal provided a constitution for the Congo. This famous document, known as the Regimento of 1512, can perhaps be described as the first essay in neo-colonialism. It provided that the Portuguese should help the King of the Congo in organising his kingdom. The Portuguese were to introduce a system of European law and to train the Congolese Army in their methods of warfare. They were to teach the royal court the correct etiquette to observe and they were to build churches and to provide missionaries. In return for this the Congo would fill the Portuguese ships with valuable cargo. In his letter of instruction to the Ambassador who was to present the Regimento, the King of Portugal wrote:

> This expedition has cost us much; it would be unreasonable to send it home with empty hands. Although our principal wish is to serve God and the pleasure of the King of the Congo, none the less you will make him understand, as though speaking in our name, what he should do to fill the ships, whether with slaves or copper or ivory.

The mention of copper is interesting as showing that the products of the Zambia and Katanga copper belt were already well known. At this time, surviving records show that Katanga copper was also being marketed on the East Coast, though the main African trade in the metal was internal. Dom Affonso accepted the Regimento and provided the Portuguese with 320 slaves. Thus began an unequal trade between the Congo and the West. The evil effect of this trade was not immediately apparent and the Kingdom of the Congo was at first able to treat other European nations on equal terms. In 1513 a mission from the Mani Congo led by his son, who had been baptised Dom Henrique, visited the Pope, traveling overland from Portugal and carrying with them gifts of ivory, rare skins and the fine woven raffia textiles then manufactured in the Congo. Dom Henrique, who was at this time 18 years old, was able to address the Pope in Latin and five years later, on the formal proposal of four Cardinals, he was elevated to the rank of Bishop of the Congo.

In the end Dom Affonso was prepared to sacrifice all Portuguese trade if he could suppress slaving. In 1526 he wrote to the King of Portugal:

> We cannot reckon how great the damage is, since the above mentioned merchants daily seize our subjects, sons of the land and sons of our noblemen and vassals and our relatives . . . Thieves and men of evil conscience take them because they wish to possess the things and wares of this Kingdom . . . They grab them and cause them to be sold: and so great, Sir, is their corruption and licentiousness that our country is being utterly

> depopulated. And to avoid (them), we need from (your) Kingdoms no other than priests and people to teach in schools, and no other goods but wine and flour for the holy sacrament: that is why we beg of Your Highness to help and assist us in this matter, commanding your factors that they should send here neither merchants nor wares, because it is our will that in these kingdoms (of Congo) there should not be any trade in slaves nor market for slaves.

But by then his power had been undermined. The traders of São Tome went over his head to his nominal vassals from whom they procured the slaves, even fomenting civil wars in which Portuguese subjects served on both sides. Thus whichever way the war went, an ample supply of captives was assured for sale to São Tome and Brazil.

With Dom Affonso's death the Congo Kingdom broke up. Portuguese troops, acting under the terms of the alliance, drove out invaders in 1570 and the Mani Congo of the time acknowledged Portugal as the protecting power. The ancient Congo capital of São Salvador was raised to the rank of city and was made the seat of the Bishop of the diocese of the Congo and Angola. But by 1700 the Bishops had departed, its twelve churches were in ruins and São Salvador was a deserted city. The Portuguese turned their attention to the area farther south, the Portuguese colony now known as Angola.

The first attempt to construct an African State by an African leader in alliance with a European power had foundered in anarchy and confusion.

In the last official Handbook of the Congo published by the Belgian Government in 1959, the results of western slave trading are thus described:

> By the end of the 17th century the slave trade, which had started as a Portuguese monopoly, had become a gigantic international undertaking. The places where slaves were kept became more and more numerous and profitable. The French appeared in their turn, drove the Portuguese away from the port of Cabinda and installed their slave markets chiefly beyond the north bank of the river toward Loango and Malemba, while the English traded in the estuary.
>
> In the course of a single year, in 1778, 104,000 slaves had been exported from Africa; one third of them came from the Congo and Angola.

During the nineteenth century there began what is often described as "the age of African exploration." The term is misleading. The travels of great nineteenth-century European "explorers" in Africa followed long-established lines of communication which had been in use by African peoples for hundreds of years. There was a network of well-defined trails from the Katanga copper mines along which the African-mined and smelted copper was distributed throughout Africa.

In 1877 one of these "explorers," the United States journalist Henry Morton Stanley, arrived at Boma at the mouth of the Congo, having started from Zanzibar and in his journeying traced the course of the river from source to mouth. Stanley was typical of a class of nineteenth-century freebooters, very similar in outlook to the mercenaries who are operating in the Congo today. He was born in very poor circumstances in England, and his real name was John Rowlands. He worked his way across the Atlantic and acquired a wealthy American benefactor whose name he adopted. In the United States Civil War he served with the Confederate Army of the South. He was taken prisoner and in return for his freedom agreed to fight for the North. Later he served with various United States expeditions against the Red Indian people and then adopted the profession of journalist explorer. He had newspaper assignments in Tibet, the Caucasus and Ethiopia. He was asked by the *New York Herald* to go out to Africa to find the missing missionary David Livingstone. This he did in 1871 and stayed on in Africa. It was on behalf of his newspaper that he crossed the continent.

Stanley at once appreciated the possibilities of European exploitation of the Congo. "I could prove to you," he wrote to the London *Daily Telegraph,* "that the Power possessing the Congo . . . would absorb to itself the trade of the whole enormous basin behind. The river is and will be the grand highway to commerce to West Africa."

Stanley's discovery was just what King Leopold II of Belgium was looking for. Some time earlier he had written:

> Since history teaches that colonies are useful, that they play a great part in that which makes up the power and prosperity of States, let us strive to get one in our turn. Before pronouncing in favour of this or that system let us see where there are unoccupied lands . . . where are to be found peoples to civilise, to lead to progress in every sense, meanwhile assuring ourselves new revenues, to our middle classes the employment which they seek, to our army a little activity, and to Belgium as a whole the opportunity to prove to the world that it also is an imperial people capable of dominating and enlightening others.

He had already founded, as a cover for his colonialist ambitions, an international African Association and Stanley was employed by him to return to the Congo and make treaties with the local rulers as a preliminary to its take-over by the Belgian King.

Leopold's plan was to run the Congo as a private domain, uncontrolled by even the Belgian Government, and to exploit it on an international scale. He succeeded because the powers of Europe were unwilling to see any other among them control the Congo.

The British at one time hoped to establish a type of neo-colonialist state working through Portugal and Leopold's organisation. A treaty between Britain and Portugal handing over the Congo to Portugal had been signed in 1884. There was so much opposition from other powers excluded from this arrangement that finally the whole issue was referred to the Berlin Conference which sat from November 1884 to February 1885. At this Conference a compromise was worked out awarding the Congo to Leopold in a personal capacity but providing that it should be open to the trade of all those participating in the Berlin Conference. Thus the monarch of a small European State was made the absolute ruler over a territory equal to the area of Europe, excluding Russia. Leopold had never visited the Congo and was never to do so. Nevertheless, he was its sole lawmaker and the owner of all its land.

The Belgians declared that their first objective on entering the Congo was to suppress the slave trade. Up to the time of the Belgian occupation, some fifteen million Congolese had been shipped out by the western route alone. Ten million of them had died en route as a result of bad treatment.

In fact, the object of Leopold II of Belgium was not to suppress slavery, but to change its nature. His object was to make slavery more profitable by employing the slave in the Congo and thus avoid the difficulties caused by the international abolition of the trade in its old-fashioned form. That he was able to do this was due to the divisions between the Congolese people and the imperial rivalry between the European powers.

In a pamphlet *The Crime of the Congo* published in 1910 Sir Arthur Conan Doyle analysed the effects of Leopold's policy and denounced the European nations who refused to intervene.

He quoted extensively from Stanley's account of the Congo as he had found it in 1877 and contrasted it with its condition in 1910. He wrote:

> One cannot let these extracts pass without noting that Bolobo, the first place

named by Stanley, has sunk in population from 40,000 to 7,000; that Irebu, called by Stanley the populous Venice of the Congo, had in 1903 a population of fifty; that the natives who used to follow Stanley, beseeching him to trade, now, according to Consul Casement, fly into the bush at the approach of a steamer, and that the unselfish sentiment of King Leopold II has developed into dividends of 300 per cent per annum. Such is the difference between Stanley's anticipation and the actual fulfilment.

Describing Leopold's method of rule, Conan Doyle continued:

Having claimed, as I have shown, the whole of the land, and therefore the whole of its products, the State—that is, the King—proceeded to construct a system by which these products could be gathered most rapidly and at least cost. The essence of this system was that the people who had been dispossessed (ironically called "citizens") were to be forced to gather, for the profit of the State, those very products which had been taken from them. This was to be effected by two means; the one, taxation, by which an arbitrary amount, ever growing larger until it consumed almost their whole lives in the gathering, should be claimed for nothing. The other, so called barter, by which the natives were paid for the stuff exactly what the State chose to give, and in the form the State chose to give it, there being no competition allowed from any other purchaser. This remuneration, ridiculous in value, took the most absurd shape, the natives being compelled to take it, whatever the amount, and however little they might desire it . . .

By this system some two thousand white agents were scattered over the Free State to collect the produce. The whites were placed in ones and twos in the more central points, and each was given a tract of country containing a certain number of villages. By the help of the inmates he was to gather the rubber, which was the most valuable asset. These whites, many of whom were men of low morale before they left Europe, were wretchedly paid, the scale running from 150 to 300 francs a month. This pay they might supplement by a commission or bonus on the amount of rubber collected. If their returns were large it meant increased pay, official praise, a more speedy return to Europe and a better chance of promotion. If, on the other hand, the returns were small it meant poverty, harsh reproof and degradation. No system could be devised by which a body of men could be so driven to attain results at any cost. It is not to the absolute discredit of Belgians that such an existence should have demoralised them, and, indeed, there were other nationalities besides Belgians in the ranks of the agents. I doubt if Englishmen, Americans or Germans could have escaped the same result had they been exposed in a tropical country to similar temptations.

And now, the two thousand agents being in place and eager to enforce the collection of rubber upon very unwilling natives, how did the system intend

> that they should set about it? The method was as efficient as it was absolutely diabolical. Each agent was given control over a certain number of savages drawn from the wild tribes but armed with firearms. One or more of these was placed in each village to ensure that the villagers should do their task. These are the men who are called "Capitas," or head-men in the accounts, and who are the actual, though not moral, perpetrators of so many horrible deeds. Imagine the nightmare which lay upon each village while this barbarian squatted in the midst of it. Day or night they could never get away from him. He called for palm wine. He called for women. He beat them, mutilated them and shot them down at his pleasure. He enforced public incest in order to amuse himself by the sight. Sometimes they plucked up spirit and killed him. The Belgian Commission records that 142 Capitas had been killed in seven months in a single district. Then came the punitive expedition, and the destruction of the whole community. The more terror the Capita inspired, the more useful he was, the more eagerly the villagers obeyed him, and the more rubber yielded its commission to the agent. When the amount fell off, then the Capita was himself made to feel some of those physical pains which he had inflicted upon others. Often the white agent far exceeded in cruelty the barbarian who carried out his commissions. Often, too, the white man pushed the black aside, and acted himself as torturer and executioner.

The Report of Roger Casement, British Consul in the Congo, published in 1904, provides further information about the nature of Leopold's rule in the Congo.

> . . . Perhaps the most striking change observed during my journey into the interior was the great reduction observable everywhere in native life. Communities I had formerly known as large and flourishing centres of population are today entirely gone, or now exist in such diminished numbers as to be no longer recognisable. The southern shores of Stanley Pool had formerly a population of fully 5,000 Batekas. These people some twelve years ago decided to abandon their homes, and in one night the great majority of them crossed over into French territory. Where formerly had stretched these populous native African villages, I saw today only a few scattered European houses.

Questioning some Congolese about the rubber trade, they told him they had to produce twenty baskets of rubber four times a month:

> We got no pay. We got nothing . . . It used to take ten days to get the twenty baskets of rubber. We were always in the forest, and then when we were late we were killed. We had to go further and further into the forest to find the rubber vines, to go without food, and our women had to give up

> cultivating the fields and gardens. Then we starved. Wild beasts—the leopards—killed some of us when we were working away in the forest, and others got lost or died from exposure and starvation, and we begged the white man to leave us alone, saying we would get more rubber, but the white men and their soldiers said, "Go! You are only beasts yourselves; you are nyama (meat)." We tried, always going further into the forest, and when we failed and our rubber was short the soldiers came up our towns and shot us. Many were shot; some had their ears cut off . . . We fled because we could not endure the things done to us.

Professor Ritchie Calder in his book *The Agony of the Congo* has estimated that in the twenty-three years of Leopold's personal rule five to eight million Congolese had been killed by his security forces and agents engaged in the collection of rubber and ivory. When it is remembered that in 1960, when the Congo became independent, its population was around thirteen million, the extent of Leopold's tyranny and inhumanity can be realised. E. D. Morel in his famous book *Red Rubber, the Story of the Rubber Slave Trade of the Congo,* first published in 1906, has described in detail with innumerable quotations from actual observers the depopulation and the devastation of the country. It was not only that the inhabitants were massacred wholesale. Those who survived were often mutilated. It was a common practice to cut off a hand or a foot.

Public outcry against Leopold's personal rule reached such a height that by 1908 the Belgian Government had to take over the Congo, the state compensating the King handsomely for the loss that he had thus sustained. Before however relinquishing control Leopold had parcelled up the country into areas to be exploited by various international concerns.

Leopold was primarily a financier who employed any capital that came to hand and used any agent, whatever his nationality. It was thus that the Southern Rhodesian company, Tanganyika Concessions Ltd., came to be so closely concerned with investment in the Congo. The "Tanganyika Concession" from which it takes its name was the transport concession which Rhodes wished to obtain on Lake Tanganyika for his proposed Cape to Cairo railway. Otherwise it has never had any connection with Tanganyika but was formed solely to exploit the mineral wealth of Northern Rhodesia and Katanga. The company established in 1899 was financed from Britain and one of Rhodes's associates, Sir Robert Williams, was its Chairman and Managing Director. On the formation of the Union Minière he became its Vice-President and Technical Manager. In order to export the Katanga copper he founded another English company, the Benguela Railway Company, to link Katanga with Atlantic ports of Portuguese Angola.

It was to consolidate these and other international interests that in 1906 Leopold set up the three great international companies which have dominated the Congo ever since.

These three great enterprises were known as "the companies of 1906." They were the Compagnie du Chemin de Fer du Bas-Congo (the BCK); the Société Internationale Forestière et Minière du Congo (Forminière); and L'Union Minière du Haut-Katanga.

The Belgian Government régime which succeeded that of Leopold, even if it wished to do so, could have done little to restore the devastation of the country or repair the exploitation of the preceding four hundred years. Actually Belgium had neither the will nor the means to redress the evil that had been done. Leopold's soldiers were recruited in the official Belgian Congolese Army, the "force publique." The same administrators remained in power and the same system continued, the worst abuses only being suppressed.

The First World War prevented further European criticism of Belgian policy. Belgium had been the victim of unprovoked aggression by Imperial Germany, and the Allied powers who won the war turned their attack on the German colonies which, as Conan Doyle had pointed out, were at least better administered than the Congo. Nevertheless, this did not prevent Belgium being awarded a slice of former German colonial territory, the present states of Rwanda and Burundi. In the inter-war years the Congo was developed as a source of raw materials, copper and diamonds in particular. The need to industrialise and to employ African skilled labour made it impossible to continue repression in its old form. Instead the Belgians imposed a paternalist régime beneath the surface of which many of the old evils continued.

The Belgian system of colonial government differed in several ways from that of the British and French. A Governor-General was appointed, responsible to the Belgian Parliament, but he had no Legislative Council or Assembly to check his power, and no Congolese sat in the Belgian Parliament. Colonial law was made in Belgium by the King, acting on the advice of a minister for colonial affairs and a colonial council. Nobody in the Congo, white or black, could vote, and the Congolese had few, if any, civil rights. The essence of the Belgian colonial system, as later developed, was to buy off any discontent by giving a certain amount of material comfort. The Congo became a model colony.

Belgian district commissioners ruled their various localities in the same authoritarian manner as the Governor-General in Leopoldville. The Roman Catholic Church and big business were the other, no less powerful, rulers of the Congo. The Belgian Government, in fact, shared considerably in the investment holdings of the interlocking combines which monopolised the Congo's economy, often to the extent of as much as fifty per cent.

In 1957 the first elections, carefully controlled and limited municipal elections, were held in the Congo. They were a belated attempt by the Belgians to prevent rising national feeling from expressing itself in violence. By then the first Congolese parties demanding political liberty had already been formed. In 1958 several of these parties published programmes calling for independence and in the following year, after serious trouble in Leopoldville, the Belgian Government was compelled to face squarely the new situation. A Round Table Conference met in Brussels early in 1960 and passed resolutions, later approved by thc Belgian Parliament, fixing the date of independence for 30 July 1960.

Prior to the assumption of independence by the Congo I sent two separate missions with the object of making known to the Belgian authorities my government's desire that progress to independence in the Congo should be orderly and peaceful, and that the Ghana Government was willing to do everything in its power to assist.

It will therefore be seen that Ghana's interest in the Congo's success and her transition to independence is of long standing.

If the political domination of the Congo by the Belgian Government between 1908 and 1960 was complete and the Congolese deprived of political experience, the economic stranglehold exercised by foreign firms was no less damaging to the interests of the Congolese people.

It was after 1908 that the great mining companies began to develop their power and influence. The Union Minière du Haut-Katanga (founded in 1906) produced its first ton of copper in 1911. Seventeen years later, in 1928, its copper output had reached seven per cent of world production. In 1907 diamonds were discovered in Kasai by a prospector of Forminière (Société International Forestière et Minière). By 1929 the Congo was the second largest producer of diamonds in the world, the largest being, of course, South Africa. Mineral products had by then taken the place of rubber as the mainstay of the Congo economy.

Today, the Congo produces sixty per cent of the world's output of cobalt, eight per cent of copper and four per cent of zinc. Among the most valuable commodities mined in the Congo are iron ore, coal, tin, uranium, radium, germanium, manganese, cadmium, gold and silver. There is hardly a country in Africa, Asia or Latin America which has such rich and varied mineral resources. Agricultural resources are no less great, and there are tremendous reserves of water power which can be used for the production of power and electricity.

Under Belgian rule, the Congo's wealth was used to serve the interests of foreign monopolists. With independence, the position remains much the same. Tanganyika Concessions, Société Générale de Belgique, L'Union Minière du Haut-Katanga, to name only a few, still make great profits and exert pressures on the young Republic which serve the interests not of the Congolese people but of foreign investors. The book *Trusts in the Congo,* published in Brussels in 1961, gives the net profit of the Union Minière between 1950 and 1959 as 31 billion Belgian francs. The shareholders of the corporation pocketed 30.5 million dollars in 1961 alone, reckoned to be a bad year for the firm because of the fighting in Katanga.

The comparatively recent entry of American big-business interests into the Congo has further strengthened the neo-colonialist hold on the country. American interests are particularly strong in Forminière, which besides participating in the mining of gold and silver owns vast plantations of cotton, oil-bearing palms, cocoa and rubber trees, as well as cattle stations and farms, forests, sawmills and even shops. When it is remembered also that in 1950 the American "International Basic Economy Corporation" bought up 600,000 shares of Tanganyika Concessions it will be realised that this American firm created by the Rockefeller family group became a partner in the profits of the Union Minière.

Seen in the light of the vast complicated web of foreign economic interests in the Congo, the disastrous years since independence are not difficult to explain. The richer the natural resources of a country, the more determined the neo-colonialists to tighten, and extend if possible, their hold over it. Under the guise of "aid," or in some cases, as in the Congo, by encouraging political disunity, they have sought to perpetuate the colonial-type economy in which Africa remains the great provider of primary materials for the industries of the metropolitan and other industrial powers.

Before independence, Belgian and British business interests predominated in the Congo and American capital was not able to penetrate very far. This explains to some extent the initial enthusiasm of the foreign business world for an independent Congo where it was hoped free competition would benefit private enterprise, and the subsequent disillusionment when Lumumba made it clear that he did not intend to become the puppet of any foreign interests.

But to leave for a moment the tangled economic situation in the Congo on the eve of independence and to turn to the way in which national sovereignty was achieved is to see that in this respect also the Congo was unique. No other country except the French colonies of Africa attained its independence so quickly, or was subjected to such suffering once independence had been achieved.

The revolt towards colonial freedom had begun in rather an unusual way through the formation of what may be described as Old Boys' Clubs. As political associations in the Congo were illegal under the Belgian colonial régime, the handful of educated *élites* made provision for their welfare through the ADEPES (Association des Anciens Elèves des Pères de Scheut) which followed a rather tranquil course from 1925. The activities of this association were fostered by other organisations, notably the Marist Brothers (UNELMA), the Christian Schools (ASAMEF), the school for the Jesuit Fathers, the UNISCO (l'Union des Intérêts Sociaux Congolais), whose members were mainly secondary school pupils. These bodies, which formed the circles of *évolués,* were devoted primarily to the study of religious and social questions, and the Belgian authorities and the Church naturally watched their development with great admiration. The only political organisations which flourished in the Congo were "tribal" associations that occasionally emerged in the rural areas.

Thus for a long time "independence" was a new word to the Congolese people, for no nationalists dared to use it in public. As one writer put it, "Independence was released as a bullet into the brittle silence of Congo politics by a Belgian professor, Dr. A. A. J. van Bilson," a liberal of the Christian Democratic wing of the Catholic Party in Brussels. Criticising Belgium, at first cautiously and later boldly, for allowing the Congo to be governed with virtually no parliamentary control, he attacked the unbalanced growth of agriculture and industry and the dismal state of Congolese social development. Congolese leaders were quick to seize this all-important opportunity to voice their grievances.

Independence for the Congo was, however, more than a national affair. It was part of the world ideological struggle. But it was more particularly an African affair from the colonial standpoint. To Africans everywhere the movement was part of the general drive towards freedom from colonial domination on the African continent. I have often said "the independence of Ghana is meaningless unless it is linked up with the total liberation of Africa." This in part explains why Ghana became a vigorous partner of the Congolese cause, especially at the time of their national crisis.

Ghana-Congo solidarity began with the All-African Peoples' Conference held at Accra in December 1958. Among the hundreds of delegates who attended the Conference were Patrice Lumumba, who became the President of the MNC (Congolese National Movement), and two associates of his party. It was at this memorable Conference that the Congolese nationalists had their baptism of fire as apostles of the impending struggle for Africa's liberation.

On returning home to Leopoldville, a mass meeting was convened on 3 January 1959 at which Lumumba with fiery oratory announced the objectives of immediate and total independence for his country. No doubt the new year was accompanied by new resolutions. Tension was already mounting in the Congolese capital. On 4 January some 30,000 riotous demonstrators, mainly unemployed workers, marched through the streets of Leopoldville and publicly demanded independence. The spontaneity of the event gave the impression that the whole nation had risen in concerted action.

Though certain political leaders, particularly those of the influential ABAKO party, had been arrested, it became abundantly clear that the Belgian colonial administration could no longer placate the rapidly growing political discontent. The All-African Peoples' Conference had made an immediate and dramatic impact on the Congo political scene. And there was no turning back.

Some diehard imperialists, after their usual fashion, sought to explain the riots in Leopoldville in terms of communist influence. In particular, a Belgian paternalist, Edward Mendiaux, went to the length of writing a book called *Moscow, Accra and the Congo.* Glorifying Belgian paternalism in the Congo as "the greatest thing since Adam," and condemning the African personality as an instrument of international communism, he proudly asserted that "in 50 years, Belgium has radically transformed the savage Congo into a modern state." Students of colonial history are familiar with the outworn practice of branding all nationalist movements as communist-inspired. Even the Congo, which had been looked upon by the Belgians as a model colony in Africa, could not escape this label.

The year 1959 was an important year in the struggle for freedom in the Congo. Riots followed unrest in several parts of the country and whenever the colonial administration endeavoured to save the situation, the repressive measures were disproportionately brutal. In a declaration handed to the Press Agencies for communication to the United Nations, the Belgian Senate and King Baudouin, the Committee of the National Liberation Front, ABAKO, alleged that the Belgian Government, continuing its repressive measures, had threatened and forced the natives of the hinterland to sign the Belgian Ministerial Declaration of 13 January 1959. Soldiers, it was said, had occupied the whole of the Bakongo and Kwango districts and had made several indiscriminate arrests. Among the arrested were Chief Bahunhu, "the uncontested owner of Leopoldville lands," formerly called Mpumbu, and Mr. Gonda Samuel, a leader of the ABAKO African Democratic Party. Besides the arrests, searches had been made resulting in the seizure of vehicles and office materials belonging to the party, under the pretext of non-payment of taxes.

Such was the gravity of the situation that nationalist students of the Congo found it expedient to proceed to Ghana in September 1959 to mobilise public support for their just cause. A petition testifying the brutalities perpetrated by the Belgians in the Congo was presented to the Ghana Ministry of Foreign Affairs on 28 September, imploring me to use my good offices to communicate the contents to all independent African States, the Afro-Asian Movement and all world organisations sympathetic to their cause, urging immediate action:

1. To demand from the UNO an international commission to investigate the events in Leopoldville on 4 January 1959 and their consequences and further to examine the charges preferred by the Belgian Government against the ABAKO party;
2. To protest against the political activities of the Belgian Government on 13 January 1959 and the policy unilaterally decided upon by Belgium with the intention of creating a Belgium-Congo community contrary to the wishes of the Congolese people;
3. To protest against the proposed elections of 5 December 1959, forced upon the people for the purpose of implementing the Belgian policy which would lead to the formation of a Belgian-Congolese community;

4. To send observers to the Congo in case the Belgian Government were to maintain and impose their will on the conduct of the December elections.

The long and explicitly written petition represented the sentiments of the Congolese *élite,* particularly of the ABAKO party, which at this time was the most important mouthpiece of the freedom fighters.

Ghana's support for the Congo took a new turn with the consolidation of the new and more dynamic party, the MNC (Congolese National Movement) led by Patrice Lumumba. The MNC from the end of 1958 became the forerunner of the smaller nationalist groups and parties. Its aims, in brief, were "to prepare the masses and *élite* to take control of public affairs; to speed up the process of democratization; to implement the Declaration of Human Rights, and by peaceful negotiation, to do everything possible to free the Congo from colonialism and imperialism."

The ABAKO party or the Association des Bakongo pour l'Unification, l'Expansion et la Défense de la Kilonga was led by Mr. Joseph Kasavubu. Formed in 1950 by Edmond Nzeza-Landu, it was originally a purely cultural society which gained adherents partly because of the fear that the Bakongo tribe of the Lower Congo would be swamped by the influx of other tribes coming into the industrially booming Leopoldville and partly because of its dynamic leadership. The Bakongo had been averse to Belgian rule and, still conscious of their own identity, they had set up tribal and religious movements which sought to preserve their culture. Other tribal groups which maintained their own political interests were the Bangala of the Equatorial Province, the Balubas of Kasai and Katanga, the Balunda, Beyeie and others.

Like the CPP of Ghana, Lumumba's MNC was the first Congolese political organisation to recognise the need for a national leader and a national movement in accordance with the principles of Pan-Africanism. Perhaps Patrice Lumumba's own peculiar advantage in organising a national movement was the fact that he hailed from a relatively unimportant tribe, the Batelela, a sub-group of the Mongo tribe which has affiliations in three of Congo's six provinces. From his boyhood he had been brought up by his Christian parents among the *évolués* of Stanleyville and was never under the influence of tribal affinities, nor tied down by any particular interest of a tribal character.

During the turbulent year of 1959, Patrice Lumumba, whose Pan-

Africanist views had won the admiration of many Ghanaians, maintained close and continuous contact with me. In a dispatch dated 9 October 1959 he wrote through our Foreign Ministry, "May I please ask the Prime Minister to give me the necessary guide in respect of the plan to follow in our struggle? His experience means a lot to us." He went on to ask for copies of my political speeches for publication in the influential Congolese journal *Independence.*

Two main factors explain his request. The kind of divisions which beset political parties in the Congo soon after the Brussels Conference were not new to Ghana. The trends of national movements in both countries, though fundamentally different in points of detail, had certain basic characteristics in common; their struggle for national independence was to some extent the struggle between nationalism and tribalism; more explicitly, between a unitary system of government and federation. The situation which faced the Congo on the eve of independence did not differ profoundly from that which threatened Ghana's independence at the period of the ascendancy of the National Liberation Movement of Ashanti, the Togoland Congress, the Anlo Youth Association, the Northern People's Party and the Moslem Association, all of which were designed to destroy the CPP movement. As in Ghana, I was convinced that the Congo needed a strong unitary form of government. Events in the Congo since independence have only strengthened this conviction ... An African solution to the problem of the Congo was, and still remains, the only hope for bringing about a lasting peace. Recent events in the Congo emphatically support this view.

Part 7
LAW AND SOCIETY

INTRODUCTION

One of the cornerstones of modern society is the legal apparatus that sits as an appendage to the state. It is, among other things, through the law that the state legitimizes its control and its use of physical coercion. An understanding of the modern world thus necessitates an understanding of the law as a living institution.

In recent years there has burgeoned a plethora of studies and treatises on the law in action. These studies have been largely concerned with three issues: (1) how laws emerge, (2) how laws are enforced, and (3) what effect law has on society. In this section we have articles dealing with each of these issues as they are reflected in the criminal law. None of the articles represents an attempt to say that the law always and only works in the ways described, but each article points to an important characteristic of the legal system which is ordinarily missed when the law is viewed as simply reflecting the values of "the society." The articles represent examples of legal studies from the conflict perspective. We begin with an article which, by tracing the history of a particular law (vagrancy), documents how the law comes to reflect the interests of the state. The article by Yale lawyer Charles Reich shows the relationship between the needs of the state and the erosion of "basic legal principles," and the final article by the psychiatrist Thomas Szasz shows how mental-illness laws come to serve as tools for the suppression of ideas and life styles that conflict with the interests of the modern bureaucratic society.

ELITES AND THE CREATION OF CRIMINAL LAW

William J. Chambliss

Conventional myths notwithstanding, the history of the criminal law is *not* a history of public opinion or public interest being reflected in criminal-law legislation.[1] On the contrary, the history of the criminal law is everywhere the history of legislation and appellate-court decisions which in effect (if not in intent) reflect the interests of the economic elites who control the production and distribution of the major resources of the society.[2]

The ways the criminal law reflects these elite interests are generally through (1) direct involvement in the law-making process, (2) influence and control over the law-enforcing bureaucracies[3] and (3) the mobilization of bias.[4] The latter process, which is the subject of this paper, is nicely illustrated by the history of the law of vagrancy in England and America. The vagrancy laws are particularly interesting because they emerged, were altered, and shifted focus during historical periods when different economic elites held sway in western society. The degree to which the interests of these changing elites were reflected in the law of vagrancy is a good illustration of the mobilization of bias which characterizes the historical process of criminal-law legislation.

LEGAL INNOVATION: THE EMERGENCE OF THE LAW OF VAGRANCY IN ENGLAND

There is general agreement among legal scholars that the first full-fledged vagrancy statute was passed in England in 1349. As is generally the case with legislative innovations, however, this statute was preceded by earlier laws which established a climate favorable to such change. The most significant forerunner to the 1349 vagrancy statute was in 1274 when it was provided:

This is a revised version of "A Sociological Analysis of the Law of Vagrancy," which first appeared in *Social Problems,* **12**, Summer 1964, pp. 67-77.

> Because that abbies and houses of religion have been overcharged and sore grieved, by the resort of great men and other, so that their goods have not been sufficient for themselves, whereby they have been greatly hindered and impoverished, that they cannot maintain themselves, nor such charity as they have been accustomed to do; it is provided, that none shall come to eat or lodge in any house of religion, or any other's foundation than of his own, at the costs of the house, unless he be required by the governor of the house before his coming hither.[5]

Unlike the vagrancy statutes this statute does not intend to curtail the movement of persons from one place to another, but is solely designed to provide the religious houses with some financial relief from the burden of providing food and shelter to travelers.

The philosophy that the religious houses were to give alms to the poor and to the sick and feeble was, however, to undergo drastic change in the next fifty years. The result of this changed attitude was the establishment of the first vagrancy statute in 1349 which made it a crime to give alms to any who were unemployed while being of sound mind and body. To wit:

> Because that many valiant beggars, as long as they may live of begging, do refuse to labor, giving themselves to idleness and vice, and sometimes to theft and other abominations; it is ordained, that none, upon pain of imprisonment shall, under the colour of pity or alms, give anything to such which may labour, or presume to favour them towards their desires; so that thereby they may be compelled to labour for their necessary living.[6]

It was further provided by this statute that:

> . . . every man and woman, of what condition he be, free or bond, able in body, and within the age of threescore years, not living in merchandize nor exercising any craft, nor having of his own whereon to live, nor proper land whereon to occupy himself, and not serving any other, if he in convenient service (his estate considered) be required to serve, shall be bounded to serve him which shall him require. . . . And if any refuse, he shall on conviction by two true men,. . . be commited to gaol till he find surety to serve.
>
> And if any workman or servant, of what estate or condition he be, retained in any man's service, do depart from the said service without reasonable cause or license, before the term agreed on, he shall have pain of imprisonment.[7]

There was also in this statute the stipulation that the workers should receive a standard wage. In 1351 this statute was strengthened by the stipulation:

An none shall go out of the town where he dwelled in winter, to serve the summer, if he may serve in the same town.[8]

By 34 Ed 3 (1360) the punishment for these acts became imprisonment for fifteen days and if they "do not justify themselves by the end of that time, to be sent to gaol till they do."

A change in official policy so drastic as this did not, of course, occur simply as a matter of whim. The vagrancy statutes emerged as a result of changes in other parts of the social structure. The prime-mover for this legislative innovation was the Black Death which struck England about 1348. Among the many disastrous consequences this had upon the social structure was the fact that it decimated the labor force. It is estimated that by the time the pestilence had run its course at least fifty per cent of the population of England had died from the plague. This decimation of the labor force would necessitate rather drastic innovations in any society but its impact was heightened in England where, at this time, the economy was highly dependent upon a ready supply of cheap labor.

Even before the pestilence, however, the availability of an adequate supply of cheap labor was becoming a problem for the landowners. The crusades and various wars had made money necessary to the lords and, as a result, the lords frequently agreed to sell the serfs their freedom in order to obtain the needed funds. The serfs, for their part, were desirous of obtaining their freedom (by "fair means" or "foul") because the larger towns which were becoming more industrialized during this period could offer the serf greater personal freedom as well as a higher standard of living. This process is nicely summarized by Bradshaw:

> By the middle of the 14th century the outward uniformity of the manorial system had become in practice considerably varied . . . for the peasant had begun to drift to the towns and it was unlikely that the old village life in its unpleasant aspects should not be resented. Moreover the constant wars against France and Scotland were fought mainly with mercenaries after Henry III's time and most villages contributed to the new armies. The bolder serfs either joined the armies or fled to the towns, and even in the villages the free men who held by villein tenure were as eager to commute their services as the serfs were to escape. Only the amount of "free" labor available enabled the lord to work his demense in many places.[9]

And he says regarding the effect of the Black Death:

> . . . in 1348 the Black Death reached England and the vast mortality that ensued destroyed that reserve of labour which alone had made the manorial system even nominally possible.[10]

The immediate result of these events was of course no surprise: Wages for the "free" man rose considerably and this increased, on the one hand, the landowner's problems and, on the other hand, the plight of the unfree tenant. For although wages increased for the personally free laborers, it of course did not necessarily add to the standard of living of the serf; if anything it made his position worse because the landowner would be hard pressed to pay for the personally free labor which he needed and would thus find it more and more difficult to maintain the standard of living for the serf which he had heretofore supplied. Thus the serf had no alternative but flight if he chose to better his position. Furthermore, flight generally meant both freedom and better conditions since the possibility of work in the new weaving industry was great and the chance of being caught small.[11]

It was under these conditions that we find the first vagrancy statutes emerging. There is little question but that these statutes were designed for one express purpose: to force laborers (whether personally free or unfree) to accept employment at a low wage in order to insure the landowner an adequate supply of labor at a price he could afford to pay. Caleb Foote concurs with this interpretation when he notes:

> The anti-migratory policy behind vagrancy legislation began as an essential complement of the wage stabilization legislation which accompanied the breakup of feudalism and the depopulation caused by the Black Death. By the Statutes of Labourers in 1349–1351, every able-bodied person without other means of support was required to work for wages fixed at the level preceding the Black Death; it was unlawful to accept more, or to refuse an offer to work, or to flee from one county to another to avoid offers of work or to seek higher wages, or go give alms to able-bodied beggars who refused to work.[12]

In short, as Foote says in another place, this was an "attempt to make the vagrancy statutes a substitute for serfdom."[13] This same conclusion is equally apparent from the wording of the statute where it is stated:

> Because great part of the people, and especially of workmen and servants, late died in pestilence; many seeing the necessity of masters, and great scarcity of servants, will not serve without excessive wages, and some rather willing to beg in idleness than by labour to get their living: it is ordained, that every man and woman, of what condition he be, free or bond, able in body and within the age of threescore years, not living in merchandize, (etc.) be required to serve. . . .

The innovation in the law, then, was a direct result of the afore-mentioned changes which had occurred in the social setting. In this case these changes were located for the most part in the economic institution of the society. The vagrancy laws were designed to alleviate a condition defined by the lawmakers as undesirable. The solution was to attempt to force a reversal, as it were, of a social process which was well underway; that is, to curtail mobility of laborers in such a way that labor would not become a commodity for which the landowners would have to compete.

Statutory Dormancy: A Legal Vestige. In time, of course, the curtailment of the geographical mobility of laborers was no longer requisite. One might well expect that when the function served by the statute was no longer an important one for the society, the statutes would be eliminated from the law. In fact, this has not occurred. The vagrancy statutes have remained in effect since 1349. Furthermore, as we shall see in some detail later, they were taken over by the colonies and have remained in effect in the United States as well.

The substance of the vagrancy statutes changed very little for some time after the first ones in 1349–1351 although there was a tendency to make punishments more harsh than originally. For example, in 1360 it was provided that violators of the statute should be imprisoned for fifteen days[14] and in 1388 the punishment was to put the offender in the stocks and to keep him there until "he find surety to return to his service."[15] That there was still, at this time, the intention of providing the landowner with labor is apparent from the fact that this statute provides:

> . . . and he or she which use to labour at the plough and cart, or other labour and service of husbandry, till they be of the age of 12 years, from thenceforth shall abide at the same labour without being put to any mistery or handicraft: and any covenant of apprenticeship to the contrary shall be void.[16]

The next alteration in the statutes occurs in 1495 and is restricted to an increase in punishment. Here it is provided that vagrants shall be "set in stocks, there to remain by the space of three days and three nights, and there to have none other sustenance but bread and water; and after the said three days and nights, to be had out and set at large, and then to be commanded to avoid the town."[17]

The tendency to increase the severity of punishment during this period seems to be the result of a general tendency to make finer distinctions in the criminal law. During this period the vagrancy statutes appear to have been fairly inconsequential in either their effect as a control mechanism or as a generally enforced statute.[18] The processes of social change in the culture generally and the trend away from serfdom and into a "free" economy obviated the utility of these statutes. The result was not unexpected. The judiciary did not apply the law and the legislators did not take it upon themselves to change the law. In short, we have here a period of dormancy in which the statute is neither applied nor altered significantly.

A SHIFT IN FOCAL CONCERN

Following the squelching of the Peasants' Revolt in 1381, the services of the serfs to the lord "tended to become less and less exacted, although in certain forms they lingered on till the seventeenth century. . . . By the sixteenth century few knew that there were any bondmen in England . . . and in 1575 Queen Elizabeth listened to the prayers of almost the last serfs in England . . . and granted them manumission."[19]

In view of this change we would expect corresponding changes in the vagrancy laws. Beginning with the lessening of punishment in the statute of 1503 we find these changes. However, instead of remaining dormant (or becoming more so) or being negated altogether, the vagrancy statutes experienced a shift in focal concern. With this shift the statutes served a new and equally important function for the social order of England. The first statute which indicates this change was in 1530. In this statute (22 H.8.c 12 1530) it was stated:

> If any person, being whole and mighty in body, and able to labour, be taken in begging, or be vagrant and can give no reckoning how he lawfully gets his living; . . . and all other idle persons going about, some of them using divers and subtil crafty and unlawful games and plays, and some of them feigning themselves to have knowledge of . . . crafty sciences . . . shall be punished as provided.

What is most significant about this statute is the shift from an earlier concern with laborers to a concern with *criminal* activities. To be sure, the stipulation of persons "being whole and mighty in body, and able to labour, be taken in begging, or be vagrant" sounds very much like the concerns of the earlier statutes. Some important differences are apparent however when the rest of the statute includes those who "can give no reckoning how he lawfully gets his living"; "some of them using divers subtil and unlawful games and plays." This is the first statute which specifically focuses upon these kinds of criteria for adjudging someone a vagrant.

It is significant that in this statute the severity of punishment is increased so as to be greater not only than provided by the 1503 statute but the punishment is more severe than that which had been provided by *any* of the pre-1503 statutes as well. For someone who is merely idle and gives no reckoning of how he makes his living the offender shall be:

> . . . had to the next market town, or other place where they [the constables] shall think most convenient, and there to be tied to the end of a cart naked, and to be beaten with whips throughout the same market town or other place, till his body be bloody by reason of such whipping.[20]

But, for those who use "divers and subtil crafty and unlawful games and plays," etc., the punishment is "whipping at two days together in manner aforesaid."[21] For the second offense, such persons are:

> . . . scourged two days, and the third day to be put upon the pillory from nine of the clock till eleven before noon of the same day and to have one of his ears cut off.[22]

And if he offend the third time "to have like punishment with whipping, standing on the pillory and to have his other ear cut off."

This statute (1) makes a distinction between types of offenders and applies the more severe punishment to those who are clearly engaged in "criminal" activities, (2) mentions a specific concern with categories of "unlawful" behavior, and (3) applies a type of punishment (cutting off the ear) which is generally reserved for offenders who are defined as likely to be a fairly serious criminal.

Only five years later, we find for the first time that the punishment of death is applied to the crime of vagrancy. We also note a change in terminology in the statute:

> . . . and if any ruffians . . . after having been once apprehended . . . shall wander, loiter, or idle use themselves and play the vagabonds . . . shall be eftfoons not only whipped again, but shall have the gristle of his right ear clean cut off. And if he shall again offend, he shall be committed to gaol till the next sessions; and being there convicted upon indictment, he shall have judgment to suffer pains and execution of death, as a felon, as an enemy of the commonwealth.[23]

It is significant that the statute now makes persons who repeat the crime of vagrancy a felon. During this period then, the focal concern of the vagrancy statutes becomes a concern for the control of felons and is no longer primarily concerned with the movement of laborers.

These statutory changes were a direct response to changes taking place in England's social structure during this period. We have already pointed out that feudalism was decaying rapidly. Concomitant with the breakup of feudalism was an increased emphasis upon commerce and industry. The commercial emphasis in England at the turn of the sixteenth century is of particular importance in the development of vagrancy laws. With commercialism came considerable traffic bearing valuable items. Where there were 169 important merchants in the middle of the fourteenth century, there were 3,000 merchants engaged in foreign trade alone at the beginning of the sixteenth century.[24] England became highly dependent upon commerce for its economic support. Italians conducted a great deal of the commerce of England during this early period and were held in low repute by the populace. As a result, they were subject to attacks by citizens and, more important, were frequently robbed of their goods while transporting them. "The general insecurity of the times made any transportation hazardous. The special risks to which the alien merchant was subjected gave rise to the royal practice of issuing formally executed covenants of safe conduct through the realm."[25]

Such a situation not only called for the enforcement of existing laws but also called for the creation of new laws which would facilitate the control of persons preying upon merchants transporting goods. The vagrancy statutes were revived in order to fulfill just such a purpose. Persons who had committed no serious felony but who were suspected of being capable of doing so could be apprehended and incapacitated through the application of vagrancy laws once these laws were refocused so as to include "any ruffians . . . [who] shall wander, loiter, or idle use themselves and play the vagabonds. . . ."[26]

The new focal concern is continued in 1 Ed. 6. c. 3 (1547) and in fact is made more general so as to include:

> Whoever man or woman, being not lame, impotent, or so aged or diseased that he or she cannot work, not having whereon to live, shall be lurking in any house, or loitering or idle wandering by the highway side, or in streets, cities, towns, or villages, not applying themselves to some honest labour, and so continuing for three days; or running away from their work;

> every such person shall be taken for a vagabond. And . . . upon conviction of two witnesses . . . the same loiterer (shall) be marked with a hot iron in the breast with the letter V, and adjudged him to the person bringing him, to be his slave for two years. . . .

Should the vagabond run away, upon conviction, he was to be branded by a hot iron with the letter S on the forehead and to be thenceforth declared a slave forever. And in 1571 there is modification of the punishment to be inflicted, whereby the offender is to be "branded on the chest with the letter V" (for vagabond). And, if he is convicted the second time, the brand is to be made on the forehead. It is worth noting here that this method of punishment, which first appeared in 1530 and is repeated here with somewhat more force, is also an indication of a change in the type of person to whom the law is intended to apply. For it is likely that nothing so permanent as branding would be applied to someone who was wandering but looking for work, or at worst merely idle and not particularly dangerous *per se.* On the other hand, it could well be applied to someone who was likely to be engaged in other criminal activities in connection with being "vagrant."

By 1571 in the statute of 14 El. c. 5 the shift in focal concern is fully developed:

> All rogues, vagabonds, and sturdy beggars shall . . . be committed to the common gaol. . . . he shall be grievously whipped, and burnt thró the gristle of the right ear with a hot iron of the compass of an inch about; . . . And for the second offense, he shall be adjudged a felon, unless some person will take him for two years in to his service. And for the third offense, he shall be adjudged guilty of felony without benefit of clergy.

And there is included a long list of persons who fall within the statute: "proctors, procurators, idle persons going about using subtil, crafty and unlawful games or plays; and some of them feigning themselves to have knowledge of . . . absurd sciences . . . and all fencers, bearwards, common players in interludes, and minstrels . . . all juglers, pedlars, tinkers, petty chapmen . . . and all counterfeiters of licenses, passports and users of the same." The major significance of this statute is that it includes all the previously defined offenders and adds some more. Significantly, those added are more clearly criminal types, counterfeiters, for example. It is also significant that there is the following qualification of this statute: "Provided also, that this act shall not extend to cookers, or harvest folks, that travel for harvest work, corn or hay."

That the changes in this statute were seen as significant is indicated by the following statement which appears in the statute:

> And whereas by reason of this act, the common gaols of every shire are like to be greatly pestered with more number of prisoners than heretofore hath been, for that the said vagabonds and other lewd persons before recited shall upon their apprehension be committed to the said gaols; it is enacted. . . .[27]

And a provision is made for giving more money for maintaining the gaols. This seems to add credence to the notion that this statute was seen as being significantly more general than those previously.

It is also of importance to note that this is the first time the term *rogue* has been used to refer to persons included in the vagrancy statutes. It seems, *a priori,* that a "rogue" is a different social type than is a "vagrant" or a "vagabond"; the latter terms implying something more equivalent to the idea of a "tramp" whereas the former (rogue) seems to imply a more disorderly and potentially dangerous person.

The emphasis upon the criminalistic aspect of vagrants continues in Chapter 17 of the same statute:

> Whereas divers *licentious* persons wander up and down in all parts of the realm, to countenance their *wicked behavior;* and do continually assemble themselves armed in the highways, and elsewhere in troops, *to the great terror* of her majesty's true subjects, *the impeachment of her laws,* and the disturbance of the peace and tranquility of the realm; and whereas many outrages are daily committed by these dissolute persons, and more are likely to ensue of speedy remedy be not provided. [Italics added.]

With minor variations (*e.g.,* offering a reward for the capture of a vagrant) the statutes remain essentially of this nature until 1743. In 1743 there was once more an expansion of the types of persons included such that "all persons going about as patent gatherers, or gatherers of alms, under pretense of loss by fire or other casualty; or going about as collectors for prisons, gaols, or hospitals, all persons playing of betting at any unlawful games; and all persons who run away and leave their wives or children . . . all persons wandering abroad, and lodging in ale-houses, barns, out-houses, or in the open air, not giving good account of themselves," were types of offenders added to those already included.

By 1743 the vagrancy statutes had apparently been sufficiently reconstructed by the shifts of concern so as to be once more a useful instrument in the creation of social solidarity. This function has apparently continued down to the present day in England. The changes from

1743 to the present have been all in the direction of clarifying or expanding the categories covered but little has been introduced to change either the meaning or the impact of this branch of the law.

We can summarize this shift in focal concern by quoting from Halsbury. He has noted that in the vagrancy statutes:

> . . . elaborate provision is made for the relief and incidental control of destitute wayfarers. These latter, however, form but a small portion of the offenders aimed at by what are known as the Vagrancy Laws, . . . many offenders who are in no ordinary sense of the word vagrants, have been brought under the laws relating to vagrancy, and the great number of the offenses coming within the operation of these laws have little or no relation to the subject of poor relief, but are more properly directed towards the prevention of crime, the preservation of good order, and the promotion of social economy.[28]

Before leaving this section it is perhaps pertinent to make a qualifying remark. We have emphasized throughout this section how the vagrancy statutes underwent a shift in focal concern as the social setting changed. The shift in focal concern is not meant to imply that the later focus of the statutes represents a completely new law. It will be recalled that even in the first vagrancy statutes there was reference to those who "do refuse labor, giving themselves to idleness and vice and sometimes to theft and other abominations." Thus the possibility of criminal activities resulting from persons who refuse to labor was recognized even in the earliest statute. The fact remains, however, that the major emphasis in this statute and in the statutes which followed the first one was always upon the "refusal to labor" or "begging." The "criminalistic" aspect of such persons was relatively unimportant. Later, as we have shown, the criminalistic potential becomes of paramount importance. The thread runs back to the earliest statute but the reason for the statutes' existence as well as the focal concern of the statutes is quite different in 1743 than it was in 1349.

VAGRANCY LAWS IN THE UNITED STATES

In general, the vagrancy laws of England, as they stood in the middle eighteenth century, were simply adopted by the states. There were some exceptions to this general trend. For example, Maryland restricted the application of vagrancy laws to "free" Negroes. In addition, for *all* states the vagrancy laws were even more explicitly concerned with the control of criminals and undesirables than had been the case in England. New York, for example, explicitly defines prostitutes as being a category of vagrants during this period. These exceptions do not, however, change the general picture significantly and it is quite appropriate to consider the U.S. vagrancy laws as following from England's of the middle eighteenth century with relatively minor changes. The control of criminals and undesirables was the *raison d'être* of the vagrancy laws in the U.S. This is as true today as it was in 1750. As Caleb Foote's analysis of the application of vagrancy statutes in the Philadelphia court shows, these laws are presently applied indiscriminately to persons considered a "nuisance." Foote suggests that "the chief significance of this branch of the criminal law lies in its quantitative impact and administrative usefulness."[29] Thus it appears that in America the trend begun in England in the sixteenth, seventeenth and eighteenth centuries has been carried to its logical extreme and the laws are now used principally as a mechanism for "clearing the streets" of the derelicts who inhabit the "skid rows" and "Bowerys" of our large urban areas.

Since the 1800's there has been an abundant source of prospects to which the vagrancy laws have been applied. These have been primarily those persons deemed by the police and the courts to be either actively involved in criminal activities or at least peripherally involved. In this context, then, the statutes have changed very little. The functions served by the statutes in England of the late eighteenth century are still being served today in both England and the United States. The locale has changed somewhat and it appears that the present day application of vagrancy statutes is focused upon the arrest and confinement of the "down and outers" who inhabit certain sections of our larger cities but the impact has remained constant. The lack of change in the vagrancy statutes, then, can be seen as a reflection of the society's perception of a continuing need to control some of its "suspicious" or "undesirable" members.[30]

A word of caution is in order lest we leave the impression that this administrative purpose is the sole function of vagrancy laws in the U.S. today. Although it is our contention that this is generally true it is worth remembering that during certain periods of our recent history, and to some extent today, these laws have also been used to control the movement of workers. This was particularly the case during the depression years, and California is infamous for its use of vagrancy laws to restrict the admission of migrants from other states.[31] The vagrancy statutes, because of their history, still contain germs within them which make such effects possible. Their main purpose, however, is clearly no longer the control of laborers but rather the control of the undesirable, the criminal and the "nuisance."

DISCUSSION

The foregoing analysis of the vagrancy laws has demonstrated that these laws were a legislative innovation which reflected the socially perceived necessity of providing an abundance of cheap labor to landowners during a period when serfdom was breaking down and when the pool of available labor was depleted. With the eventual breakup of feudalism the need for such laws eventually disappeared and the increased dependence of the economy upon industry and commerce rendered the former use of the vagrancy statutes unnecessary. As a result, for a substantial period the vagrancy statutes were dormant, undergoing only minor changes and, presumably, being applied infrequently. Finally, the vagrancy laws were subjected to considerable alteration through a shift in the focal concern of the statutes. Whereas in their inception the laws focused upon the "idle" and "those refusing to labor" after the turn of the sixteenth century, emphasis came to be upon "rogues," "vagabonds," and others who were suspected of being engaged in criminal activities. During this period the focus was particularly upon "roadmen" who preyed upon citizens who transported goods from one place to another. The increased importance of commerce to England during this period made it necessary that some protection be given persons engaged in this enterprise and the vagrancy statutes provided one source for such protection by refocusing the acts to be included under these statutes.

Shifts and changes in the law of vagrancy show a clear pattern of reflecting the interests and needs of the groups who control the economic institutions of the society. The laws change as these institutions change.

What is true of the vagrancy laws is also true of the criminal law in general. To be sure, not all criminal laws so clearly follow the economic interests of the ruling classes. Some laws are irrelevant or tangential to economic interests. Other laws serve the interests of some elite groups and not others. In these latter instances the study of criminal-law legislation should be pursued to determine how competing economic interests fare in efforts to influence criminal law creation. It is also important that studies be undertaken to investigate how criminal-law legislation creates legitimacy for the established economic and political structure of the society.

NOTES

1. For a discussion of the various schools of thought which assume "public interest" or "value consensus" as the source of criminal law, see William J. Chambliss and Robert B. Seidman, *Law, Order, and Power,* Reading, Massachusetts: Addison-Wesley Publishing Company, 1971. See also William J. Chambliss, *Crime and the Legal Process,* New York: McGraw-Hill Book Company, 1969, Part I and Jerome Hall, *Theft, Law and Society,* Indianapolis: Bobbs-Merrill, 1937.
2. This argument is spelled out in detail in William J. Chambliss, "The State, the Law and the Definition of Behavior as Criminal or Delinquent," in Daniel Glazer (editor), *Handbook of Criminology,* Chicago: Rand-McNally Co., 1972.
3. See William J. Chambliss, "Vice, Corruption, Bureaucracy and Power," pp. 353-379.
4. I am indebted to Ann Lunden for pointing out the utility of this concept for an understanding of the criminal law process. The concept was originally suggested in the work of F. E. Schattschneider, *Semisovereign People: A Realist's View of Democracy in America,* New York: Holt, Rinehart & Winston, 1960. See also Peter Bachrach and Morton S. Baratz, *Power and Poverty,* New York: Ford University Press, 1970.
5. 3 Ed. l. c. l.
6. 35 Ed. l. c. l.
7. 23 Ed. 3.
8. 25 Ed. 3 (1351).
9. Bradshaw, F., *A Social History of England,* p. 54.
10. *Ibid.*
11. *Ibid.,* p. 57.
12. Foote, C., "Vagrancy-type Law and Its Administration," *Univ. of Pennsylvania Law Review* (104), 1956, p. 615.
13. *Ibid.*
14. 34 Ed. 3 (1360).
15. 12 R. 2 (1388).
16. *Ibid.*

17. 11 H. & C. 2 (1495).
18. As evidence for this note the expectation that "the common gaols of every shire are likely to be greatly pestered with more numbers of prisoners than heretofore . . ." when the statutes were changed by the statute of 14 Ed. c. 5 (1571).
19. Bradshaw, *op. cit.,* p. 61.
20. 22 H. 8. c. 12 (1530).
21. *Ibid.*
22. *Ibid.*
23. 27 H. 8. c. 25 (1535).
24. Hall, *op. cit.,* p. 21.
25. *Ibid.,* p. 23.
26. 27 H. 8. c. 25 (1535).
27. 14 Ed. c. 5 (1571).
28. Halsbury, Earl of, *The Laws of England,* Butterworth & Co., Bell Yard, Temple Bar, 1912, pp. 606-607.
29. Foote, *op. cit.,* p. 613. Also see in this connection, Deutscher, Irwin, "The Petty Offender," *Federal Probation,* XIX, June 1968.
30. It is on this point that the vagrancy statutes have been subject to criticism. See for example, Lacey, Forrest W., "Vagrancy and Other Crimes of Personal Condition," *Harvard Law Review* (66), p. 1203.
31. Edwards *vs* California, 314 S: 160 (1941).

THE LAW AND THE CORPORATE STATE

Charles Reich

Law is supposed to be a codification of those lasting human values which a people agree upon. "Thou shalt not kill" is such a law. The Corporate State is a distinctively legalistic society. It utilizes law for every facet of its activity—there has probably never been a society with so much law, where law is so important. Thus it might be expected that law would represent a significant control over the power of the Corporate State, and a source of guidelines for it. But law in the Corporate State is something very different from a codification of values. The State has transformed it.

During the New Deal period the law was gradually changed from a medium which carried traditional values of its own to a value-free medium that could be adapted to serve "public policy," which became the "public interest" of the Corporate State. This produced law that fell into line with the requirements of organization and technology, and that supported the demands of administration rather than protecting the individual. Once law had assumed this role, there began a vast proliferation of laws, statutes, regulations, and decisions. For the law began to be employed to aid all the work of the Corporate State by compelling obedience to the State's constantly increasing demands.

One area in which this can be demonstrated is the field of constitutional rights. The first point that must be made is that despite the vast growth of corporate power the courts, except in the area of racial discrimination, have failed to hold that corporations are subject to the Bill of Rights. A mere statement of this fact may not seem very significant; corporations, after all, are not supposed to exercise the governmental powers with which the Bill of Rights was concerned. But this has been radically changed by the emergence of the public-private state. Today

---

private institutions do exercise government power; more, indeed, than "government" itself. They decide what will be produced and what will not be produced; they do our primary economic planning; they are the chief determinants of how resources are allocated. With respect to their own employees, members, or students, they act in an unmistakably governmental fashion; they punish conduct, deprive people of their positions within the organization, or decide on advancement. In a sweeping way they influence the opinions, expression, associations, and behavior of all of us. Hence the fact that the Bill of Rights is inapplicable is of paramount importance; it means that these constitutional safeguards actually apply only to one part (and not the most significant part) of the power of the Corporate State. We have two governments in America, then—one under the Constitution and a much greater one not under the Constitution. Consider a right such as freedom of speech. "Government" is forbidden to interfere with free speech, but corporations can fire employees for free speech; private organizations can discriminate against those who exercise free speech; newspapers, television, and magazines can refuse to carry "radical" opinion. In short, the *inapplicability* of our Bill of Rights is one of the crucial facts of American life today.

But does the Bill of Rights afford protection even where it directly applies? The Supreme Court decisions of the last few decades are not reassuring. In its adjudications the Court gives heavy weight to the "interest of society." It defers to what the legislature-executive-administrators have decided. The commands of the state are to be overturned only if there is no "rational" basis for them or if they contravene an express provision of the Constitution, and that provision is not outweighed by "the interest of society." The result over the years has been that virtually any policy in the field of economics, production, planning, or allocation has been declared constitutional; that all sorts of decisions classifying people in different and unequal statuses for tax or benefit purposes have gone unquestioned; that peace-time selective service has been upheld; that free speech has been severely limited.

A second area where law has been made to serve the state is that of federal regulation of economic activity. Here, if anywhere in the law, one might expect control to be exercised over corporate power. But the story is the same as the story of constitutional law. In the first place, most regulation is either very superficial or does what the regulated industry really wants to be done anyway. Regulation polices the outlaws, prevents unruly competition, limits entry into a field, and in effect rationalizes and stabilizes industry. Gabriel Kolko, in *The Triumph of Conservatism,* suggests that regulation began performing this function as long ago as the so-called Progressive Era; and surely regulation performed largely this function under the New Deal. Food in interstate commerce must be properly labeled, inspected, and not adulterated. Stocks must not be sold in a misleading way. These are regulations with which any industry can feel comfortable. Moreover, regulation has to a large extent been taken over by personnel representing the thinking and interests of those supposed to be regulated.

The inadequacy of regulation shows most clearly in the decisions made concerning allocation of valuable resources. Consider the television channels, owned by the public and licensed free of charge to various applicants (who can make a fortune out of them, and then sell them for millions of dollars). The FCC could have distributed these channels to a wide spectrum of applicants; there could be stations controlled by blacks, by the poor, by students, by universities, by radicals, by groups with various cultural interests. The opportunity was there. What did the FCC actually do? A large number of stations, the most desirable of all, were given to the three giant networks, which proved a crucial aid to the networks in establishing domination over the entire industry. Most of the remaining stations were given either to already established powers in the mass communications field, such as newspapers (with the result that in a given town the principal station would be given to the principal newspaper, so that the sources of information in the town tightened rather than loosened), or they were given to giant corporations. Moreover, the FCC failed to make any adequate provision for truth, objectivity, or balance in the programs of those to whom it turned over the airwaves. Has anyone ever been able to see a program prepared by the Black Panthers, or migratory workers, or student draft resisters, or New Left economic critics, or women's liberation groups presented on a major network? Yet, at the same time, the law actually forbids any of these unrepresented groups to attempt to broadcast their views without a license. Regulation, proceeding strictly according to law, thus had the effect of giving a television monopoly to the power groups in the Corporate State, and excluding all others *by law.*

The role of the law with respect to the Corporate State, and particularly with reference to technology, can be further illustrated by the circumstances surrounding the introduction of chemical Mace as a police weapon. Developed by a private company whose motivation was presumably to make a profit and expand its market and organization, it was purchased by many police departments and presently sprayed in people's faces, causing temporary and/or possibly lasting injuries, plus that more profound injury to the nation as a whole that comes from the use of technology in a way that dehumanizes both policeman and victim. The law authorized the company to market this product, and the police to adopt it and start using it on human beings, without: any tests or studies by a scientific or government agency; the kind of review by the Food and Drug Administration required for other drugs used on people; approval by any legislative body; any vote by the public; any disclosure of information concerning the properties of Mace; any information on long-term effects of Mace, or its effects on people with special infirmities or allergies; setting any general standards as to what weapons are appropriate for what circumstances; requiring any special training for the use of Mace. At the same time, the law gave Mace its full protection and sanction. The law bars any redress to victims, any lawsuit for injuries, any criminal proceedings against the police—unless the most unusual circumstances are present. Thus the use of Mace has the full power of the law behind it, and those who oppose its use have never been given a chance.

While furthering the power of the Corporate State, the law has also served the function of advancing private interests. As the nation has become a legalistic society, law has increasingly become the medium in which private maneuver for power, status, and financial gain could take place. It has become a huge game board, like Monopoly, on which expert players make intricate moves to positions of advantage. The game of law is played with all of the legal powers of government to provide benefits, subsidies, allocate resources and franchises, and grant special exceptions and favors. It is played with the whole property-status system in which a move from one status to another provides different and increased benefits. It is played with all the duties imposed by law on citizens, including the tax laws and the draft. Lawyers are the professional strategists for this game and vast amounts of energy and activity are poured into playing it.

The legal game board builds up into structures that embody, *in the law itself,* almost every inequity, injustice, and irrationality that has become accepted in our society. Among the greatest examples are the federal tax laws and the draft. The tax laws are surely one of the most intricate and remarkable structures of inequity that the human mind has ever devised. There are hundreds of pages of inequities; special privileges of every imaginable sort. It seems accurate to say that the one overriding principle of the tax laws is that inequality and special favors are the rule that governs all. If possible, the draft law is even worse. For it sends some young men off to risk their lives and lose long years which might be spent in ways of their own choosing, while others are privileged to escape any military service. We need not linger here on facts that are so well known; the point is that the tax structure and the draft are not unusual examples of how the law works; they are entirely characteristic examples of what is true of the law as a whole.

Viewed in a broader perspective, it can be seen that for each status, class, and position in society, there is a different set of laws. There is one set of laws for the welfare recipient, one for the businessman. There is one set of laws for the government employee, another for the congressman. There is one set of laws for the farmer, another for the writer. These differences are not limited to any particular area or subject matter; for example, the constitutional right of privacy is treated differently for a businessman or farmer than for a welfare recipient. A person receiving Medicare is required to take a loyalty oath; others are not. If "law" means a general rule to govern a community of people, then in the most literal and precise sense we have *no* law; we are a lawless society.

As administered, the law becomes lawless in an even deeper sense. A motorist is stopped by a policeman who is on the lookout for a stolen car of that description. The motorist soon proves he is driving his own car, but in the course of events the officer calls the motorist by his first name (obtained from the automobile registration) in a way which the motorist deems insulting. "Please call me Mr.____," the motorist says. The officer says, "You want to be arrested?" "For what," says the motorist. The policeman says, "I can arrest you for having a dirty license plate, or for a faulty windshield wiper, or for failing to signal when you pulled over, or disrespect to an officer, or jaywalking." The driver realizes that at best he will lose several hours, perhaps be subject to a fine, a record, even a jail term if the magistrate is in a vindictive mood. He apologizes profusely to the officer.

When the heavyweight champion Muhammad Ali refused to submit to induction into the army, the New York State Boxing Commission, a public body operating by authority of law, revoked his title. The Commission held no hearing at which Ali presented his case. It did not wait to see whether the courts would convict Ali of a crime or hold that, by reason of his religious views, he had a right to refuse induction, or that his draft board was illegally constitued. In Seattle the legal authorities started proceedings to revoke the license of a G.I. coffee house because it supposedly encouraged anti-war thinking among young G.I.'s; the license official said that he did not want such activities around the Seattle area. Through the law, his arbitrary personal view became a governmental act.

Behind this lawless use of law lies the fact that the greater the quantity of legal rules, the greater the amount of discretionary power is generated. If a licensed pharmacist is subject to fifty separate regulations, he can be harassed by one after another, as soon as he proves himself to have complied with the first. One school of legal philosophers has long advocated a society in which precisely drawn laws would give everyone the freedom of knowing his exact rights. But in practice, experience has shown that the greater the number of laws, the greater the resulting discretion, and the more lawless the official part of the state becomes. Laws that are widely violated, that represent cultural differences, such as the marijuana laws, especially lend themselves to selective and arbitrary enforcement.

For blacks, for anyone with long hair or nonconforming dress, and even for youth in general, the law and the police have become something to be automatically feared. The long-haired youth who drives a car is likely to be stopped, searched, and harassed by police over and over again because of his appearance alone. Blacks have experienced a similar arbitrary discrimination for years. Youth in general find curfews and other laws specially designed to "keep them in their place." All of these groups feel the law to be their enemy in two ways. First, because of the way it is enforced against them. Second, because in a larger sense it is constructed against them; tax favors, subsidies, and privileges are denied them and given others; special penalties are reserved for them alone.

What we fail to realize is that there is a basic pattern to this kind of lawless law. When police lawlessness is revealed, such as the "police riot" in Chicago or unnecessary brutality at a university, everyone is shocked as if this were an *aberration* in our society. But the police have always been brutal and lawless to the powerless; we know this from how blacks were and are treated by the police in the South, and from the way young people, the poor, blacks, and outcasts are treated in the North. The cry of police lawlessness misses the point. In any large city the bureaucracies are also lawless; the building inspectors make threats and collect bribes, the liquor licensing authority is both arbitrary and corrupt, the zoning system is tyrannical but subject to influence. An individual in a small town criticizes the mayor and the zoning board rezones his house, the assessor raises his taxes, the police arrest him for minor violations, and the sanitation department declares his sewage system unsafe. Impossible? No, it has all happened to unpopular and powerless people. An aberration? Not at all. It is not the misuse of power that is the evil; the very *existence* of power is an evil. Totalitarianism is simply enough power, of whatever sort, to exercise full control over those within the system.

The point is this: there can be no rule of law in an administrative state. The ideal of the rule of law can be realized only in a political-conflict state which places limits upon official power and permits diversity to exist. Once everything is subject to regulation, the rule of law is inevitably lost, for the rule of law cannot stand as an independent principle of society; it is always tied to the question of power. The real issue in any society is the degree of power. Is that power divided or massed? Is it controlled? In a managerial society, where the individual is subject to the vast regulatory power of the state, the rule of law becomes an empty, hollow concept.

With the advent of deep cultural conflict in the United States, the law has lost any pretense of neutrality and become a major element used by one side in the struggle. The way law is employed in the ghetto, in cases involving war protesters, and in drug-possession cases among the young has made almost the whole new culture "illegal." During the summer of 1970, nearly every attempt to hold an outdoor rock festival anywhere in the United States was subject to repression by legal means. An instructive example was the Powder Ridge Festival, supposed to be held at a ski resort in Connecticut on the weekend of August 1. A judge declared the whole festival to be a "nuisance" because of the traffic congestion it might create, and issued an "inappealable" injunction against it. Of course, the rock fans responded by coming anyway, perhaps in part to show their contempt for this species of law. Equally instructive was a recent action by the Board of Regents of the University of California. Ignoring the recommendations of faculties and administrators, the regents delayed promotions for two professors deemed to be left wing and at the same time gave extraordinary and unrequested salary raises to two professors who had been vocal in a way that appealed to right-wing sensibilities. Both actions carried with them, of course, the full sanction of the regents' legal authority.

One further thing needs to be said concerning the function of law in the Corporate State. In any society, there is some medium that intervenes between the individual values, choices, and needs of people and the social structure that results. In a primitive society, this mediator is the cultural-social tradition; it provides a society that is encrusted with many uses of the past, but in a long-range sense reflects the beliefs and values of the people in it. Beginning with the market system and the industrial revolution, a new mediator appeared: money. As Marx said, money became the pimp between man and his values. Money did not, of course, provide as accurate a reflection of socially felt needs as the old culture did; you only got what you paid for, and so there commenced the terrible erosion of values. . . . But money was not totally unresponsive to values either; perhaps it reflected 50 percent of them; it enhanced some while neglecting others, but it remained true that what an individual or society wanted, it could (if it could pay for it) succeed in getting.

As we have described the American Corporate State, it is a society very different from both a primitive culture and from the early market system. It is a society which is entirely indifferent to human needs and values, which can be wholly irrational, which can indeed make destructive war on its own people. What medium could possibly furnish a way for human needs to emerge so utterly distorted and ignored, and yet keep the people believing that it was "their" society?

Law is such a medium. Far more than money, law is capable of intervening between man and his humanity. Why? Because law is a medium that is capable of being wholly external to the self. Primitive culture is a reflection of self, modified by time and tradition. Money is a medium which is compelled to reflect the self if the individual happens to have enough of it. But law can be given any form at all; it is capable of being made the servant of interests wholly indifferent to man. Thus it is perfectly suited to the Corporate State. And law has a second great advantage: it is the very means by which standards are carried forward by any human community. When law is employed to serve the Corporate State, the people do not know what has been done to them, for law gets into the individual's mind and substitutes its external standards, whatever they may be, for the individual's own standards. We are taught that it is our moral and civic duty to substitute the law's standards for our own. It is a virtue to obey the law, a sin to ignore it in favor of one's own personal desires. That doctrine serves a community well as long as law is formed in a human image. But what if the law becomes the betrayer of the people? Its use then is diabolical. The people's best instincts are then used to disable them from fighting an enemy; they are told it is morally right to surrender. Thus the people are led to deny their own inner values in favor of law which has become, unknown to them, corrupt, unjust, and antihuman, the servant of an enemy of man—the Corporate State.

Diabolically, law can teach that what is wrong is right, that what is false is true. It does this by supplying the sole normative standard in a society become so complex, so confused, so divided, where people know so little about each other, that they can have no other standard. And so we have today the fact of law that says to a young America, "Thou shalt kill," and a people who believe that it is their moral duty to obey such a law. When a "not" was accidentally left out of one of the Commandments in an early Bible, it was called the Wicked Bible; today it is our law which has become wicked, and which has robbed us of the ability to know what is just and what is human.

Behind the law stands that even more basic element of the Corporate State, "reason." It is a state built upon "reason." But just as what is denominated as "law" has been distorted to fit the ends of the state, so reason itself has been distorted to become merely an expression of the state's values. The "reason" of the Corporate State leaves out so many values, ignores so many human needs, and pushes its own interests so singlemindedly that it amounts to this: the state has called its own insanity by the name of reason.

Ultimately, what the Corporate State does is to separate man from his sources of meaning and truth. To humans, the cosmos cannot be a source of truth. Nor can an entity such as the state. For human beings, the only truth must be found in their own humanity, in each other, in their relation to the living world. When the Corporate State forces its "public interest" truth as a substitute for man's internal truth—for the truth man creates—it cuts him off from the only reality he can live by. We say a man is mad when he believes he is Napoleon, or kills someone because an outside voice told him to do so. A society is mad when its actions are no longer guided by what will make men healthier and happier, when its power is no longer in the service of life. It is this fact that stands back of the fury and rebellion of youth. That anger is based on much else besides. But perhaps its deepest basis is the sense that the

State has cut man off from his sources, cut him off from his values and from knowledge. The State is the enemy not merely because of oppression, injustice, and war, but because it has become the enemy of life itself.

TOWARD THE THERAPEUTIC STATE

Thomas S. Szasz

Valeriy Tarsis is a literary critic, translator, and writer. In 1960 he sent an English publisher a manuscript which was highly critical of life in Khrushchev's Russia. This work, *The Blue-bottle,* appeared in England in October, 1962, under the pseudonym Ivan Valeriy. Actually, Tarsis had opposed the use of a pseudonym and made no secret in Russia of having sent his book abroad. In August, 1962 two months before the appearance of *The Blue-bottle* in London, Tarsis was arrested and committed to the Koshchenko psychiatric hospital in Moscow. News of his fate soon reached the West and an article about it by the British journalist Edward Crankshaw appeared in *The Observer* for February, 1963. In March, Tarsis was released.

Ward 7[1] is Tarsis' account of what happened to him in the "mental hospital." It was written shortly after his release and smuggled to England in the summer of 1964. In this autobiographical novel, Valentine Alamazov, a Russian writer, is arrested and incarcerated in a psychiatric institution for the same offense as Tarsis had been; he is held in the notorious Russian insane asylum, the "Villat Kanatchikov," the nickname in Moscow for the Koshchenko Hospital; and he was released after protests from the West.

This, in bare outline, is the plot of *Ward 7* and the story of the events behind it. The question is: What shall we make of it?

I have seen many English and American comments on this book; all deal with it as political criticism. Nearly a year before the book's American publication, such an interpretation was offered by Mr. C. L. Sulzberger, in *The New York Times* for October 28, 1964:

> Khrushchev . . . conducted a running battle with writers who felt sufficiently revitalized by his reforms to fight for total freedom. Khrushchev

---

> struck back by restraining some of the boldest of these spirits—not in prisons or concentration camps, but in mental homes and sanatoriums.

After briefly reviewing the book, and noting that "The material conditions of Ward 7 are not too bad. . . . All they (the 'patients') lack is freedom," Mr. Sulzberger concluded:

> When contemplating this strange book one cannot but wonder if in any way the system that invented *Ward 7* under Khrushchev as a halfway house to prison might now be affecting Khrushchev himself. In Stalin's day, political disgrace terminated in torture cells, execution cellars or Siberian barbed wire enclaves. Khrushchev, to his enduring credit, virtually did away with all that. . . .

The supposition that *Ward 7* should be read as political commentary on contemporary Soviet society is further borne out by Mr. Elliot Graham of E. P. Dutton & Co. Tarsis was eager to have *Ward 7* published in the West, writes Mr. Graham, "because although the Soviet government claims that there are no political prisoners in the Soviet Union, the practice of putting inconvenient citizens into lunatic asylums seems to have become fairly widespread and is all the more shocking because this can be done without putting them on trial and because the term of their detention is indefinite."

These comments do not, in my opinion, penetrate to the significant lessons in this book. Approached as a piece on psychiatric hospitalization—as an exposé, as it were, of the Soviet mental hospital system—what do we find? The same claim—that they have been incarcerated improperly and unjustly—is made by people in mental hospitals all over the world. How do we judge whether such a claim is valid or not?

The irony of *Ward 7* will elude those who do not mentally substitute a German, a Frenchman, or an American for Valeriy Tarsis. Suppose an American poet were committed to a mental hospital and were to claim that he is sane; who would believe him? Valeriy Tarsis was confined for 6 months; Ezra Pound, for 13 years.

Our logic concerning involuntary mental hospitalization is evidently this: If a Russian is committed as insane, it is because he is sane but loves liberty too much; if an American is committed as insane, it is because he is insane but loves liberty so little that by depriving him of it we provide him with a "therapeutic milieu." "This is the only court," said a judge in Chicago, "where the defendant always wins. If he is released, it means he is well. If he is committed, it is for his own good."

Pity the poor Russians, deprived of such guarantees of the "civil rights of mentally ill."

Actually, Tarsis' comments about psychiatry and psychiatrists are far more detailed and damaging than his observations about Soviet society or the Soviet political system. Here are a few examples:

The hero, Alamazov, has been taken to the hospital by force: "In the morning Alamazov was examined by the head city psychiatrist, exactly as a prisoner is examined by a magistrate. He was brought to Dr. Yanushkevich's consulting room under guard. The doctor made no attempt to treat him as a patient; illness was never mentioned. Pink and smug, he seemed to take his role as prosecutor for granted."

Alamazov's view of the situation is this: "I don't regard you as a doctor. You call this a hospital, I call it a prison to which, in a typically fascist way, I have been sent without trial. So now, let's get everything straight. I am your prisoner, you are my jailer, and there isn't going to be any nonsense about my health or relations, or about examination and treatment. . . . " Clearly, Alamazov has no insight into his condition: the poor fellow does not even realize he is sick!

Then there is this revealing exchange between Alamazov and Professor Stein, one of the nastier psychiatric types in the hospital:

> [Stein] "We shall get acquainted, Valentine Ivanovich. . . . Tell us why you are here—what are your symptoms?"—Alamazov glared at him with such contempt that Stein looked uncomfortable. "I have not the slightest wish to get acquainted with you, but evidently I must. The reason I am here is that I was brought in by the police. My health is excellent. It's your job to make me ill. But I warn you, you won't succeed."—"How you actually got here is irrelevant. The point you should keep in mind is that healthy people are not in hospitals."—"That's exactly what the Cheka interrogators used to say to their victims: 'Innocent people are not in prison. You say you are innocent, that means you are anti-Soviet, so prison is the place for you.' The only difference is that now it's the madhouse,"—"I see. . . . You don't sound exactly sane!"

It would be a grave mistake to believe that *Ward 7* is populated only by political dissenters. Many of the inmates are ordinary people, like the elderly husband who stood in the way of his wife's fuller sexual life. This is Tatyana speaking to her friend Anna:

> "It's quite simple. You write to the clinic. You tell them that your husband, who is much older than you are and beginning to be impotent, is insanely

> jealous and has been threatening your life."—"It's true. He said 'I'll kill you'."

I was intrigued, and pleased, by the views Tarsis put in the mouth of Professor Nezhevsky. Nezhevsky is an elderly psychiatrist, at odds with the police methods of his Soviet colleagues. In a conversation with a French psychiatrist, René Gillard, Nezhevsky says: "I told them at the Ministry that you avoid drugs, . . . your staff are forbidden to talk about 'illness,' the patients . . . are free to come and go. . . ." Replies Gillard: "So you stick to happiness pills?" "Yes, exactly," says Nezhevsky. "Happiness pills. Andaxin, aminodin, and the rest of the muck—our doctors think the world of it." And so on, until at the end, Gillard says: "I must say, the idea of compulsory treatment really revolts me. We'd never stand for it."

On the day I write this—responding partly to CORE demonstrations and draft-card burning by a Syracuse youth—Mayor William F. Walsh of Syracuse offered a "six-point legislative program beamed at reducing youthful crime and *civil disobedience.* . . ." Walsh asked that "a treatment and research center for juvenile delinquents be included in the new multi-million-dollar *mental health center* to be built here."

No, *Ward 7* is not only in Moscow. Nor is *Ward 7* a recent phenomenon. Psychiatric sanctions have been with us for centuries. Successors to the witch hunts, they are one of the manifestations of a passage, in Western societies, from theological to secular, and from magical to "scientific," methods of *social control.* However, only through the creation of vast psychiatric bureaucracies in modern mass societies has involuntary mental hospitalization become a major force in the police powers of the state. To attribute this evil to Communism, or to Capitalism, would thus be both an oversimplification and an evasion.

Indeed, by alluding to Chekhov's *Ward No. 6,* Tarsis admits that he knows this. Chekhov, himself a physician, had as his protagonist not a patient, but a psychiatrist—Dr. Andrei Yefimich. The psychiatrist is honest and soon cannot tolerate the task he has unwittingly assumed. He then commits the fatal mistake of actually engaging a patient in *conversation*—as if such a thing were possible with one who is insane! The dramatic end follows swiftly: the psychiatrist is declared insane, is commited to the hospital, and following a near-fatal beating by an attendant, dies of a stroke. Before he is declared insane, Chekhov's psychiatrist has this to say:

> I am serving an evil cause, and receive my salary from people whom I dupe; I am not honest. But then I, by myself, am nothing; I am but a particle of necessary social evil: all the district bureaucrats are harmful and receive their salaries for nothing. Therefore it is not I who am to blame for my dishonesty but the times.

It is necessary to be absolutely clear about two points, lest *Ward 7* be misread: (1) Neither involuntary mental hospitalization as such, nor its political uses and abuses, was discovered by the Soviets. (2) The fundamental logic behind commitment has been accepted throughout the world for several centuries, and is still widely accepted today: according to it, it is "humane" and "helpful" to deprive a person of his *liberty*—a right second only to his right to his life—on the ground of a "mental illness" (or because such "illness" renders him "dangerous to himself and others"); if so, the only question is to define and determine what mental illness is or who is mentally ill.

Thus, Tarsis explains, it is "assumed, by doctors and politicians, writers and ideologists, that anyone dissatisfied with the socialist paradise must be a lunatic. . . ." Every one of the modern nation-states has, in the course of the last century-and-a-half, produced its own definitions and theories of lunacy. It is in this way that both a political and a psychiatric analysis of *Ward 7* must come to the same thing: a better understanding of secular society, its bureaucracies, and its methods of social control—among them, institutional psychiatry.

The list of famous persons deprived of liberty by means of psychiatric incarceration would run to several pages; for example, Secretary of State Forrestal, Governor Earl Long, General Edwin Walker, Ezra Pound, Norman Mailer, and Mary Todd Lincoln in the United States; in Germany—Marga Krupp, the wife of Fritz Krupp, committed by the Kaiser for making a nuisance of herself with complaints about her husband's homosexual orgies; and, in Austria-Hungary, Ignaz Semmelweiss, discoverer of childbed fever, for upsetting his colleagues and the public with the view that the disease was caused by the doctors' dirty hands.

Only a short time ago, men believed that slavery was a good institution, so long as only the proper people were enslaved: in historical order, the proper persons were the enemy vanquished in battle, the heathen, and the Negro. At long last, mankind concluded that slavery was a basic human wrong, regardless of who was placed in the class of slaves or why. I consider involuntary mental hospitalization also a basic human wrong.

No adult should ever be cast in the sick role through the power of the state. The only deviance of which a person should be accused by the government is law-breaking; and once so charged, he should, of course, enjoy all the protection of the Constitution.

Many years ago, Lord Russell predicted that the Communist East and the Free West will, under the pressure of the forces of collectivism, drift even closer together until the differences between the two will be indistinguishable. Years later, Orwell warned of the same dismal future in *Animal Farm.* The concluding paragraph reads thus: "Twelve voices were shouting . . . and they were all alike. No question, now, what had happened to the faces of the pigs. The creatures outside looked from pig to man, and from man to pig, and pig to man again; but already it was impossible to say which was which."

The nature of the "machine" that homogenizes man and pig now seems clear: it is the modern state, regardless of whether it is the police state of the East or the bureaucratic state of the West. By substituting "private happiness" for "public happiness," all modern societies tend to wean the individual from the *polis,* and thus deprive him of a voice in the decision of all but his most trivial interests. The result is depoliticized man. It is small wonder, then, that the "Psychological Man" of today is more interested in mental health than in liberty. Thus it is inevitable that the individual seems less a citizen and more a patient.

But not only is the nature of modern bureaucratic mass society as a depoliticizing apparatus clear. It is also clear that institutional psychiatry is an important cog in it: the Russians call it Ward 7 and Villat Kanatchikov; we call it the state hospital and the community mental health center. Totalitarian tyranny and popular (non-constitutional) democracy thus rush to meet each other in the Therapeutic State.

NOTES

1. *Ward 7, An Autobiographical Novel,* by Valeriy Tarsis, translated by Katya Brown (Dutton).

Part 8
CONCLUSION

Were the eye not attuned to the sun the sun could never be seen by it

GOETHE

The idea prevailed a few years back that science was concerned primarily with the task of accurately describing the world without prejudice. The dictum was very wrong both as a rule to be followed and as a description of how science accomplishes its purpose. Indeed, if it were necessary to describc the world without prejudice in order to be scientific, then science would be impossible. Believing it to be possible has led to some very unscientific researches.

First let us take up the question of whether it is possible to describe the world without prejudice. The world is not composed of naturally occurring lumps and lines; the world is a complete and utter chaos until we impose some order on it. What the scientific effort does is to create order out of chaos by creating abstract concepts and relationships which explain some of the events that make up the chaos. What we choose to look at, from amidst all those movements, nuances, and facts, depends on the theory through which we do our looking. Take this for example: Would Johannes Kepler and Tycho Brahe see the same thing if they watched the sun at dawn? Kepler believed the sun was fixed and that the earth moved. Tycho believed the earth was fixed and that the sun moved. Although the "objective reality" of the sun at dawn might be the same for both men, what they see and, for that matter, whether they even attend the sunrise at all, is conditioned by the theory they believe in.[1] The Pope would not have seen the same things had he been at Darwin's side during the voyage of the Beagle. The Pope would not even have gone on the voyage.

Consider the following:

> . . . it takes a special perspective to "see" what is happening. . . . one does not simply "see" what is going on unless one has a theoretical perspective which the events taking place make sense. A chimpanzee cannot see what a physicist sees and two physicists see different things if they operate with different theories. Thus theories are not only things that order our data; they determine what we see and what we count as data. The view that it is possible to have a science that is purely descriptive is nonsense. What one describes, what one sees as important, how one interprets what is seen and ultimately how one explains the events observed, all depend on the theory (or more generally on the theoretical perspective) that one carries to and away from the observations. To deny that one has a theory is to admit that one does not wish to articulate precisely what the theory is; but observation is impossible without a theory, and nothing can be described without theory operating at all stages of the descriptive process.[2]

Ironically, it has often been asserted that the most scientific procedure is to eschew any theoretical preconceptions in order to free oneself from bias. By so doing we do not free ourselves from bias —we become slaves to bias; by so doing we do not become more scientific —we make science impossible. By failing to specify our theoretical preconceptions we avoid the possibility of exposing our theories to either logical or empirical scrutiny, but the theory remains a dominant, albeit unassessed, component of the research process.

It has sometimes been assumed that explanations will arise when "all the facts are in" and that the "scientific" procedure is to go forth equipped with the necessary techniques and gather in "all the facts." Such a procedure generally takes the form of establishing statistical associations between certain selected features of the environment. Thus, one interested in gathering "all the facts" about delinquency might attempt to measure the degree of association between juvenile delinquency and numerous other variables, e.g., the type of discipline found in the home, median income in the area of residence, and the general health level of the child. But philosophers of science warn that such a procedure is not the method which has proved successful in other disciplines in building explanatory theories. Thus Hanson warns:

> [Causal laws] . . . are not built up in the manner: $(A \text{ then } B)_1$, $(A \text{ then } B)_2$, $(A \text{ then } B)_3$; therefore all A's are followed by B's. This obscures the role of causal laws in our conceptions of a physical world . . . The causal structure of the universe, if such a thing be, cannot be grasped simply by

counting off event-pairs, Noah fashion, and then summarizing it all with an umbrella formula.[3]

Those who defend the enterprise of description without explanation generally end by arguing that the sole purpose of science is prediction. But prediction alone is a poor test of a scientific contribution. It is possible to predict (or more accurately to forecast) out of ignorance. Forecasts may be accurate without touching on variables that have causal significance. Sunspots on the moon may forecast a good crop but have no relationship whatsoever to the outcome. Although not always perfectly accurate, one of the best predictors of what people will do is what they say they will do. Thus when a man in a rural village in Tanzania tells us that he will move to Dar es Salaam next spring, we can predict with considerable statistical confidence that he will do this. But the reason why he moves will not be touched on by this prediction. Indeed, relying only on the respondent's own view we may well miss the importance of social forces of which he himself is unaware because of the theory which he uses to explain his behavior.

Furthermore, some of the most important theories in the history of science have not been particularly good predictors.[4] Darwin's Evolutionary Theory predicts only hypothetically; that is, we can only predict the survival and extinction of a species if we can predict environmental changes. We can predict the extinction of Irish Elks only if we can predict the Irish flood which will drown them all. But the biological theory of survival need not be held in limbo until we have a climatic-geographical-geological theory that accurately explains environmental changes, although such a theory would be necessary if we insisted that all theories must predict. A good theory must have deducible, testable assertions about empirical events, but these may be events that have occurred in the past or events that can be anticipated only hypothetically.

Science is not an inhuman enterprise that requires us to dismiss the human qualities of bias and selectivity. Science is, in fact, the very human enterprise of selecting things to see and seeing them with a bias. The touchstone of science is to articulate the bias and clarify explicitly why we choose to see what we are looking at.

The articles and comments in this book have approached the study of human behavior from the bias of the conflict perspective. The utility of this perspective has been assessed against the empirical data of researches, using most of the research tools of contemporary social science.

If the book has been successful, you should now be in a position to use sociology as a way of understanding the world around you. You should also be able to move on to more intense inquiry into social life if such a quest shows promise of being worthwhile. Ultimately you will want to become as familiar with other theoretical perspectives as you now are with the one covered in this book. Hopefully, this book will serve as a springboard to further study and, in so doing, it will help you to contribute to the continuation of the accumulation of knowledge.

NOTES

1. Norwood Russell Hanson, *Patterns of Discovery,* N.Y.: Cambridge University Press, 1958.
2. *Ibid.,* p. 7.
3. *Ibid.,* p. 4.
4. Michael Scriven, "Explanation and Prediction in Evolutionary Theory," *Science,* 28, August 1959, Vol. 130, #3374, pp. 477-481.

INDEX

SUBJECT INDEX

NAME INDEX

ABCDEFGH798765432